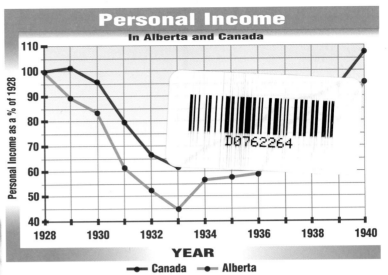

Personal Income
In Alberta and Canada

Canada — **Alberta**

This graph measures the amount of personal income earned by Canadians every year. The amount earned by Canadians living in Alberta is also used to show how Alberta compared to the Canadian average during the Depression. Canadian personal income did not fall until after 1929, whereas Alberta's fell after 1928. Both reached their bottom in 1933, but Canada's personal income fell to slightly more than 60% of its 1928 level, while Alberta's fell to about 45%.

Average Monthly Farm Wages
In Alberta for an adult male

Canada — **Alberta**

Shown are the average monthly wages on a farm in both Canada and Alberta as a percentage of 1928's wage level. The Canadian average did not fall until after 1929, whereas Alberta's began its decline after 1928. Alberta's dropped by more than the Canadian average by 1933, when it reached less than 50% of 1928's, whereas Canada's remained slightly above 50%.

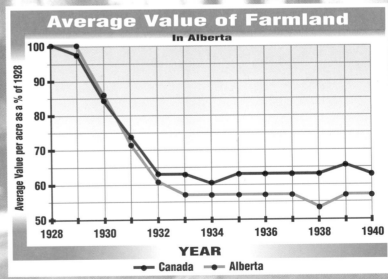

Average Value of Farmland
In Alberta

Canada — **Alberta**

This graph shows the average value per acre of farm land in both Canada and Alberta as a percentage of their 1928 levels. The Canadian average fell after 1928, while Alberta's did not fall until after 1929. However, the drop in Alberta was sharper when it happened, and it fell further than the Canadian average. Canada's reached a low of 60% of its 1928 value, while Alberta's reached a low of slightly less than 55% of its value in 1938. The average value per acre of farm land both in Canada as a whole and in Alberta is charted here as a percentage of 1928 levels.

ALBERTA IN THE 20TH CENTURY

A JOURNALISTIC HISTORY OF THE PROVINCE IN THIRTEEN VOLUMES

VOLUME SIX

FURY AND FUTILITY:
THE ONSET OF THE GREAT DEPRESSION

United Western Communications Ltd.
Edmonton
1998

Consultive Committee: Donald Graves, Calgary businessman; Martin Lynch of Kaslo, B.C., former chief of the copy desk of the Globe and Mail; Richard D. McCallum, president, Quality Color Press Inc., Edmonton.

Editor: Ted Byfield
Associate Editor: Jan Tyrwhitt
Photo Editor and Production Co-ordinator: Moira Calder
Photo Research: Philippa Byfield

Writers:
Ted Byfield
Virginia Byfield
Fred Cleverley
Hugh Dempsey
Ric Dolphin
George Oake
J.F.J. Pereira
Davis Sheremata
Jan Tyrwhitt

Illustrations:
Lyle Grant

Maps:
David Cristall

Charts:
Barry Hebb

Researchers:
Ron Ardell
Ardith Beley
Ed Buskel
Norm Fennema
Eleanor Gasparik
James Leech
Bill Lysak
Mircea Panciuk
Don Spratt
Dustin Tkachuk

Proof Readers:
Joanne Hatton
Wendy Tang
Kathleen Wall

Page Production:
Lawrence Richard
Dave Stevens

Lithography:
Screaming Colour Inc., Edmonton

The publisher acknowledges the generous contribution of the Provincial Archives of Alberta, the Glenbow Archives, the City of Edmonton Archives, the Edmonton Public School Board Archives, the Medicine Hat Museum and Archives, the Fort Vermilion Archives, the Lethbridge Archives, Peace River Centennial Museum and Archives, the National Archives of Canada and the Saskatchewan Archives Board.

FURY AND FUTILITY: THE ONSET OF THE GREAT DEPRESSION

© Copyright 1998
United Western Communications Ltd.

(Alberta in the 20th Century v.6)
Includes bibliographic references and index
ISBN: 0-9695718-6-0
Second Printing
Printed in Canada

1. Alberta—History—1905-1945.* 2. Depressions—1929—Alberta. 3. Alberta—Social conditions—1905-1945.* I. Byfield, Ted. II. Tyrwhitt, Janice. III. Series

FC3673.F87 1998 971.23'02 C98-910447-8
F1078.F87 1998

Alberta in the 20th Century

Table of Contents

Section Four FURY ON THE PRAIRIES: THE FALL OF THE UFA AND THE SOCIAL CREDIT EXPLOSION

Provincial Archives of Alberta, A.5148

Glenbow Archives, NC-54-2037

The Cover:

The front cover photo on this volume is from one of the 5,054 negatives and 1,085 prints made by Thomas Gushul, his wife, Lena, and their son, Evan. Gushul came to Canada from Ukraine in 1906, worked for the railways for three years, then for the coal mines in Blairmore until he was laid off in the big bust of 1914. He and Lena then opened a photo studio, and their work provides a superb record of social and economic life and strife in the Crowsnest area. This striking photo of Len Neuman of Leduc atop a freight bespeaks the sense of futility that tens of thousands of Canadian youths felt as the Depression set in. On the back cover protesters in the On-to-Ottawa march of 1935 pass through Medicine Hat on their way to Swift Current and then to Regina.

Foreword

History, I'm beginning to discover, doesn't lend itself to neat packaging. When this series began we had a very simple plan. We would divide Alberta into ten parts, begin with a volume covering the period before the 20th century, then devote one volume to each of the ten decades in the century itself, making an eleven-volume series in total.

Unfortunately this doesn't work. History, like everything else about human nature, is obstreperous. It doesn't cheerfully categorize, compartmentalize, digitalize, or organize into compact, manageable, uniform segments. As with our lives, in some decades very little happens, in others altogether too much.

We initially encountered this problem in the third volume, which as originally planned would have covered the period 1910 to 1920. But that decade saw two cataclysmic events — the first great boom and the Great War. To have fit them both into one volume, we found, would simply cheat the reader and cheat history as well. Either we would fail to adequately describe the incredible explosion of growth that occurred between 1910 and 1914, or we would be forced to omit the epic deeds of valour and self-sacrifice during that war, prints Albertans left upon the sands of time for other generations to contemplate and at which we can but marvel.

Hence Volume 3 became Volumes 3 and 4 and we were able to cover both these phenomena much more adequately.

The 1920s posed no difficulty and became Volume 5. But then came the Thirties and the same difficulty arose. I knew, of course, we must cover the Great Depression, with all that implied, and also the extraordinary rise and triumph of the Social Credit movement. I assumed this could all be dealt with adequately in a single volume.

What I did not know, did not in fact have the least idea of until I got into it, was the astonishing attendant events these developments brought about. I knew the Depression was tough; I knew there had been a considerable migration of people out of the Dust Bowl from the Twenties onward. I did not realize (though I should have guessed) the personal tragedy that this in so many cases involved. Such stories needed to be told. Neither did I know the extent to which radical ideas of every political persuasion, left and right, had permeated the minds of tens of thousands of people. Alberta verged on revolution, and that is the fact of it.

Neither did I understand the degree to which Social Credit, as originally advanced in William Aberhart's famed Yellow Pamphlet, was a radical revolutionary movement. Its proposals, read nearly seventy years after they were made, are at least as extreme as Marxism and in many ways far more extreme than fascism.

What people noticed, understandably, was Aberhart's promise of $25 a month for all adults. Other incidental elements they did not notice: hoarding of wealth and credit was to be banned. People who had money in the bank would have to turn it over to the state in return for provincial bonds, payable only in Social Credit certificates. When they died, their bonds would revert to the government. Those who moved out of Alberta could redeem their bonds for Canadian dollars only when those bonds reached maturity. And on and on.

This, believe it or not, is what we voted for in the greatest landslide in our electoral history on that famous date, August 22, 1935, when we elected a Social Credit government. That we did not get it was due in no small measure to Aberhart's own reluctance to enforce such things. For his failure to do so he came within a hair's breadth of being ousted as premier.

None of this I was aware of until we began researching the volume. Something else I did not take into account was the magnificent photography stored in the Provincial Archives and the Glenbow Archives, which records the trials, agonies and occasional violence of this period as nothing else could. These photographs, some of which have never been printed, certainly belong in any history of this magnitude.

So as the assignments went out to the writers I told them to include all the stories they felt needed to be told. Then, as I combined the chapters with the pictures, the problem asserted itself implacably.

"How many pages is this volume likely to run?" asked Richard McCallum, who has been printing adviser on the series since it began. "At least 460," I replied. He breathed deeply and spoke with an unusually measured gravity. "Then there are a couple of things you might take into account," he said. "One is the fact that we will go very, very broke if we print a book this size. The other is the fact it will be practically impossible to bind it."

I brought the problem up with John Scrymgeour, one of the owners of United Western and a man with many decades of business acumen. "Simple," he said. "Just split it. Put out two volumes to cover the 1930s."

"You don't seem to understand, John," I said. "The Thirties are an entity. They have a beginning point with the stock market crash and an ending point with the outbreak of the Second World War. You can't just arbitrarily break them in two."

I kept repeating this to myself while I turned over and over in my mind the impracticability of such an idea. Then it occurred to me. For Alberta, anyway, there is a decisive turning point in the middle of the decade. It can be pinpointed to that same single date, August 22, 1935. This made it possible to split the Depression in two — the first half being what the Depression did to us; the second what we tried to do about the Depression. We have called this first volume, No.6, "Fury and Futility" because that is what it aroused in us.

But we have changed the name of the second slightly. It was to have been called "Aberhart and the Social Credit Explosion" because a political explosion was what most assuredly occurred on that August day in 1935. But it was more than an explosion; it was a rebellion, indeed an insurrection, and that is the word we have used in the title of Volume 7: "Aberhart and the Alberta Insurrection." That volume is due to come out October 15, this year.

I doubt, by the way, that many old Social Crediters would argue with the word "insurrection." According to Oxford, it means "a rising in open resistance to established authority." Yes, they would say, that is exactly what we intended. The fact that in many constituencies the Communist party unofficially backed the Social Crediters in 1935 comes as astonishing to people who knew the Social Credit government in its later conservative manifestation. On August 22, 1935, however, it surprised nobody. On that day, Alberta launched out onto its own. Whether it was for good or for ill, people still argue about. In fact, nothing has ever divided us so fiercely. Our internecine struggle appalled and fascinated reporters from all over the country. We became distinct, unique, "crazy" according to a headline in the *Boston Globe*. Yet it also defined us. Alberta's reaction to the Depression was different. We would not capitulate and let it hammer us. We would fight back. That is our reputation.

"So how many volumes is this thing likely to wind up at?" asked one sceptic. "As the century goes on, things keep getting more complex. Are you sure you won't have to split them all?"

Yes, I'm sure we can now stay with the plan in every decade but perhaps one other, the 1970s. Much happened then, more of an economic than a political nature. We grew into a more urban, impersonal place in the 1970s, just as we did in the first big boom sixty years before. But I hope we can get it all into one volume.

One other thing needs to be noted. We have covered the Brownlee case — unquestionably the most celebrated trial, civil or criminal, in the whole legal history of the province — in all possible detail. Since it was a sex scandal, we can be accused of appealing to prurient interest. And yet when we considered the whole astonishing spectacle it represents, a 22-year-old stenographic clerk bringing down a powerful premier and his government too... Well, as a work of fiction it would be unbelievable. Yet that too is part of Alberta and how it happened is a story that surely must be fully told.

The splitting of the volume has made something else possible. With the 1930s, we begin to enter the period which some people, still alive and lucid, well remember. They were there; they took part; it lives in their memories. In Volume 7, we will begin a feature, "Reminiscences," that will appear in all the subsequent volumes. Here people will give their impressions of those events, sixty years later. This element too would not have been possible in a single volume.

Ted Byfield,
April, 1998

List of Contributors for Volume VI

Ted Byfield is the founder of *Alberta Report, Western Report* and *British Columbia Report* newsmagazines. After seventeen years on daily newspapers, he helped found the St. John's Boys' Schools in Manitoba and Alberta where he taught history for ten years. He started *St. John's Edmonton Report*, the ancestor of *Alberta Report*, in 1973.

Virginia Byfield, mother of six, is a senior editor of *Alberta Report* newsmagazine who over a twenty-five-year period has edited its political, educational, cultural and religious departments. She previously worked as a reporter for the *Ottawa Journal* and the *Timmins Daily Press*, shot television news film for CBC in the early 1960s, and taught French, English and Latin in the St. John's schools.

Fred Cleverley was a reporter and member of the editorial board at the *Winnipeg Free Press* for more than twenty years. He currently writes a weekly column for the *Free Press*.

Hugh Dempsey is a well-known western historian. He is chief curator emeritus of the Glenbow Museum in Calgary and has written many books and articles on Indians and the history of Alberta. He began his journalistic career as a reporter and later editor of the *Edmonton Bulletin*.

Ric Dolphin is a former executive editor of *Alberta Report*, a contributor to western and national magazines, managing editor of Volume 2 in this series, and a staff member of the *Edmonton Journal*.

Lyle Grant is a Calgary-based illustrator and art director who has lived in Alberta since 1974.

George R. Oake is a born and bred Albertan. He is the former western bureau chief of the *Toronto Star*, managing editor of the *Edmonton Journal*, and for many years covered western Canadian politics for Southam News. He is retired and living in Edmonton.

J.F.J. Pereira is a retired newspaper editor and columnist, amateur railway historian and model railroader.

Davis Sheremata is a freelance reporter whose contributions have appeared in *Alberta Report*, the *Edmonton Sun* and *Canadian Geographic*. He grew up near Grassland in northern Alberta.

Janice Tyrwhitt, a writer and editor with a particular interest in Canadian social history, is the author of *Bartlett's Canada* and *The Mill*. She lives in Toronto.

Section One

THE GRIM YEARS BEGIN

For tens of thousands of young men, 1930 began a decade of futility and despair as they hopped freights from town to town in search of work. This group was photographed by the Edmonton Journal as they awaited an outbound freight beside the Canadian National mainline.

1930, the year when everything went to pieces throughout Alberta

AS THE FIRMS SHUT DOWN, THE BANKS FORECLOSED, THE JOBS VANISHED, IT SOON BECAME PLAIN THAT AN UNPRECEDENTED CALAMITY WAS OCCURRING

by TED BYFIELD

When the Great Depression came to Alberta, nobody knew it. It did not arrive as an event, but as a hundred little events, few of them unprecedented. In 1929 there had been the stock market crash. Very bad in New York, no doubt, but hardly a disaster way up here in Alberta. Then throughout 1930, there was bad news about collapsing grain prices, terrible enough for the farmer, only hypothetically terrible in the city. And anyway, the grain market had gone sour before. Construction was definitely down. Too bad about that contractor going broke. Wonder who all those idle guys were downtown? Funny, there was this fellow going door to door last week begging for food.

Then one day it would become immediate. The boss would call in the staff and announce the business was folding. Or there was no more credit at the general store. Or the bank took over the farm on the next section, then the one just across the road. Or you saw whole families in the cities, their belongings piled onto a trailer behind the car, and unable to buy gas. Lines of single, increasingly surly, men were becoming commonplace. So were the signs, "No Help Wanted." Gradually, ever so gradually, you came to realize that what was happening had never happened before. The word "depression," which used to mean a low spot on a field, acquired a new and terrible meaning.

For the next nine years that word would enter nearly every conversation, become the chief term in every business issue and the decisive factor in most personal decisions — from where people lived, to whether they worked or got married, to what they ate and whether they ate. This was the world that Albertans were entering in 1930, though for most people, its trials, agonies and horrors were well beyond their worst foreboding.

By May 1930 some newspaper editors began to suspect that the economic downturn was something more than merely transitional. "To see so many young men looking for work in town is most regrettable," said the *Ponoka Herald*. "The change has come so suddenly... How work is to be found for our unemployed is a great big problem."

Three days later the Calgary *Albertan* reported that city garbage collectors were selling the clothes they had collected from their routes to the destitute. That information followed hard on a plea to city council not to stop providing free milk to the schoolchildren during the summer holidays because many were plainly undernourished.

Then Alberta's liquor commissioner, R.J. Dinning, declared that no one on relief (i.e., on welfare) would be allowed to purchase

Signs at Edmonton's relief headquarters, 99th Street and 102nd Avenue, give conflicting messages to those forced to frequent it.

City of Edmonton Archives, Hollingsworth Collection, EA-160-691

Some men grew weary of the endless urban struggle for relief and hit the rails; others were lured by the romance of the wandering life. Whatever the reason, the Edmonton Journal of June 16, 1931, estimated that 200 men were "hooking a drag" in or out of the city every day. This pair was photographed at Edmonton's Calder Yards.

Unemployment was a problem in Alberta from the onset of the Depression until the outbreak of the Second World War. But no accurate measure of its severity is available because some published figures took account only of those registered, while others were estimates. Using comparable figures, however, a pattern can be seen. The number of registered unemployed appears to have risen from 3,148 on January 8, 1930, to a peak of 12,000 some time during 1931, then fluctuated until it reached 11,410 in October 1936, after which it tapered slightly until the declaration of war in September 1939, when it began to fall dramatically.

liquor; anyone applying for relief was required to turn in his liquor permit. The Alberta Hotelmen's Association agreed not to permit the unemployed, or anyone on relief, to buy beer. Such a decision, sniffed the *Edmonton Journal*, was like placing the unemployed on the Interdict List. "The Jobless," headlined the paper, "Are Drinkless."

Something else became notable. Calgary's transit system reported that streetcar revenues "went to pieces" in April, either because people were walking to work or, worse still, because they weren't working at all.

All through 1930, demands for "action" were being voiced everywhere. Unemployment was reaching crisis proportions and required federal intervention, said a convention of Prairie mayors meeting on the problem in Winnipeg. Prime Minister Mackenzie King disagreed. He had not once been approached by any province to such an end, he said, while the Calgary *Albertan* called current unemployment purely "seasonal" and warned against "hysteria."

So did others, like Sir Herbert Holt, president of the Royal Bank. "In spite of the losses incurred by thousands of investors," he said on January 9, 1930, "there is no reason to look forward to more than a moderate recession in business." He promised a rosy year ahead for bank shareholders. Premier John Brownlee assured a Lethbridge audience on July 2 that things were looking up. There is "too much pessimism extant on the economic problems," complained the *Albertan*. "There are comparatively few people in this province who cannot take care of themselves," said the *Edmonton Bulletin* in June.[1]

This optimism seemed belied by the statistics. Auto registrations fell by 20 per cent in 1930, and coal production was down 11 per cent. Alberta exports to the United States fell 14 per cent. Demand for eggs, pork, and cheese was down. Wheat prices had gone through the floor and wool

[1] **Undeterred by bad news. Edmonton declared "Prosperity Week," in October 1930 with the slogan, "Buy It Now," paraded in the streets, encouraging the idea that the Depression was being caused by consumer caution. "Mr. Prosperity" wandered the streets handing out $5 gift certificates. But the people did not "buy it now," and retail business continued to decline.**

To be on the "dole" was a source of great shame in the Thirties, and most Albertans tried to provide for themselves with whatever resources were available. Competition for waste coal was fierce at this disposal dump at Coalhurst, near Lethbridge.

When railway police were cracking down on hoboes, or when there were no empty boxcars, desperate men often crawled under the cars and lay on the linkage that worked the brakes, leaving only inches between themselves and the rails. This was called "riding the rods" and was extremely dangerous. To fall off when the brakes went on, or to fall asleep, meant almost certainly losing life or limb.

[2]While some scientists claim that such stories are exaggerated, Dr. Dan Johnson, the crop protection entomologist at the Lethbridge Experimental Station (Agriculture Canada), said in an interview with Philippa Byfield on March 23, 1998, that during the 1986 explosion, he saw a farm building where 'hoppers had stripped the paint and eaten 1/4" into the wood.

dropped 50 per cent. All these trends would continue for the next four years, then flatten and stay flat.

Day by day events became ever more alarming. In May, 500 unemployed miners in Drumheller besieged Premier John Brownlee for direct aid because, they said, their families were starving. Eight months after that, the largest meeting of farmers ever held in Lloydminster passed a resolution advocating that all three prairie provinces get out of Canada.

Soon hunger marches and sit-ins became ubiquitous, and the communists were blamed for organizing them. In Blairmore and Coleman, citizens' leagues were formed to get rid of the leftists and the local papers printed pledge forms inviting people to join. But not all the demonstrations were organized. After a New Year's Eve party a mob, screaming what police called "foul language," assembled spontaneously at Calgary's Eighth Avenue and First Street, hurled chunks of ice at the buildings, and pushed parked cars into the middle of the street. These were mere revellers, but many were unemployed and there was in the incident an element of defiance. In the same mood, idle men would walk into restaurants, order meals, then declare themselves unable to pay. This meant jail, but jail meant three or four weeks with steady meals.

December's cold weather saw the jobless begging door to door for food. "The men seemed most grateful for any food given them," said the *Ponoka Herald*. This easy sympathy for the unemployed and their gratitude for help extended them, however, soon wore thin. What in the 1990s would be called "workfare" was instituted and resented by those on relief. In 1933, 500 Calgary

---

For the next nine years that word 'Depression' would enter nearly every conversation, become the chief term in every business issue and the decisive factor in most personal decisions — from where people lived, to whether they worked or got married, to what they ate and whether they ate.

---

unemployed flatly refused to work for relief because the pay was too low. When they called a protest meeting, 4,000 more joined them.

Edmonton designated the "old pen" site, on which a new stadium and athletic park were to be built, as a temporary garden. Unemployed married men were allocated plots and seeds and told to grow vegetables. Families on relief were required to plant vegetable gardens.

In the country came a host of new scourges. The drought, which drove almost 17,000 people out of southern Alberta in the early Twenties (see Vol.5, Sect.1, ch.1), then eased in the latter part of the decade, returned with a vengeance. In June 1930 the *Calgary Herald* reported that Moosejaw Creek in Saskatchewan was carrying a twentieth of its normal water flow, the Battle River less than a sixth, and both the North and South Saskatchewan were at their lowest level in memory. The *Medicine Hat News* reported that 1930 was a record year for drought in twenty American states.

Then came another horror — the grasshoppers. Alberta had always had them, of course, but in the Thirties they arrived as never before, most blown in from Montana and North Dakota. They would descend in a roaring whir, devour everything in sight and move on. "They ate the handles off pitchforks, armpits out of shirts on farmers' backs, clothes off lines." writes James Gray in his

THE GRIM YEARS BEGIN

Men Against the Desert (Saskatoon, Western Producer Prairie Book, 1967).[2] A single flight was once trapped by a cold wind over Lake Winnipeg, fell into the water and when blown toward land covered the shoreline for twenty miles (thirty-two kilometres) to the depth of an axe handle. In Alberta the area hit hardest initially lay along a line from Lethbridge to Drumheller, but soon the whole province south of Red Deer was under siege.

By 1933, writes Gray, every farm and garden between Brandon and Calgary had been damaged. Millions of acres of crops were gone. The disappointment in the farm community intensified because in the spring it looked as if the long drought had been broken. The grasshopper invasions of late June and July ruined the dream. Newspaper accounts itemized the toll. In June 1931 the *Lethbridge Herald* reported the destruction of 60 acres of new wheat. In June 1933 the *Calgary Herald* described widespread destruction of grain fields across the prairies, and on June 29 the *Ponoka Herald* called the grasshopper situation "acute." In 1934 a full tenth of Alberta's crop was lost.

Southern Saskatchewan, said the *Medicine Hat News* in 1934, "has become a wilderness of

Home for many was where you could find or make it. The Edmonton Journal ran a feature on thirty-odd single men who had dug shacks into the side of the river bank below Grierson dump [A]. Most of these unidentified men supported themselves [D]. [C] This man took up residence by the North Saskatchewan River in 1938. [B] T.J.L. Wilkinson (left) and Bob Fraser were photographed having a treat at the Cranbrook, B.C., relief camp, which accommodated many Albertans.

UNRESERVED

AUCTION SALE

Having received instructions from Willms Brothers, who are giving up farming, I will sell by public auction at the farm, situated - 3 miles north and 5 miles east of Carseland then 2½ miles south. 7 miles south & 2½ miles west of Namaka

TUE. MAR. 22

1938, at 10 a.m.

18 Head of horses

36 HEAD OF CATTLE

12 FEEDER HOGS - 140 - 150 lbs.

FARM MACHINERY

HOUSEHOLD EFFECTS

TERMS CASH   Lunch at nominal fee   NO RESERVE

A. Layzell, Auctioneer License, 6434

Phone 91-3311   Box 353, Calgary

8   THE GRIM YEARS BEGIN

Glenbow Archives, NA-3597-65

Glenbow Archives, NA-1869-5

The abandoned dream

Farm abandonment in southern Alberta began with the drought in the 1920s (see Volume 5), but was renewed again in the Dirty Thirties. For most families, leaving the farm meant the end of a lifetime dream. Left behind would be the old farmhouse, sheds and barn, standing like tombstones over the last vision, the auctioneer's poster their last desperate effort to gain enough money to move north and start again. While the location of most of these scenes is not known, some were recorded. At the upper left is what remains of the store at Eagle Butte, about 30 miles south of Medicine Hat. The farm immediately to the left was adverised for sale at Nevis, Alberta, for $1,800 down with an $800 mortgage. It had a 100-acre wheat acreage. The deserted barn (inset above) was near Hanna. The auction sale was on a farm at Carseland.

R. Ross Annett was principal of the school at Consort when he created the farm family whose escapades started appearing in the Saturday Evening Post. The members of this fictional family were Big Joe, his orphaned children, Little Joe and Babe, and Uncle Pete. This charcoal sketch for the first installment, It's Gotta Rain Sometime, which earned Annett $500, was drawn by Amos Sewell, a Connecticut artist who would have worked from photographs provided by the author.

drought, cutworms and grasshoppers." In 1931, Alberta had grown more wheat than Saskatchewan, a rare occurrence before and since. By 1937, 18 million acres of the Prairies, roughly a quarter of the arable land in Canada, was suffering from moisture deficiency, between three million and six million were deemed damaged by wind erosion, and as much as 300,000 acres were listed as returning to desert. On the productivity of these lands the livelihood of 900,000 Canadians depended.

On the farms this meant gaunt families trudging away from homes they had spent a lifetime creating. Cardboard had long replaced glass in the windows; lard pails had replaced kettles; clothes were made from flour sacks; farm machinery had been worn out and abandoned. In 1932 Charles Stewart, former premier of Alberta, now a Liberal MP, predicted that forty per cent of the farms in western Canada would soon be up for tax sale. In 1933 H.J. Montgomery, Liberal MLA for Wetaskiwin, counted eighteen mortgage foreclosures in his district in four days; the *Edmonton Journal* reported 137 between January 1 and February 28.

By 1931 the Red Cross was appealing in eastern Canada for clothing to help 125,000 destitute prairie farm families. By then 1,590 rural municipalities had cut off interest payments on their debentures, and crop averages were down to two bushels an acre where they had once been twenty and some as high as forty. In 1934 northern Alberta shipped fifty carloads of vegetables and potatoes to the south, carried free by the railways. Only fifteen years earlier, southern Alberta had been a veritable breadbasket.

Diversification became the commonly-preached panacea, and farmers, driven from business by the collapse of wheat prices, surged into cattle. Herd numbers rose wildly, creating a crisis; pastures were already burnt out by the drought. The outcome was hundreds of thousands of half-

Day by day events became ever more alarming. In May, 500 unemployed miners in Drumheller besieged Premier John Browlnee for direct aid because, they said, their families were starving. Eight months after that, the largest meeting of farmers ever held in Lloydminster passed a resolution advocating that all three prairie provinces get out of Canada.

starved animals across the West, most of which would be sold off at one cent a pound in 1937. By then, said R.H. "Dick" Painter, one of the scientists who would eventually save dryland farming in western Canada, cattle were dying from "hardware disease." The cattle, he said, "would eat doorknobs or pieces of iron, or hinges that fell off gates, they were that desperate to get something into their stomachs."

In 1931 a vast resettlement plan was launched to transfer farmers out of southern Alberta and into the North, chiefly into the Peace River country with the province, Ottawa and the railways sharing the costs equally. In one week of that hot August, Northern Alberta Railways handled 39 carloads of settlers and their effects. The stock was offloaded at Edmonton, fed, watered, and reloaded. The *Edmonton Bulletin* described the scene:

> Long trainloads of bawling cattle crawling across the sun-baked prairies... tired women with lack-lustre eyes and grimy children, looking out of the dusty windows of day coaches... Their cattle are better off than the women. They call the cattle dumb animals, but they at least can bawl their hunger and thirst; the women and children cannot do that — not loud enough to be heard by the world.

"They had good outfits and they were good men," A.W. Burrell, an Edmonton stockyard hand, told the *Bulletin*. "They were just beaten by the breaks of the game. Some of them lost their crops for three years straight. Most of them said they had come from south of Hanna." New provincial regulations in 1931 allowed women, married, single or widowed, to claim homesteads. By the end of the next year, 2,292 women had done so, as had 5,012 men.

But the program encountered continuing problems. In 1934, for instance, their crops were unharvestable because they lacked binder twine for the wheat sheaves. The banks wouldn't extend credit and the province wouldn't extend a guarantee. Charles W. Frederick, owner of the *Peace River Record*, deplored the situation volubly. 'They are without twine and they can't get it," he told the *Edmonton Journal*. "They are homesteaders and they are getting their first real crop off the land they have cleared. This crop would enable them to get off relief, that is if they could harvest it." But without the twine they could not. (For life in the Peace country in the 1930s, see Sect.3, ch.3.)

Mr. and Mrs. John Daynaka, immigrants from Poland five years before, who had worked as farm laborers at Ranfurly, were photographed in Edmonton on May 6, 1933, with their children, Teddy, 7, Mike, 5, and baby Marie, as they headed north to High Prairie where they had at last acquired their own land. What happened to the Daynakas is not known, but the photo bears a striking resemblance to the famous picture of the Fehr family, taken the following year as they headed home from the Peace, their hopes dashed (see page 20).

Glenbow Archives, ND-3-6343

A population on the move

As the expanding drought crept northward farms were abandoned and towns disappeared off the map. As a result, much of the population was set on the move. Some crossed the border into British Columbia, some headed for the Peace River country, some edged into central Alberta or simply moved to more promising locations within the drybelt itself. Thus in photo [A], teams driven by George Conley and Earl Hoffman tow a house from Alderson to Scandia in 1931. [B] In 1934 Richard and Arthur Swanson were photographed in a tent at Clearwater, B.C., where their father, John Rudolph Swanson, had moved from Alberta to find work. [C] Gerald and Betty Groves appear optimistic in their covered wagon on the trail at Champion in 1937. [D] These homesteaders decided to try their luck in the Peace country in 1930; the man on the left is identified as Marshall Barber. [E] After the Canadian Pacific station burned down at Castor in 1937, the railway put the Loyalist station on a flatcar and moved it to Consort. Loyalist had ceased to exist.

Glenbow Archives, NA-3069-2

Glenbow Archives, NA-3657-33

[3]According to the Dominion Bureau of Statistics 1931 census, there were 32,767 abandoned farms in Canada. The largest percentage increase occurred in Alberta where the number of abandoned farms jumped 17.7 per cent between 1930 and 1931.

Such problems seemed endless. By May 1935 hardly a week passed without new revelations about northern farm abandonment by resettled families. "The pioneers who undertook the development of this vast area are in reality giving it back to the Indians," said the *Peace River Record* in 1936. It said one in eight farms was being abandoned. Provincial statistics put the ratio at closer to one in three — of 1,000 resettled families, 300 gave up.[3]

Everywhere in Alberta bartering returned to the agricultural economy. In 1932 the *Lethbridge Herald* reported prairie farmers regularly travelling through the Crowsnest Pass to swap wheat for vegetables, fruit and eggs with B.C. farmers. At Coronation in 1932, farmers were trading wheat for almost anything they could get. The following year, the B.B. Hoyt hardware store in Lethbridge said it would accept payment in wheat for anything it sold. In March 1933 Alberta Government Telephones (later Telus) announced it would accept wheat for payment of any bill, and at ten per cent above the market price.

With the drought came the duststorms. They began in the spring of 1930 when searing winds picked up both the soil and much of the new seed on farms from Calgary to Hanna. These continued for the next eight years, some so severe they damaged buildings. In 1934 a duststorm ripped the roof off a boxcar at Calgary, throwing two transients off with it, and killing one. In May 1937 a dense storm hit Strathmore, injuring two Montreal motorists. Historian Gray tells of a barber who quit offering shaves because dust particles embedded in men's faces had ruined his razors. He describes dust being driven into a strawstack at Shaunavon, Saskatchewan, to a depth of three feet.

In January 1938 a Calgary pilot said he had encountered thick dust at 9,000 feet. Three months later, the *Edmonton Journal* reported winds hitting the city at seventy to eighty miles an

Nine women fight for the right to scavenge coal

They also beat up the designated scavenger, even if he was kind of cute

by FRED CLEVERLEY

The shortage of money, food and fuel that beset many Albertans as the Depression tightened its grip occasioned some bizarre situations, not just among men. Nine Lethbridge area women spent a night in jail in December 1931 with no evident regrets and even less remorse.

The nine were arrested on charges of unlawful assembly and theft when they attempted to take coal from a dump at Coalhurst. They ran into trouble not with the company, Coal Producers Ltd., but with a man named Robert Adams Jr. The coal they were taking, he testified, belonged to him. That is to say, the company had given him the exclusive rights to pick over its coal pile, so they were trying to take what he had a right to scavenge first.

Miners living in Coalhurst objected to this implied contract with Adams. They too needed coal, they said, but when three of them attempted to take it they were charged with theft and briefly jailed. This outraged their wives and neighbours, nine of whom arrived at the dump on a December morning, poured oil on the coal and set it on fire.

Alberta Provincial Police from Lethbridge were dispatched, but when they arrived the women had vanished. They put out the fire and returned to Lethbridge for lunch, only to be interrupted by a call that the women were back and had set the dump on fire again.

By now the indignant Adams had arrived on the scene.

When he ordered the women to stay away from his property, they said that if they couldn't pick coal, then nobody else could. Then all nine piled on him, Adams testified. "They pulled my hair, jerked my cravat, and kicked me from the rear."

He couldn't exactly say which of the nine did what, he told the court. And when he wrote down their names on a cheque book, the women seized it. Then he took out a note book and they got that too. This wasn't the first time people had stolen his coal, said Adams. He had complained to the police, but the stealing continued.

There had been other indignities. One of the women, notably Mrs. Rosie Boychuk, had "patted me on the cheeks and said she rather liked me. I gave her no encouragement to continue her advances. So she called me an opprobrious name."

When the police returned to the dump, they sized up the situation immediately and sent for "the wagon," meaning the van used by the Lethbridge department to haul in drunks and prostitutes. The women were unceremoniously loaded into it and taken to the jail where they were kept overnight. "Never before had so many women been imprisoned at one time," reported the *Lethbridge Herald*, always alert to historical precedent. The women, if anything, seemed proud of all this.

The next day Sophie Hlushko, Minnie Tymchuk, Effie

THE GRIM YEARS BEGIN

hour (115-130 km/h) and dust so thick on the city streets that visibility was down to three feet. By now the storms were known as "black blizzards." As black as the blizzards was the humour. Standard tall tale: During dust storm, farmer takes gopher out of box under bed and tosses it out window. If gopher falls to ground and runs in door, farmer can go out. If gopher starts burrowing while still six feet in the air, farmer cannot go out.

Water shortages sometimes made rural firefighting almost futile. On February 19, 1931, a fire took out a third of the business district in Chipman. On March 4, 1931, first a blizzard and then a

---

Then came another horror — the grasshoppers. In the Thirties they arrived as never before, descending in a roaring whir, devouring the handles off pitchforks, armpits out of shirts on farmers' backs, clothes off lines, writes historian James Gray. A single flight fell into Lake Winnipeg and covered the shoreline for twenty miles to the depth of an axe handle.

---

fire swept the freight yard at Rocky Mountain House, destroying fifty carloads of wood and coal and eighteen other freight cars. In February 1932 fires wiped out a general store and pool hall at Magrath, a store at Vulcan, and a grist mill at Coalhurst. Magrath was hit again September 29 when a café, hardware store and shoe repair shop went up in flames.

Fire could be similarly devastating on the open prairie. On April 15, 1933, a twenty-five-mile-

Drawing by Lyle Grant

Boychuk, Rosie Boychuk, Nancy Slemko, Jessie Yakiwcyuk, Mary Wasinski, Grace Horchuk and Anna Farmos appeared in magistrate's court, all charged with unlawful assembly, Mrs. Slemko, mother of two, with setting the fire and Effie Boychuck, mother of one, with assault. She was accused of forcibly removing Mr. Adams' counter check book and note book.

Bail proved to be a problem. Many people were eager to help, but few had personal property worth $250. One man said he had two horses and 13 pigs. The magistrate, described as an experienced farmer, declared this collection not worth any $250. Another offered his 1921 automobile but was refused.

The *Herald* reported: "Miss Mary Wasinski, the only spinster accused, had no difficulty getting bail. One man paid the magistrate the sum of $170 in cash and gave a cheque for the balance, testifying to the esteem in which he held the lady." The newspaper also reported that the women had been jailed by the police on short notice, and with no time to prepare themselves. "They appeared rather dishevelled."

As they left, each was asked by police if she had left any property with the constable downstairs. "One lady had left her baby with the policeman on duty and promised to call

for the wee fellow who was somewhat dismayed by the proceedings."

On March 16, 1932, the nine women were convicted by a jury of unlawful assembly. Alberta Chief Justice William C. Ives gave them each six months' suspended sentences on their own recognaissance in the sum of $100. Effie Boychuk was also convicted of assault. The charges against Nancy Slemko appear from court records to have been dropped.

While the single unemployed could usually shift for themselves, those who were unable to provide for their children ended up driven to extremes. On September 28, 1934, the Edmonton Journal *told of the plight of these children, identified only as Fred, 10, Gordon, 3, Ernest, 6, Wally, 4, and Virginia, 8. Their mother had turned them over to the RCMP at Rimbey (the RCMP handled relief in rural areas), asking that winter homes be found for the children because she feared that they would not survive. The family homestead was not within an organized municipality so she and her husband could not obtain relief. Such fears were well founded, as the story of the Zins family from the same area (see text) attests.*

wide prairie fire destroyed five farms and killed three people near Drumheller. On November 19, 1936, a brush fire destroyed four Cochrane area ranches, sent children running for their lives from their flaming school, killed or devalued hundreds of head of cattle and at one point threatened Calgary itself. Meanwhile the forest service announced that forest fires in 1932 had been the worst in provincial history.

When the rain did come, it often fell in a deluge, replacing drought problems with flash flood problems. On April 29, 1930, rain-fed floods took out much of the gravel highway at High River. On June 17, 1931, a mother and son were killed in Drumheller by a sudden cloudburst that swept their home away. On the same day floods left many homeless at Wayne (where flood waters rose to three feet above the street) and Rosedale when Rosebud Creek flooded two days later. That week 150 were left homeless by floods across Alberta, said the *Edmonton Bulletin*. Highways were washed out, but for the first time in 12 months sloughs were brimming with water.

What alarmed people far more than the weather, however, was the grinding poverty and squalor they saw around them or read about. "'Misérables' Seek Shelter in City's Storm Sewers," said the *Edmonton Journal* on October 21, 1930, noting the parallel between Hugo's novel and the "homeless wanderers" who had gained access from the North Saskatchewan riverbank to a large tunnel under Edmonton's business district. Vigilant city fathers evicted them and padlocked the entrance. So the unemployed built shelters by burrowing into the riverbank itself, then furnished them. George Miwlisch, who lived in such a cave for three years, had glass windows, linoleum on the floor, and a back porch, said the *Journal*. He had also fenced his property, and gave his address as "Seventh Tee, Mayfair Golf Links," which was just above his head.

Calgary also had its hobo jungles on the banks of the Elbow River near Victoria Park, where makeshift shacks housed hundreds of unemployed people. As early as May 1930, Calgary, albeit

Everywhere bartering returned to the agricultural economy. In 1932, farmers travelled through the Crowsnest Pass to swap wheat for vegetables, fruit and eggs with B.C. farmers. At Coronation farmers were trading wheat for whatever they could get. Alberta Government Telephones announced it would accept wheat for payment of any bill.

reluctantly, allowed a tent city to be set up on the Bow Bend riverflat immediately west of the CPR tracks, where "children are revelling," according to the *Albertan*. Eleven days later a flood of applications to move into "Tent City" so alarmed aldermen that they capped the number of tents

Everybody who could kept a garden in the Thirties. (Some who couldn't were still required to do so as a condition of their relief.) (Left) Mrs. Hattie Matilda Spearman came to Okotoks to stay with her daughter, Mrs. Coultry, and seemed determined to do her share. She is shown here hoeing in the backyard garden. (Above) This couple is cutting potatoes for seed in the Hanna area.

at twelve and the number of dwellers at sixty. The city generously ran in a communal water pipe.

Living conditions could be much worse. A letter found in Prime Minister R.B. Bennett's Calgary constituency files read: "Officials of the city Health department have found it next to impossible to prevent men and women carting away spoiled food from the dump at Nose Creek... On several occasions sanitary inspectors herded persons away from the dump only to find that they had returned later in the day."

Other desperate people made direct appeals to newspapers, which published their pleas and invited donations. "I am a mother of seven children," said a letter to the *Albertan*. "My children are in bad need of shoes and stockings. We need a stove and some underwear. We are alone here, in a poor house, on a homestead 180 miles north of Edmonton. My husband went away four months ago and has never come back... Trying to look after seven children makes you nearly

---

'Homeless wanderers' had gained access from the North Saskatchewan riverbank to a large tunnel under Edmonton's business district. Vigilant city fathers evicted them and padlocked the entrance. So the unemployed built shelters by burrowing into the riverbank itself, then furnished them. One had glass windows, linoleum on the floor, and a back porch.

---

crazy. We are in bush country. We have no stove and no heater." People almost always responded lavishly.

Similarly the *Edmonton Journal* of December 14, 1932, portrayed a family: "Rough boards, straw-filled sacks and a few rags form the bed of an 11-year-old girl who is recovering from a severe attack of painful rheumatic fever... Her parents managed to get an old bed but no springs or mattress. The father has not worked for many months." The *Calgary Herald* of January 14, 1932: "A family of four, a man, his wife and two children, transported to Calgary because they were thought to be residents of this city. They are now being shipped back to Winnipeg by order of provincial authorities." Said Calgary Mayor Andy Davison: "The taxpayers of Calgary should not be asked to support this family." Callous, he knew, but his city bordered on bankruptcy.

Some gave city officials no choice. They simply abandoned their children. One mother left her four at the Edmonton police department. She told Desk Sergeant Reg Jennings: "My husband left me a year ago. Here are my children. They are hungry and I have no money to feed them." Before Sergeant Jennings could reply, she rushed from the building and vanished down the street.[4]

The *Calgary Herald* interviewed men who were sifting through garbage cans on a cold day in

Then there was the humble gopher. A little animal--much the size of a squirrel; almost the colour of the sun-bleached prairie—its chief function in life was to help reduce our bushelage by eating or storing our grain where we couldn't get at it. Sometimes—if the gophers got very hungry—they would even eat each other. During the worst years in the dust bowl, some of our neighbours were reduced to salting gophers in barrels, to be placed later on the family table as a special treat. Not very pretty, I admit—but true.
—from *Palaces in the Dust Bowl*, by N.B. James, *in The Alberta Golden Jubilee Anthology*

[4]The *Medicine Hat News* reported from Calgary in November 1934 that the unemployed were threatening to "park" their children in city hall corridors unless food allowances were increased. In July 1936 Medicine Hat families who had been dropped from relief lists occupied city hall. Women and children took over the council chamber. They left only when their previous level of assistance was restored.

During two desperate months travelling from Peace River to Edmonton, the Fehrs subsisted on cold tea, breadcrusts, syrup, the occasional sip of milk and strawberries picked beside the road. From left to right are: Abram Jr., 4; Helen, 6; John, 2, standing in front of his father; Agatha, 3; Cornie, 10; Herman, 8; and Elizabeth holding Peter, aged 3 months.

The story behind a famous Depression photograph

AN EDMONTON POLICEMAN SNAPPED THE PICTURE OF THE STARVING FEHRS

by DAVIS SHEREMATA

When a police constable photographed an unemployed blacksmith named Abram C. Fehr and his family in Edmonton's Market Square in 1934, he little realized he was creating probably the most famous image to come out of the Great Depression.

His picture of the family fleeing poverty and starvation in Peace River ran in several newspapers. "It's an important photo," says Barry Broadfoot, who nearly 40 years later put it on the cover of *Ten Long Years* (Toronto, Doubleday, 1973) his best-selling oral history of the 1930s. "It symbolized the Canadian Okie fleeing nature's fury and God's wrath."

Behind the picture lies a story that epitomizes, if not what Westerners always are, at least what most think they ought to be.

Abram and his young family were living in the tiny village of Hague, 30 miles north of Saskatoon, when the Great Depression set in. He heard work and land were plentiful in northwestern Alberta, and decided to start anew in Carcajou, a settlement of fellow Old Colony Mennonites, about 225 miles north of Peace River.

In the fall of 1933 he and Elizabeth held an auction sale and sold everything except their truck, a kitchen table and chairs and some bedding. In that truck, besides the Fehrs and their six children, were Abram's brother Isaac, his wife and their five children.

At Peace River the two families rented a cabin while Abram and Isaac built a barge powered by the truck motor. They then set out on the river. Encamped the first night, "it snowed real heavy and in the morning there was about a foot of snow on the blankets," Cornie recalled in 1976, when the family was interviewed by Paul Grescoe for *The Canadian Magazine*.

Then things got worse. A huge ice floe punched a hole in their boat and forced them to land 125 miles short of their destination. Abram broke his left leg when he slipped on the ice unloading the boat. The Fehrs lived in a bachelor's hunting shack while Abram recovered and Isaac built a rudimentary house with branches and dirt for a roof. That winter the family lived on noodles, biscuits and some moose, elk and deer meat while Abram earned money shooting squirrels for 12 to 18 cents a skin.

One night Elizabeth gave birth to child number seven, Peter, forever known in the family as the Peace River Kid. "It was hard when I was pregnant," Elizabeth recalled in 1970. "I sit and cry and sit and cry...You know who the doctor was? My man was my doctor, and we have a nice baby."

In spring the Fehrs arrived at Carcajou and found a flood had put their homestead under water. The Mennonite community they counted on for support had fled to the hills in search of dry land. "Seven kids, and then we have nothing," Elizabeth said. "Money was all gone. I was not happy."

Isaac and his family returned to Saskatchewan. With just a few dollars and no prospects; Abram decided to follow his brother a few days later. He traded his boat for a 1927 Chevrolet car and trailer and took his family south. The Fehrs got by on cold tea, breadcrusts, syrup, the occasional sip of milk and strawberries picked next to the road.

For weeks the family pushed and pulled the car through rain and mud. Barely halfway to Edmonton their money ran out. To get by, Abram did odd jobs at every farmhouse that would hire him while the children begged for handouts.

Two months after leaving Carcajou the Fehrs arrived in Edmonton. Elizabeth was so weak and starved she could not nurse Peter, just three months old. The family had not eaten for more than a day. Elizabeth and three of her children were barefoot. Within minutes of pulling into town the Chevrolet's axle broke. Abram and Cornie took it to a nearby garage, where they were told it could not be welded.

"Father's English was not too good and he told me to ask if he could weld it himself," Cornie recalls. "The foreman kind of laughed, he thought we were crazy." After Abram welded the axle back together, the foreman inspected it and offered him a job. Abram declined.

Constables Ed Kenny and Ernie Foster found Abram in the Market Square trying to sell his watch and the trailer he had towed from Peace River. The policemen fed the family at the station house and took them to the Salvation Army. A collection taken at the station house raised some money for the Fehrs and a local woman named Mrs. W.E. Simmons contributed some hand-me-down clothing and two days' worth of food.

When the Salvation Army took the Fehrs in, their undernourished baby was taken away for a while, to the horror of his mother. "They give us the meals, meat and cookies and cake, but I can't much eat," said Elizabeth. "They take away my baby. I worry... Then in an hour and a half there was the baby. Two police and two policewomen

and they have it in a white blanket and they dress it so nice and give it a bottle with milk. My blanket was all so poor. Then you know what I do? I cry. And oh, the police were so good, they say, 'No cry, no cry.' Then I say, 'Thank you very much.'"

Back in Hague the Fehrs moved into their old house (the buyer had never paid for it) and Abram took up blacksmithing again. In 1940 he bought some farmland outside of town. "We had a fairly good crop of wheat and from then on, things started looking up," said Cornie.

Although the family would prosper as farmers, nothing ever came easy. A baby born to Abram and Elizabeth after their return to Saskatchewan died in infancy. Then on July 1, 1946, Abram was drilling a well when some dynamite exploded; he lost half of his left arm and the sight in one eye. "We all had to pitch in and help. But Dad finally perked up and started working again. He got an artificial arm with a hook and a hand you could switch and he could work as well as most people who have two good arms. He was not the kind of man who gave up, says Cornie"

Elizabeth died in 1992 of complications from diabetes, followed by her husband three years later. By the century's end, most of the seven Fehr children in the policeman's photo still lived within a few miles of Hague. Peter, the

Dave Clark

Curious as to what ever happened to the Fehr family, writer Paul Grescoe tracked them down in 1976, forty-two years later, and found most of them still living at Hague, Saskatchewan. Photographer Dave Clark reassembled them in the original pose. Standing in for John is his brother-in-law John Blazzi; sister Betty represents Agatha; brother-in-law Bill Wiebe represents Herman.

Peace River Kid, lived on Abram and Elizabeth's farm. John, a retired tinsmith, was in Calgary, and Herman, a retired logger in Burns Lake, British Columbia, live far away from the family. Cornie, a retired dairy and grain farmer, explained why, 64 years after their venture into Alberta, the family stayed so close: "We learned to stick together in order to survive."

February 1933. "One announced he had found a pair of old boots which fortunately fitted him. Another stated he had found a pair of quite serviceable trousers, while others had gathered pieces of cloth, an old paint brush, a tobacco pouch and numerous small articles... One was found who admitted he was hungry enough to eat bread crusts."

Gustav Zins, a homesteader 20 miles west of Rimbey, phoned a doctor when he thought his young daughter was dying, the *Edmonton Bulletin* reported in January 1937. When Dr. J.N.C. Byers arrived he was shocked at what he found. "Three of the children, Herta, 7, Lillian, 3 (who had pneumonia and was bleeding at the mouth), and Alvina, 11, were wrapped by the doctor and Constable Fordham in their own coats and rushed to hospital suffering from intestinal flu." The farmer explained he had no money and no food. At least one of the children had not eaten for a week. Emergency relief was rushed to the family but too late to save Lillian.

Some of the clearest pictures of the poverty and desperation appeared in the letters written to Prime Minister Bennett. War veteran Richard J. O'Hearn, of Southwark, Alberta,[5] listed the food in his house: two loaves of bread, no flour, yeast, sugar, butter, fat or lard, soap, or anything to spread on the bread. He had a dozen eggs, but since the family had eaten 152 eggs in the previous nine days they could no longer keep them down. He had a wife and three children, one of them taken from school because he wasn't getting enough to eat. The Southwark council forwarded the letter to Bennett, noting everything it said was true.

Noah Norris of Calgary, who wrote to Bennett as "a brother in Masonry" and

Using all the skills and resources available to them, Albertans provided for themselves and others. Vernon Stellmaker of Thorsby (above) poses proudly with a cougar measuring six feet nine inches from head to tail. (Right) Buffalo were slaughtered at Wainwright and sent north as relief food to Indians and Eskimos throughout the Thirties. Participants in this 1939 kill are identified as (L-R): Sam Purcell; Ivan Pigeon; George Armstrong; unidentified; Murray Trefry; Blake Sharpe; unidentified; F. Cliff Saville. The truck belonged to Mr. Saville.

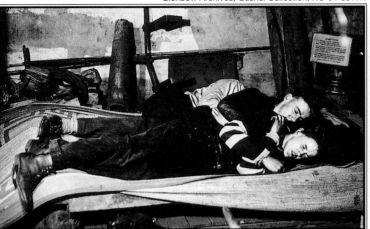

who said that in 1906 he had become the first farmer in Alberta to raise a 50-bushel-an-acre wheat crop, confessed: "It takes courage, and courage of the bravest kind, to ask for relief. I have been humiliated and sent from pillar to post, just as if I were a criminal." He couldn't go on relief because he had lived in Calgary only eleven of the requisite twelve months. But his sick wife had been put on a diet of milk, beefsteak, orange juice and "certain medicines" which he couldn't buy. "I don't want to see her die by inches before my eyes."

A.N. Starlight of Crest Willow[5]: "I had my crop completely hailed out... I am on the sick list... I have a bad ulcerated stomach... If it had not been for our storekeeper we would have starved. I have been here nearly 22 years and have never asked for anything before."

Mrs. Jonathan Forester of Brazeau wanted clothes. Everything her husband earned in the bush had been spent on food and "it isn't very nice to have to go out in 50-below weather with hardly any clothes on." She included her bust size, and said her husband was "medium" and took Size 7 boots. She also needed sheets. Bennett instructed that they be sent "a package."

This response was not unusual. Bennett often replied with money from his own pocket, like the five dollars he sent to Mrs. R. Paddy of Burton,[5] who had written: "Please help me by lending me some money and I will send you my engagement ring and wedding ring as security... My rings

Escape was not easy for those held most tightly in the jaws of the Depression. Even sleep was not readily come by, as for these men in the Crowsnest area. Photographed by Thomas Gushul of Blairmore, they may have been transients, or possibly itinerant miners. What is certain is that the accommodations that the people of the Crowsnest, who were wrestling with mine shutdowns, strikes and layoffs, were able to provide was modest, to say the least.

In 1932 the *Edmonton Journal* portrayed a family: 'Rough boards, straw filled sacks and a few rags form the bed of an 11-year-old girl who is recovering from a severe attack of painful rheumatic fever... Her parents managed to get an old bed but no springs or mattress. The father has not worked for months.'

---

[5]These place locations are cited in *The Wretched of Canada: Letters to R.B. Bennett, 1930-1935*, L.M. Grayson and Michael Bliss, eds. (University of Toronto Press, 1971). However, they are not listed as place names in Alberta Energy's Geographical Names of Alberta and likely are misreadings of handwritten letters.

cost over $100 15 years ago but what good are they when the flour is nearly all done and there isn't much to eat in the house?"

Some letters to Bennett were brief and bitter, like one dated May 20, 1931, and signed, "Sudbury Starving Unemployed." Addressed to "Mr. Bennette," it read: "Since you have been elected, work has been impossible to get. We have decided that in a month from this date, if things are the same, we'll skin you alive the first chance we get."

City families could at least stay put. Farm families were often driven from the land, and thousands of single men drifted across the country on freight trains in such numbers that the railway police frequently gave up all effort to stop them. Their quest, of course, was usually work, and usually they didn't find it. The result was a rail-riding subculture (see sidebar). But riding freights was always a dangerous way to travel.

Thus Frank Reiner, 25, a Dutch immigrant, numb with cold and hampered by a backpack, lost his balance while jumping from a train at Rocky Mountain House. Both legs were severed. Finn Dahl from Saskatchewan, 17, fell while trying to board a train at Medicine Hat and lost both feet. Edward Zimmer, Henry Greilach and Arthur Milovanov of Regina fell asleep on the tracks at Red

[6]Not all the railway accidents involved transients. In January 1936 a young construction worker in Northwestern Ontario was clearing a hose line entangled in the undercarriage of a boxcar. Suddenly he heard the click of the wheels and realized the car was moving. He rolled out, avoiding being cut in half, but the wheels ran over his right shoulder. The victim lived to become the great wildlife artist of western Canada, one-armed Clarence Tillenius.

Riding the rails was an option for the daring, provided they could avoid the CNR and CPR police. It was a risky business, but the most dangerous part of it — "riding the rods," underneath the railway cars — doesn't appear in photographs.

Deer and were decapitated by the wheels of a locomotive. The oldest was 19. When word reached J.W. McLeod of Blue Ridge near Whitecourt, who was looking for work on the Coal Branch, that one of his children was dying, he stowed away in a locomotive tender to get home. The coal shifted and buried him alive.[6]

Women too rode the freights. Police inspecting a train just arrived in Winnipeg found Mrs. Mary Donik and her 17-month-old baby trembling in the empty grain car they had ridden for nearly a thousand miles from Sudbury. They were headed for Vegreville, said the mother, eight hundred miles farther ahead, where relatives awaited her.

On October 1, 1932, on orders from Bennett himself, the RCMP joined the railway police to crack down on freight-jumpers. That day they took 147 men off the freights at Calgary. Three days later, 32 more were arrested. Some paid fines of $1, some were released, some spent 36 hours in jail, twelve were sentenced to thirty days. In Wetaskiwin police removed 27 from one train. Twelve paid fines; the others were locked up. Angry transients threatened to commandeer vehicles and force motorists to carry them. Instead they simply went back to illegally jumping the freights.

The railway crackdown forced many hundreds to remain in the cities where they created impossible problems and found themselves shunned and unwanted. RCMP watched railway yards across Alberta to turn away transients. Medicine Hat declared it would supply meals, but only to men willing to work for their room and board. Calgary did the same.

"Don't Give Money to Panhandlers on the Street," warned a 1932 headline in the *Lethbridge Herald*. Tell the beggar to "go to the police," the story advised. If he says he has already been there, "nine chances out of ten he's a panhandler who would rather beg than go to a relief camp." Edmonton spent more than $7,000 supplying 500,000 bowls of porridge, served with sugar and milk, between May and September of 1931. So it advised its citizens: Ask beggars to show their relief cards. If they have one, give them nothing. Mendicants soon learned not to have one. By the end of 1933 more than 3,000 single unemployed men had been sent to relief camps run by the Canadian army where a man earned 20 cents a day working under rigorous military discipline (see next chapter).

Many unemployed resorted to theft, often of food, and sometimes from houses. "Thieves broke in and took two plates of ice cream from the kitchen table," reported the *Albertan* on April 9, 1930. "Nothing else was touched." The *Lethbridge Herald* of June 16, 1931, reported a café in

Life atop Freight No. 404

A REPORTER JOINS THE HOBO SET AND DISCOVERS HOW AN UNDERCLASS LIVES

Through the severest years of the depression small armies of unemployed single men would arrive daily in Edmonton, hidden in boxcars or clinging to rods underneath trains. After R.B. Bennett's federal government made it illegal to ride freight trains — from midnight, September 30, 1932 — Edmonton Journal reporter R. F. MacLean spent some time with rod-riders coming and going from Edmonton's Calder railyards. The following is a portion of one of his dispatches:

FIFTEENTH CAR BEHIND ENGINE 3554, SOMEWHERE EAST OF EDMONTON, Oct. 3 — How these hoboes hate Edmonton! It's now about 3:00 a.m. and I am well on my way eastward on through freight 404.

I started my hobo hunting freight tour at midnight, September 30 at the Calder yards, when I drifted out to the first "jungle." I found five 'boes around a little fire — and they didn't even grunt when I arrived. From them I got the real low down about what the transients think about Edmonton, Mr. Bennett's ban on freight travel — and other assorted topics.

have to do is cough and you get what you want. I was making about $4 a day there.

"But take Edmonton. Now you could get the handouts easy enough if the cops would leave you alone. But the first thing you knew you are like to get the Fort for a stretch. And the meals at the Fort are ——." Dashes indicate the profane opinion that Marcus had of Fort Saskatchewan jail restaurant service, colourful but unprintable.

In the intervals of Marcus' orations and his rhetorical decision to leave Edmonton as soon as possible and as far behind as possible, the 'boes talked about their train.

They knew by the moccasin telegraph of the jungle that the next through freight east was 404, hauled by engine No. 3554 and that it was made up on track No. 12 and its time of departure. In fact they knew everything about the train but the conductor's age. Further along the line other fires with little knots of men about them showed that other groups of transients were also waiting for No. 404.

"I wonder are the bulls out to start this raid on the stiffs?" whispered a young transient in my ear as we

---

A man of about 40 with a permanent grouch joined the little knot of drifters around the fire. 'Edmonton is the lousiest place for handouts I ever did strike,' he said. 'The Dicks (police) are on your tail from the time you drop off until you book out again, and the relief system is lousy too. I wish I was back in Flagstaff, Arizona.'

In the jungle — which is hobo parlance for any place where there are more than two 'boes waiting for a freight — there aren't any names used. So in introducing the five floaters with whom I joined forces, I will have to forego the usual cognomens.

One, a man of about 40 with a permanent grouch, a boasting streak and an inclination to rhetoric, I will call Marcus Aurelius. When I joined the little knot of drifters around the fire, Marcus was discoursing about his past:

"I've drifted from New Brunswick down to Agua Caliente but Edmonton is the lousiest place for handouts I ever did strike. The Dicks (police to you) are on your tail from the time you drop off until you book out again, and the relief system here is lousy too.

"I wish I was back in Flagstaff, Arizona. When I was down there I had a real graft. I would go around to the church doors on Sundays just as church was letting out and throw a little coughing fit. That was always good for anything from a free meal to a $10 handout and a suit of clothes. You see that's the TB state down there and all you

crouched in the cover of a little clump of bushes. "I see the papers say they are going to start at midnight tonight. Look!"

He pulled out a clipping from the *Journal*, soiled and wrinkled. "I don't think they can do much, do you? There's too many stiffs here tonight. Anyway I guess if they are clipping (arresting) them I think they'll pick some of those others down the yards." And he pointed to a knot of men carrying their packsacks half a mile down the tracks toward Calder.

"What will you do if they catch you?" I asked him.

"Well they will have a job getting me," he answered. "I will just run outside the railway fence and chuck rocks at them."

"Why go outside the fence?" growled a husky Ukrainian on the other side. "Those fellows would shoot you down for a dollar-ten a day — if they come just gang up on them, and then they will beat it."

"That's all right to talk about, but I don't want no Dicks shooting me," the young hobo answered. "If they want to shoot, they can pick somebody else. I'll be a good boy."

Although immigration was at a virtual standstill by 1933, immigrants continued to be vilified by native-born Canadians for taking the jobs that were, in their minds, rightfully theirs. (Above) Olha Nakoneozhniyj, 9, and her brother, Jurij, 7, arrived in Edmonton on December 5, 1931, to be reunited with their parents, who had immigrated earlier. Their father, an Edmonton tailor, had not seen his children in four years. (Upper right) Until the early Thirties the CPR had been very active in recruiting Europeans to populate the land along their railway lines, and many came in groups. Like all homesteaders, the key to success had been in community, with neighbour helping neighbour. In 1929 two families lived with Piotr Sokol at his farm on the Gainford CPR colony until their own homes were built. (Lower right) Hutterites in particular were a target for prejudice in some farming communities.

[7] The Lloydminster case did not typify the CPR's Depression policy which was often more compassionate than that of governments. The *Calgary Herald* in May, 1931, for instance reported the company paying $700,000 in back taxes for settlers on CPR land to prevent forfeiture. It also forgave interest payments.

Fort Macleod suffered two break-ins in a week; nothing but food was taken.

In the country, wheat and livestock were frequently stolen. The *Lloydminster Times* reported in January 1932 how the Canadian Pacific took a farmer to court for selling a crop grown on CPR land and using the proceeds for winter living expenses, rather than paying his land rental.[7] The *Calgary Herald* told how a Cochrane homesteader got two years for stealing three cows and selling the beef to obtain money to buy dirt cheap fox meat to feed his family. "Ten farmers from the Rosenheim area raided a government-owned supply of wheat in [nearby] Provost to feed starving cattle," reported the *Edmonton Journal*. "Thirty-three bales of hay were taken." The farmers said they were desperate.

Even armed robbers blamed their crimes on unemployment. Police nabbed Albert Barron on a train at Unity, Saskatchewan, reported the *Edmonton Journal* of March 25, 1930. Barron had pointed a revolver at a grocery store owner the night before and escaped with the day's proceeds. Asked by the magistrate why he did it, Barron replied from the prisoner's dock. "I was out of work. I wanted to get away and didn't have the money. So I just took that way of getting it."

Others were equally desperate. When the *Lethbridge Herald* offered free space to any employer advertising a job, one such ad produced a mob at a furniture store. An elderly lady asked for work carrying furniture. Refused, she begged for the chance to scrub floors.

The job shortage was widely blamed on immigrants. As early as January 1930 Edmonton was checking relief registrants to spot newcomers to Canada. In the year ending March 31, 1930, 5,000 immigrants were registered as arriving in northern Alberta. But the immigrants were not docile. The next month a parade of them marched on Lethbridge city hall, angered by the fact they were being blamed for taking jobs. They were jobless too, they said.

At a convention in Calgary of the Imperial Order Daughters of the Empire, the president, Mrs. R.C. Marshall, worried that immigration would "severely test and perhaps even endanger our British ideals and those things we love." On the same February day, Alberta Agriculture Minister George Hoadley announced an intergovernmental conference on the effects of immigration in the prairie provinces. In August Hoadley, acting premier, protested to Ottawa that 200 German immigrants had been "dumped" in Alberta.

By October 1930 it became evident the Americans had the same attitude. They suddenly refused entry to Canadians playing in the National Hockey League, disrupting the league's operations and creating what the *Lethbridge Herald* called "a mess." In July 1931 Canada reciprocated. A number of North Dakota Hutterites had bought land in Alberta, worked it for a year, then returned to the U.S. to move their colony north. They were denied re-entry into Canada.

In January 1932 Edmonton relief superintendent Thomas Magee announced a plan to "deport" from the city all persons of foreign birth who had been in Edmonton less than five years. Several indignant immigrants reminded him that the Canadian government had invited them in as homesteaders; they had made an honest effort and now were victims of the Depression like everyone else.

But the harshest attitudes were reserved for the Chinese. In Calgary sixty-three were cut off relief after it had been reported that the Chinese community had donated $10,000 to support China in its war with Japan. If they could afford this, they could look after their own indigents, said the aldermen. The *Calgary Herald* later reported that the relief allowance for Chinese was $1.12 a week, as against the $2 a week charged by the pound to feed and shelter a dog.

> I am the flunky of the house, they call me Flunky Jim,
> You'll find me knocking around the yard in a hat without a brim.
> My overalls are shabby and I have no shirt at all,
> But I'm going to get a new outfit with my gopher tails next fall.
> —from T.B. and P.J. Rogers, Some folk songs from the Thirties, in *The Dirty Thirties in Western Canada*, R.D. Francis and H. Ganzevoort, eds.

Sometimes the worry and despair proved too much

LOST JOBS, HOMES, FARMS AND SELF-RESPECT DRIVE MANY TO END THEIR LIVES

Economic depression generated clinical depression in the Thirties, often leading to suicide. In 1930 alone, at least 71 Albertans committed suicide, compared with 23 who were murdered.

• In April, 1931, Clarence Cridland, a 53-year-old Pincher Creek farmer, shattered by losses on grain, took his own life by drinking formaldehyde.

• In May 1931, R.C. Vooght of Camrose, depressed by the loss of his job, killed his wife and two children, then drowned himself.

• In August 1931, Edgar Joseph Barnes, an unemployed transient, made a noisy protest outside a Lethbridge residence, claiming that he had not received payment for work done there. He was arrested and thrown into jail, where he committed suicide in his cell.

• Also in May 1931, John Jean Bechinet, a young farmer in the Therien area, north of St. Paul and west of Bonnyville, grew so despondent over his financial situation that he was driven to shoot his aged parents and then himself.

• In June 1931, at Rainier, southwest of Brooks, Fred Leike killed his housekeeper, Mrs. Elizabeth Irwin, and her two-year-old daughter Kathleen, doused their bodies and the house with gasoline, set the gasoline afire and finally killed himself.

• In September of 1932 the province was shocked by the suicide of Harold Huxley, long-time mayor of Lloydminster, evidently in despair over financial difficulties.

• In December 1934 Mrs. Isabel Brown, 37, of Dorenlee, between Camrose and Stettler, attempted to kill her six children by giving them candies laced with gopher poison, but only one died. The mother then shot herself.

As late as 1938 there were Depression-related suicides. Early in that year Alfred Smith, a destitute bachelor farmer of the Rose Lynn district, east of Drumheller, soaked a pile of Russian thistle with gasoline, set it alight, then shot himself so that he would fall face-down into the fire.

The Depression claimed lives in other ways.

• In 1934 Hugh McPhail, a lone homesteader of the Peace River area, froze to death in his roofless hut.

• A few weeks later Mrs. Fred Nicholls, a deserted mother in the Winfield district, was found dead in bed, where she had apparently lain helpless for five days. Her three small children were still trying to feed her.

• In April 1935, near Drumheller, Corporal Michael Moriarity of the RCMP was killed and Const. Roy Allan was wounded in a two-hour gun battle which began when the two officers attempted to serve a summons on farmer David Knox, who then opened fire. Knox fled to a granary where he was killed by police bullets which penetrated the walls.

How much other mayhem and violence had its origins in the economic calamity will never be known.

Any payment was better than no payment at all — even Alberta Government Telephones was accepting wheat in exchange for services by 1933. These farmers are grading a road in the Grande Prairie area in order to reduce their taxes.

By January 1933 immigration was at a standstill, but the resentment of immigrants remained. Some people in the Crowsnest Pass "bring shame onto the whole province," said Mr. Justice W.C. Ives of the Alberta Court of Appeal, "and always it is people of foreign birth."

One by one, familiar agricultural institutions disappeared. In 1932 the colleges at Raymond and Claresholm closed; the money to run them had run out. Organizations that had represented the pride of Alberta's farming community also began folding. At Taber, two agricultural societies were declared officially dead. Local fairs, of which 108 were held in Alberta in 1921, had dwindled to forty-nine in 1931 and to ten just three years later.

Wages were cut from the top to the bottom. Premier Brownlee chopped the salaries of provincial civil servants by a total of $320,000, and took a $1,200 reduction himself. Every member of the legislature received a pay cut of ten per cent. The Calgary city police supported a petition to have their own salaries reduced by four per cent, although the head of the police union resigned over the issue.

Squabbles over who would pay the cost of the Depression raged between governments. In April 1932 the mayors of Edmonton and Calgary met with Premier Brownlee to once more ask for relief dollars. It would be two years before the premier increased relief funding for the cities, and then by only 2.5 per cent.

The initial federal attitude was outlined in January 1930 when Interior Minister Charles Stewart in the outgoing King government wrote to Edmonton Mayor J.M. Douglas. Unemployment was a provincial responsibility, he said. Other than providing public works where required, Ottawa was not concerned. His government was defeated a few months later, but the succeeding Tory Bennett government at first took the same stand.

Meanwhile, the cities went broke. Even back in July of 1930 the Bank of Montreal warned Calgary that a combination of $150,000 overspending on relief and a growing amount of tax arrears had put the city in the red by $275,000. A *Calgary Herald* editorial the following February pointed out that eleven per cent of Canadian municipal debentures were in default in the past three years amounting to $141,150,000. Although Ottawa sent $175,000 a month to the province for relief in 1935, the federal government ended its city relief program in December of that year, and at the same time turned down a request from Calgary for a $150,000 loan.

The Depression home soon became much more self-sufficient. Newspapers carried columns showing people how to live on sparse grocery budgets. The *Edmonton Journal* told how 25 cents worth of meat could be turned into a meal for six. The meat concentrated on such items as brains and stewed heart. People preserved everything they could — first rhubarb in the spring, followed by strawberries, then peas, corn, raspberries, apples, wild blackberries, saskatoons, chokecherries and thimbleberries. From off-grade fats, they made soap. In the fall, every household was said to

smell of pickles. Every scrap of material was used to make clothing, and locally-produced wool was being washed, carded and made into quilts and comforters.

A certain ingenuity was appearing everywhere. Some actually advertised for jobs. A Calgarian offered $25 to anybody who would find him one. He described himself as single and handy with tools and machinery. Hockey teams bartered tickets for foodstuffs, one promoter suggesting a bushel of wheat as an admission fee. Eaton's department store employees voluntarily took a day off work each week to save their colleagues from layoffs. In Ponoka, one individual got eggs on credit from a local merchant, sold them to a creamery for cash and then used the cash to buy gasoline.

Fred Hranac, who farmed at Coaldale, was short of gasoline for his car and kerosene for his lamps. He rigged up a device that used wind to turn a wheel, which was then hooked up to his car's generator to charge the car battery and light the house. On November 26, 1931, the *Calgary Herald* reported that an unnamed company in a rural municipality bought food in large quantities

(Above) Edmonton relief crews clear ice from sidewalks at 118th Avenue and 95th Street. The temperature on this day in 1939 was -10°F. (Left) These men could afford to keep their sense of humour — they were employed by an oil company in the Lethbridge area in 1936.

War veteran Richard J. O'Hearn of Southwark, Alberta listed the food left in his house: two loaves of bread, no flour, yeast, sugar, butter, fat or lard, soap, or anything to spread on the bread. He had a dozen eggs, but the family had eaten 152 eggs in nine days and they could no longer keep them down. The Southwark council noted that everything he said was true.

---

at low prices and persuaded its employees to donate a percentage of their salaries to purchase clothes for the needy. It then sought volunteers to organize, package and distribute the food and clothing that had been acquired to 62 local families. Tired of living in tents and roaming the streets looking for work, three men walked into the bush near Cochrane, and cleared the land and built shelters for themselves and their families from the logs they had cut.

There was a call for men to pan for gold at Edmonton. Pay consisted of a small percentage of whatever they found. The cost of grubstakes was deducted. One of the gold-panning sites was located on the North Saskatchewan River near the Stony Plain Ferry. Existing mines, such as the one at Duffield, also offered work for men willing to take a small percentage of their production. The Red Cross offered to provide a "stake" to anyone willing to provide upkeep services to workers at the mine. Forty-two men gained employment. A farmer near Provost, identified only as T. Crouch, developed a method of boiling crawling cedar, a plant found in abundance on otherwise

We had a car even in the Depression, when the rich ones didn't... When it came licence time [my husband] would go to the elevator and borrow $10 to buy the licence. And then when he thought, "Well, that's long enough," he'd go to the storekeeper and borrow $10 and pay the elevator guy back until he'd have pigs or grain to sell, and then he'd pay it back. But always he didn't leave it too long.
—Mary Godard of Radway, interviewed on 11 June, 1976 (Provincial Archives of Alberta, Acc.No.81.279).

Glenbow Archives, McDermid Collection, ND-3-6484

Glenbow Archives, McDermid Collection, ND-3-6528

Glenbow Archives, NA-4248-1

Some gave of their abundance, others of the little they had

Costs of labour and produce went down during the Depression, which meant that the standard of living went up for those fortunate enough to stay employed or keep their businesses afloat. But Albertans seemed willing to share what they had, great or little, with the less fortunate. [A] A camp for underprivileged boys, operated by the Rotary Club of Edmonton in conjunction with the Boy Scouts of Canada, July 1931. [B] By 1933, when this picture was taken, the annual Kiwanis apple sale was already a tradition in Edmonton. Some of the men have their coats on backwards. [C] Johnnie Althen, Art Bourne, George Tipper and Ed Bussian pose with relief vegetables collected at Taber for the Del Bonita district in 1936. [D] IODE members Mrs. T.H. Mackie, Mrs. W.S. Gray, Mrs. G.M. Findlay and Mrs. Reginald Campbell put the finishing touches on baskets woven by blind workers, to be sold at the lodge's 1933 pre-Christmas sale, held at the Edmonton Hudson's Bay store. [E] The relief society of the Church of Jesus Christ of Latter-Day Saints (Mormons), Calgary ward, around 1929. This was a chapter of a relief organization founded in Illinois in 1842.

A buggy defined the era

When the prosperity that R.B. Bennett had promised to be on the horizon when he was elected in 1930 turned out to be a mirage of the encroaching desert, people all across Canada gave his name to the means of transportation they improvised when they could no longer afford to buy gasoline. Counterclockwise from the bottom left: [1] Two horses pull five people in this Lethbridge area photo. [2] Sinai and Lea Godard were photographed with the child Jeanne Soucy in the Redwater area. [3] This Bennett Buggy was seen near Dapp. [4] Jim and Stan Mayberry pose in a cart that used two Chevrolet wheels at Red Deer. [5] Alfred and Ethel Vallieres are ready to be taken to school in a car pulled by Major. [6] Mr. and Mrs. W.J. Dillane pose in the Viking area with the car they could afford neither to run nor to abandon. [7] Arthur Caldwell and his son Duncan drove from Calgary to Sundre via Cochrane in this makeshift vehicle. Hugh McLean is holding the horse's head. [8] These girls were likely too young to remember the long-gone prosperity represented by this buggy.

barren soil, to produce creosote. He made a living on it.

When Raymond couldn't pay its teachers, it issued them $25,000 in "scrip" as a substitute for money, essentially promissory notes.[8] Local merchants honoured them and they were later redeemed. When a Calgary lawyer wrote that the scrip was being used as money and was therefore illegal, the complaint was ridiculed. Among the comments: "Well, it proves that the joy-killers are not all dead yet," and, "Why can't [lawyers] apply their brains and skill for constructive purposes?" A few years later, Raymond's success would lead to one of Alberta's most celebrated and unsuccessful fiscal experiments, the Social Credit "funny money."

Few enterprises, however, could rival the ingenuity of the thousands of rural youngsters in the gopher business. Most rural municipalities paid a one-cent bounty for a gopher tail. These rodents destroyed tens of thousands of bushels of grain. Boys and girls made string-snares and sat patiently beside gopher holes, waiting for them to poke their heads up, using the revenues to finance visits to the candy store. Gophers served another purpose. People ate smoked gopher, baked gopher, pickled gopher. Children at Stettler, wrote author Gray, enjoyed bread and gopher for lunch.

On May 1, 1930, an annual provincial pest-control competition was launched, enthusiastically backed by the news media. The *Camrose Canadian* announced a "war on crows," calling for the destruction of the birds, eggs and nests. The *Ponoka Herald* reported that a "bountiful harvest" of crow and magpie feet was arriving at the municipal office. By 1933 it was printing the year's results with the previous year's in brackets: Pairs of crow and magpie feet 48,555 (43,614); crow and magpie eggs 201,499 (152,773), gopher tails 725,253 (621,786). First prize went to the Medicine Hat Fish and Game Association. Edmonton's Sportsman's Gun Club had added its own $200 prize. In

1934 the *Red Deer Advocate* advertised: "Crow and magpie eggs wanted." The rates listed were 24 cents an egg and 14 cents for each pair of feet. The offer was for children only, who were warned to leave hawk eggs untouched.

Meanwhile at Lethbridge attention was turned to rattlesnakes. One Hilda area farmer reported he had shipped 200 live ones to a buyer in Lloydminster. Why did the buyer want them, the farmer was asked. "I have no idea," he replied, though he was making almost as much on rattlesnakes as he was on grain. He wasn't alone. The *Blairmore Enterprise* reported in 1934 that squirrel skins "have become almost a standard medium of exchange." Provincial statistics credit the gopher program with killing 700,000 animals a year, about two thirds of the bounties going to children. All this effort notwithstanding, the gophers proliferated steadily throughout the Thirties.

Not all the innovations were motivated positively. When his phone was cut off for non-payment of the bill, a Red Deer area man enterprisingly retaliated by disconnecting the entire neighbourhood. In December 1930, the *Edmonton Journal* reported that an unnamed farmer near the city, informed that his revenue from a load of wheat must go to the bank, dumped the whole load into the bank manager's office. Generally, though, people tried to make light of their miseries. In November 1936 Medicine Hat held a "hard-up costume ball." Some showed up in their long underwear. (These dances were so popular that they were continued in some districts well into the 1960s.)

As always, distress prompted remarkable acts of charity. The experience of Hugh Russell of Nanton was typical of thousands. When he was hospitalized for seven weeks during seeding time in 1933, his neighbours mobilized a force of fourteen six-horse teams and four tractors, and seeded 320 of Russell's acres in a single day. In March 1932 a group of farmers in the Granum area donated 700 bushels of wheat for the benefit of the poor, if the flour mills would grind it for free. They did.

That year H.A. Walter of Raley (near Cardston) wrote the *Lethbridge Herald* offering 100 bushels of wheat for the homeless and jobless if a miller could be found who was willing to grind the wheat gratis, a trucker who would haul the wheat to the mill and a baker who would turn the flour into bread. Within days Ellison Milling and Elevator Company of Lethbridge had undertaken to mill the wheat. D. Morris and D.R. Yates of Lethbridge had volunteered to haul it and George W. Green & Company Ltd. had offered sacks. Then Western Bakery and Canadian Bakeries made a joint offer to turn the flour into loaves.

The most munificent charity, however, was extended by eastern Canada to western. The Red Cross, the United Church and other national organizations shipped into the Prairies hundreds of freight-car loads of clothing and food, including such items as apples from British Columbia and Ontario — even salt cod from Nova Scotia, much of which went uneaten because few people knew it must be soaked overnight to get rid of the salt.[9]

[8]One scrip coupon from Raymond was accepted as legal tender by five Calgary banks before it was redeemed for cash.

[9]Newspapers printed lists, sometimes daily, of local citizens' donations to those in want. In December 1931 the *Lethbridge Herald* carried, on two columns, the names of 98 individuals who had donated a total of $646.55 to the Emergency Relief Appeal. The RCMP detachment donated $72.40.

CHAPTER TWO

The decade when the weather went crazy

After the soil began blowing away in the Twenties and the grasshoppers had eaten what remained of the crops, southern Albertans with no money for warm clothing or fuel faced the winters of the Thirties that numbered among the coldest on record. At first, people could only watch helpless as their labour, hopes and dreams were swept away in black blizzards. This duststorm blew into Lethbridge in the late 1930s.

BON-TON ST
BOOTS AND SH

This duststorm blew into Fort Macleod. Farmers would be scrambling to protect their belongings, and few stopped to photograph these events.

This Thirties' duststorm was photographed near Twin Rivers, then a post office near the Saskatchewan border, ten miles south of the South Saskatchewan River.

This was the result of a duststorm near Hanna. Wind easily picks up soil like this and the ensuing storm furthers erosion.

Dust

Palliser's Triangle had been turning to dust long before the 1930s, but by the end of the decade, even the northern half of the province was experiencing black blizzards, and fear of a province-wide drought was spreading. And winter provided no reprieve as land lay bare due to low snowfall or high drifting. On January 5, 1938, the Edmonton Journal recorded that Calgary pilot Ted Holmes had encountered a duststorm at 9,000 feet over Lethbridge.

This 1930s duststorm, between Fort Macleod and Monarch, was photographed looking east. Later, homesteaders would tell of the fleas that were blown in with the sand.

This soil blew down from the north into Parkland, southeast of Calgary, in 1938, then turned east just north of the hotel, shown at left, which burned down during the Second World War.

A

B

Wind

The pioneers had planted hedges as windbreaks, but few had survived the drought. [A] Sand-blown corn near Rosthern, Saskatchewan, on August 23, 1938. [B] The Smith homestead house covered with hay, also in 1938. [C] The result of a tornado in the Viking area in August 1935. A binder is upside-down on what had been the roof of A.B. Gilpin's machine shed. [D] Railroad tracks after a duststorm near Grainger, south of Three Hills: the railways used snowplows to clear the tracks of soil. [E] A combination of sleet and strong wind blew telephone poles down at Strathmore on April 20, 1932.

C

D

Grasshoppers

These vacant farms became breeding grounds for grasshoppers. Government scientists fought back with arsenic, bran, sawdust and molasses concocted at local mixing stations. [A] Jack Crowe examines a Manitoba grain field that has been completely stripped. [B] Caterpillars in southern Alberta. [C] Adult grasshoppers in Saskatchewan. [D] Allan Egan's garage in the Bow Island area in 1935, covered with 'hoppers. [E] A grasshopper invasion near Chestermere Lake.

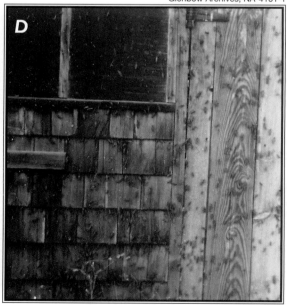

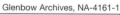

E

Fire

Drought and heat made conditions ripe for fire throughout the 1930s in the South. Blamed on electrical storms, carelessness and even arson, they were fed by strong winds that rendered fireguards ineffective. [A] The fire at Foremost in April 1930 destroyed the east side of the main street. The year 1934 saw forest fires at Willow Creek, in the Cypress Hills [B] and at Elkwater Lake [E]. [C] An elevator fire at Alderson. [D] The Cheviot Hotel at Mountain Park burned in September 1934.

A

D

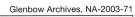

B

C

E

A

Snow

It drifted in spots 15 feet high. [A] A Greyhound bus was stuck for a month in the Crowsnest because of impassable roads. [B] A snowplow clears roads east of Cowley. [C] A snowbound train is stopped near Nobleford. [D] A sleet storm that lasted from April 20 to 26, 1932, felled telephone lines near Strathmore. [E] The main street of Cowley is blocked after a February 1936 snowstorm. [F] A Greyhound bus follows a snowplow on the Calgary-Edmonton highway in 1930. The company had its own plows. [G] The Kosior farm at Tide Lake, 1938, had snowdrifts so high that the cows could climb into the hayloft. [H] Railway engine at Bon Accord, May 22, 1930.

B

C

D

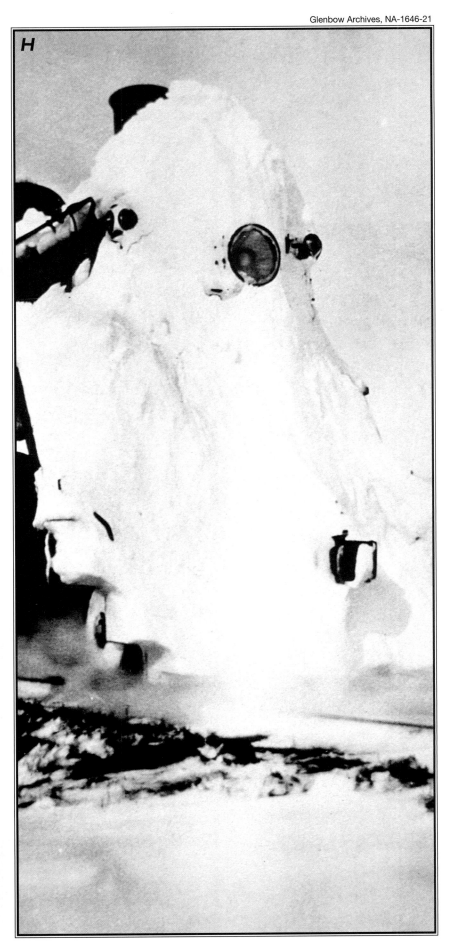

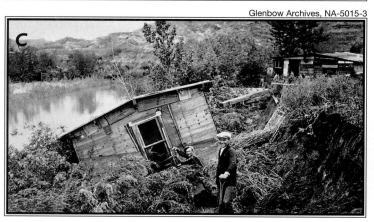

THE GRIM YEARS

Provincial Archives of Alberta, A 7919

E

Glenbow Archives, NA-2952-76

F

Floods

Land denuded by erosion or fire could not absorb water when it did come. [A, E & H] The Lethbridge Herald in June 1931 described "a cloudburst that pitched thousands of gallons of water over the town of Wayne as if poured from a giant pitcher" that killed a woman and her son and left 150 homeless. [B] Men lifting and surfacing railway tracks at Slave Lake following a flood, 1935. [C] Miners demonstrate damage done to their shack by flooding of Rosebud Creek, June 1931. [D & F] In 1930 the Highwood River overflowed, resulting in the flooding of High River. [G] Ice jams causing flooding were a recurrent problem in Calgary until the completion of the Glenmore Dam.

Provincial Archives of Alberta, A 7698

H

Glenbow Archives, NA-2179-28

G

Section Two
THE REVOLUTIONARIES

Proudly behind their hammer-and-sickle flag, striking farmers at Two Hills, in February 1931, march in support of the Communist attempt to unite country and city in an agrarian-urban revolution. The movement reached its high point in the Edmonton hunger-march riot the following year, which in turn led to the On-to-Ottawa march of 1935. Ironically, however, the only Thirties revolution that succeeded was occurring imperceptibly within the education system. By transforming the schools, Deweyist educators began a cosmic change in the value system of society.

As the Depression pain deepens, Communism launches its revolution

STRIKES, PROTESTS AND RIOTS WITH EVER-GROWING VIOLENCE SPREAD OVER ALBERTA AND THE REDS RECRUIT THE JOBLESS TO THEIR CAUSE

by **FRED CLEVERLEY**

When the Communist Party made a determined effort to seize control of Canada in the 1930s, beginning in the West, it had the support of devoted followers like Sam Bezruko, an otherwise obscure Drumheller miner who fell victim to cancer. Sam died as he had lived, a man convinced that Communism was the wave of the future. At his funeral, conducted by the party, he lay in his casket with his arm upraised in the Communist salute, his fist clenched upon his final message: "Goodbye comrades, keep up your fight against Fascism." While Sam lay in state, his arm remained in the salute position, holding his manifesto until the coffin was sealed, the *Lethbridge Herald* reported.

That was in September 1938. By then Canada's Red revolution was over and had failed. But it came much closer to success than many Canadians later in the century would realize. Its peak in the early Thirties would see hundreds of Alberta farmers marching behind the hammer-and-sickle flags of international Communism, strikes, riots and skulls routinely cracked by police truncheons at Edmonton, Calgary, Drumheller and a dozen other centres, and finally a national march on Ottawa by the unemployed of the West that would be stopped dead at Regina under a hail of gunfire from the Royal Canadian Mounted Police.

The tactics espoused by higher profile Communists like party leader Tim Buck and his colleagues in the 1930s were identical to those employed in Russia fifteen years earlier. Although most Canadians knew nothing about the Communist movement, they had lately been learning a great deal about poverty and protest. As early as 1930, those two words described the condition and mood of thousands of western Canadians. By then poverty was beginning to cover the land like asphalt on a parking lot. And protest, nurtured by the poverty, was bubbling up like tar boils, increasing in size and activity as the poverty deepened.

Among other things, of course, poverty was news. On November 20, 1934, for example, the *Edmonton Journal* painted a grim picture in a front page appeal for assistance to a widow and her five children. "The children have no footwear or winter underwear. They will suffer badly unless someone helps them." With the aid of neighbours the family had put in a crop consisting of 35 acres of wheat and fifteen of oats. But bad harvest weather, coupled with lack of a binder that could not be borrowed in time, "made what might have been a good crop nearly a total loss. The children (a boy, 15, and girls, 13, 11, 7, and 5) are going around barefooted. They have no warm clothing to protect them from winter's icy winds. A few minutes outside would turn their feet blue with cold." The family was, the paper reported, "virtually living on potatoes."

Before the end of 1930 public unrest and indignation had already become the rule rather than the exception. Leaders of the Communist Party of Canada (CPC) made good use of this disillusionment to recruit members, particularly among the growing army of unemployed. For some, like John O'Sullivan, who had recently run as a CPC candidate and had been defeated, Communism itself had become their chief vocation.

In January 1930, for instance, he harangued a crowd of 350 in Calgary. City Council was offering a mere dollar a day as unemployment relief, he shouted. Could anyone live on that? "It's like scab wages." A thousand people had been identified as unemployed in Calgary, but that

> The people's flag is deepest red,
> It shrouded oft our martyred dead,
> And ere their limbs grew stiff and cold
> Their hearts' blood dyed its every fold.
> Then raise the scarlet standard high!
> Within its shade we'll live or die
> Though cowards flinch and traitors sneer,
> We'll keep the red flag flying here.
> —*The Red Flag*, words by Jim Connell, sung to the tune of *O Christmas Tree*.

May Day in Drumheller some time in the Thirties—miners march in protest against high prices and low workmen's compensation.

meant a further seven or eight thousand would be suffering. And the answer wasn't charity and soup kitchens. It was the good, permanent jobs at 48 cents an hour being demanded by the Calgary Trades and Labour Council. But the best answer of all was the Communist Party and an organized protest against this paltry dollar a day.

In Edmonton, when the Trades and Labour Council discussed that city's unemployment policies the same month, the council's secretary, Alderman Alfred Farmilo, found himself alone in defending the Edmonton relief limit of $2 a day for married men. Since the city was trying to spread the work around, few recipients got more than three days' work a week, leaving them to support their families on less than $1 a day. One delegate, Carl Berg, claimed a war veteran had been refused emergency work because he had a $10-a-month pension.

Meanwhile the Alberta Federation of Labour tackled Premier John E. Brownlee, demand-ing a forty-hour week consisting of five eight-hour days. They called on the cabinet to end the six-day work week, and to bring in a six-hour day in the construction industry. There was so little work, they argued, that it should be shared as much as possible. That was on a Tuesday. On Saturday of the same week the premier was listening to a very different demand. Delegates from the Canadian Manufacturers' Association objected to limiting the work day to eight

Suffering and solidarity

Workers and unemployed, Reds and reliefers, all marched through the militant 1930s. (Top) Demonstrations such as this one at Calgary City Hall, staged by some of the many unemployed groups, were a familiar sight. (Below left) By mid-decade the Calgary-based United Married Men's Association mustered a poignantly impressive contingent. (Below right) Layoffs and lockouts in local mines made Lethbridge a centre of organized discontent. These workers are protesting the administration of the Workmen's Compensation Board.

Glenbow Archives, NA-2800-12

Blairmore had elected what they called the "red mayor", Bill Knight. He was a member of the UMW of A and this is after the 1932 strike, which had quite an impact on them. He had spent $5200 and bought for the town a gas Cat-30 bulldozer, which shocked the citizens no end. He got it that spring and come fall and winter and there's a vicious winter and all of the snowplows that the government had in Alberta were broke down and they put him to work with this Town of Blairmore Cat and they ploughed away for 24 hours a day. He made enough money with his tractor to pay for it, so the town got it for nothing.
—Charles V. Drain, Blairmore miner, in an interview preserved in the Provincial Archives of Alberta (Acc.No.79.192/1)

Some of these men had encountered war. Others had conquered the fear and loneliness that all emigrants face, to build lives in a new city. But by July 1929, when this photo was taken, many Albertans were facing a different challenge — being without the means of supporting themselves and their families. Men accustomed to action had nothing to do. What they did was organize themselves. These 150-odd unemployed men marched from Edmonton's Market Square to the Legislature, hoping to spur the government to action on their behalf.

hours. They wanted it longer.

Edmonton's Communists, although they had no access to the premier, were just as busy as the business-suited CMA. They held one meeting that drew close to 400, protesting dollar-a-day relief wages for single men. The local party leader, known as "Sergeant" Murphy, made a prolonged speech; another speaker addressed the gathering in Ukrainian. Those able to contribute a nickel received a card certifying their membership in the Unemployed Workers of Canada. The card, of course, was coloured red.

In early March 1930 Moscow appealed to Communists worldwide to parade in protest against unemployment. Alberta newspapers dubbed the chosen day Red Thursday. City and provincial authorities said one thing and prepared for another. They expected no trouble, they assured the media. In fact they did, and events elsewhere in Canada gave them reason. Toronto police had

---

On April 14, 1930, Agriculture minister George Hoadley announced that the province did not want immigrants without the means and ability to maintain themselves on their own land. This launched a dark and little known page in Alberta history.

---

arrested more than a dozen people after a cordon of mounted officers broke up a demonstration attended by 5,000. Winnipeg police had used their billy clubs to quell what was described as a mob. Thus mounted patrols of the Alberta Provincial Police were notified they might be needed.

They weren't. By two o'clock Red Thursday afternoon, only about seventy marchers had gathered on Edmonton's Market Square and no police were visible. Little else happened.The result was much the same in Calgary. Several hundred individuals began gathering along a proposed march route, some actually on the steps of city hall. The parade, two blocks long and featuring dozens of Communist banners, saw men marching four abreast. Near City Hall, they were met by Inspector John Cooper of the city police.

"Where are you going?"

"To the city hall steps."

"Not today, I'm afraid. Better find a vacant lot somewhere. There's lots of them around."

Although the inspector was alone, the marchers turned without a word and headed for a vacant lot on the southeast corner of Sixth Avenue and Second Street East. There, using an old automobile as a platform, John O'Sullivan led a series of speakers who earnestly described to the crowd the cause and spread of the Communist movement.

As a demonstration of irresistible proletariat might, however, it had failed. Officialdom relaxed. The Communist threat was plainly overblown, they concluded. They were wrong. As the spring weather warmed, so did the protests. On April 2 a crowd of 650 marched on the Legislature, where six of them were admitted to the office of Walter Smitten, commissioner of labour. Their demand: $25 a week for married unemployed men, plus $5 for each child; $18 a week for single men; and free light, heat, rent and gas. The six returned to tell their fellows that Smitten had promised he would pass this on to the legislative assembly, a claim Smitten later repudiated. Meanwhile twenty-five policemen had readied fire hoses in case the crowd rushed the building. The demonstrators merely marched on to Edmonton's Civic Block, where Mayor J.M. Douglas told them their demands were ridiculous and unreasonable. The response was surly and bitter but not violent.

The Communist party distributed literature to Lethbridge area school children, urging them to 'take' May 1 as a holiday. They said the 'boss class' gave them patriotic holidays like Victoria Day, Thanksgiving and Christmas, and suggested they take a 'workers' holiday' to see how workers fight for their rights.

Edmonton organizers managed to get out only 500 people for a parade to the Legislature later that month, then had to call it off and hold a meeting instead when they learned the House was not in session. The *Edmonton Journal* reported that ninety per cent of those attending were "foreign speaking." The use of the term was instructive. Newspapers of the day nearly always referred to the large number of immigrants involved in any protest demonstration. The wording was

These men were among the 300 unemployed Edmontonians who signed their names to a list on July 5, 1929, following a demonstration at the Legislature. Six of their number had been appointed at a prior meeting to present this list, along with their grievances, to Walter Smitten, the government's commissioner of labour.

Wyoming top hands discussed Sunday rodeoland's latest development — a union known as the "Cowboys Turtle Association." The association, they said, was formed to bring rodeo contestants up to a higher standard and to eliminate "would-be cowboys" and hangers-on.

The hardy sons of the West indicated the union movement started in the East, but how "Turtle" got into the association's name, they professed not to know. The organization's membership list reads like a Who's Who of rodeoland... Herman Linder... Harry Knight... Huey Long...
— *Albertan* April 19, 1937

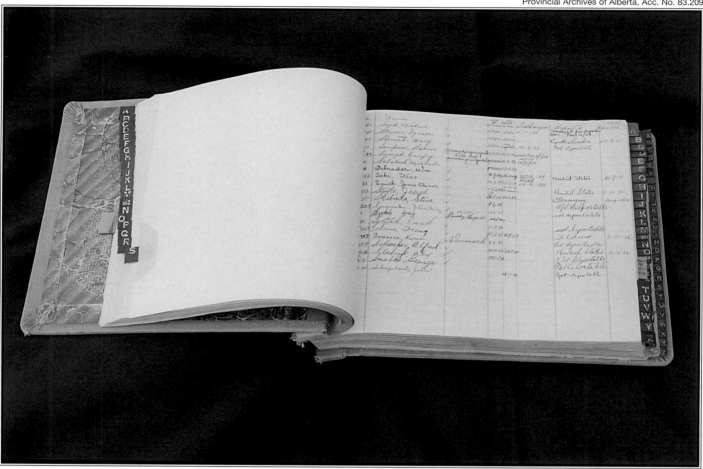

The Alberta Attorney-General's Department kept this ledger of immigrants recommended for deportation between 1930 and 1935.

seldom direct, but tended to concentrate on the inability of protesters to speak English, or on their appearance. Immigrants were in a precarious position. Those who had lived in Canada for less than five years could be deported for becoming a public charge.

On April 14, 1930, Agriculture minister George Hoadley announced that the province did not want immigrants without the means and ability to maintain themselves on their own land. This launched a dark and little-known page in Alberta history, notably the immigrant deportation program of the early 1930s. In pursuing it, civil rights were ignored, and fully legal immigrants sometimes banished.Edmonton and Calgary diligently ferreted out the "aliens" on their relief lists and forwarded deportation applications to Ottawa. Meeting Calgary mayor Andy Davison on

[1] A former Calgary newspaperman, W.A. De Graves, visited old friends there in 1930 prior to leaving for Russia to report on conditions there for a syndicate of London newspapers. One of the first Calgarians to enlist in the Great War, De Graves had returned with the rank of major; his decorations included the Distinguished Service Order and the Belgian Croix de Guerre. The fact that two other newspapermen sent to Russia by the syndicate had never been heard of again, he said, did not worry him. He was convinced he was "a match for any Bolshevik."

The inspector seized the banner Jordan was rolling up and hit him over the head with its wooden support pole. By now other police had arrived, who began wielding their batons, driving back the crowd. Before things settled down, five people had been arrested and more than 400 were milling about the police station.

November 26, 1930, federal Immigration minister W.A. Gordon promised to expedite these expulsions. In the next four years, Ottawa deported more than 2,500 immigrants from Alberta. Many were denied citizenship papers, or were deported because of their political activity.

Unemployed Chinese immigrants were especially ill-treated. Their relief allowance was only $1.12 a week, less than half that of single non-Chinese, because officials believed their standard of living was lower. In December 1936 three single unemployed Chinese in Calgary died of malnutrition after being cut off relief.

By the spring of 1930 militant action had reached Lethbridge, where 400 marched on city hall and Joe Farbey, an organizer for the Young Communist League of Alberta, was the main speaker. He told the crowd that under Canadian laws the unemployed were liable to be thrown in jail because they had no visible means of support. The marchers' demands were placed before Mayor Robert Barrowman, who said that while he was very much in sympathy, to support unlimited relief would bankrupt the city. Five days later the protesters responded with another march to City Hall, this time of only 150.

If most citizens, like Mayor Barrowman, sympathized with the unemployed, their sympathy did not necessarily extend to Communist instigators. In a letter to the editor of the *Lethbridge Herald,* James H. Moore asked how this sort of parade would be received in Russia. He also accused the organizers of deception in claiming they had the support of miners. There had in fact been no miners in the parade, he said. "Sooner or later," an April 30 Calgary *Albertan* editorial predicted, "unemployed men will find that there is nothing to be gained by parades, demonstrations and the presentation of sheaves of unreasonable and out-of-the-question demands to authorities." The Communists themselves were reaching the same conclusion. Parades and marches were not enough. The party distributed literature to Lethbridge area school children, urging them to "take" May 1 as a holiday. The pamphlets told the children that the "boss class" gave them patriotic holidays (it named Victoria Day, Thanksgiving and Christmas) and suggested they take a "workers' holiday" to see how workers demonstrate and fight for their rights. Lethbridge communists, augmented by Coalhurst miners and their wives, held a May Day demonstration at Galt Gardens opposite the provincial unemployment office.

The first incident that resulted in violence occurred in Calgary. A crowd of about a thousand, marching in protest through the downtown area, was stopped by a Calgary police inspector who asked for their parade licence. They had none. The inspector and Chief David Ritchie tried to lead them back to CPC headquarters. The trouble started when the two policemen ordered the banner carriers to take them down and roll them up. Felix Jordan of the Young Communist League, shouted, "Comrades and fellow workers! This is your day! Fight for it!"

The inspector seized the banner Jordan was rolling up and hit him over the head with its wooden support pole. By now other police had arrived, wielding their batons and driving back the crowd. Before things settled down, five people had been arrested and more than 400 were milling about the police station. By nine, however, everybody had left. Mayor Andrew Davison, elected as a labour man, announced himself as already fed up with local Communists and offered to facilitate a return to the land of their birth, or better still "to the land for which they have displayed a long-distance love," meaning, of course, to the Soviet Union.[1]

When Calgary police jailed eleven Communist supporters the following month for attempting another parade, a missive was delivered to city hall two days later which read: "Forewarning. In regards to action taken by your tools, I am warning you to let those men that were arrested go before 48 hours or we will blow your headquarters to hell. Signed C.P." City officials assumed the signature stood for the Communist Party, but Mayor Davison dismissed the threat, declaring: "Mob law is not

to be effective in Calgary, as we proved Saturday [the day of the arrests]. The civic authorities are not seeking trouble but we will take care of trouble if it arises." He returned to his deportation theme. "The vast majority of this class appear to have come here from foreign lands... They fully realize that they are better off in Canada than in their home lands. Their departure from the countries from which they came was a gain for those countries, but has been our loss."

However, whether or not many people were better off in Canada was becoming debatable. The Calgary Trades and Labour Council, meeting in November 1930, endorsed the principle of supplying three meals daily and a bed for every unemployed man. They quickly and diplomati-

With wheat at 45 cents, farmers call a boycott; fists fly at the elevators

MOUNTIES CLASH WITH STRIKERS ACROSS EAST-CENTRAL ALBERTA; THE SOUTH REFUSES ITS SUPPORT

Farmers are rarely strikers but when Alberta's farmers did go on strike in 1932, it was neither tranquil nor orderly. Fists flew, a Communist was tarred and feathered and the grain commissioners came running.

Hunger marches, mine strikes and relief camp walkouts became almost routine as the Thirties unfolded, but a farmers' strike seemed an unthinkable paradox. Farmers were self-employed businessmen, to whom radicalism was anathema. Yet the myth of the inevitably conservative farmer was belied in the Depression. By November 1932 world wheat prices had slipped to 45.4 cents a bushel, about 25 cents below the cost of production. For more than two years farmers had watched their livelihood melt away. The provincial government in Edmonton — *their* government run by the United Farmers of Alberta — was broke, and the Conservatives in Ottawa didn't seem to care that the banks were foreclosing upon them.

"Farmers of Rumsey Decide on Spring Strike Against Sowing of Wheat" was the banner headline in the *Medicine Hat News* on November 5. It was an early warning of a new militancy that would unsettle rural Alberta for the next two years. More than 90 per cent of district wheat growers attended a raucous mass meeting in Rumsey and unanimously voted for nationwide farm strike action before the spring seeding season, unless the Dominion government guaranteed the cost of producing the 1933 crops.

Unperturbed, Brownlee announced that he thought Westerners could work out a solution without resorting to extreme measures. He underestimated the farmers of Rumsey, who took their strike resolution to the United Grain Growers' annual convention in Saskatoon, attended by 400 delegates representing 30,000 farmers. UGG officials,

appalled by such radical action, refused to discuss the proposal. Beaten but not broken, they now carried their resolution to the annual Alberta Wheat Pool convention. There it was effectively shelved when delegates decided to consult other farm organizations before considering it.

While these latter shied away from a strike, the idea took root among fed-up farmers. At a UFA district association convention, more than 100 delegates from the hamlets of Morrin, Munson, Rowley and Rumsey in the Big Valley area southeast of Red Deer voted to sow no wheat in 1933. At the meeting in Morrin, speakers declared that strikers would resort to picketing, and might even destroy the crops of

cally added that they were not really criticizing the city council's recent decision to provide only one meal, which was better than no meals at all.

In Edmonton, the lot of the single unemployed grew worse. The city could hardly let these men freeze and starve. It had hurriedly turned over the old immigration hall to the Hope Mission, which was run by the Rev. Henry Edwardson and his wife, to enlarge its operations. When close to 500 men paraded in Market Square, Mayor Douglas directed them to the mission. About 150 took his advice. Crowded it unquestionably was, but when trade council member Carl Berg complained about it, the mayor and the Edwardsons defended themselves in the *Edmonton Journal*.

As part of Soviet-backed International Struggle Day, Edmonton Communists organized demonstrations on February 25, 1931, among local farmers. This group was from St. Paul.

farmers who opposed the strike.

On December 28 several hundred farmers at Leduc endorsed the principle of the proposed strike. When the strike resolution was again presented, at the UFA annual convention in Calgary on January 20, 1933, it found few supporters. Instead, a huge majority of delegates proposed a national wheat board to control marketing and production.

Even though Alberta's two most influential farm organizations, the Wheat Pool and the UFA, had rejected any notion of a strike, the idea didn't die. It was revived in December 1933 by Ukrainian farmers in the Myrnam area, northeast of Edmonton. Accusing grain buyers at the town's five elevators of downgrading their crops at purchase,[A] they began picketing the roads and threatening to dump grain, slowing deliveries to a trickle by Christmas.

Early in the new year, 1934, the embattled farmers stepped up their campaign, and soon clashes occurred on the back roads. Hauling wheat to a local elevator, Gus and Ivor Berg managed to break through a ten-man picket on January 6, but the strike was so effective that only three

"I tasted the [breakfast] porridge myself," Mayor Douglas assured the newspaper. "It was quite good. I know something about porridge too." Mrs. Edwardson said that Mr. Berg had never visited the hall, adding that there were no complaints when the Hope Mission was operating privately and it was only now, after the city had got involved, that agitators felt free to complain. Furthermore, the soup she served was thick and rich enough to jell when it was cold. The last batch contained fifty pounds of shank beef, sixteen or seventeen pounds of split peas and fifteen pounds of onions, she said. As for keeping the hall clean, the men themselves did nothing. Mostly, she said, "they pile off as soon as they are fed. They don't seem to do much

loads of grain got through the pickets that day.

After police warned the striking farmers that they would not tolerate intimidation, the protest on the back roads might have petered out but for support from an unexpected quarter. Reversing its previous stand, the UFA 1934 annual convention decided to support the Myrnam strike. Two days later, district farmers came by sleigh to a meeting in the village. After hearing impassioned speeches and collecting a large sum of money, they decided to prolong the strike, now in its eighth week. All local grain deliveries stopped.

The strike gained momentum as organizers headed for other farming communities. Mass meetings in towns such as Mundare and Innisfree vowed to join if the elevator companies and the government refused redress. Soon eight other towns joined the strike: Warwick, Royal Park, Fitzallen, Lavoy, Innisfree, Inland, Haight and Willingdon.

Internationale' as they marched along. The banners were mainly directed against war and fascism, but Bennett's 'Iron-Heel Government' and tax sales came in for their share of abuse."

However, in the optimistic summer of 1934, the Myrnam parade failed to inspire any strikes. Wheat prices began rising and by the end of May and No.1 grain futures for October climbed to more than 80 cents a bushel. This subdued the movement for the summer, but come fall it was on again, centred in Mundare. The grain farmers there launched a protest on November 6, citing the same issues of undergrading, excessive dockage and low prices that had galvanized the farmers of Myrnam into action the year before.

Again, hot disputes broke out between those who supported and opposed the strike. On the evening of November 8, fists began to fly when the picket line of twenty farmers

---

Fists began to fly when the picket line of twenty farmers clashed with the RCMP as an anti-striker tried to deliver his grain. Ten picketing farmers were arrested; released on bail the next morning, they were cheered by a crowd of 500 fellow strikers and spectators.

No longer an isolated protest, it showed signs of sweeping the province, and apprehensive provincial and federal authorities decided to intervene. On a recommendation from the federal Board of Grain Commissioners, Myrnam elevator operators agreed to change their buyers. But when the board published results of its investigation into charges that crops had been downgraded by the grain buyers, it not only exonerated the dismissed agents, but showed that, if anything, their grading had been overly generous. For some eighteen months the elevator companies had taken a loss on those sales.

Within two months, however, the farm unrest had attracted communist organizers, who descended on Myrnam, organized the Farmers' Unity League under the direction of Carl Axelson of Bingville, and paraded into the village from three directions. "Each line was led by small children scarcely old enough to walk. Some were carrying banners demanding free school books," reported the *Edmonton Bulletin*. "Many were carrying banners advertising the district from which they came and singing the 'Red

clashed with the RCMP as an anti-striker tried to deliver his grain. Ten picketing farmers were arrested; released on bail the next morning, they were cheered by a crowd of 500 fellow strikers and spectators.

The Board of Grain Commissioners immediately promised that all the grain held in Mundare's eight elevators would be regraded. Led by chairman E.B. Ramsey, the board hastened to the village for a noon meeting with the farmers' strike committee. "While trebled picket forces of striking grain farmers blocked all deliveries and a detachment of RCMP stalked the town streets to preserve order, fur-capped Ukrainian farmers loitered without the Mundare Hotel," the *Edmonton Bulletin* reported.

Though the authorities assured the farmers that the board was there to see that they were treated fairly, the *Bulletin* suggested that their approach was condescending rather than conciliatory. Back in Edmonton, Ramsey told a Calgary *Albertan* reporter, "I got a very unfavourable view of their complaints. It was a sad spectacle to see a farm woman, bringing in a few sacks of grain, being attacked. When men

cleaning up after themselves."

The Edwardson effort was not the city's only such endeavour. The widespread misery was typically eliciting a variety of responses from the churches. The Salvation Army was operating along its usual lines, much like the Edwardsons' mission. In a January 1930 appeal for funds to keep its Calgary operation up and running, the Army said it had provided 29,776 free meals and 10,900 temporary jobs in 1929.

In May a mainstream Protestant charity, Wood's Christian Home, began a campaign for $10,000 to build an extension; it had fifty needy boys waiting for space. Both Catholics and

FARMERS DEMONSTRATION
AGAINST WAR + FASCISM
Aug 5 1934 Two Hills
Alta

Within a month of Richard Gavin Reid's swearing-in as premier, the farmers who had elected his government were serving notice that their patience had run out. This demonstration took place at Two Hills on August 5, 1934.

grabbed her horses, police had to club them off and make further arrests. I was not at all impressed."

Official warnings had little effect on spreading discontent. On November 12 strikers used railway ties to block the market road near Kaleland, west of Two Hills; one man was arrested by an RCMP patrol. Pickets at Hairy Hill, Norma and Andrew closed a CPR branch line. By November 14 the strike was joined by Myrnam and eight other towns north and east of Edmonton.

But the protest was confined to the Ukrainian centres of north-central Alberta. It won no support from conservative Anglo-Saxon farmers in the south. Rallies at six other communities failed to provoke grain boycotts, and at least one agitator was chastened. George Palmer, described in the press as a "Moscow newspaperman,"[B] came to Vegreville from Calgary to help incite a grain strike. On the night of November 16, according to the *Medicine Hat News*, "Palmer claims he was seized by a group of men, loaded into a truck,

and taken for a 'ride.' Parts of his clothing were stripped from him and he was liberally daubed with tar and feathers. About two miles from Innisfree he was released and the truck drove away, leaving him to make his way to town as he best he could."

The indignities suffered by Palmer hinted at the underlying ethnic tensions in the strike. Palmer told the *Edmonton Bulletin* that his assailants were "young English-speaking men," an unusual description in a district dominated by Canadians of Ukrainian descent. Most of the anti-strike farmers and businessmen in the area east of Edmonton came from British stock. German, French and Scandinavian settlements also resisted overtures from strike organizers. Reporting that at least two Anglo-Saxon farmers planned to run the pickets' blockades at Mundare, the *Medicine Hat News* quoted Mundare Mayor H.A. White and local farmer J.D. McAllister as saying that the strike was organized by Communists who talked the Ukrainians into following their line.

[2]Wayne boasted the largest membership of any branch of the Canadian Defenders League, suggesting there was more interest around the Drumheller area in promoting the employment of people of British ancestry than anywhere else in the province. However, it was also a big United Mine Workers town.

Protestants were trying to help the Indians, who were as badly off as everyone else, if not worse. The Calgary presbytery of the United Church (See Vol.5, Sect.3, ch.2), meeting in Banff in September, for example, was told that their Morley congregation couldn't get harvesting jobs that year because the demand for labour was so slack. And many Protestants, clergy and laymen as well, were more interested in instigating government social action to alleviate distress than they were in Christian charity.

Then too there was the Canadian Defenders League, which favoured neither church charity nor government aid. Its declared function was to oppose Communism and to promote the employment of people of British ancestry.[2] The league's national president, Lewis McDonald, an ex-CPC stalwart, was present at a league meeting in Calgary on November 18, 1930, where he

The province's daily newspapers charged that Communist agitators from the cities were trying to use the farm strike as a stepping stone to a much wider provincial disruption. The hapless George Palmer's mission had been to co-ordinate the strike with an attempted Alberta-wide relief worker strike, according to the *Medicine Hat News*. The *Edmonton Bulletin* reported that organizers were promoting a general strike covering beef, poultry, eggs and other agricultural products. The *Bulletin* also said that agitators intended to counter anti-strike stories by putting out their own paper and using radio to spread propaganda.

Although the strike had spread to 21 different points by November 23, it was slowed by reports of Communist involvement and tough jail sentences for violent pickets. Two men convicted of intimidation were sentenced to two months in jail, and four others were each fined $40 and costs for obstructing police officers and wilful damage. The convicted men immediately appealed the sentences.[C]

By November 26 grain was flowing to elevators in Mundare and Willingdon. Gradually the strike shrank to an 80-by-50 mile area with an 85 per cent Ukrainian population. It lost all impetus on December 6, when the federal grain commissioners issued a report that charges of undergrading and excessive dockage at Mundare elevators were groundless. That day, anti-strike farmers at Myrnam challenged pickets by escorting several loads of grain to the elevators. The first farmer to bring in a load of grain was cheered by his comrades and booed by the strikers. When a picket tried to

board a farmer's load and seize the reins, the farmer's wife knocked him off. Four days later strikers met in Myrnam's Ukrainian Temple and decided to end the strike.

In Mundare, Mayor White called a meeting where local businessmen vowed to arrest the activities of "foreign-born strikers." While the strikers doubled their picket lines, six special policemen were sworn in to protect farmers delivering their grain in convoys.

It was the last attempt at an Alberta farm strike of the Depression. Was it a "front to cover up a campaign of radicals of foreign birth against capitalism," as the Calgary *Albertan* alleged? Communist agitators certainly tried to exploit the strike for their own ends, but the grain commissioners and the judiciary — the Anglo establishment — showed little sympathy for the Ukrainian farmers who were the ultimate pawns in a larger game.

—*G.O.*

Provincial Archives of Alberta, A 13912

Carl Axelson was president of the Farmers' Unity League and a leader of the 1934 Myrnam strike.

[A]Farmers often feared and mistrusted grain buyers employed by private companies. These all-powerful "elevator agents" could downgrade a load of wheat for many of reasons. If the grain had been frozen it might be classified as feed grain. The wheat might be "dirty," contaminated with dirt or weeds. Downgrading meant a lower price.

[B]George Palmer was on the executive of the Communist party in Calgary and a former editor of the city's Communist paper, according to the *Medicine Hat News*. A Great War veteran Palmer joined the Communist party in 1925 and spent two years in Moscow. When he returned to Canada he wrote a series of articles on life in the Soviet Union.

[C]On December 12, 1934, Peter Kleparchuk and William Zasebida appealed the two-month sentences handed them for intimidation, obstructing the police and wilful damage of property. The judge increased the sentences to three months.

Farmers at Acadia Valley line up for relief feed grain. Central Alberta farmers refused, however, to join in the farm strike that broke out north and east of Edmonton.

We worked out a taxation system whereby (the mines were working very short and most of the miners were on relief, and they couldn't pay taxes so we encouraged them not to pay taxes, but the town had to operate) the whole burden of taxation fell on the company, who had property inside the town limits of Blairmore. And then under law, we had to put up these miners' houses and shacks for auction, but nobody would bid when we told them not to. These miners lived there and they drew relief rent. Then they'd give it to the Council and we applied it to their debts, and in two or three years they got their houses back, with taxes paid off...

We passed one law that I liked very much — it was on dog taxes. We allowed mongrels to get away without being taxed and we taxed thoroughbreds. Only the bosses had thoroughbreds!
—*Harvey Murphy, in an interview with Warren Caragata preserved in the Provincial Archives of Alberta (Acc.No.80.218)*

read a letter he had received from the CPC executive in central Canada several years before. It urged him to concentrate on Communist propaganda at workers' meetings, not on workers' wages.[3]

McDonald said that he had "suffered for eight years on behalf of the Communist Party and upon my release from jail, following a three-year term for doing their dirty work, received no gratitude but was termed a renegade... The Communist Party is directed from Moscow and its only purpose is to sow dissatisfaction so that the workers will rebel and fall into the hands of the dictators at Moscow."

The Defenders offered to help break up Communist demonstrations. Calgary's Mayor Davison said he wasn't interested. "We will not interfere with an open air meeting so long as the traffic is not tied up or the rights of pedestrians or motorists is not interfered with," he declared. And no,

---

The Defenders League offered to help break up Communist demonstrations. Calgary's Mayor Davison said no. We will not interfere so long as the rights of pedestrians or motorists are not violated, he declared. And counter-revolutionaries couldn't have parade permits either.

---

counter-revolutionaries couldn't have parade permits either.

Edmonton Communists found Mayor Douglas equally formidable. When a delegate identified only as "Comrade A. Farmer" told the city council he wished to lay a number of grievances before them, Mayor Douglas snapped: "I'll tell you what I think. If men like you would get out of town we might be able to do something for the unemployed. You hinder our efforts by your continual agitating."

A recurrent point of contention was the singing of *God Save the King* at public rallies — or the failure to sing it. In Willingdon, 30 miles northeast of Edmonton, on January 30, 1931, anti-Communist farmers threw rotten eggs to disrupt a meeting called by the Farmers Unity League, an organization that included what the *Edmonton Journal* described as "Red leaders from Mundare." The eggs began flying when Unity League president Carl Axelson of Bingville refused to open the meeting by singing *God Save the King*.[4]

[3] In June 1931, anti-Communist Lewis McDonald reported that he was fired on three times through a window at the headquarters of the Canadian Defenders League, on Seventh Avenue, just east of Centre Street in Calgary. McDonald took refuge behind furniture. An off-duty policeman heard the shots. They were never explained.

The Alberta town that went Communist

IN ITS BRIEF RED HEYDAY BLAIRMORE HAD A TIM BUCK BOULEVARD

The coal-mining community of Blairmore became a national spectacle in 1935 when its citizens elected both a Communist town council and a Communist school board. One of the council's first actions was to declare a civic holiday in March to honour Tim Buck, leader of the Communist Party of Canada (CPC), and another on November 7 to mark the anniversary of the Bolshevik revolution in Russia. It also changed the name of the main thoroughfare, Victoria Avenue, to Tim Buck Boulevard.

However, as explained in a *Lethbridge Herald* article, none of these newly elected dignitaries considered himself a Communist. Said British-born Mayor William "Bill" Knight: "I am not a member of the Communist party. There is not a real Communist on either the council or the school board. We are in sympathy with the Communist party — that is true — and I think the way out lies in Communism. But this is a Workers' government that Blairmore has."

Knight elaborated on the links that tied him, his council and the school board to Communism. They were all nominated and elected by the Mine Workers Union of Canada (MWUC), a Communist union which had broken from the United Mine Workers of America (UMWA). It was also affili-

Tim Buck, Secretary of the Communist Party of Canada.

ated with the Workers' Unity League (WUL), which in turn was connected with the Third Internationale in Russia. "I hold a card in the union and so do all my associates... We belong to the union and in that sense are affiliated with the Third Internationale, which I consider mighty good leadership."

When asked just how "Red" Blairmore was, the mayor replied: "Red is a state of the stomach. Back in 1929 there were no Reds. Things were prosperous — everybody was well fed. It is different today. You talk about Communists — the Communists in Canada were made by [Prime Minister R.B.] Bennett. We have Reds today but we won't have any here in 1940 if they'll leave us alone, if we can carry out our plan."

Part of this plan had already been carried out, he added. Blairmore had better roads in sections where workers lived, and new sidewalks. The town was debt free, although it had a new snow plough, a new road maintainer and an automatic fire alarm system. It had also rebuilt its water system. Garbage was being collected. On Tim Buck Boulevard a water sprinkler system kept things green and reduced summer dust. The future, the mayor said, would see $40,000 worth of new housing built, as well as a plan allowing workers to retire

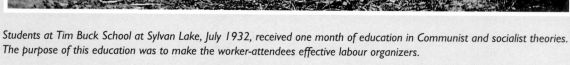

Students at Tim Buck School at Sylvan Lake, July 1932, received one month of education in Communist and socialist theories. The purpose of this education was to make the worker-attendees effective labour organizers.

(Above) Tim Buck addresses a Crowsnest Pass meeting shortly before being jailed for three years for his Communist leanings.

at 50, thus providing employment for younger men.

Even some of Blairmore's businessmen expressed reluctant approval for the mayor and his program, the *Lethbridge Herald* reported. "Knight has not done a bad job," was a typical comment. However, they did question council's habit of proclaiming new holidays.

Mayor Knight had little time for the fledgling Social Credit Party or the new democratic socialist CCF, the Co-operative Commonwealth Federation, which he described as the last leg of capitalism. He also expressed great praise for his council (listed as Evan Morgan, Joe Krkosky, Joe Aschacher, Ole Olsen, Jack Packer and Angelo Pagnucco) and for the school board (Chairman Albert Bosetti — born in Italy and now a naturalized Canadian — Joe Krkosky Jr., Sam Patterson, Mrs. Gaston Bazzil and Enoch Williams).

As for Communist influence in the classroom, it was true that when the national leader of the Communist Party of Canada visited the community that had so honoured him to open the Tim Buck Shower Baths, he wrote on a school blackboard: "For working class solidarity in training our children. Tim Buck." (The large portrait of King George V that hung just above it reportedly afforded Buck an ironic smile.)

Harvey Murphy, with Blairmore mayor Bill Knight at his side, speaks at the 1931 May Day gathering.

Blairmore's workers' town council, 1933: Back row, l-r: Robert Horne; Harvey Murphy; Joe Krkosky, Jr. (Police chief); Ole Olsen; Albert Bosetti. Front row, L-R: Joe Aschacher; R. Peressini, Sr.; Bill Knight; Fitz Patrick; Joe Krkosky, Sr.

Communism received support not only in the Crowsnest, but from miners all over Alberta. Nordegg, a coal town about 60 miles south of Edson, welcomed Tim Buck in 1935, not long after his release from prison.

But *O Canada* was sung daily. There were no "Red" songs, and the Lord's Prayer was recited regularly.

Blairmore's Communist notoriety was short-lived, however. By 1937 the Tim Buck Boulevard beautification program had failed, according to a *Calgary Herald* report. Mayor Knight's successor, former school trustee Enoch Williams, decided the boulevard was serving no good purpose and was too expensive to maintain. He and his new council ordered the removal of the two large neon signs that identified it. Again it became Victoria Avenue.

Tim Buck was born in Suffolk, England, in 1891, came to Canada in 1910 and was an early member of the Communist Party. He received training in Moscow in 1924, which resulted in his expulsion from the Machinists' Union. Arrested under Section 98 of the Criminal Code of Canada in the early Thirties, he spent three years in Kingston Penitentiary. There he was involved in a prison riot, and an attempt allegedly was made on his life by guards firing into his cell.

When he was paroled he resumed leadership of the CPC, which gained some support between 1936, when it was allowed to function as a legal party, and 1939. He then went into hiding following a non-aggression pact signed between Germany and the Soviet Union. In 1943, with the USSR now an ally of Canada, he re-formed his political party under the name of the Labour-Progressive Party. He was defeated in the Ontario election of 1929 and in the federal elections of 1935, 1945 and 1949. However, as national leader he toured Canada and was honoured by communities

such as Blairmore. He retired from politics in 1962 and died at the age of 82 in 1973. The section of the Criminal Code under which Buck was prosecuted was one of the most draconian measures ever introduced into Canadian law. It was designed to terminate the Winnipeg General Strike in 1919, but never actually invoked until the Thirties when it was used to jail Buck and seven other radical leaders.

The section made it a crime, punishable by up to 20 years in prison, to belong to any association whose purpose was to bring about governmental, industrial or economic change by force or which advocated the use of force for such purposes. Property belonging, or suspected to belong, to such an association might be seized without warrant and forfeited to the Crown.

If it could be shown that a person had attended meetings of such an association, spoken publicly in its support or distributed its literature "it shall be presumed, in the absence of proof to the contrary, that he is a member of such unlawful association." Persons printing, distributing, selling or importing material advocating or defending the use of force might also be imprisoned for up to 20 years. The effect was to make the Communist Party and organizations affiliated with it *de facto* illegal in Ontario and any other province where provincial authorities chose to enforce section 98.

Five times, from 1926 to 1930, the House of Commons had voted to repeal it, but the Senate (Conservative majority) had killed the move every time, once by only three votes. It was finally removed from the code on August 17, 1945.

—*F.C.*

Axelson ran into the same kind of trouble in Edmonton four months later. A crowd of 250 had gathered in Market Square when Axelson climbed up on a box to begin the meeting. There were calls from the crowd for him to sing the anthem. He replied that he could not sing and suggested the crowd start and he would join in. The audience insisted that he begin, saying that if "the King" was not sung there would be no meeting. He then protested that he did not know the words. The crowd offered to write them down for him. Police watched, ready for any violence. Axelson finally left in an automobile.

However disagreeable to civic officials, parades and demonstrations continued and with 1931 tempers reached the point of exasperation. By now the dilemma of the cities was all too plain. If a municipality denied the transient unemployed food, this fomented trouble. If it fed them, word soon spread and scores more would arrive with every freight. So Calgary's Davison had an idea. To receive relief a single man had to put in one day's labour a week on some city make-work project. At the end of June he increased this to two days, hoping that would spur some men to move on.

Instead it gave the Communists a new grievance. In effect, they said, the city's paltry pay scale was being cut in half. "We are already undernourished and starving," said one Communist handbill. "Many of us are too weak to work even one day. We demand to have relief tickets issued once a week, rather than once a day, and three meals and a bed per day." With that, they called a "relief strike," a term that would rapidly become familiar, refusing to work at all. Some crews obeyed the strike call, some didn't.

To enforce the strike a crowd of about 1,000, adhering to what had declared itself the National Unemployed Workers Association (NUWA) which had been denied a parade permit, assembled on the vacant lot at 6th Avenue and 2nd Street NE, by now known as "Red Square." It was May Day, 1931. For more than two hours they heard speakers deplore their plight as the inevitable consequence of the capitalist system whose failings were proclaimed on various cardboard placards fastened to poles and held aloft by the spectators.

At some point in the afternoon a squad of about 90 policemen, obviously forewarned of trouble, filed

(Above) These demonstrators gathered in front of the Legislature in October 1933 to vent their frustration with Ottawa's inaction on relief. As the Depression wore on, demonstrations started to take a violent turn. (Below) Harold Dake, a relief worker, was struck on the head, knocked down and trampled by supporters of a the May 1934 UMMA-backed relief strike in Edmonton after he crossed their picket line.

[4]The singing of *God Save the King* at political meetings served several purposes. Among these was the determination of British Canadians to maintain their links to the Crown, links which they saw as in jeopardy at the hands of more recent immigrants. In some meetings, there was a rivalry between those who insisted on *God Save the King* and those determined to give *The Internationale* equal status. In Calgary, on May 15, 1931, the Communist anthem was the only one sung as 500 protesters gathered to demand unemployment insurance.

The faces of destitution

(Left) "Old Joe," as this man identified himself to the Edmonton Journal on June 16, 1931, claimed to have been travelling freights for 60 years. (Bottom left, L-R) S. Menard, P. Lefrencas and John Mtak were part of the leadership of one of the groups of unemployed men who demonstrated in Edmonton on July 5, 1929. (Below) Edith Swanson posed in 1934 in the clothing she wore to ride the rails with her husband and children. The family travelled extensively in search of work and later settled down in Calgary.

into the intersection and lined up on the opposite side of the street. They did nothing else because a crowd on a vacant lot did not constitute a "parade."

Finally Phil Luck, 32, the designated chairman, protested the denial of a parade permit. "We should ask [Mayor] Andy Davison to come down here and state his reasons why we should not walk on city streets. I ask for three volunteers." Three men came forward, then headed for City Hall to demand an interview with the mayor. As some of the crowd began to follow them, they urged them to stay put, since moving along the street could constitute a parade and signal the police to move in.

When the three got to City Hall, Davison ordered them admitted with an escort of two policemen. His policy remained firm, said the mayor. There would be no parade permit for Communists. Neither would he come and address them.

So they trudged back to the lot where Luck announced that the meeting would now adjourn to the association's headquarters to receive their report. Thereupon the crowd began to move from the lot onto the sidewalk. No sooner had their feet touched it than the police charged. Billy clubs swinging, they burst into the throng, grabbing their placards.

Police hauled Luck off the improvised platform, while the mob fought back with sticks and

---

There were calls from the crowd for Axelson to sing the National Anthem. He replied that he could not sing. The audience insisted that if 'the King' wasn't sung there'd be no meeting. He then protested that he didn't know the words. The crowd offered to write them down for him. Axelson finally left in an automobile.

---

stones. When APP Const. J.M. Carter was knocked out with a brick, city constable Alex McCulloch clubbed and handcuffed the attacker, a striker named Andrew Grant. Soon five other bruised and bleeding strikers were arrested. The *Calgary Herald* described the encounter:

> Emil Jensen and Fred Levenotsky, carrying banners in the front rank, dropped their poles into a fighting position and the battle was on. Levenotsky went to his knees from a baton blow over the head, while Jensen ducked one baton but caught another over the shoulder. As Sergeant George Millen reached for Levenotsky, a woman clubbed him over the head with a stick, driving his helmet over his eyes. [Calgary police at the time wore bell-shaped helmets like London bobbies.] She then dodged behind a tree on the vacant lot and disappeared.
>
> By this time Sixth Avenue was a milling mass of Communists and police officers. The police soon showed that they meant business. Batons were swung freely and after six men were placed under arrest, the Communists, disheartened by the action of their leaders in running when the first signs of trouble commenced, dropped their banners and sought safety in the lanes.
>
> Most of the crowd fled in every direction. The police then started a real cleanup of the crowded streets. Four abreast they forced the crowd from the scene of the battle, while another detail of officers smashed the banner poles and ripped the cardboard placards to shreds.

In this fifteen-minute mêlée, about 25 people were injured. Some were bloodied, none seriously hurt. The six men were charged with unlawful assembly, one with assaulting a peace officer.

That evening, thirty policemen setting out to raid NUWA headquarters in the David Block on Eighth Avenue SE were followed by a crowd of more than a thousand spectators. Someone on Eighth Avenue began hurling stones and Sgt. C.W. Cox was felled by a chunk of concrete. When police entered the basement headquarters the communists switched off the lights, and a fierce fifteen-minute battle in the dark cellar ended with benches and chairs reduced to kindling and eighteen strikers lined up against a wall. By midnight, police jailed six alleged agitators and 21 others, most of whom were fined and released. The strike collapsed and the unemployed grudgingly accepted the two-day work week.

In 1931 Premier Brownlee ordered 43 troopers of Lord Strathcona's Horse to Edmonton as a manifestation of government muscle to increasingly militant strikers. Steel helmets, rifles, sabres and Hotchkiss machine guns were part of the show of force.

A labour journal reporter described the scene after police had left Communist headquarters: "All the benches used as seats were smashed to pieces, all the windows were broken, doors were wrenched from hinges and broken, the floor was bespattered with blood and I was told by a few of the men who refused to give their names that the police entered both doors with truncheons in their hands and clubbed over the heads about 100 men and women who, they claim, were driven into the rear of the basement where some of them were badly hurt."

Ten days later Communist Bert Ley led some sixty followers into a city council meeting demanding to know why his protest of "police brutality" at the May Day meeting had simply been "filed" by city council, rather than acted on.

When Ley was not given the opportunity to address council, he addressed it anyway, out-shouting Mayor Davison's demands that he sit down and be quiet while his followers stomped their feet and brought the meeting to a halt. Finally the mayor ordered the police be called. After Police Chief Ritchie arrived with four other officers, Ley and his followers filed from the chamber. Thereafter a police detail was assigned to city council meetings.

Worse trouble was meanwhile brewing at Edmonton where men were arriving in the city in a flood, one thousand in a single week, 150 on a single train. The first indication of trouble came at a meeting in the Ukrainian Institute at 10564 98th Street on May 12 where 500 came to hear an anti-Communist speech on behalf of the Ukrainian Self-Reliance League. As the meeting ended chairman Paul Tkachuk called for the national anthem. Communists in attendance put on their hats and began to walk out. Others attacked them, trying to rip the caps from their heads in respect for the King. Soon the meeting dissolved into a brawl in which a rock came smashing through a window. When police poured in, the fighting abruptly ended. There were no arrests.

Another more violent incident soon followed. Police fought a battle with 100 or so men in front of the police station. Two policemen were hurt slightly and seventeen of their adversaries were charged. The demonstrators were protesting the arrest of one of their leaders, Jack Nicholson, who had been picked up following a police raid on Communist headquarters, where five old rifles and three revolvers had been found, though no ammunition.

The Communists claimed these weapons were used in theatre plays, but the discovery prompted police to attend a Nicholson meeting, at which he told the crowd they would have to fight the same way as their comrades had fought in Winnipeg. "Three Cheers for the Soviet Union," he reportedly shouted, "and to hell with the police force." He was thereupon arrested and charged with inciting to riot.

The next day, when the provincial cabinet was meeting with Alberta mayors, some 500 men marched on the legislature demanding "full maintenance." The premier and Edmonton Mayor

Douglas summoned police and read the Riot Act, and the protesters dispersed. But their march so alarmed the authorities that Mayor Douglas banned all parades, forbade banners and red flags with messages such as "Defend the Soviet Union," cut off relief to transients, and ordered them to leave town within two days.

In response an estimated 800 single unemployed stormed city hall, filling the corridors and stairways of three floors, and besieged the mayor's office. When he came out to speak to them, they said they were starving and the city relief office wouldn't give them meal tickets. He asked them to leave the building. They refused. He promised them immediate aid that afternoon. Meanwhile a squad of police hurried to the building and pointed fire hoses at them. They then left and 1,900 meal tickets were handed out.

Only two small restaurants, however, were willing to accept the tickets, so the following day things grew uglier. A fistfight broke out between a war veteran and an immigrant at the old immi-

Emil Jensen and Fred Levenotsky dropped their banner poles into a fighting position and the battle was on. Levenotsky went to his knees from a baton blow over the head, while Jensen ducked one baton but caught another over the shoulder. Then a woman clubbed Sergeant Millen over the head, driving his helmet over his eyes.

gration hall where men were lining up for food. This began a general brawl, which ended when police arrived. About 100 men crossed the road to a nearby restaurant, four of whom went inside and demanded to be fed. When they were turned down, they seated themselves in a booth and ordered food. Outside, the entire crowd began shouting and jeering. Police arrived and arrested the four, one a noted Communist agitator.

Hurried conferences were meanwhile under way between city and provincial officials and local restaurant operators who finally agreed to feed the men for the 12 1/2 cents the city provided when a restaurateur turned in the meal ticket. At the same time Premier Brownlee and Mayor Douglas issued a statement warning the public that the city was being deluged with single unemployed and that Communist agitators were active among them.

A day later there was another outbreak in Calgary where 300 men gathered at the police station and demanded the release of six who had been arrested for obtaining a meal at the Club Café without paying for it. After their arrest, Communist Phil Luck had followed them to the station

Of course to lose a job then was a real serious thing. And to illustrate that point, in the seven years I worked in Greenhill [collieries] there were 220 men employed, and two quit and two hired, if you want to talk about labour stability, you know. My theory is that the value of a job is directly related to the availability of it.
— *Charles V. Drain, Blairmore miner, in an interview preserved in the Provincial Archives of Alberta (Acc.No.79.192/1)*

and demanded their release. When police refused, he left the building. Almost immediately the mob descended upon the station, shouting Luck's reply to the police: "All right! We'll get them out!"

It was then midnight, shift-changing time, so two platoons of police were on hand. Led by twelve baton-swinging officers, the police charged at the crowd. Some briefly fought back, but soon they all fled. The police then formed a shoulder-to-shoulder line and swept up the street striking out at anyone who still resisted. When they returned to the station, however, so did some of the crowd who spent the rest of the night throwing stones at the building. The encounter lasted about 10 minutes and there were only superficial injuries.

Alberta authorities by now were becom-

Radicals had abundant opportunity to foment discontent among the jobless, who gathered together to apply for assistance, or work on relief projects, and sometimes to eat. (Above) A 1933 soup kitchen in Edmonton feeds men who by this time were becoming increasingly dissatisfied with handouts. (Below) In September 1931, the Army and Navy Department Store opened in Edmonton, stocked with goods from a Saskatchewan bankruptcy sale. Locals lined up by the hundreds, first to apply for the half-dozen store clerk positions advertised, and second in hopes of snagging bargains.

ing so edgy that Premier Brownlee decided to deliver the strongest possible message to revolutionaries by calling in the cavalry. Forty-three troopers of Lord Strathcona's Horse therefore journeyed from their Calgary barracks to Edmonton. Under the command of Major F.W.M. Harvey, who wore the Victoria Cross ribbon, they made a brave spectacle and an effective show of force, when they emerged from the train at the 109th Street yards on July 13. Equipped with steel helmets, rifles, sabres and Hotchkiss machine guns, they immediately mounted their horses and rode, sabres drawn, to the Prince of Wales Armouries. After spending a few days there, passing the time playing cards, they quietly slipped out of town. The show of arms cost the provincial government almost $1,700.

Premier Brownlee issued a statement denying he had summoned the militia because he expected further trouble; he was simply determined to let everyone know law and order would be maintained. "As long as there are so many unemployed from elsewhere overrunning the city, and with agitators operating in their midst, there is the possibility of some incident which might lead to violence," he explained.

The rumour mill was busy, however. The *Medicine Hat News* speculated in a front-page story that the troops had been activated because Communists had marched under the flag of the Soviet Union. Another report suggested the government was worried about demonstrations when the federal Labour minister, Senator G.D. Robertson, paid a scheduled visit to Alberta's capital. The Edmonton Trades and Labour Council condemned Premier Brownlee's action as "a disgrace to the community."

The "get tough with the drifters" policy was not confined to Edmonton, of course. Medicine Hat Mayor Isaac Bullivant almost simultaneously served notice on nonresident unemployed that his city would no longer feed men who refused to work. City relief work admittedly did not match the harvest season wages that would soon be available, but it did provide room, food and $10 a month.

Alberta cities also had to develop and enforce policy on the parades of which Communist supporters were so fond. The organizers of one such event in Edmonton, for instance, celebrating International Struggle Day in August 1931, were forbidden to carry signs reading "Defend the Soviet

Union." So they reworded the message and got the approval of Police Chief Anthony G. Shute for: "Young workers defend, do not attack the U.S.S.R." Four hundred men left Market Square to be joined by others as they marched to 109th Street, singing the *The Red Flag*, then returned to the square for speeches condemning what they were told was a worldwide movement to attack Russia.

In Drumheller that August, on the other hand, when members of the National Unemployed Workers tried to parade after being refused a permit, seven men were charged with unlawful assembly. Five of the seven, including council candidate John O'Sullivan, drew one-year jail terms. Two others got two years each, one for the additional charge of carrying a concealed weapon and the other for assaulting a provincial police officer.

Fellow citizens could be tough too. At Rocky Mountain House a public meeting called by Fred G. Bray, a Communist MLA candidate, was broken up by spectators. Bray was yanked down from his speaker's box, tossed into the crowd and told to start his revolution immediately. Two other scheduled speakers ran up the street, with the crowd in full pursuit. That part of the country, they were told, had many veterans in it and they were dead against any Red propaganda.

Other allegedly Communist enterprises also ran aground. A highway project near Blairmore was halted when relief workers, after one day on the job, struck for higher pay. This was blamed on the mine union, since many of the men were out-of-work miners. In keeping with the new tough stance, the response from the provincial government was swift. Get back to work, the government warned, or the project would be cancelled and the names of those involved would be removed from the relief eligibility list. They went back to work.

In the mining industry itself, Communist organizers had already lost a major fight in the Lethbridge coal fields in April 1930. Although the Lethbridge-published *Western Miner* openly favoured their demand for strike action, most of the miners favoured conciliation. The proposed strike got little support at Fernie, Michel and the Alberta Crowsnest Pass and was scuttled when the Galt local in Lethbridge voted two-to-one against it. That vote vindicated provincial United Mine Workers president Frank Wheatley, a former president of the Alberta Federation of Labour. Thereafter, however, the mood changed. Support for strike action grew and Wheatley paid for his opposition to it. In a province-wide vote in June 1,484 Alberta miners voted for his recall, while only 887 supported him. He resigned.

After that, labour trouble spread rapidly through the mining regions. In October 1931, in what was thought to be a move toward a general industry strike, United Mine Workers' acting president L. Maurice called a 24-hour protest walk at Estevan, Saskatchewan, which he described as a demonstration against "the slaughter of miners there."[5] In December workers at the Sovereign Coal Company's mine at Wayne, Alberta, struck over working conditions.[6] Alberta miners also turned thumbs down on a proposal from Premier George Henry of Ontario to ship coal for $2 a ton as a relief measure. Henry's idea was that the company would receive no profit, and the workers would receive relief wages to keep the mines open. The miners objected that any such arrangement would eventually depress wages everywhere.

That officialdom by now actively feared revolution on the Soviet model was plain. In February 1931 the appearance of seditious propaganda throughout Alberta had triggered an RCMP investigation, and some of the material was read to the legislature by Dr. W.A. Atkinson, the Conservative member for Edmonton who demanded to know Premier Brownlee's views on Communist endeavours in Alberta. The premier cautioned that his reply would have to be carefully worded, and he then took four days to carefully word it. Responsibility for such matters, the premier said

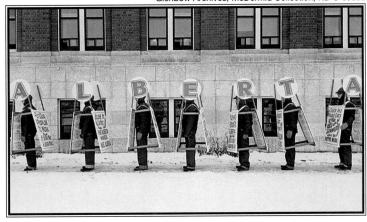

In the fall of 1933 the Edmonton Chamber of Commerce launched a campaign urging people to support local industry. This signboard demonstration was part of the campaign.

[5]At a protest in Estevan, Saskatchewan, by Mine Workers Union of Canada members from Bienfait, Sask., on Sept. 29, 1931, the town's mayor banned the demonstartion and called the RCMP to help local police crush the march. In the riot that followed three miners were killed and several more injured.

[6]The *Calgary Herald* on January 14, 1930, told of housing conditions in what were described as "closed" mining towns such as Cadomin, Rosedale and East Coulee. Miners, mostly Hungarian, were living in hovels made of old railway ties, plastered over with mud and straw, with sod roofs. They lived on land owned by the mine companies where everyone, including the police, was under company jurisdiction. The men had to contribute $5 from each week's wages to an organization that sent the money back to Hungary, a convention of the Alberta Federation of Labour was told.

The Crowsnest Pass was under police vigilance in the spring and summer of 1932 due to violence and threats of violence stemming from strikes in the coal-mining industry and from internecine rivalries within and between unions. (Top) An RCMP mounted detachment is alert for trouble at a strike meeting at Blairmore on June 4. (Above left) Workers demonstrate at Coleman on May 19 against the backdrop of the coke ovens. (Above right) An RCMP patrol in Blairmore on May 27.

delicately, rested with the RCMP. The police had complete information on Communism in Canada, thoroughly tabulated. There had been correspondence with the prime minister on the subject. Finally, the consideration of the provincial departments of justice and of the attorney-general would be brought to bear on the information, which was being accumulated.

That summer of 1931 the Communists announced they would hold classes in Marxism and Leninism, both for new members and also for "comrades who have already shown some promise of becoming real party leaders." The latter would contain higher levels of political instruction. The school promised variety, with one course in Canadian history and another in the history of trade unions and the labour movement.

Elsewhere in the world that year violence was appreciably increasing. A German mob shot and wounded a policeman; in Lisbon soldiers assisting police used the flat of their swords against the crowds; 21 demonstrators were arrested in Winnipeg.

As 1932 began, strikes and rumours of strikes were everywhere. At Coleman in the Crowsnest Pass, 200 employees of McGillivray Creek Coal, operated by West Canadian Collieries, walked off in sympathy with 400 of their fellows at International Coal & Coke. All were demanding equal distribution of available work. In the last week of February, 300 men at West Canadian's Greenhill mines near Blairmore quit on Tuesday, and 400 more at the same company's Bellevue mines joined them on Wednesday. In Saskatchewan officials of National Mines in Estevan denied rumours of a strike over hiring there.

By March a thousand miners were on strike. The *Edmonton Journal* reported that "observers" detected Communist influence, and were expecting a showdown in April, when existing agreements expired. On the 24th the United Mine Workers convention in Edmonton passed a resolution calling for a general strike April 11 to oppose any wage reductions. The ballot sent out posed just one simple question: "Are you in favour of a strike if the coal operators make a reduction in pay?" Miners at Beverly, on the eastern edge of Edmonton, had already declared their support. When the ballots were counted more than 1,300 favoured a strike, with just 115 opposed.

The strike did not last long, however. The first return to work took place at Bellevue, when West Canadian Collieries offered what was called an open-shop policy. One hundred and twenty-five workers signed up, but the reopening that followed was neither smooth nor simple. The mine had been temporarily manned by about fifty older employees. Hundreds of pickets surrounded it, including women and children, and another fifty or so climbed aboard a truck to support their union brethren. More than 300 pickets remained in place all night

Mounted police, already present in force and heavily armed, were reinforced from Lethbridge. The new miners arrived and were intercepted by the pickets. (A

A sodden RCMP detachment files past Brunetto's store in Blairmore on June 2, 1932.

newspaper report said the most active and most noisy were women.) At first there were no actual clashes and only one arrest, for interference. Coffee and sandwiches were distributed to the pickets, many having decided to remain another night. Next day was a different story, however. Police had to swing their batons to get the strikebreaking miners through the lines. Two women were injured and one man, John Bezille, was charged with assault.[7]

West Canadian Collieries thereupon reversed its decision to start up again on an open shop basis. The pickets announced they would remain until a definite agreement was reached. The company issued an ultimatum. It would have no further dealings with the Mine Workers Union of

---

Alberta authorities by now were becoming so edgy that Premier Brownlee decided to deliver the strongest possible message by calling in the cavalry. Forty-three troopers of Lord Strathcona's Horse journeyed from their Calgary barracks to Edmonton.

Canada, a UMW rival, because, it said, the union was dominated by the Workers Unity League, which it alleged was a Communist organization. Get rid of this, the company threatened, or the mines will be closed indefinitely. The standoff continued. Miners began a boycott of merchants who, they claimed, had tried to break the strike. The company stood firm.

On May 14 the MWU announced that miners at Coleman had voted to return to work, extending for two years the contract that had expired in 1932. That night a fiery cross was burned on Goat Mountain, clearly visible to Crowsnest Pass residents. A note was tacked to the door of union headquarters at Blairmore. Signed KKK, it carried the message "Beware Reds," and had a cross drawn in its centre. And although no direct connection was proven, John Stokaluk,

[7]**The United Mine Workers convention in Edmonton in March 1932 dispatched a telegram to Premier J.E. Brownlee describing RCMP officers in the strike areas as "armed thugs." Telegrams to the premiers of Ontario and Saskatchewan called for release of "working class prisoners" from jails.**

The unions and their politics were a part of the lives of both the miners and their families, and all seem to take an interest as this speaker addresses a 1931 May Day gathering outside Coleman.

secretary of the Mine Workers Union of Canada, reportedly was the target of a drive-by shooting while travelling by car from Bellevue to Blairmore. Just east of the Frank Slide, his car was shot at and the windshield pierced, but Stokaluk was not injured

The UMW was not easily purged, however. On May 17 some 600 miners gathered in the Coleman opera house in an attempt to change the leadership, and elected two former UMW officials, David Gillespie and William White, as provisional chairman and secretary of what was described as a local mine workers' organization. But then, says one newspaper report, tempers flared and for a time the hall was filled with flying chairs and the sound of breaking glass. Police had to be called and three miners were arrested. Nearly every window in the opera house was broken.

Meeting with company officials a few days later, Gillespie and White were told that the mines would open again as soon as negotiations had been completed. They dragged on, however, and picketing and some violence continued for five months longer. Meanwhile citizens' leagues were

---

At Rocky Mountain House a public meeting called by Fred G. Bray, a Communist MLA candidate, was broken up by spectators. Bray was yanked down from his speaker's box, tossed into the crowd and told to start his revolution immediately. Two other scheduled speakers ran up the street with the crowd in full pursuit.

---

organized in Coleman and Blairmore for the express purpose of getting rid of Communist agitators. Mayor George Pattinson of Coleman had urged this move. Residents had been insulted and abused by the agitators, who were clearly "Reds." Without their activity, many people believed, mine operators and miners could reach an amicable agreement.

Miners had generally come to believe themselves caught in a fight they could not win. In a printed message to Premier Brownlee they made a number of points. They complained about the enthusiasm of police when it came to arresting miners. They informed the premier that the Ku

Klux Klan ("an organization based on ignorance and bigotry")
kept sending death threats. They pointed out that the Communist
party, although outlawed in Ontario, was still legal in Alberta. But
they denied membership in the Communist party. They complained about government subsidies to the mine operators. They
vowed to continue the strike.

The appointment of miners' committees June 20 to end the
four-month shutdown at Bellevue suggested progress, but
another month passed and word came that no end was yet in
sight. But at Newcastle (which later amalgamated with
Drumheller) the mines were running, and were close to declaring an open mine policy of hiring anyone willing to work. In
August agreement was reached at Drumheller, with the old contract continued for a year. A conciliation board had called for a
three-year agreement, but mine operators would not accept it
because of depressed market conditions. And on September 6,
1932, the remaining miners decided to accept what were known
as the "Brownlee awards" because the premier's office had negotiated the settlement with the UMW and West Canadian Collieries.

The awards included no checkoff but no open shop, and what
was in effect a two-year contract at the same wages as in the old
contract. The settlement called for no discrimination, a temporary
layoff with no definite time set for re-employment, and the right
of miners to belong to any organization they wanted. Still, unrest
continued. In October, for example, mounted police officers were
called to disperse 300 pickets at Wayne, and they arrested one
man who had his pockets full of stones. But the main action was
very much over.

Readers of the *Lethbridge Herald*, however, had a chance the
following month to assess some of the thinking behind all these
troubles. The paper published, in almost 50 inches of type, an
interview with Harvey Murphy, an unapologetic Communist who
had come west from Ontario and helped organize the Mine
Workers Union of Canada. It outlined how Murphy's politics differ from those of his parents and
his views on how the Communists would attain power. When asked directly if he was in favour of
overthrowing the government and monetary systems by armed revolution if peaceful progressive
evolution fails, Murphy said: "Yes, by all and any means." Found guilty of unlawful assembly during the strike, Murphy was later sentenced to three months in jail at hard labour.

The role of the RCMP was changing radically, partly because of an agreement under which the
force took on provincial police duties in six provinces, including Alberta, Saskatchewan and
Manitoba. Effective April 1, 1932, the federal government added responsibility for enforcing the
collection of customs (transferred from National Revenue). Later that month, in preparation for
May Day when Communists had threatened militant demonstrations, the RCMP started a coun-
try-wide roundup of Communists, beginning with one arrest, and the issuing of several warrants
in British Columbia.

Meanwhile, the national debate over bolshevism and communism was, of course, becoming
increasingly heated. Felix Walter, a writer for *Canadian Forum*, took the position in October 1930
that the threat of Communism in Canada was exaggerated. When Communist candidates ran in
the dominion elections that August, none was elected and most lost their deposits. He suggested
that total Communist support in Canada could be counted in five figures.

Walter was particularly critical of the Canadian press for its fascination with communism; certain (unnamed) newspapers were making steady efforts to prejudice their readers against what he
called the "Russian experiment." This was unnecessary, however, since Canadian Communists
"had neither the will nor the ability to harry Rideau Hall with fire and sword, and instead
immersed themselves in doctrinal discussions about various heresies within the movement." The

*May Day was the traditional day
of celebratiion and protest among
organized labour. These workers
from both sides of the Pass joined
forces on May 1, 1934, to protest
perceived injustices such as
unemployment, police actions,
and vagrancy laws.*

Walter article suggested that the real danger, from the Tory point of view, lay in the nonexistence of a genuinely reformist third party. Lacking such a safety valve, reformers could be forced into the arms of extremists.

At no time did Westerners appreciate being labelled as Bolshevik, however, particularly by the eastern press. An editorial in the *Medicine Hat News* on January 19, 1931, took issue with the *Financial Post*. It appeared to be common Toronto practice, the News complained, to represent what was clearly propaganda by small groups as indicative of westerners as a whole. This, the News said, was clearly untrue: "The Western farmer is not a frantic Bolshevik, he is not a radical theorist, he is not a continuous grouser, he is not a politician, nor is he an economic weakling. The newspapers of Canada might give the Western farmers recognition at least for what most of them are, decent, hard-working sons of the soil... capitalist rather than socialistic because their chief aim... is to win by individual effort property for themselves and their families. But no one would recognize such men in the picture of the Western farmer that must be conjured up by

How it all looked to a 1930s' Communist

THE COPS WERE KIND, THE JAIL GREAT, BUT OH THAT JUDGE IVES

Born in Ireland, Pat Lenihan worked in Calgary during the 1930s as an organizer for the Communist Party. He rejected democratic socialism and the Co-operative Commonwealth Federation as "a joke." It was the Communists, he said, who were "out in the streets trying to do something." He served as a Calgary alderman in the late Thirties, and as a cook in the Canadian Army in the Second War. By then he had quit the party, joined the NDP and become one of the founders of the Canadian Union of Public Employees. He was interviewed at Calgary in 1978 by Warren Caragata for his history of the Alberta labour movement, Alberta Labour: A Heritage Untold *(James Lorimer, Toronto, 1979). Lenihan died in Calgary in 1981. This is taken from the interview, which is on file at the Provincial Archives of Alberta.*

Courtesy of Dennis Lenihan

CPC organizer Pat Lenihan.

Lenihan: In 1931 Calgary was becoming radical. See in those days we had four or five labour aldermen on city council, and we had three or four on the school board, see. [Mayor] Andy Davison was a labour man when he first started out. He came to Calgary without a second pair of pants, the same as I did. But he left a big millionaire... He was a small-l liberal, but he was kind of humanitarian at the same time.

We were sent to Drumheller to organize there among the miners... The living conditions were terrible. They had nothing. Poverty, extreme. The only thing that was good about it was their little houses. You could eat off the floors. Spotless. And this pertained to all nationalities — Italians, Belgians, French, every nationality was there. Somehow or other they had a deep love of their little shacks. But very little to eat.

And nothing for social enjoyment, nothing.

Caragata: Some people used to live in piano boxes too, is that right?

Lenihan: What the hell are piano boxes?

Caragata: You know, those big huge boxes that pianos come in.

Lenihan: No, I never came across it. And I was in practically every mining camp in this province before I got finished. But anyway, we called a demonstration. It was a worldwide demonstration against fascism and against war. The communists knew at the time that the war was coming, and the rise of fascism in Italy, you know, and in Germany and all this.

And I went to see the chief of police... and asked him for a permit. I told him what we were going to do, that we were going to march in Drumheller. And all over the valley. And we'd have a meeting up on the hill across from the White House Hotel. And that was it; he wrote out a permit...

And then as we came in we'd pick up the Wayne miners, and then within three miles of Drumheller we'd pick up the Rosedale miners. We must have had a thousand anyway, or more, by the time we got to Drumheller. Then the Drumheller people, they had come to meet us there. And as we got closer, here we see the police. Mounted police. It was a hot, hot summer's day. August 1932.

And the chief of police says, "Well, Mr. Lenihan, you'll have to call off your meeting." I says, "Why? You gave me a permit." He says, "Yes, but don't you see what's in front of you?" He says there's going to be trouble. And the Mounties.

Anyway, it's a good thing they were all drunk. The coal companies had opened the Legion Hall that morning, and

Eastern businessmen reading some of the interviews and statements recently appearing in news-papers."[8]

Justifiably or otherwise, many westerners blamed the immigrant population for bringing Bolshevism with them. A letter to the editor of the *Lethbridge Herald* in December 1931 was quite typical. M.T. Halliwell of Coleman wrote that many immigrants had been unable to achieve the material wealth they expected when they came to Canada. Admittedly, of course, their discontent was encouraged when "staid publications such as *The Church Times* of London editorially states that the capitalistic system has broken down and that capitalism will leave nothing but class hatreds."

Some western Canadian churchmen also adopted a tolerant attitude to "the Russian experi-ment." In January 1932, for instance, the Rev. J.S. Woodsworth, Labour member of Parliament, addressed the annual convention of the United Farmers of Alberta. Woodsworth, back from a trip to Russia the previous summer, contrasted construction activity in Russia, where there was work for everyone and no difficulty finding money, with the depression and unemployment in Canada.

[8] In Saskatchewan the issue of western separation had been raised by the Last Mountain Provincial Progressive Association at Strasbourg, which passed a resolu-tion stating that Eastern and Western concerns over the Depression were diametrically opposed. The association called for a policy under which Western Canada would become a separate and distinct unit of the British Commonwealth of Nations.

---

gave free whiskey to all the right-wingers. They were so goddam drunk, you know, the most of them, that they didn't know what they were doing. There was the Mounties and the right-wing miners behind them. And they were all armed with clubs and pipes, cut two feet long.

And I jump on this pole [presumably a power pole] and I started off: "Comrades! Fellow workers!" And I had no more than two sentences out of my mouth when all around me the battle broke. I don't know whether our people charged first, or the other side charged first. But the other side were drunk. Because, you know, when the crowd started mixing they beat each other up. There was none of our people hit. We had nothing but our fists. The chief of the fire depart-ment had his arm broke. All the injuries were on their side and they beat themselves up.

came, and as I'm going out the door, the chief says, he whis-pers to me: "Lenihan, don't come back." I said, "Thanks chief, but don't worry. I'll be back."

And they took me to Drumheller, and I was out on $5,000 bail. The local people put up their homes, arranged it, like Fred White did here, the labour alderman.[A] They used to do it all the time. And the surprising thing, the great thing that makes you think, was that here were poor people mortgaging, you might say, everything they had on the basis of trust in strangers. All the people here in Calgary who were getting arrested, they were transients. And these peo-ple would come out and put up $20,000 bail for them. It was out of this world.

And we finally appeared in court. And I'll never forget, a Justice Ives. Oh boy, he was full of class. Chief [John]

'The coal companies had opened the Legion Hall that morning, and gave free whiskey to all the right-wingers. They were so goddam drunk, you know, the most of them, that they didn't know what they were doing. And they were all armed with clubs and pipes.'

There was a warrant for my arrest. Illegal assembly. They put me in the can in Medicine Hat and you never seen such a dungeon in all your life. It must have been built a hundred years ago, and the cells are in the basement. The door opens and in comes the chief. He says, "Lenihan, are you hungry?" And I said, "Sure, chief. Sure I'm hungry." "What would you like, a steak or a chicken?" So I figured this was going really far, so I said, "Look, chief, I'll eat anything." "All right. Do you want some magazines?" I said, "Yes, I'd like them." "Okay." Away he goes, and I thought it was a bloody joke, you know, part of the torture or some other thing. And in about an hour he comes back, and he has a platter of chicken that big, and four or five magazines.

Taylor was his name, Chief [James] Taylor. And he says, "Well, enjoy yourself. You'll be here for a couple of days anyway until an escort comes for you from Drumheller." And sure enough, they treated me fine. And the escort

Duncan of Drumheller got up on the stand and swore that if it wasn't for the way we behaved ourselves, there'd have been more bloodshed in Drumheller. He really exonerated us, you know. Trial was over. The old judge looks at us. "Stand up! I sentence you to twelve months hard labour in Fort Saskatchewan." He threw the book at us, and he didn't listen to half the evidence. He was reading a bloody book through half the proceedings.

But the prison guards treated us as human as they could, I think, in the main. Even the warden understood our position.

[A] Calgarian Fred White served simultaneously as alderman for 17 years and MLA for 14 years. He also held the full-time job of President-Treasurer of the Calgary Trades and Labour Council from 1927 until 1941, when he was appointed regional superintendent of the Unemploy-ment Commission. He died in Guelph, Ontario, where he had moved in 1942 to become Treasurer of the Guelph Labour Council, in 1967.

As markets evaporated, men for whom the mines had been their life raged against the cutbacks and layoffs endemic to the entire coal industry in the 1930s. This demonstration took place at Mercoal, 70 miles southwest of Edson, on July 24, 1930.

Premier Brownlee, who spoke at the same convention, took vehement issue with this. All the work in Russia, he observed, resulted from the need for material things with which Canada was already provided.

Moreover, Brownlee argued, Canadians also had civil and religious liberty, universal suffrage and a high standard of living, things still singularly lacking in Russia. Another reason for Russia's full employment was its low standard of living; every Canadian could be put to work if standards were ignored. The premier did not apologize for the fact he had himself advised Albertans to study Russia. He simply believed they should look at all the facts and ensure that their judgements were sound.

Premier Brownlee meanwhile remained opposed to any moratorium on debt, arguing that such a move would destroy credit and reduce the economy to a cash basis. UFA president Robert Gardiner, however, expressed more radical ideas at that convention. He proposed confiscation by government of any earnings beyond $20,000 or $25,000 a year, an income level he said should be sufficient for any Canadian. One Alberta editorialist asked the obvious question. If no one could

keep more than $25,000, why would anyone work to make it?

But as economic distress deepened, radical ideas were one of the few commodities not in short supply in 1932. In July an "On to Ottawa" movement appeared in Regina. It would be three years before it actually happened, but posters and handbills urging the unemployed to visit Ottawa were distributed, and Toronto news outlets reported that thousands of unemployed were riding the rails to the capital. Mounted police in Regina reversed their policy of allowing men to ride on freight cars and began ordering off anyone caught on an eastbound train.

A month later, on August 15, Premier Brownlee wrote to Calgary's Mayor Davison to assure him that RCMP officers were within their rights to remove transients from trains. The police, the premier said, had received their instructions from Ottawa, not from Edmonton.

The violent unrest of 1932 was far from over, however, and Communist insurgence far from exhausted. At both Calgary and Edmonton a sullen fury kept rising within the minds and hearts of desperate men and these were about to result in the most violent two-year span in the history of Alberta.

The relief camps became schools for Communism

ANGRY YOUNG MEN, UNWANTED BY SOCIETY, MADE FINE RECRUITS
AND WHEN THE DISCONTENT EXPLODED A MOUNTIE OFFICER PERISHED

Communist organizers, anxious to spread their revolutionary message, must have been pleased indeed when the Canadian government in effect provided them with a school system where they could conveniently do just that — namely, a network of relief camps for single, unemployed men.

Men poured into the cities to find work, couldn't find it and then stood about on vacant lots and railway yards, hungry and angry. Something unquestionably had to be done.

the Department of National Defense (DND). In charge of parks camps was James Wardle, an engineer who had run "enemy alien" work projects during the Great War. The men found them a welcome change "from the nightmare they had been living for several months, if not longer," Bill Waiser wrote in *Park Prisoners* (Saskatoon, Fifth House, 1995). "They discarded their worn-out clothes for a new winter outfit, slept in a bed — and the same one at that —

Inmates of relief camps, whether administered by local or national agencies, were paid "gratuities," rather than wages, to perform backbreaking manual labour far from their friends and families. These breeding grounds of political unrest exploded in violence within months of their opening. This camp was in the Drumheller area.

General A.G.L. McNaughton, hero of Vimy Ridge (Vol.4, Sect.3, ch.1), toured the country and was appalled, fearing insurrection. It was he who first proposed the relief camps, to get the men out of the cities and into a controlled setting. Moreover, the camps could provide military installations at no cost to the regular defence budget.

In October 1932 the federal cabinet authorized the defence department to go ahead with the project. More than a hundred relief camps ultimately housed thousands of unwilling young men, most of them sent there because they were hungry and ineligible for city relief.

The camps came in two varieties. Some, operated by the National Parks, had a better reputation for living conditions, morale and what they accomplished than did those run by

every night, and could eat all they wanted three times a day... and could enjoy something of a settled life in a place where they — or at least their labour — were wanted."

Parks camps had better food, more of it, and slightly better pay than the 20 cents a day offered in the military camps. They provided recreational items like hockey sticks and footballs, and organized boxing tournaments. Each had a concert company, some had orchestras. Turk Broda, the National Hockey League's legendary goalie, got his start guarding the net at Manitoba's Riding Mountain relief camp.▲

They were also more efficient. For their $400,000 they housed more than double the number of men, and accomplished much more work, than did the DND for $500,000. General McNaughton complained of their "unnecessary extravagance" and demanded the parks camps reduce their rations (which they didn't) and their pay (which they did). Soon the bitterness of the army's camps was evident in the parks camps as well.

That bitterness was not hard to explain. Once in the camps, the men were in effect inmates. No leave periods were permitted. There was no machinery to speed the construction projects in which the men were engaged. The government saw the camps as first-class bush camps, which they arguably were. But they lacked two components: men did not choose to go there, and the vision of making a stake and getting out to spend it was absent. Some army camp supervisors scrounged correspondence courses and recreational equipment, but in most there was little to relieve the boredom and loneliness.

So they offered no future and represented defeat and futility. Not only had these men failed to find jobs, their confinement to the camps delivered the message that the country didn't want them. And as an activity of the Department of National Defence the camps were subject to semi-military regulations. This, as historian James Gray observed, "guaranteed that whatever grievance did develop... would be bottled up until it reached explosive proportions. Anyone who tried to organize a protest in the camp faced expulsion and in some camps that meant being expelled in midwinter at the camp gates a hundred miles from the nearest habitation."

Camp inmates tended to rely on the Communists as spokesmen. The Communists would stand up to camp authorities, seemingly unafraid of being thrown out, and demand to be paid a wage for their work. (The 20 cents a day was considered a gratuity.) They also demanded better food. Standard army rations, the food was generally of good quality but, also as in the army, the cooks could be very poor indeed.

The Communists demanded the right to organize, something strictly forbidden under the military administration. Even "collective consultation" among the men was forbidden. When the Communists began putting together protest groups, camp authorities usually called the police, who rounded up the agitators and any men holding positions in any organization and evicted the lot. Often, however, new organizations were being born and new officers elected while police were interrogating members of the old ones.

At their peak a report that used military terms such as "authorized strength" showed there were 108 camps, holding a total of 19,917 men — nearly 10,000 fewer than they were designed to hold. They included 41 devoted to high-

way construction, 34 building airports, twelve on military bases and the remainder engaged in municipal projects.

By then many of these had become scenes of unrest and defiance. The camps were beset by work stoppages and prolonged strikes, often well organized, disciplined and carefully co-ordinated so that authorities were confronted with demonstrations at several camps at the same time.

These incidents mounted until a major confrontation with police occurred at a provincial relief camp in Saskatoon on May 8, 1933. The history of the Saskatoon camp had scores of parallels across the country, but it was this one that attracted great public attention because the trouble there claimed the life of a senior RCMP officer.

The Saskatoon camp had been established by the city early in 1930 on the Exhibition Grounds in the southeast corner of the city at the end of Ruth Street. The city appointed ex-army officers to run it to prevent it from becoming a Communist hotbed. They failed. From the start,

Part of the Jasper-Banff Highway was built by relief-camp workers.

radical labour leaders appeared among the camp residents protesting its conditions. "No efforts were made to isolate venereally-diseased men from the others," said a report in the *Canadian Labor Defender*. "A foul stench pervaded the place at all times. Ventilation of the crudest kind. Bunks and dinner tables all jumbled together... Adjoining the living room were swill tubs, bathtubs, toilets, dryers and boilers, with the floor generally flooded and a foul odour permeating the living quarters."

After nearly two years' operation the place became the scene of repeated demonstrations. On November 1, 1932 the men paraded beneath a red flag through downtown Saskatoon, protesting "Bennett's Slave Camps." Two leaders were arrested for parading without a licence and "carrying a red flag without a Union Jack." A week later 200 unemployed men and women gathered at the city relief office and blocked traffic. When they refused to clear the street, ninety city police and RCMP appeared and waded into the crowd, swinging their truncheons. The crowd fled, but only after a dozen people were injured, some of them policemen, and five had been arrested for unlawful assembly.

By February 1933 "bunk committees" were organized and confronting the camp management with demands for "union wages." The police arrived and arrested the leaders, then had to release them because they hadn't broken any law. On April 5, forty workers carried their soup bowls into the superintendent's office to protest the unvarying food menu. When they were refused they began smashing the furniture until the police arrived.

This brought Premier J.T.M. Anderson to inspect the camp, which by now had been taken over by the province. He agreed the conditions were bad and named a new superintendent. This man proved tougher than his predecessor. Consequently on April 10 another food protest saw further damage done and a squad of 35 Mounted Police were dispatched to Saskatoon because Mountie "plants" among the inmates were warning that real trouble was afoot.

the crowd. The *Saskatoon Star-Phoenix* described what followed: "Stones began to fly and the officers, swinging their long cavalry batons, put their horses to the gallop and started to scatter the crowd, chasing them away from in front of the building, while their quarry scattered and took shelter in the corners of various buildings and behind fences. Wheeling their horses again and again, the policemen chased the fugitives all over the grounds, striking right and left."

In the midst of this RCMP Inspector James Lorne Sampson either fell or was knocked from the saddle and was dragged by his horse across the field, banging his head against a pole. He died soon after in hospital. Twenty-eight workers were arrested and hauled away in a furniture van. For various offences from rioting to assault, all received sentences ranging from fines to up to a year in prison. No charge was laid in connection with Sampson's death, though an inquest found he fell from his horse after being hit by a flying stone.

The government, torn between demands that the camps be abolished or that they be brought under better control,

---

The bitterness of the men was not hard to explain. The camps delivered the message they were unemployable. And once there, they were in effect inmates. No leave periods were permitted. Anyone who walked out found himself at the camp gate, miles from the nearest town.

One cause was grotesque overcrowding. Hundreds of men were now pouring into the place. In February it had accommodated 391, by April 630, and by May 870. Hence the camp's managers planned to move fifty inmates, notably the agitators and leaders, to a similar camp at Regina. They refused to go, and instead called a protest meeting on the camp premises on May 7, where a leaflet was passed among the inmates, headed "WAR IS DECLARED. BE PREPARED." The meeting adjourned with the singing of the *Red Flag*.

The following day the situation exploded. About 5:30 p.m., the fifty men designated to go to Regina instead went into the buildings for dinner. Three hundred more milled about outside. At least 400, fearing a bloody riot, left the camp entirely. Two troops of mounted RCMP officers arrived on the scene and took up positions about a hundred yards from the crowd outside the hall. Three police officers entered the building and gave the fifty ten minutes to go outside and board waiting buses for Regina. They responded by booing and jeering and declaring they were staying. The three returned with more police reinforcements, repeated the demand, and were told by one of the leaders to leave the building. The police chief grabbed the man by the scruff of the neck and hustled him to the door, then hit another leader over the head with a truncheon.

This signalled the mounted police outside to plunge into

had secretly decided on drastic action against strikers. Preparations were started under the "peace, order and good government" clause of the Relief Act to set up what were called Camps of Discipline. General McNaughton instructed his quartermaster-general to draw up plans for these jail camps, each to house about 100 men sentenced to "detention," another army term. He envisioned that several such camps would be necessary. (The parallel with the labour camps of the Soviet "Gulag" did not escape later writers.)

An order-in-council was prepared, providing for the incarceration of anyone refusing employment or refusing to perform "duties required of them." These persons "should be subject to special disciplinary measures, notwithstanding the provisions of any [other] statute or law." Sentences would range from fourteen to sixty days, and proof of physical inability to perform the required duties would rest with the accused. Alternatively, an accused person would have to prove he was not unemployed or homeless.

Detention camp punishments were to include solitary confinement, bread-and-water diets, and the revoking of such privileges as having a mattress to sleep on, receiving visitors and writing letters. Privileges could also be revoked for talking without authority to other inmates, carelessness at work, not attending church or the use of obscene language.

Since British Columbia relief camps were more troubled

than those in other provinces, McNaughton attempted to acquire East Thurlow Island, at the north end of the Strait of Georgia, as the site of the first jail camp. Provincial officials were initially told it was to be used as a forestry experimental farm; only later did they learn it was to become a Camp of Discipline for 250 inmates.

But the project remained a plan. The violence that McNaughton feared did not spread, and the government waited to make sure it had a political base for such a drastic measure and found it did not. So the order-in-council was never proclaimed.

By now McNaughton had critics even among his own officers. Brigadier J. Sutherland Brown, after failing to persuade McNaughton to adopt a more generous policy towards rations and allowances, resigned from the army and publicly criticized the defence department and federal relief policy generally.

McNaughton brushed off such criticisms and did some complaining himself. He was particularly irritated by the "constant sniping" of Alberta Public Works officials, he said. In September 1933, for instance, a confidential memorandum on the camps circulated in the Alberta bureaucracy had found its way to the *Edmonton Journal*, which intended to publish it. He had taken up the matter with Premier Brownlee who "communicated with the Prime Minister... and after a great deal of trouble we persuaded the paper that no good purpose would be served and it was suppressed."

What finally doomed the camps was a much bigger Communist project. In the spring of 1935 many young men began walking away from British Columbia camps and headed for Vancouver, some to seek work there and others to catch freight trains east in the great March on Ottawa described in the next chapter. Many of the marchers had been trained in the camps by the Communists.

Furthermore, by this time the relief camps were becoming a political liability to Bennett. Since 1932 the Conservatives had lost three provincial elections (British Columbia, Saskatchewan and Ontario) and, by the fall of 1934, five important federal by-elections. The camps were only part of the cause, but an important one.

Moreover B.C. Premier Duff Pattullo was advocating they be closed in favour of a massive federal public works program that would pay regular wage rates, like those that the Roosevelt administration was enacting in the U.S. under its New Deal. Even Conservative backbenchers were complaining about the camps. H.J. Barber of Chilliwack said the time had come to pay $2 a day, with a deduction of 60 cents to cover food. Then Liberal leader Mackenzie King campaigned in the 1935 election on a promise to abolish them.

In May 1933 RCMP on horseback charged a relief-camp demonstration group, and Insp. J.L. Sampson was killed in the ensuing mêlée.

Once elected, he established a committee under the labour department to study the situation, while strikes and unrest continued. The committee recommended they be shut down immediately. The new government began phasing them out in March 1936. On June 2 Labour minister Norman Rogers announced that the last had been closed and with it an unhappy chapter in Canadian history.

—F.C.

▲One of the first parks to benefit from the new funding was Elk Island in east-central Alberta, which provided one of the Depression's more curious relief projects: the park golf course. When the local golf club president wrote to Ottawa about their "very immediate need," Parks Commissioner J.B. Harkin agreed perhaps because he himself was an avid golfer.

85

As Communism turns to violence, its first big riot hits Edmonton

BUT THIS WAS JUST THE FORERUNNER FOR THE DECISIVE MARCH ON OTTAWA THAT SAW THOUSANDS RIDE THE FREIGHTS TO A BLOODY CLIMAX AT REGINA

by FRED CLEVERLEY

The year 1932 found Canadian Communists in something of a dilemma. They had a powerful influence over the hordes of single men who wandered across the country, unemployed, unwanted, and frequently confined in semi-military camps, which were breeding grounds for unrest and radicalism. But at the same time, three-quarters of the country was still working, and this three-quarters controlled the forces of law and order. Only by somehow sufficiently disrupting the social order, therefore, could they possibly instigate a Marxist revolution. But how could such a disruption be achieved? There seemed only one answer: by engendering a public perception of mayhem and chaos. The consequence was three years of riotous violence that would crescendo to a destructive finale on the streets of Regina in the summer of 1935.

This new militancy first appeared in Alberta in December of 1932, when the Communist-led Workers' Unity League (WUL) staged what would be known to Alberta history as the Edmonton

The Workers' Unity League's aim was to unite industrial workers and farmers in the overthrow of the government when it organized the December 1932 Edmonton Hunger Strike. Here would-be marchers assemble in Market Square prior to this defiant promenade that set off the Edmonton riot.

Hunger March. It was carefully planned, extensively promoted and achieved its immediate purpose, which was to stimulate publicity and attract attention.

The ultimate aim of the WUL, according to a booklet published after the event by the Canadian Labour Defense League (another Communist group), was to encourage solidarity between industrial workers and farmers, and to convincingly demonstrate that their interests were similar if not actually identical. It was also meant to show that democratic socialist and semi-socialist organizations, such as the moderate trade unions, and political parties like the United Farmers, the Progressives and the newly founded Co-operative Commonwealth Federation (CCF) (see sidebar) could not and would not solve the problems of either workers or farmers.[1]

Look at Alberta, argued the Communists. It was governed by the United Farmers' party, which expressed great sympathy with the CCF. In its capital, the mayor and five aldermen were Labour Party members and controlled the city council by one vote. Yet when a delegation of unemployed approached Mayor D.K. Knott and his council before the projected Hunger March, seeking the requisite parade permit, the mayor equivocated. Even the threat of "a bloody battle" didn't move him. Neither did the observation of one alderman that the no-parade policy was "dangerously anti-social and stupid." Mayor Knott would only reply: "If the premier is agreeable, the [police] chief will grant a permit." UFA Premier John Brownlee was not in the least agreeable, as Knott well knew. So much for the "moderate" approach, argued the Communists.

Direct, decisive action was what was needed, they said, and as the winter of 1932 set in they prepared to provide some. The Edmonton office of the Communist-led National Unemployed Workers' Association announced that the 5,000 unemployed men in the capital city would be on the march, joined by hundreds of others from across the province. By December 16, despite winter conditions, people were arriving by truck, car, sleigh and on foot from Calgary, Lethbridge, Drumheller, Vegreville, Ranfurly, Smoky Lake and points between. Many were farmers, like the three trucks full of men from Myrnam and another three from Tiger Hills. Many were city boys.

There would have been more by far from both country and city, claimed a booklet published by the Communists after the event, entitled *The Alberta Hunger-March and the Trial of the Victims of Brownlee's Police Terror*, if organizers had had more time to mobilize them, and if the RCMP had

[1] Economic conditions in 1932 could hardly have been more suitable for a grand gesture by the hopeful Communist Party of Canada. As reported by S.A. Saunders in his *Nature and Extent of Unemployment in Canada* (1939), unemployment was estimated at nearly 13 per cent of the work force in 1930, it reached a peak of nearly 27 per cent in 1933 and thereafter it gradually declined to about 13 per cent during the partial economic recovery of 1937.

[2] "No Charity — But Solidarity" was the slogan of the Workers' International Relief, which advertised itself as "a workers' self-help organization — aid from the workers for workers, distinct and apart from capitalist charity." It would do its best within the present system, the WIR promised, but workers must realize "that complete emancipation of the working class cannot be achieved within the capitalist system."

Provincial Archives of Alberta, A 9217

not been doing its best to block the roads. Even so, by December 20 there were an estimated 2,000 out-of-towners in Edmonton.

Whatever other qualities the hunger marchers might have had, hunger was not one of them. Farmers brought truckloads of meat, vegetables and flour. Kitchens were set up by the Workers' International Relief, another Communist affiliate.[2] RCMP and city police searched Hunger March headquarters and various halls for firearms, but found none. Police spies ("paid out of the pockets of farmers and workers") were everywhere.

Early on the afternoon of the 20th, some 2,000 would-be marchers assembled at Market Square, the area south of City Hall that would one day accommodate the city's central library. It was bounded on the north by 102nd Avenue, on the west by 100th Street, on the south by 101A Avenue (which many still called by its old name, Rice Street) and on the east by 99th Street. Down the centre of the square, north to south, stretched the one-storey Market Building. Across 101A Avenue from the Market Building, where in the 1970s the Westin Hotel would be built, stood the old Post Office Building with its distinctive clock tower.

The purpose of the assembly was to protest the denial of a parade permit by Mayor Knott and the premier. To stand in the square and talk about it was not an offence under the law. To leave the square and embark on a parade was.

This the organizers had been volubly threatening to do, and provincial and city authorities knew that if they successfully defied the law, control would become impossible. Formidable preparations had therefore been made. Lined up along 102nd Avenue to the north of the square were 75 blue-uniformed city policemen, each armed with a truncheon. Across 100th Street west of the square stood 22 mounted RCMP officers, their horses in perfect control. Occupying the Market

THE REVOLUTIONARIES

Twenty-two mounted police officers stand ready at Edmonton's Market Square. Nearly 10,000 people showed up to witness what promised to be the best show in town.

In one work gang (at Bragg Creek), a former bank clerk works side by side with a former canned heat artist. The banker had quit to enter a brokerage house. The brokers went to jail. He lost his job, well nigh starved to death and then hit for the brush camps. He traded off his tuxedo for two pairs of overalls and two pairs of shoe packs. He's well and happy and healthy. The canned heat artist almost died the first week. He's one of the best men on the gang now. Three square meals a day and good Alberta sunshine worked wonders with him. —Calgary Herald, January 20, 1931

Building were thirty RCMP officers on foot.

For more than an hour, the crowd heard increasingly strident appeals from their Communist leaders. Finally Hunger March Committee chairman Andrew Irvine took the platform. "There is no law in Canada that can prevent us from walking peacefully along the sidewalk," he declared. "We don't want violence and I want you to refrain from violence. If there's any violence, let it be the police who start it." Then, raising his voice to its highest pitch, he cried "Now let's go!"

There were cheers and roars of approval. Out came the banners and immediately the vanguard of the parade moved out of the square and onto the sidewalk bordering the north side of 101A Avenue, one of the two flanks of the square not guarded by a police squad. After forming up in pairs the paraders moved west along the sidewalk towards 100th Street, then began to wheel south. They got that far and no farther.

By then the mounted policemen had trotted south on 100th Street and met the paraders at its intersection with 100A. There was as yet no violence. Riding knee to knee, the phalanx of horsemen simply moved into the front of the parade and began working it backwards along 100A Avenue to the point where it had begun.

Then out of the Market Building streamed the Mounties on foot while the city policemen on 102nd Avenue came across the square and into the crowd. For the next eight minutes a fierce fight ensued between the police on foot and the paraders, the latter armed with brickbats and stones, the police with their truncheons and batons.

Newspaper accounts describe a broiling mass of humanity, and a din of men shouting curses, women screaming abuse at the police, cudgels cracking skulls, people sprawled on the pavement, blood streaming from their heads (see sidebar). But the worst complication had yet to occur.

As well as the estimated 2,000 paraders in Market Square the advance publicity had attracted

In the calm before the storm city police, billies at the ready, line up along the north side of 102nd Avenue as marchers assemble across the street in Market Square. Within minutes they would cross the street and engage hunger strikers in an eight-minute battle that would degenerate into two hours of isolated free-for-alls around the Market Square area.

The night of December 21, fifty policemen raided the Hunger March headquarters in the Ukrainian Labour Temple at 96th Street and 106A Avenue (known to later generations as "the Blue Hall"). They found women busy cooking turkey dinners in the basement for the "hungry." The Ukrainian Presbyterian Church stood beside the temple.

City police chase marchers and spectators east along the sidewalk on the north side of the Post Office, just after mounted police had charged into the throng of demonstrators. The Edmonton Journal reported that the police had swung their "billies" freely, forcing people to seek refuge between or on top of automobiles.

thousands of spectators, for whom this promised to be the best show of the year. (The *Journal* put their numbers at 7,500, the *Bulletin* at 10,000.) Behind the mounted police came the cudgel-swinging foot police and behind the foot police came the curious onlookers in their thousands. Not long after the initial eight-minute clash it became impossible to distinguish the citizenry from the demonstrators.

During the ensuing two hours 101A Avenue, 100th Street, Market Square and the Market Building became the locale of scores of individual fights between policemen, paraders and, occasionally, bewildered citizens mistaken for protesters. Soon, observed the *Bulletin*, the spectators were making as much noise as the paraders, greatly spreading the confusion. The paraders meanwhile made their way to the roofs of the buildings and hurled stones at the police below.

By nightfall the riot was over and the news media counted the toll: no deaths, scores of minor injuries to police, paraders and some citizens, but no serious ones. No store windows smashed. Serious damage to Christmas trees on sale, which had been stripped of their limbs for weaponry. Also heavy damage to cars parked on the affected streets — their windows broken, and roofs and fenders dented because of the numerous people who climbed on top of them.

That night fifty policemen raided the Hunger March headquarters in the Ukrainian Labour Temple at 96th Street and 106A Avenue. They found more than 400 men in the building and more than 100 in the church next door. They also found an enormous supply of food contributed by farmers from the area east of Edmonton. Women were busy cooking turkey dinners in the basement. Thirty-two men and one woman were arrested as suspected leaders of the parade. Only the woman resisted arrest; she was wrestled into a police car by two constables. All were charged with unlawful assembly and later acquitted. Andrew Irvine wasn't there, but he was apprehended in Calgary two months later.

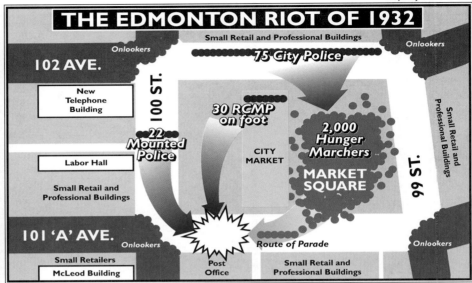

THE EDMONTON RIOT OF 1932

Small Retail and Professional Buildings

Onlookers — Onlookers

75 City Police

102 AVE.

New Telephone Building

100 ST.

30 RCMP on foot

2,000 Hunger Marchers

99 ST.

Small Retail and Professional Buildings

22 Mounted Police

Labor Hall

CITY MARKET

MARKET SQUARE

Small Retail and Professional Buildings

101 'A' AVE.

Onlookers

Route of Parade

Onlookers

Small Retailers

McLeod Building

Post Office

Small Retail and Professional Buildings

Meanwhile Premier Brownlee agreed to meet a delegation from the hunger marchers, who asked $4 million in assorted benefits. Brownlee proved unsympathetic. "Are you hungry?" he asked one delegate, a farmer. "No, I'm not hungry," the young man answered, obviously surprised at the question. "And you aren't wanting clothing, are you?" persisted Brownlee, adding: "You are better dressed than many young men who come to my office."

"No, I'm not asking for clothes," the man replied. "How did you come to the city?" asked Brownlee. "In my car," the farmer replied. Brownlee had made his point. "The 'hunger march,'" observed the *Edmonton Bulletin*, "accomplished nothing, for the reason that there was nothing for it to accomplish. Misnamed, misplanned, and mishandled, the demonstration was born of pretence and died of exposure. The marchers were not hungry and desperate men and the public knew it. That killed any chance it might have had of arousing popular sympathy."

But the *Bulletin* was wrong. The Edmonton affair accomplished exactly what the Communists wanted. It spurred Ottawa to act, and it thereby became the indirect cause of the grand finale of Communist insurgency in Canada, the On-to-Ottawa March of 1935.

SAME AREA AT CENTURY'S END

Winston Churchill Square

102 AVE.

Telephone Building

100 ST.

Stanley Milner Library

99 ST.

Winspear Centre

101 'A' AVE.

McLeod Building

Westin Hotel

Citadel Theatre

(Above left) The sense of excitement visible in the faces of these strikers of all ages would soon turn to horror, as confusion turned to chaos. (Top) Map of the riot scene. (Below) The same block at the century's end.

Whatever other qualities the Edmonton Hunger Marchers might have had, hunger was not one of them. Farmers brought truckloads of meat, vegetables and flour. Kitchens were set up by the Workers' International Relief, another Communist affiliate.

Alarmed by the Edmonton experience, the federal government established the isolated work camps for unemployed single men described in the last chapter. An organization called the Relief Camp Workers' Union (RCWU), affiliated with the WUL, was soon in operation inside them[3] and over the four years of their existence the camps recorded 359 "disturbances," these being strikes, demonstrations and riots occasioned by dissatisfaction with work and living conditions. Out of all this fevered activity arose the On-to-Ottawa March.

Although the RCWU was a national organization, or at least had national pretensions, both its leadership and its activity were largely concentrated in British Columbia where 53 camps — more

[3]Communist-affiliated organizations concerned with the unemployed proliferated in the 1930s. They were also mostly affiliated with one another. Among them were: The Workers' Unity League (WUL); the Farmers' Unity League (FUL); the Workers' Ex-Servicemen's League (WESL); the Canadian Labour Defence League (CLDL); and, not least, the Relief Camp Workers' Union. For reading material, members could subscribe to *The Worker*, *The Furrow*, *The Canadian Labour Defender*, *Young Worker*, *Canadian Miner* or *Workers' Unity* — among others.

Christmas trees on a nearby lot were stripped of their branches for makeshift weapons.

This RCMP constable (left) was cut on the face during the fracas.

An assembly of excited bystanders, some young, like the Edmonton Bulletin carrier on his bicycle, confronting policemen inexperienced at riot control, made violence inevitable. The cyclist escaped.

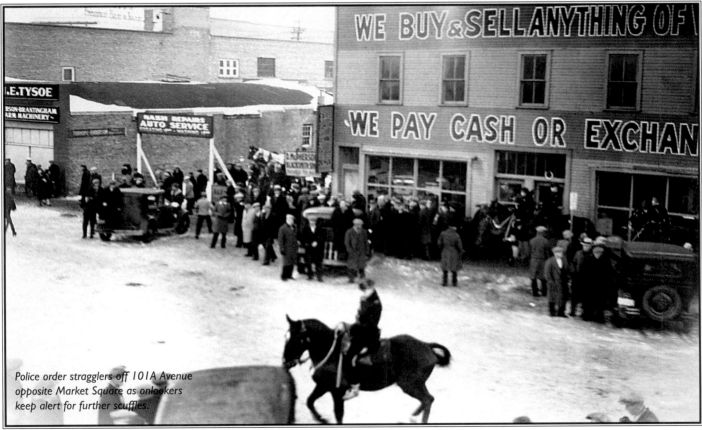

Police order stragglers off 101A Avenue opposite Market Square as onlookers keep alert for further scuffles.

than in any other province — were situated. The first B.C. disturbance was in June 1933. When ten men were discharged for causing it, nearly 400 more walked out in sympathy. In 1934 there were at least a hundred such incidents in the province, 27 of them in December alone, when the RCWU orchestrated a mass walkout to Vancouver. Close to a thousand camp workers congregated in that city in early December, and a six-man delegation went to Victoria to present their demands: for removal of the camps from Department of National Defence jurisdiction, for payment of the B.C. minimum wage rather than twenty cents a day, for unemployment insurance, for abolition of camp blacklisting of troublemakers, for pottery dishes not tin ones, and assorted

An eye-witness describes Edmonton's 'Hunger-March' riot

SKULLS ARE CRACKED BY FLAILING POLICE BATONS, AND THEN THERE WAS THIS DEPARTMENT STORE SANTA WHO CAME TO WATCH AND GOT CAUGHT IN THE BRAWL

The following is excerpted from the Edmonton Journal's *description of the "Hunger March" riot published on December 21, 1932.*

Riding in perfect line the mounted men met the foremost marchers and slowly pushed them back. Fast in the wake of the horsemen came a swarm of city police on foot and it was this force and the dismounted RCMP that were confronted with the task of dispersing the mob.

It was then that the police were forced to use their batons on the heads of unruly paraders and in some instances on sympathizers in the crowd of onlookers who became jammed in a wild, swirling mass of humanity which confused marcher with bystander.

Charging into the crowd, their batons used with telling effect, police caused demonstrators and bystanders to rush helter-skelter. Hand-to-hand battles between small groups of police and paraders were frequent, the latter snatching pieces of boards and engaging the officers in individual contests that resulted shortly in many battered heads.

Police on foot, following up the mounted men, cleared the street as far as the lane, and then spent a few moments in chasing men up the lane. Turning, they paid more attention to the crowd in the centre of 101A Avenue. It was here that the fiercest fighting took place. At a dozen points at once, marchers tangled individually with policemen and above the shouts could be heard the "whack-whack" of the sticks on skulls.

Hundreds viewed the battle from the roofs of surrounding buildings and through windows of blocks commanding a view of 101A Avenue. The roof of the McLeod Building was black with humanity.

Long before the trouble broke, people in the Post Office, McLeod Building and other places offering a semblance of safety were at the windows to watch events. "We could hear the sound of the police batons at this distance," said one spectator whose office is on the fourth floor of the McLeod Building.

Several of the demonstrators fell to the pavement under well directed blows from night sticks. Boards or tree limbs

Provincial Archives of Alberta, A 9214

RCMP wait on horseback at the corner of 100th Street and 101A Avenue, ready to charge the crowd again if need be. Some onlookers hurled stones, others just booed the police.

proved a popular weapon with the marchers, dozens of spruce bows being torn from a large number of Christmas trees piled in Market Square.

At one time four of the marchers were lying on the ground, but only one needed assistance as he walked away. His face was extremely pale and he was assisted along the sidewalk in front of the Market Building stores.

Several of those injured by blows from the police clubs hurried over to the McLeod Building with blood streaming

other improvements.

Premier Duff Pattullo told them the province could not afford to consider their economic demands, but he himself was sympathetic. He was also acutely conscious that the movement had wide public sympathy. The province would provide the strikers with food and lodging during their stay in Vancouver, he promised, and he would ask Ottawa to investigate their complaints.

Dissatisfied, dispirited and disillusioned, the men filtered back to their camps in mid-January 1935, but by then something else was in the works. Arthur Herbert "Slim" Evans, a veteran union and Communist Party activist, had been released from Oakalla Prison, where he had been serving

down their faces to get medical attention. Three marauders were treated at the provincial clinic for minor scalp injuries.

Frank Hyduk of Ranfurly was one who received a bad cut on the forehead. It was found on examination by Dr. Clyde Macdonald that this man had a severed artery. The wound being stitched, he walked away to rejoin his comrades.

Another casualty was an Edmonton citizen, Reg Healey, who evidently was struck by a baton when caught in the police charge. Examination by Dr. Walter Morrish showed that Healey had a wound over the right side of his head. The cut required four stitches. According to Healey he was merely watching the fight when he was cracked by the police billies.

The fight was not without its amusing incidents, however. Just after the first charge of the Mounties, the troop had re-formed at the Post Office corner. The crowd was packed tight around them and city police were trying to clear a path along the sidewalk. It was a tense moment.

before the charging police.

As the mounted police moved through the crowd the flank of one trooper's horse flicked a man's hat from his head. The latter raised his clenched fist and struck the horse a blow and it reared on its front legs. Two city police pounced on the wearer of the hat and he went down under the combined weight of the constables to the pavement. When the struggling mass became untangled, the civilian arose with a couple of large bumps on his head but smiling for all that. He made his way to the sidewalk unmolested.

One of the most amusing sights was two banner carriers ducking for cover beneath two parked cars. Two city policemen went down on their hands and knees, reached in and hauled the banner carriers out. These two marchers showed fight for a moment, but a couple of whacks on their skulls sent them scurrying for safety.

A dozen men scampered under Christmas trees erected in tent-like style and the horsemen found that they could

During the ensuing two hours 101A Avenue, 100th Street, Market Square and the Market Building became the locale of scores of individual fights between policemen, paraders and, occasionally, bewildered citizens mistaken for protesters.

Suddenly a report like a pistol shot rang out. As one, the faces of the police and the crowd turned and looked up 100th Street. Almost immediately it was realized that an automobile, standing outside the Post Office with its engine running, had backfired and everyone laughed.

Another amusing spectacle was the sight of Santa Claus, white whiskers and red coat and all, hopping about in the thick of the fight. It was the Santa of one of Edmonton's big stores and he had become mixed with the crowd evidently with the idea of seeing the show.

Many of the marchers who were the first to experience the feeling of night sticks and batons on their heads beat a hasty retreat and climbed to the roof of the Market Building. Noticed by their comrades still battling in the streets, the deserters were subject of derisive shouts. Cries of, "You yellow cads, come back and fight!" were hurled up at the marchers on the roof.

A fish store in the Market Building proved a popular haven for hundreds of spectators who fled at top speed

not ride in there. City policemen with billies raised walked in. Onlookers saw the trees shudder violently and then each policeman emerged with a man who was told to "get going." They did. One man shouted angrily, "I'm a taxpayer. I've got a right to be here." The policeman told him, "Taxpayer or not, you're going to get out of here," and he shoved him along.

J. Alan McNeil of the Alberta Motor Association was in the crowd of spectators which scampered up the lane behind the Post Office Building. "I can't understand it yet," he said. "The man on my right was hit, and the man on my left, but I didn't get it. Maybe I ran too fast."

There were several women caught in the crowd. One woman, coming out of the fish shop in the Market Building, was caught in the maelstrom as the mounted men first started to break up the parade. She screamed and, throwing her parcel of fish high in the air, ran across the street in the thick of things and apparently, and amazingly, made it to the other side.

[4]Oscar Ryan, in his biography of the Communist Party of Canada leader, *Tim Buck, a Conscience for Canada* (Toronto, Progress Books, 1975), claims that Arthur Meighen rammed Section 98 of the Criminal Code through Parliament to wreck the Winnipeg Strike of 1919. It was not used then, but in 1931 it served to jail Buck. Section 98, which was finally replaced in 1937, made it a crime punishable by up to 20 years in prison to belong to any association that aimed to bring about governmental, industrial or economic change by force. Its property could be seized without warrant, and anyone attending its meetings or publicly supporting it was "presumed, in the absence of proof to the contrary" to be a member. Thus the successful prosecution of Buck made the CPC *de facto* illegal in any province that chose to enforce Section 98.

a one-year sentence under Section 98 of the Criminal Code for membership in an unlawful organization. (Evans had been trying to set up a local of the WUL-affiliated Mine Workers' Union of Canada at Princeton, B.C.)[4] Now, as district organizer for the WUL, he called a meeting in Kamloops in March to plan another and better walkout. Attended by delegates from WUL and its affiliates, the Kamloops meeting expanded the demands of the December-January strikers to include repeal of Section 98, of two clauses of the Immigration Act and of all vagrancy laws, and scheduled a major relief camp strike and walkout April 4.

This time an initial 1,600 or so men quit the camps and headed for Vancouver, often — according to union legend — assisted by friendly police. There Evans divided them into four divisions and bivouacked them in various halls, and there they remained for the next two months. They kept busy. They raised $5,500 at an illegal tag day. They marched 5,000 strong (counting sympathizers) across the city. They infiltrated department stores — peacefully for the most part, but in late April the Hudson's Bay store somehow got trashed.

At that point Mayor Gerald McGeer decided to put his foot down. In response the strikers staged a mammoth May Day rally, with a parade that featured a caricatured Mayor McGeer reading the Riot Act. Some of Vancouver's active unions began to rally to the campers' support, but by May 16 they were running out of money and everyone was getting edgy. In desperation they forcibly occupied the Vancouver Public Library and Museum, which still brought no results. By June 1 the decision to take their grievances straight to Ottawa had been made.

It was a decision that made everybody in Vancouver — well-wishers, long-suffering municipal and provincial officials, and bitter opponents too — very happy. Jack Cosgrove, a Great War veteran from Calgary, was appointed to maintain order on the trek to Ottawa. On the evening of June 3 he supervised the boarding of freight cars in the Canadian Pacific yards by the first 800 participants in the On-to-Ottawa Trek. As they climbed atop the boxcars at Cosgrove's direction, friendly Vancouverites rallied round with cheers and songs and gifts of food. There was an equally friendly welcome at Golden, B.C., where they stopped over for a rest. Then came the harrowing trip through the Spiral Tunnels, no happy experience on a freight car behind a steam locomotive.

THE REVOLUTIONARIES

Many had equipped themselves with goggles, which offered some protection from cinders, soot and dust, and they all survived the passage.

On June 7 they reached Calgary, where municipal authorities, fully aware of what had gone on in Vancouver, were close to panic. They had believed the march would take the northern route through Edmonton.[5] Disabused of this idea, Mayor Andrew Davison of Calgary sent a telegram to Major-General Sir James MacBrien, commissioner of the RCMP, asking that the marchers be stopped at the Alberta border. If not, he warned, Calgary would require additional police to prevent disorder. Nor could Calgary accept any responsibility for care of these men, "as we are finding it increasingly difficult to finance the care of our own *bona fide* citizens." From Ottawa, however, Prime Minister Bennett replied that he could authorize federal police only if provincial authorities asked him to.

Mayor Davison was unaware of the brilliant public relations strategy of the march organizers, who were determined there would be no disorder. Anxious to avoid anything that might alienate the public, they planned to spend two or three days in Calgary, holding a tag day to raise more travel money (they had left the coast with only $800), and persuading Alberta citizens of the justice of their demands. Disembarking at the railway yards, the soot-grimed men marched in parade formation, escorted by a police motorcycle officer, to the exhibition grounds, Calgarians cheering them on from their windows. The city had offered them use of the civic stadium, with a kitchen range and with water and gas supplied, so long as they only stayed the weekend.

While there could be no official authorization for a tag day, organizer Bill Hammill many years later told Victor Howard, author of *We Were the Salt of the Earth: The On-to-Ottawa Trek and Regina Riot* (University of Regina, 1985), that members of city council assured him they would look the other way. In any event, a tag day that Saturday raised $1,302. The province contributed an additional $600, caving in after relief officials were confined to their offices by hundreds of trekkers doing a snake dance round and round their block. Some eighty trekkers invaded the office of relief commission chairman A.A. MacKenzie and held that terrified official prisoner for two hours until he agreed to send to Edmonton the telegram they dictated urging compliance with their demand for funds. Edmonton instructed him to issue two fifteen-cent meal tickets a day for the weekend. This was the sole untoward episode, however. Trek veterans were also occupied with integrating and indoctrinating some hundreds of eager Alberta recruits, three hundred of whom arrived from Edmonton.

Eight hours down the line, Medicine Hat was also apprehensive about these uninvited guests. However, the *Medicine Hat News* was reassuring. In a report from Calgary, the *News* described the

This "hunger march" in Calgary in the summer of 1932, prior to the Edmonton Hunger March the following December, occasioned few headlines and attracted little attention, persuading the organizers of the Edmonton demonstration they had to bring farm workers into the protest if it were to achieve its purpose. (Left) This group assembled at City Hall. (Right) They proceed along 7th Avenue East.

[5]The On-to-Ottawa organizers did their best to soothe concern in Calgary by distributing leaflets before the trek arrived there and by a broadcast on radio station CFAC on the previous evening. Both leaflet and broadcast assured Calgarians that the relief camp marchers would be in their city for only a few days, and their appeals for help were very carefully worded.

[6]Newspaper attitudes as the trek moved across the country often depended on whether the trekkers were coming or going. The *Vancouver Province* benignly described their departure as a migration unique in the history of Canada. In Ottawa, the target city, the *Ottawa Journal* criticized provincial governments (presumably Alberta and Saskatchewan) for not stopping them. The *Calgary Albertan* consistently supported the trek, however, and one of Prime Minister Bennett's supporters used to send him clippings. One *Albertan* editorial, discussing whether the march was Communist-led, concluded: "To be quite frank, we don't care much," since the main purpose was to demand work and wages to make relief camps unnecessary.

[7]In deciding to stop the march at Regina, the Bennett government took advantage of some of the preparations made to counter the anticipated labour unrest that had resulted in the establishment in the relief camps. These preparations had included the issuing in October 1931 of 300 bayonets and 30,000 rounds of .303 ammunition to the RCMP at Regina. The armed forces had also made bayonet instructors available to the police in Regina and Winnipeg.

[8]A report carried in the *Calgary Herald* said that many of the jobless were Canadian born, scores of them youths sixteen to twenty years of age. While there was a strong representation of southern Europeans, and although one division contained two Negroes, "all the leaders appeared to be Anglo Saxon." This observation appears to have been quite accurate, though there were plenty of eastern Europeans among the trekkers as well. Nor did an Anglo name always mean much; some found pseudonyms a useful expedient.

marchers thus: "Mostly young men, nearly all well under 30 years, they appeared a carefree, happy lot, on adventure bound. Through the streets they sang as they marched."[6] It was exactly the impression for which the trek organizers were striving. Even so, Mayor Isaac Bullivant offered them $200 not to stop at the Hat, but they declined. They would spend a day in his city, they said.

The trekkers departed Calgary as promised, in the early morning of June 10; by Victor Howard's estimate they numbered 1,400 by then. Trek marshal Jack Cosgrove continued to maintain discipline in the boarding order; local supporters provided them with 2,400 sandwiches; and railwaymen seemed to be warming to their cinder-begrimed passengers.

The city police amiably escorted them to the yards and CPR officials showed them how to board without being injured. The newspapers portrayed some touching scenes — a mother searching for her son in the crowd to dissuade him from going, but failing to find him; a small boy proudly pointing to his father, who had joined the march because he couldn't find a job to support the youngster's twelve brothers and sisters.

At Medicine Hat, too, matters remained amicable. Bullivant announced that the province had contributed $250 toward food, a tag day produced $224.88 and the trekkers played a football game against members of the Legion. Speakers at an evening rally made the usual charges that the relief camps were slave camps, and uneconomic at that. Their manual labour cost the government $5 for every yard of highway built, it was alleged, whereas full wages and adequate machinery would cost only 60 cents a yard.

The trek's appeal to the public was clearly a continuing success. Future plans included one-day stops at Moose Jaw, Regina and Brandon, followed by four days each at Winnipeg and Toronto for

---

It seemed that Ottawa, having ignored the trek as it rolled through British Columbia and Alberta, had suddenly discovered that hitching a ride on a freight train was trespassing.

---

more of the same: garnering favourable publicity, raising money, and adding recruits. Then it would be time to confront the Bennett government in Ottawa itself. But in Medicine Hat came the news that would stop the trekkers cold. They would not be allowed to proceed beyond Regina, Ottawa informed the leaders, and the government was prepared to use whatever force was deemed necessary.

This was a shock — a complete turnaround from the previously reiterated dominion government policy of no interference in a provincial problem unless specifically asked to do so by the provincial government involved. It seemed that Ottawa, having ignored the trek as it rolled through British Columbia and Alberta, had suddenly discovered that hitching a ride on a freight train was trespassing. James G. Gardiner, the Liberal premier of Saskatchewan, had not asked for help. On the contrary, he was furious at this Ottawa move — both because he was naturally reluctant to have a potentially lethal confrontation set up in his capital city, and because the "necessary force" would be supplied by the RCMP, who in Saskatchewan were under contract to his government as provincial police.

The federal order to hold the marchers in Regina, Gardiner fumed, was "the most diabolical conspiracy ever perpetrated upon the people of any province or any city." R.B. Bennett should "keep his hands off the policing of this province." Having taken no steps to prevent the March from leaving Vancouver, the dominion government had no business stopping it in Regina. His own government had not even been consulted, and he vehemently objected "to the police force, which acts in matters of law enforcement under the instructions of this government, being used for any such purpose and will so instruct them. The Canadian Pacific Railway delivered these men in Saskatchewan en route to Ottawa and we expect them to carry them through."

Ottawa, ignoring the question of authority to direct the RCMP, blandly replied that the trek must be stopped in Regina because the RCMP training depot was there, and sufficient men were therefore available. Although this was true so far as it went, there was much speculation both then and later about Bennett's possible further motives.[7] A *Lethbridge Herald* editorial, for instance,

observed that the Tory prime minister appeared ready enough to extend his authority into many other provincial fields as well, such as unemployment insurance, hours of work and the regulation of industry — although he preferred to dodge the vital matter of unemployment by hiding behind the constitution.

Another indignant *Herald* editorial questioned the position of any province that depended on the RCMP for its police services, if Ottawa could still retain authority to order the force to do something the province did not want done. When the attorney-general of Saskatchewan directed the RCMP to keep its hands off transients in Regina, the newspaper declared, then surely the RCMP must do just that, particularly since the British North America Act assigned to the provinces responsibility for the administration of justice.

The trekkers themselves surmised — no doubt correctly — that federal authorities were greatly relieved to have them out of British Columbia, where the labour element was regarded as entirely too powerful. This same reasoning, however, would argue against letting them reach Winnipeg, where additional recruits, especially from the immigrant population there, could double their strength.[8] And who would expect Bennett to halt the march of the unemployed in or near his own constituency of Calgary? As for Ottawa, it was hardly likely he ever intended to let it get that far.[9] So that left Regina.

The Saskatchewan government issued countermanding orders forbidding the RCMP to participate in any move to stop the marchers, but the RCMP had no apparent difficulty in deciding whose orders to obey. The first consequence was that at Chappell Junction, just west of Saskatoon, they arrested 22 recruits trying to board a train to join the trekkers in Regina. Meanwhile Regina businessmen prepared for the worst. When they tried to get riot insurance, they found that rates for one day had jumped to the price normally charged for a year's coverage.

The arrival of the On-to-Ottawa trek at 6 a.m. on June 14, however, provided yet another example of order and discipline. When a dozen men jumped off the train early, probably to get out of the driving rain, they were sternly rebuked by their division commanders. Once off the trains, the trekkers as usual "formed fours," giving the appearance, one newspaper account observed, of "wartime troops moving into the front lines." But there was only a single police officer on duty at the Regina Exhibition Grounds, where the trekkers found hot coffee being served by a Citizens' Emergency Committee, and the floor inside the stadium bedded with straw. Wet and

The introduction of relief camps aroused immediate opposition that grew increasingly strident until it burst forth full blown as the On-to-Ottawa Trek. This 1935 Mothers' Day picnic at Stanley Park in Vancouver was part of a campaign to abolish the camps.

[9]An exchange of telegrams between the two mayors, reported by the *Vancouver Sun* June 6, 1935, nicely represents prevalent municipal attitudes. "You ought to be fair-minded enough to see that your troubles should not be forced on other communities," wired Mayor P.J. Nolan of Ottawa to Mayor Gerald McGeer of Vancouver. "...and as far as I am concerned I shall refuse to deal with such a question." Replied Mayor McGeer: "Vancouver has suffered enough and you ought to be willing to bear your share of the national grief... Most of these men came from eastern Canada and ought to return there."

On June 7 the trekkers reached Calgary, where Mayor Andrew Davison was close to panic, having failed to convince the RCMP to stop the marchers at the Alberta border.

cold, they cheered in appreciation of the coffee, while some began a good-natured mooing in reference to the straw.

In the stadium they got their orders. No cigarettes or pipes in the building, soap and water would be found in the corridors, breakfast would be served at 9 a.m. Slim Evans, who had not ridden with them from the coast but had now rejoined them, set up a committee to deal with their new problem: what to do if and when the police tried to stop them leaving Regina.

With scarcely a by-your-leave to Premier Gardiner, two Bennett cabinet ministers shortly arrived, armed with authority to negotiate with the strikers. Railways Minister R.J. Manion and Agriculture Minister Robert Weir, who represented the Saskatchewan constituency of Melfort, set up in the Hotel Saskatchewan, where they conferred briefly with Gardiner and his attorney-general, T.C. Davis. Manion later reported to Bennett that Gardiner increasingly became "very resentful;" his attitude and that of his government was in general "very ugly and anything but helpful." Since Manion was undoubtedly convinced that the On-to-Ottawa Trek was a subversive tactic which might well end in bloody revolution, he thought Gardiner was behaving irresponsibly.

At this point public sympathy unquestionably remained with the marchers; a public subscription list was opened in Saskatoon to raise money to pay the fines of the 22 men arrested at Chappell. For various somewhat contradictory reasons, however, Regina citizens were eager to see the trekkers on their way east. Efforts were being made to have a large body of citizens gather at the railway station when the departure took place. Alternatively, officers of four service clubs (Rotary, Kiwanis, Gyro and Lions) were making plans to move the strikers by car and truck should they be prevented from boarding trains.

The two federal ministers next proposed to talk with the trek leaders themselves. "We are willing to negotiate," Evans had declared. He and his Strike Committee — Jack Cosgrove, Tony Martin, Peter Neilson, Stewart "Paddy" O'Neil, Mike McCaulay, James "Red" Walsh and Robert "Doc" Savage — were easily persuaded to come to the hotel. Also present were several dozen other people, including Regina's Mayor, Cornelius Rink, delegates from Premier Gardiner and a whole range of functionaries from railway officials to school trustees.

After the obligatory opening speeches, Manion made his offer. The strike committee, he proposed, should proceed to Ottawa as a delegation, all expenses paid by the railways, to confer with Prime Minister Bennett himself. The rest of the marchers would await the outcome in Regina, receiving twenty cents a meal to eat at restaurants. The government agreed not to intimidate or disrupt the trekkers during negotiations. The trekkers agreed not to encourage others to join them (except for some 300 already on their way from the relief camp at Dundurn) or to attempt to board trains. Since Manion's proposal was essentially what they had been asking for all along Evans accepted, and that evening the trekkers ratified his decision by vote.

The eight delegates went to Ottawa by train, of course — only this time they were travelling first class. Evans would later describe how the waiters set the dining car tables with three knives, four forks and as many spoons, and how at his Ottawa hotel he had a bath in a real bathtub for the first time in five years. As promised, they met with the prime minister and cabinet, but all they got out of the meeting was a lecture from Bennett and considerable abuse. He rejected all their demands, telling them that they and their supporters should return to the relief camps and await, as others were doing, "the opportunity of securing employment."

Mayor Davison's fears were ill-founded. March organizers were anxious to avoid anything that might alienate the public. Disembarking at the railway yards, the soot-grimed men marched in parade formation, escorted by a police motorcycle officer, to the exhibition grounds, Calgarians cheering them on from their windows.

The relief camps provided shelter as good as that enjoyed by the average employed Canadian, Bennett insisted. His government had taken care of its unemployed as well as any country in the world had done, and "in most of these camps contentment prevails, if not real happiness." He dismissed their demand for a five-day, six-hour-a-day work week at fifty cents an hour. In some instances, he observed, the men had shown no great desire to get work. In any case, the relief camps were not meant as a work-and-wages program, which was something the country simply could not afford, he said. The twenty cents a day they gave the men was a humanitarian gratuity; there could be no question of wages.

As recollected by the trek delegates, exchanges between Bennett and Evans became both heated and personal. The prime minister set the tone with a remark to the effect that "except for one with a record we will not discuss [meaning Evans], you were all born outside Canada, most of you in a country where a million men have had no work for years and may never have work again." It was true that only Evans was Canadian-born. The origins of most of the rest, however, were hardly what the future Viscount Bennett of Mickleham and of Calgary and Hopewell might be expected to classify as "foreign." Five were British immigrants — Cosgrove from Scotland, Walsh from Ireland; Martin, Savage and McCaulay from England — while O'Neil hailed from the British colony of Newfoundland. Neilson was from Denmark, a nation not noted for revolutions. And as Evans observed, among them they counted 112 years as Canadians.

[10]Trek organizer Arthur "Slim" Evans was convicted of fraudulent conversion of union funds at Drumheller, and in January 1924 was sentenced to three years in penitentiary. Secretary of the United Mine Workers of America local, he had distributed about $2,500 in union funds to the striking miners as relief, instead of sending it on to international headquarters in Indianapolis. His release in March 1925 may have been hastened by a petition to the Minister of Justice, signed by about 8,700 people and presented by E.J. Garland, UFA MP for Bow River.

Trek organizers declined Medicine Hat mayor Isaac Bullivant's offer of $200 if they passed through without stopping, and the marchers arrived on June 10th. But the Medicine Hat News described them as a youthful, carefree group, for whom the revolution was an adventure. They made time for a football game, Trekkers vs. the local Legion, then continued eastward.

Provincial Archives of Alberta, A 5146

Provincial Archives of Alberta, A 5148

When Evans called for work and wages, Bennett jibed, "I come from Alberta where you were arrested for stealing the funds from your union."

"You're a liar," Evans replied. "It was for fraudulent conversion."[10]

"Well, call it what you like," retorted the prime minister.

"It was for fraudulently converting money to feed starving miners — instead of sending it down to the pot-bellied international officers in Indianapolis. I am going to go out and tell the people of Canada that I had to call the prime minister a liar."

"That is your privilege," Bennett responded. "So long as you keep within the law. When you go beyond the law you will find yourself back where you were."[11]

Arthur Evans did carry out his threat to call the prime minister a liar, and in doing so he seemingly overstepped the line defining what Canadians would then tolerate from a group that had embarked on what they saw as a noble cause, but which was now showing signs of becoming a disturbing mob. Evans himself apparently was unaware of this, and in statements to the press he dug himself deeper into the hole of public disapproval. When his train stopped in Sudbury he predicted that the streets of Regina would run red with blood if police clashed with marchers. Back in Regina he promised that the march would continue, likely by freight cars, "but if they are denied us we will walk to the capital if necessary." If Premier Gardiner wanted them out of the province,

[11] By no means illegal, but also not likely to appease an already indignant prime minister, was the ditty the trekkers were singing in Regina — to the tune of Home on the Range — while their leaders faced R.B. Bennett in Ottawa. One verse went:

"And we're on the tramp
From Bennett's slave camp,
Our demands before him we will place.
We will soon be there
And we want no hot air
And he won't get no thirty days' grace."

he added, "perhaps he will hire a freight train to take us."

Such cockiness rapidly eroded sympathy for the cause. The *Calgary Herald*, in a June 25th editorial, said the march had been exposed as a dangerous challenge to law and order. "What originally purported to be an effort to draw public attention to conditions in relief camps by spectacular means has become, under Communist leadership, a definite hostile movement against peace, order and good government in this country." It praised the tolerance shown by the prime minister "in view of the epithet applied to him by the leader of the delegation."

That same day the strike leaders announced that the march would resume, and the *Medicine Hat News* quoted an unnamed trekker as saying, "The only way the police can get us off that train will be to shoot us off. Clubs won't do it." For its part, the federal government opened registration for a proposed new relief camp at Lumsden, thirty miles north of Regina. Premier Gardiner again objected, strongly urging that out-of-province marchers be moved out of Saskatchewan and back to their homes. The Lumsden camp never was set up; the strikers boycotted the registration.

Instead, in the belief that the police were now determined to prevent them from boarding trains, they began lining up trucks and cars. The RCMP, searching for some law that would make this move illegal, seized on a provincial traffic regulation that required trucks carrying passengers to obtain permits. The Public Utilities Board of Saskatchewan pointed out that permits were required only if passengers were charged a fee. The RCMP decided to use reliable old Section 98, and set up roadblocks. On June 27 five men were arrested when the first truckload of trekkers tried to break through a blockade.

Then the RCMP raised the stakes by announcing that anyone holding a membership in any strike organization would be considered to be Communist, and that anyone trying to trek from one province to another would also be classified as such and liable to arrest. "Furthermore," RCMP headquarters in Ottawa announced, "any person giving aid or comfort" to any striker or trekker would also be liable to prosecution. They remained silent about reports that a new, secret, federal order-in-council had been passed to give the force additional powers. Much later Ottawa

By June 1 the decision to take the camp strikers' grievances straight to Ottawa had been made. It was a decision that made everybody in Vancouver — well-wishers, long-suffering municipal and provincial officials, and bitter opponents too — very happy.

denied that such an order ever existed.

For the men still bivouacked at the Regina Exhibition Grounds the situation was becoming acute and the fuse growing short. They were out of money, almost out of food and stymied in every direction. The leaders called a public meeting in Market Square on the evening of July 1, Dominion Day, where they could tell local residents the results of their trip to Ottawa. Some thousand townspeople initially appeared; there is disagreement about how many trekkers were there, and how many were back at the Exhibition grounds watching a ball game. Nor is it entirely clear — despite the scores of accounts that have been written about it — precisely what happened on Market Square that fine summer evening after a platoon of city police and three RCMP troops burst upon the scene.

Some of the results, of course, were plain enough next day: one Regina police officer killed; twoscore policemen (city and RCMP) injured, mostly by rocks and makeshift clubs; threescore civilians (trekkers and residents both) similarly injured; Regina's city centre a litter of abandoned cars, damaged shop-fronts, pieces of two-by-four, stones, bricks and broken glass.

But just who did what, and who was to blame for it all, was another matter entirely. Not unnaturally, many trekker recollections differ sharply from the conclusions reached by the Regina Riot Inquiry Commission later established by the Gardiner government to look into it. Leftist lore generally blames the RCMP for firing on the crowd. The officials who testified at the inquiry, on the other hand, claimed the federal officers were carrying their revolvers but had no bullets. This left them only their batons, which, for men on foot, were of little use when the trekkers began hurling stones. What many accounts appear to agree upon, however, is that the riot need not have happened — that by this time the marchers had made up their minds to admit defeat and to disperse, but that the federal government was determined not to let them go without getting the leaders into jail.

A graphic account from the trekkers' viewpoint was preserved by Ronald Liversedge, who had joined the British army at 16, served in the Great War and become a Communist soon afterward. A founding member of the RCWU, he kept a diary on the march, which was edited by Victor Hoar and published in 1973 by McClelland and Stewart as *Recollections of the On-to-Ottawa Trek*. For its coherence and detail it becomes a central source document on the incident, though most of its facts were challenged by other evidence given at the subsequent commission of inquiry.

"By the first of July, 1935, our plans were made to call off the trek," Liversedge wrote. "Most of that day our committee had been in the Parliament Building conferring with the premier and cabinet, and a public meeting was scheduled for that evening... to acquaint the public of our decision. All that was left to do was working out the details of our retirement. The Saskatchewan government had promised to help, but the federal government had other plans."

Liversedge is confirmed in this by documents attached to the inquiry commission report. A telegram sent by Premier Gardiner to Prime Minister Bennett on July 1 reads in part: "We wish to state that the men had interviewed us at 5 p.m. They stated that they had advised your government through your representatives they were prepared to disband and go back to their camps or homes provided they were allowed to go under their own organization. They state this was denied them. They asked our government to take responsibility for disbanding them to their own camps and homes. While we were meeting to consider their proposals and any suggestions we might make to you, trouble started down town between the police and strikers without notification to us of police intervention which has resulted in at least one death in the police force and scores of citizens, strikers and police wounded. We are nevertheless prepared to undertake this work of disbanding the men, without sending them to Lumsden. Will you consider negotiations on basis of this proposal?"

The inquiry commission also noted that Assistant Commissioner S.T. Wood, commander of the RCMP's Regina-based F Division, was seriously concerned about the legality of arresting the leaders. It reported:

On the morning of the 28th Colonel Wood was advised by the [RCMP] Commissioner by telephone that the government desired the arrest of the leaders as soon as possible. During the conversation Colonel Wood stated that so far as he knew the leaders had done nothing in Saskatchewan to warrant their arrest. On the same day, however, his superior in Ottawa instructed him by telegram that the Government desired proceedings taken under Section 98 of the Criminal Code against those arrested on the evening of the 27th and also against the known leaders, Evans, Black, O'Neil, Shaw and "others you think necessary."[12] He was also advised that a special agent named Leopold, who had experience in

After a harrowing trip through the Spiral Tunnels in B.C., the Trekkers must have found the Prairies in June a welcome sight.

[12]Among the men targeted by Ottawa, George Black was a Glasgow-born veteran of the Scots Guards, a member of the Workers' Ex-Servicemen's League, and Arthur Evans' principal lieutenant during the trek. Matt Shaw, a young man from Saskatchewan, was a founding member of the RCWU and was spokesman for the deputation that approached Premier Duff Pattullo during the December 1934 relief camp strike. Newfoundlander Stewart O'Neil, also active with the WESL, was a member of the trekkers' Strike Committee.

[13]Under the identity Jack Esselwein, Sergeant John Leopold had been sent to spy on radical political groups, as well as trade unions, as far back as 1921. Oscar Ryan in his biography of Tim Buck describes Leopold's appearance at Buck's trial in Toronto in November 1931: "The man who had been exposed in 1928 as a stool-pigeon strutted smartly to the witness stand and snapped to attention." Buck himself wrote that "many were sickened" at the sight of this "police agent bearing false witness against men who had given him food and shelter and friendship in their homes." Leopold's background data was to prove crucial to the RCMP in breaking up a Soviet spy ring disclosed in Ottawa immediately after the Second World War by a cipher clerk in the Soviet embassy.

Communist activities, would arrive in Regina on Monday morning, July 1st, with documents for perusal by counsel.[13] At his request information in the possession of the officers commanding at Vancouver and Edmonton was forwarded to Colonel Wood and on the morning of July the 1st was placed before counsel for consideration.

Had Colonel Wood been allowed some latitude, the Royal Commissioners suggested, an agreement on disbanding the trek might have been reached. However, the colonel could only offer the men a billet at Lumsden, and this they refused. At 5 p.m. that day he was surprised to find that the lawyers had already decided to issue warrants for the men Ottawa wanted. Having been instructed to act on their advice, he decided he should do so as quickly as possible; the trekkers were reported to be making clubs and preparing for a battle with police. He would try to arrest them at their headquarters or, if that failed, in Market Square soon after their meeting began.

This decision lit the fuse on the dynamite that would explode a few hours later. The Liversedge diary takes up the account:

> There were probably fifteen hundred men and women, townspeople, some with their children, on that nice summer evening. It hadn't been thought necessary for a full turnout of the trekkers, as the meeting was to inform the people of Regina what we, the trekkers, already knew [that Ottawa had ordered that the march be disbanded].
>
> There were probably four or five hundred of us on the Market Square, and there would be two or three hundred still having supper, or walking around town. The vast bulk of our men were watching two ball games out at the Exhibition grounds. The meeting wasn't long under way. Evans was speaking when four large furniture vans backed up, one to each corner of the Market Square. A shrill whistle blasted out a signal, the backs of the vans were opened and out poured the Mounties, each armed with a baseball bat.
>
> In their mad, shouting, club swinging charge they killed Regina City Detective Millar, who had evidently come onto the Square to help them. In less than minutes Market Square was a mass of writhing, groaning forms, like a battlefield.
>
> As we retreated I saw one woman standing over an upturned baby carriage, which had been trampled by these young Mounties. I saw four Mounties pulling at the arms and legs of one of our men, whom they had on the ground, while a fifth Mountie continued to beat viciously at the man's head.

Some eighty trekkers invaded the offices of relief commission chairman A.A. MacKenzie and held that terrified official prisoner for two hours, until he agreed to send to Edmonton the telegram they dictated urging relief to the strikers.

Pierre Berton in his book *The Great Depression* (McClelland & Stewart, Toronto, 1993) adds more details of the police charge, all from the striker viewpoint, or that of sympathetic Regina residents. "The moment the whistle blew, the steel-helmeted Mounted Police... poured from the big vans and waded into the crowd. In less than a minute the scene in Market Square was transformed into a confused melée, marked by scenes of unmitigated savagery. The people in the square who had no idea of what was happening and saw the police coming towards them began to flee in panic."

Berton describes the stampeding crowd, the police behaving as though they were fighting a raging mob, women stumbling and being trampled down, baby carriages being knocked over, the fear-crazed crowd caught between the city police and the Mounties, somehow finding stones and other missiles to throw back (none having been forearmed), mere spectators being knocked down and beaten up by the ruthless police, beaten men being dragged off the field by the police, another innocent bystander being clubbed down by two policemen, the frantic effort of a Regina barber to find his child lost in the midst of all this (the child turned up unhurt), and finally the police using tear gas to clear the square.

Even Berton, however, concedes that it was not entirely one-sided. He describes one group of strikers forcing two Mounties against a wall and battering them with fists and sticks. When a bystander intervened he was struck by an angry citizen wielding an automobile spring, but the Mounties were then left alone.

After the police cleared Market Square, says Berton, the riot spread six blocks westward down Regina's 11th and 12th avenues and a series of further altercations broke out where the two avenues meet Scarth and Cornwall streets. Police harassed the strikers as they moved along the streets, hurling stones back at the mounted officers.

The Market Square fray, continues the Liversedge account, "was a victory for the Mounties, the only one they had that night. Even at that, they were unable to follow up, as there were also not a few Mounties writhing on the ground, and it took about half of their number to arrest Evans and the few boys on the platform.

"The word went out quickly for the trekkers to assemble on one of the main streets to march back to the stadium... I think it was either Eleventh or Sixth Avenue... On that street we assembled under group leaders. Hilton and Paddy O'Neil took the head of the column and we had just started our march when somebody told us there were two hundred horsemen lined across the street ahead of us... We were not going to be allowed to get out of town. We were to be smashed up. How incredibly stupid.

"Immediately orders were given to us to build barricades. The streets were lined with parked cars and we simply pushed them into the streets, turned them on their sides and piled them two high. It was then, before the first futile charge was made by the Mounties, that the miracle happened. The young boys, and even some girls, of Regina organized our ammunition column. Without being asked, they came riding bicycles in from the side streets, their carrier baskets loaded with rocks, which they dumped behind the barricades, and then rode off for another load."

This altercation occurred on Eleventh Avenue between Scarth and Cornwall as the crowd moved west from Market Square. Berton tells how Wilfred Woodhill, a radio reporter for station CJRM, had shinned up a pole to the roof of a building at Eleventh and Cornwall and provided his listeners with a play-by-play account of the fracas in the street below. The mob by then was smashing store windows along the street and the sound of the shouts and shattering glass went out of the air. "Here's a good one!" someone shouted, pointing to the Willson Stationers store. Every window in it was thereupon smashed. Woodhill was particularly impressed by what he called the "restraint" of the police who, though being pelted with stones, did not counter-attack. He was finally ordered off the air by his station manager, who apparently feared an adverse public reaction to his broadcast. Berton describes a single streetcar on Eleventh Avenue running a gauntlet of flying stones and debris.

Shortly after Woodhill quit broadcasting, a squad of city police moving north on Scarth Street nearby was caught between one mob in front of them and one behind, all hurling stones and other debris. Drawing their .38 revolvers they fired at the crowd. One man fell and was taken to hospital by ambulance. Another man, trying to make his way home from a friend's house, was hit by a ricocheting bullet, which went through his abdomen and emerged near his spine without hitting any vital organs. Doctors called his escape miraculous.

In that encounter, forty strikers and five Regina citizens were wounded, eleven seriously. The effect of the gunfire was to bring the riot to an end. The strikers fled in terror and by midnight were back at their camp on the Exhibition grounds, which was encircled by police until the following afternoon.

What disaccords with the striker version of the affair and casts doubt on Berton's account of uncontrolled police brutality was the final toll, which was suffered chiefly by the police. One Regina policeman was dead and sixteen were wounded. Twenty-nine members of the RCMP went to hospital with injuries inflicted by stones, clubs and other weapons. Apart from those wounded in the gunfire on Scarth Street, striker injuries were minimal. More than 100 strikers were

Hear the Reply of the authorities to Strikers' Delegation requesting immediate Relief and opening of negotiations on counter-proposals to Bennett Government's offer of Concentration Camps

MASS MEETING TONIGHT

Market Square 8 p.m.

(If wet will be held in Stadium)

Several Speakers representing local organizations will address the crowd

Winnipeg Strike Camp situation will be outlined. Latest developments will be given

Strikers' Funds are Completely Depleted

Support the Strikers and Force the authorities to grant immediate Relief

A scheduled one-day stop at Regina grew into two weeks, and Trek leaders scrambled to respond to R.B. Bennett's warning that his government would use any force necessary to prevent them from continuing to the capital. This poster advertised the meeting that set off the Regina Riot.

Two weeks of smouldering tensions, fanned by increasingly rancorous negotiations between R.B. Bennett and Arthur Evans, erupted in Market Square as the Regina Riot on July 1, 1935.

Regina detective Charles Millar lay dead or dying, felled by a blow to the head from an assailant whose identity was still unknown at the end of the 20th century.

arrested, but most were released without charge. Twenty-two came to trial, and eight received jail terms. All charges laid under Section 98 were dismissed for lack of evidence.

The commission of inquiry into the riot, appointed by the Gardiner government, disputed the striker version at virtually every point. Claims made by ten witnesses that "police were swinging their batons and knocking down any persons they could get hold of" were considerably shaken by cross-examination and many admitted, reluctantly, that they did not actually see anybody struck in the first police advance. They were talking about subsequent events, they said.

The commission accepted the version of the RCMP inspector who testified that the first police advance was orderly, that the crowd parted before the squad of uniformed men, and that by the time they reached the speakers' platform there was nobody within fifty feet of them. In fact, according to the commission report, in five minutes Market Square was clear of people.

The claim recorded in the Liversedge diary that the RCMP killed Regina detective Charles Millar was repeated many times by Arthur Evans, who stated that he personally saw the Mounties beat Millar to death. It fell apart upon examination, however. Evans had been taken to the police station long before Detective Millar appeared. Millar died, the commission found, from a blow on the head during the riot. It did not pretend to know who delivered it.

Of another man, allegedly beaten by five Mounties, police testified that he had actually thrown a piece of iron pipe with a jagged end which struck the arm of a Constable Gibbons. "This was thrown... from a distance of about 12 feet [at the constable's head, who put up his arm to deflect it]. The edge of the iron struck his elbow, cutting it to the bone and inflicting a wound from which [when the commission sat] he had not fully recovered." Two policemen, not five, followed the assailant and knocked him down; then one guarded him while the other went to disperse a group who were still throwing stones at them.

"One of the fundamental principles in connection with the reliability of evidence, as applied to human actions," the commission declared, "is the reasonableness of the act described. True it is that in moments of excitement or stress human beings will often act unreasonably... but there must always be an underlying motive for the action. What object, for instance, would a policeman have in chasing and beating a woman with a baby in her arms, whose only apparent object was to escape? Why should three or four policemen continue to club a man when he was lying on the ground begging for mercy?"

The commission dismissed the charges of police brutality and decided the federal government was justified in halting the march, which it described as a menace to peace, order and good government. Berton calls the inquiry a whitewash, without explaining why an inquiry called by arch-Liberal Jimmy Gardiner would want to whitewash a police action directed by arch-Tory R.B. Bennett.

Premier Gardiner and Attorney-General Davis took charge, and within three days as many as 1,500 trekkers were dispersed. Some seem already to have moved out on their own. Gardiner

---

But in Medicine Hat came the news that would stop the trekkers cold. They would not be allowed to proceed beyond Regina, Ottawa informed the leaders, and the government was prepared to use whatever force was necessary.

---

arranged for a CPR passenger train to take men to Moose Jaw, Medicine Hat, Calgary and Vancouver by the southern route, and a CNR train to cover Saskatoon, Edmonton, Vancouver and points between. The strikers made good use of the trip for more publicity. An Edmonton newspaper photographer who wanted to know if any of them had been wounded in the riot, for instance, found them most co-operative. Unfortunately they had not, they replied, but this could easily be fixed. First aid workers were called and soon had men swathed in bandages and ready to pose.

Their provincial compatriots remained largely sympathetic. Twenty cents a day plus board was still no solution to unemployment, the *Edmonton Bulletin* reminded its readers. The majority of the marchers were not to blame, said Col. Gilbert Sanders, a member of the Alberta Relief Commission, when he testified at the Regina trial of the strike leaders. Most of the men, he said, were "dupes in the hands of revolutionaries."

The Big March, as it would later be known, slowly receded in memory to become part of socialist mythology in Canada. Most historians do not regard it as a Communist revolution designed to take over the country, but as a rehearsal for such a takeover. It provided a chance to perfect techniques of gaining public support for just grievances, to sort out the logistics of moving a thousand or more men across Canada, to practise maintaining order and discipline under trying circumstances. The Communists well knew that most of these young Canadians had no idea they were being converted to Communism. Most thought what they were asking for was simply reasonable. They believed they could get decent work, decent wages and acceptable living conditions without a violent insurrection.

But that the men who planned and led the Big March were dedicated Communists has never been in doubt. Nor is there any question that their message was spreading. It is noteworthy, for instance, that when the Spanish Civil War broke out the following summer, Liversedge, Martin, Walsh and O'Neil quickly joined the Mackenzie-Papineau Battalion of the Fifteenth International Brigade to fight for the Republican cause against the fascist insurgents. Victor Hoar quotes Mac-Pap survivors as estimating that a probable 400 trekkers did the same. Many, including Paddy O'Neil, did not survive.

Medicine Hat is back to normal after... about 1,200 On-to-Ottawa marchers camped here during a 24-hour stopover.

The trekkers slept at the arena last night and early this morning they marched over to the athletic park, where breakfast was served... After breakfast the entire body lined up and marched to the railway yards, where they swarmed on to the fast freight train of 52 cars due to depart shortly for the east.

About 6:30 a.m. the train pulled out for Swift Current. The marchers gave three lusty cheers as they got under way, jubilant shouts that were heard in distant points of the city. All the movements were orderly, there being no disorder at any time. A group left behind to clean up the athletic park and arena made a good job of the task and left these points as clean as they found them. This group will leave during the day to join their comrades on their eastward trek.

No complaints of the marchers during their stay in the city have been received by the police, which bears out the statements made by the advance agents that the men were under control at all times. There was a possiblilty that some of the recruits who joined the marchers in Calgary might be the cause of trouble before they were imbued with the spirit of discipline and order that animates the majority of the On-to-Ottawa army, but nothing of this sort developed.
–*Medicine Hat News*, June 12, 1935

As the Thirties wear on, Communism wears down

The March on Ottawa proved the high water mark of Communist activity in Canada, and from then on the party slipped steadily in public support. May Day was still celebrated as this parade (upper left) at Edmonton's Jasper Avenue and 101st Street in 1937 evidences, and the children of Communist parents lined up (below) to demand "free text books." There were occasional "sit-down strikes" like the one at Swift's in April of that year, where a committee (centre left) prepares food for the strikers. But labour papers like the Daily Clarion, promoted by a May Day billboard, did not long survive, and the gradual recovery of the economy eroded Communist support.

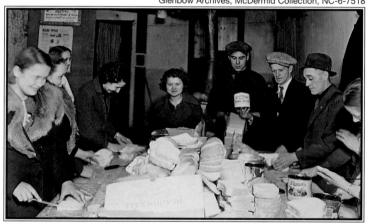

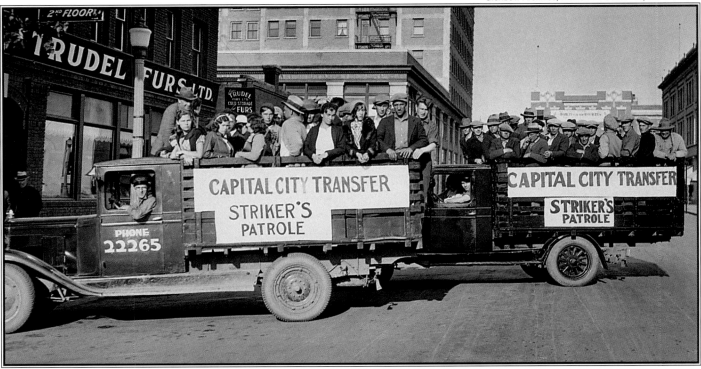

As relief became more commonplace, people resented working for it

At first cities provided mere make-work projects on which relief recipients were required to work, but gradually relief workers began replacing regular city employees. This brought on relief strikes, such as this one in Edmonton in 1934, wherein relief recipients refused to do the required labour. Above, truck-borne "relief patrols" set out to make sure that relief recipients are respecting the strike. When they encountered people picking potatoes on the city patch in Forest Heights, atop the riverbank southeast of the Dawson Bridge (below right), they marched over the field and assaulted the pickers. The city responded by calling out a patrol of Mounties to trot around the field and protect the strike breakers. (Above left) A strike patroller is loaded with his bike into a paddy wagon.

The CCF, ancestor of the New Democratic Party, was born in Calgary, vowing not to become political

Under the saintly James Shaver Woodsworth it envisioned a paradise of socialism, but its link with the UFA crippled it in Alberta

Like the farmers' movement before it and the Social Credit movement that developed alongside it, Canada's democratic socialist political party, which would form governments in four provinces before the century's end, came into being with the determined avowal it would never become a political party.

Its birth occurred at Calgary on August 1, 1932, and its non-political intention was spelled out unequivocally by its founder, the saintly James Shaver Woodsworth, socialist ideologue, Labour member of Parliament and Methodist minister, whose eloquent exposition of the theories of democratic socialism inspired it into life.

The movement must not be political, he said. It must not be a party. It must be a "federation," and he carefully articulated the difference. His listeners, awed by the clarity and moral authority of his message, solemnly named themselves the "Co-operative Commonwealth Federation," the CCF. They then promptly went about making it a purely political organization that would later declare itself frankly to the nation as the NDP, the New Democratic Party.

What they wanted, however, had also been set forth by Woodsworth and was in no sense ambiguous. Before the cheering 1,300 assembled at Calgary's Labour Temple he portrayed a Canada with a planned economy that would dispense equal economic and social opportunities, free from discrimination based on sex, nationality (the 1930s word for race) or religion. He called for socialized health services available to all, for insurance against crop failure, illness, accident, old age or unemployment. He spoke of secure land tenure for farmers and a time when the federal government would be responsible for full employment.

He also called for the socialization of banking, credit and financial systems in Canada, and public ownership, development, operation and control of natural resources.

The speech carried everyone along with it and the following day, when representatives met to formally launch the new CCF, there was no doubt in anyone's mind that J.S. Woodsworth should be the first leader. He spent much of his first year vigorously denying that the CCF was a political party and for a highly political reason.

One of the largest groups represented at the founding meeting had been the United Farmers of Alberta. It had elected the government of Alberta in 1921 and it now was

keeping Premier John Brownlee in power. Robert Gardiner, who had chaired the nominating committee that recommended the executive council for the new federation, was also president of the UFA. UFA vice-president Norman F. Priestley was chosen as secretary. Agnes Macphail and two other MPs from the Progressive movement were involved, the Progressives being the federal arm of the farm movement.

So there could be no denying that the UFA had already immersed itself in the new group. And if the CCF was also a party, then implicitly it must be opposed to the UFA, which had been so instrumental in founding it. Understandably, therefore, the news media and the public tended to regard the CCF not as a new political movement but as a late manifestation of the old UFA. As sex scandals and the Depression assailed the UFA, this would prove fatal to it in Alberta.

Immediately after the founding meeting, a membership drive was begun aimed at organizing every federal constituency in the country. The membership committee included an Alberta Progressive member of Parliament, William Irvine of Wetaskiwin. He joined Woodsworth and Macphail to recruit anyone who agreed with the CCF's political policies. At the same time the CCF's first annual national convention was scheduled for Regina.

Within the UFA, however, there were problems. Many members were not socialistically inclined, including Brownlee himself and his cabinet. But the socialists controlled the UFA's monthly publication, which strove to explain and justify its affiliation with the CCF even though support for government-paid crop insurance was not UFA policy. Neither had the

The first CCF National Convention, which produced the famous Manifesto, was held at Regina on July 19-21, 1933. Appropriately, J.S. Woodsworth is front and centre.

UFA ever called for the socialization of the banks.

The Conservative *Calgary Herald* did not shrink from pointing out Brownlee's dilemma. How did he get along with his new socialistic colleagues, the paper wondered. "Should the UFA of Alberta become part and parcel politically of the new Western party, formed at Calgary this week — and it would appear that there is quite a possibility that that might happen — Mr. Brownlee must sooner or later divulge his attitude towards it."

The Conservative *Edmonton Journal* echoed these thoughts. Where exactly, it mischievously asked, did the UFA government stand, now that the UFA had affiliated with the CCF? Gardiner vehemently maintained that as long as he was president of the UFA it would not be submerged in or dictated to by any other organization. Like it or not, replied the *Journal*, in the public mind this affiliation had already taken place.

Other UFA members and the official publication didn't trouble to deny it. So what, asked their opponents, did this UFA-CCF stand for? Was it defending the status quo, like Brownlee, or calling for radical change, like Woodsworth? Communist publications meanwhile exacerbated the problem by referring to the Brownlee administration as "the CCF government of Alberta."

There were other confusions. Between the founding convention and the one in Regina, would-be supporters were presented with conflicting views not only of what the CCF would do if elected, but of how it would do it. Party leader Woodsworth was always the voice of reason. Not so William Irvine, the Wetaskiwin Progressive MP. In May 1933, just two months before the convention was scheduled to open, Irvine told a audience in the Majestic Theatre in Lethbridge that the CCF intended to transform, not reform, Canada's social system. The idea that change should be gradual must be abandoned. It was no use trying to reform capitalism. The system must be entirely changed. The reaction was swift. The *Lethbridge Herald* said Irvine had left no doubt that, under the CCF, the state would be an economic and social dictator.

On July 20, 1933, the first CCF convention opened in Regina with a 4,000-word policy declaration founded clearly on Woodsworth's ideology. It called for a planned, socialized economic order, the socialization of all banking, currency, credit and insurance, as well as all federal, provincial and municipal transportation, communications, electric power and all other industries and services essential to social planning. Farmers were to be given security of tenure. A national labour code was to be introduced ensuring maximum incomes for workers, insurance against illness, accidents, old age and unemployment, as well as freedom of

(Above) The federal CCF caucus confers with its secretary some time in the late 1930s. (L-R): T.C. Douglas, Angus MacInnis, A.A. Heaps, J.S. Woodsworth, M.J. Coldwell, Grace MacInnis, and Grant McNeil.

association. There would be state health, hospital and medical care services throughout the country. The declaration was approved with but one dissenting vote, that of delegate W.C. Good of Paris, Ontario, and would go down in the history of Canadian socialism as the Regina Manifesto.

Far less unanimity, however, attended the proposed methods of its implementation. A dispute over how its objectives were to be achieved surfaced almost immediately. A Toronto labour proposed an amendment which would remove from the manifesto the words "we do not believe in change through violence." He preferred, "If the ruling class opposes the will of the people, we must use a method suitable to the occasion."

His amendment did not succeed, and the non-violence clause remained, but only after Alfred Speakman, the Progressive member of Parliament for Red Deer, reminded the convention that it would be the job of the CCF to convince people they did not need force. "History shows no case where force did not delay progress," he said. Former judge Lewis St. George Stubbs of Winnipeg told delegates that violence would be fatal to the new movement. "Let us get no Russian bee in our bonnet," he said.

It was no surprise that newspapers picked up the split, and commented on it. The *Medicine Hat News* said that a "fog

of verbiage" had surrounded some clauses of the CCF program. While it may be argued by the CCF leaders that certain rights in individual property would remain, said the *News*, there was no guarantee of anything of the sort. The CCF was a socialist party, under which ownership and control of all property, industry and services would pass into the hands of the state.

The *Calgary Herald* said the convention showed that "Mr. Woodsworth was already feeling that conservatism that comes with responsibility," and that "he is not so violent in his language as he used to be. He is more placatory, as becomes a party leader seeking votes."

The eastern press was less generous. Harsh criticism of the CCF and its policies came from the *Montreal Star*: "The platform clearly envisages the ultimate socialization of all industry and it promises to get along ultimately without taxation, without paying interest on any public loans — and yet it outlines a most ambitious and costly programme of public expenditures. Only a totally socialized state could do these things... Until [Agnes] Macphail converts the whole world to her gospel there will, however, always be plenty of places where money can earn interest.

"The farmer will be sacred. His debts will be progressively removed. He will be insured against crop failures. The prices of his products will be raised... In a word, the farmer will be the bully boy with the glass eye. And he will need two glass eyes if he does not see through this buncombe... But if the CCF is to sweep the prairies and cut into rural Ontario, obviously the farmer must be promised an earthly paradise."

The *Star* also raised the spectre of communism. "Still the enlightened Canadian farmer may have noted that Mr. Woodsworth's friends in Russia do not think much of 'security of tenure for the farmer.' He is collectivised when he is not nationalized. If he dislikes the system, he is promoted to a new job — cutting lumber in Siberia. If he gets a little more comfort than he had, he is called a 'kulak' and treated as a public enemy — and they know how to treat enemies in Russia. In short, the home-owning farmer is a 'capitalist' and is 'eradicated.'"

The convention ended with an optimistic Woodsworth's predicting that the federation would hold the balance of power in Ottawa after the next election. Woodsworth was named chairman of the federation for the coming year. The Alberta representatives on the CCF's governing council were Irvine, Gardiner and Edmonton's Elmer Roper.

Soon after the CCF manifesto was presented by Woodsworth to the House of Commons, the federal Liberal leader, Mackenzie King, said that the party's aim was to crush all Canadians into the same mould. Liberal lawyer George Van Allen, addressing members of the Young Liberal Association in Edmonton, described the CCF as a "chocolate-coated variety" of Communism.

The convention established Saskatchewan, and not Alberta where the federation came into being, as the CCF's natural home. Twenty years later, only the dedicated historians in Canada's third party were aware of the fact that the Co-operative Commonwealth Federation began not in Regina, where its first annual convention was held, but in Calgary.

National Archives, Karsh Collection, C85705

James Shaver Woodsworth was captured in a reflective moment by Yusuf Karsh.

The suspicion that it was Communist would haunt the CCF for years, in spite of its denials and despite even more vehement denials from the Communists themselves. From the start Woodsworth strove to combat the Red tag. Declaring that CCF clubs had become "happy hunting grounds" for various cranks and Communists, he warned them in 1934 against the activities of leaders of the labour section of the CCF in Ontario. The Ontario executive responded with a resolution calling for the expulsion of the entire labour section, strongly backed by the United Farmers of Ontario.

When the labour leaders protested, the UFO withdrew from the association and Woodsworth announced the suspension of the Ontario provincial council, declaring it had proved incompetent to unify, control and direct the activities of the three affiliated bodies: Labour, UFO and the CCF clubs.

Another touchy point, one that guaranteed future trouble was the inclusion, in July of 1934, of a neutrality clause in the federation's principles. "The CCF is unalterably opposed to war," the statement read. "If the great capitalist powers drift into another world war Canadian neutrality must be rigorously maintained whoever the belligerents may be." The federation also decided not to provide any military assistance to the League of Nations, as it was then constituted. In the war against Nazi totalitarianism that lay a mere five years ahead this would divide Woodsworth from his own party.

Another early adversary was the Catholic church, in the person of Father Athol Murray, principal of Notre Dame College at Wilcox, Saskatchewan, whose makeshift school was providing an almost free education for hundreds of Saskatchewan youngsters after the Depression had closed the public school system over much of the drought-afflicted South. In March 1934 Father Murray ousted two students for their CCF membership. When the left protested, the priest replied: "The socialist system of thought is utterly alien to Catholic thought." M.J. Coldwell, the provincial CCF leader, said he considered Father Murray's action as a "distinct threat to the CCF and if the gauntlet is thrown down, we shall assuredly pick it up."

The CCF confidently expected to become the official opposition in Ottawa in the election which followed its formation, and to form the government of Canada four years after that. This was not to occur in the 20th century. It would form provincial governments in Saskatchewan, Manitoba, British Columbia and Ontario, and it would once almost become official opposition in the Commons. But in the Conservative national sweeps in 1958 and 1984 it almost disappeared, and its pragmatic venture late in the century into abortion advocacy and assorted sexual liberation movements would separate it from its religious roots, thereby fulfilling, as many would point out, Father Murray's contentions.

— *F.C.*

CHAPTER THREE

In one revolution that worked Deweyism captures the schools

WITHOUT MARCHES, RIOTS, PROTESTS OR STRIKES A QUIET CONVULSION
RADICALLY TAKES ALBERTA EDUCATION IN AN ENTIRELY NEW DIRECTION

by VIRGINIA BYFIELD

The unemployed marched, the Communists organized strikes, the world's radical leaders talked of revolution. Yet as the 20th century unfolded these convulsions would lead to little permanent change in the social and economic order. But meanwhile, with no furore and hardly any headlines, a very real revolution was quietly taking place that would have deep and lasting effects indeed. The locus of this revolution was the North American classroom and not least the Alberta classroom. Its seemingly unlikely leader was a slight, somewhat reclusive American philosopher named John Dewey, a man regarded by most in academe as a major seer and by some as a monster of perversity.

In 1930 this unspectacular revolutionary was 71 years old and still going strong; he would live to be 93. By then he would have been promulgating his theories for some 45 years in books, articles and lectures. Although never a teacher himself, he radically influenced several generations of teachers, and he thereby created legions of followers who were dedicated with evangelical fervour to promoting his ideas on "progressive education."[1]

In essence, Dewey's philosophy required a foundational change in the perceived purpose of education. What, he asked, were the schools there to do? Before the Deweyist revolution, any teacher knew the answer. The purpose of education was to pass on to the next generation the wisdom, knowledge and skills gradually amassed by their ancestors. Above all, it was to transmit to the young the value structure upon which western civilization had been built, with its perceptions of good and bad, true and false, beautiful and ugly. Therefore young people must become acquainted with its history, its classic literature and its religious faith (within the limits of their aptitude, of course). Thus would they become worthy members of their society, prepared to carry on its cultural traditions. In the pursuit of this goal the teacher stood, indisputably and unmistakably, as the authority.

After the Deweyist revolution, that goal would have radically changed. Henceforth the pre-eminent purpose of schooling would be to produce young people who were happy and fulfilled. This would be accomplished by enabling them to develop their individuality and to give free rein to their creative capabilities. Therefore they must be freed from what progressive educators liked to refer to as "the dead hand of the past." Liberated from the oppressive authority of religion, of textbooks and lectures that forced upon them masses of "mere information," young human beings would grow naturally into their true potential. Clear-eyed and unhampered by past misconceptions, they would be able to construct a new and better society. In this process the teacher became a mere guide or counsellor. The ultimate authority lay in the child himself.[2]

Obviously any school founded on this new premise would be radically at odds with one founded on the old. And so parents from the 1960s onward would find that their children's school vastly differed from the one they had attended. The values that their children espoused were often different as well, and the society that their children came to establish was in many respects very different indeed. Its assumptions were different; its expectations were different, and its ideas on manners and morals were the most different of all. All this was the achievement of the revolution. It did not take place at street barricades, however, but in the offices and corridors of bureaucracy,

[1] John Dewey's enormous influence in the United States cannot be over-stated, and the same is true of Canada. However England and other European countries were contemptuous of Dewey's ideas, according to his colleague and follower William H. Kilpatrick, head of the Foundations of Education Department at Teachers College, Columbia University, New York. They interpreted him "narrowly," said Kilpatrick. But his influence was strong in Soviet Russia from 1923 to 1933. It was also discernible in Turkey, Iraq, India, China and Mexico.

[2] "Indoctrination" appears to have been a progressivist preoccupation. When University of Ohio education professor Boyd H. Bode addressed the ATA's 1938 convention, his topic was "Who shall set the patterns in education?" Bode's answer, according to *The A.T.A. Magazine*, was that the pupil should set them, because "passing out patterns is just another name for indoctrination. Therefore, while I am very sensitive about the shortcomings of the progressive method... I think it keeps the door open for self-determination and the basic principle of democracy; it keeps the door open for a new social order."

in academic conferences, in education faculties all over North America and, most visibly, in teachers' conventions, educational publications and guest lectures by forward-thinking visiting academics.

Whether its strategists actually intended to overturn their society would remain unclear even half a century later. Probably not, in most cases. In some, definitely yes. Whatever the educator's final intention, however, his immediate goals and methods were altogether clear. "If I had my way I would do away with every grade in our schools today," was Henry D. Ainlay's ringing declaration to a January 1930 Gyro Club lunch meeting, the Edmonton Journal reported. Ainlay was an Edmonton high school teacher at the time. He would go on to become a leading educator, mayor of Edmonton, and a major city high school would commemorate his name.

That same month Elmer Luck of Edmonton's Victoria High School explained in a speech to another Edmonton service club, the Lions, that "the old idea of education was to know the book... to cram masses of facts and figures into the students' heads." He quoted Dr. R.C. Wallace of the University of Alberta on the merits of "the new system," according to which education must do four things: 1. Teach the laws of health; 2. Provide vocational training; 3. Train for

These lads were sent off to an Edmonton public school in 1933, where they were expected to obey rules similar to those listed at the left. If they didn't, there was always the strap.

"The old idea of education was to know the book... to cram masses of facts and figures into the students' heads," explained Elmer Luck of Victoria Composite High School in Edmonton an early proponent of "progressive" eduction.

citizenship and home life; 4. Teach how to make worthy use of leisure.

Similarly, in the February 1931 *A.T.A. Magazine*, Dr. C. Sansom undertook to explain the "New Education."[3] Essentially, he wrote, it is "the educational correlate of the entire social revolt against external authority which is characteristic of our time. Just in proportion as adult individuals assert the right to break away from the traditional social and religious sanctions are they insisting that their children also shall be set free from imposed tasks and limiting prescriptions."

The following April the *Camrose Canadian* reprinted an article by an Ontario teacher who castigated homework as the expression of "secret resentment on the part of grown-up people towards the happy and carefree state of childhood... a positive detriment to the child's physical and mental advancement, and the last word in pedagogic imbecility." A year later Dr. K.W. Coffin, principal of Calgary Normal School, declaimed in a speech to the Calgary Rotary Club, "How can intellectual freedom be obtained under a despotism?... Nothing short of an upheaval will shake this system." He was talking about the educational system, but his words carried distinct implications for larger systems, economic ones, for instance.[4]

If Albertans generally were discontented with the defined purpose of their schools as they were, they were not making their unhappiness at all obvious. The impetus for change was coming entirely from the province's educational leaders, who kept insisting that the existing school system was sadly deficient, and that they knew the cure. "Progressive educational leaders no longer believe that the educational process consists in conveying to the children their so-called 'racial inheritance' of skills and knowledges, of attitudes," wrote W. Wallace MA, FRSE, in the January 1930 *A.T.A. Magazine*, "... but rather in providing such conditions as each child, individually, requires in order to grow naturally into his part in the Play of Life..."

Many an outside expert was also invited to preach the progressivist doctrine. In January 1930, for example, Mrs. Beatrice Ensor, described by the *Calgary Albertan* as a "noted educationist" from London, England, told a meeting of teachers in Central United Church that standardized education, rigid curriculum and examinations were "at the root of the evil of the present system." Moreover, she added, how any child could develop his creative instinct in a classroom "presided over by a stern disciplinarian" was utterly beyond her comprehension.

All of these critics perceived the schools of the time — representing "traditional education" — as stultifyingly authoritarian. The tone was set immediately by the elementary school custom of

---

Parents from the 1960s onward would find that their children's school vastly differed from the one they had attended. The values that their children espoused were often different, and the society their children came to establish was very different indeed.

---

[3] The initials A.T.A. in 1931 stood for Alberta Teachers' Alliance, a voluntary organization founded in 1917. Among other purposes, it was to "unite members for their mutual improvement, protection and general welfare." Not until the late 1930s, however, would it make significant progress in achieving compulsory membership and other measures, at the same time changing its title to Alberta Teachers' Association. It would become one of the most powerful labour organizations in the province.

having children march to their classrooms to the strains of gramophone music; sometimes it was even martial music. In class, pupils must then stand quietly by their desks (which were arranged in rows and usually bolted down) until all were assembled. Before receiving permission to seat themselves, they had to formally greet their teacher by chorusing "Good morning, Miss Jones."

Curricula were ancient, immutable and largely irrelevant, progressivists complained. Text books were collections of facts meaningless to children, which they were forced to memorize. Teaching consisted of lectures which bored the pupils and, more deplorable yet, drills that forced "rote learning" of such things as multiplication tables, historical dates, provinces and their capitals.

And instead of being encouraged to work together, children were pitted against each other competitively. In a spelling "bee," for example, the class was divided into two teams; as soon as a youngster missed a word he must return ignominiously to his seat. The last speller standing was the winner.

Even more damaging to young psyches were the intimidating examinations in almost every grade, many of them set and marked by provincial authorities, and with individual results in the upper grades of high school actually published in the newspapers. Teachers talked and gave orders; pupils passively listened and obeyed. Failure or disobedience brought prompt punishment:

Even more damaging to young psyches were the intimidating examinations in almost every grade, many of them set and marked by provincial authorities, and with individual results in the upper grades actually published in the newspapers.

---

detention at recess or after school, and for more serious misdemeanours a strapping administered across the palm with a 14-inch piece of leather.

In startling contrast to this grim picture, the Deweyist-progressivist reformers envisioned a veritable children's paradise that could scarcely have differed more in method and appearance. The only effective teaching technique was to ensure that children "learn actively by doing." True education could only be acquired through personal experience, not from books, and it must start with what interested the child. "Coercion" was bad. Most effectively, the pupil should make his own decisions on what to learn, and when. Teachers might subtly influence the process, perhaps, but must take great care not to "impose" ideas and values. Only if pupils were left free could every individual, each in his own way and at his own pace, maximize his unique personal potential. The academic air was thick with slogans that would survive the century, such as "Teach the child, not the subject" and "The whole child goes to school."

There was obviously little place in such a scenario for formalized marching in lines, rigid rows of bolted-down desks, competitive spelling bees, coercive examinations or punitive leather straps. Dewey's disciples argued for years over just how the master meant his philosophy to be applied. His writing style being more than a little ambiguous, there remained room for variety of interpretation. But clearly a progressive school had to be at least something like the aptly named Laboratory School, which John Dewey founded (but did not himself run) at the University of Chicago in 1896.[5]

At the Laboratory School pupils and teachers pursued their self-directed interests "wherever they intelligently might lead, across conventional subject matter lines, across the threshold of the school house door," writes Dewey disciple William H. Kilpatrick of Columbia University. At one early stage, Laboratory School pupils spent considerable time growing wheat, grinding it into flour and finally baking it into bread. This was meant to let them "experience life" as it had been experienced by their ancestors, to encourage teamwork, and to integrate the moral, the social and the intellectual.

Although it lasted only seven years, Kilpatrick writes, the Laboratory School inspired many "to new hopes and a new vision." Eschewing any artificially constructed

City of Edmonton Archives, EA-10-1471

Edmonton teacher Harry Ainlay waxed enthusiastic about the new trends in education. "If I had my way I would do away with every grade in our schools today," he declared in 1930.

4 Whether from school or home, 1930s students were picking up the social action message. An article in the March 3, 1938, *Medicine Hat News* described threatened strike action by Grades 7 to 11 in nearby Redcliff over midterm curriculum changes: "In fact no work was accomplished for two days, although the pupils attended school." But a pupil delegation had interviewed the school board "and with the help of Inspector Sweet matters were straightened out last night."

5 John Dewey, beholding the way his disciples had interpreted him, was towards the end of his life appalled at the result. He vehemently denied advocating that schools be "child-centred" to the extent of leaving the entire planning of their education to the children themselves. His intention, he protested, was that the teacher should manage the process—but unobtrusively. His ardent disciples, however, routinely created progressivist classes of the sort that elicited from one befuddled small boy the plaintive query: "Do we have to do what we want today?"

[6]**Not all John Dewey's educational colleagues at Columbia University found his theories beguiling. Representing the Essentialists, William C. Bagley complained that Deweyists would be well advised to spend less effort trying to teach children to think and more effort giving them something to think about, in the form of real subjects like mathematics and history. The Essentialists emphasized a rigorous traditional curriculum. Bagley was also opposed to limiting educational opportunity on the basis of IQ tests.**

curriculum of reading, arithmetic and so on, it began its pupils on "those fundamental types of activity which make civilization what it is," such as cooking, sewing and manual training. Although little of this found its way into the schools of North America in its original form, elementary education was nevertheless being completely remade on underlying Dewey doctrines in the early 1930s. Among the first watchwords were: "Education as a process of living." Educators spoke of the "inherent" subject matter, or the "problem approach," and rejected the "slavish" use of textbooks.[6]

Soon they were advancing whole curricula based upon "themes." In 1938, for example, the *Calgary Herald* described a lecture delivered to the American Women's Club by Miss T. Baxter of

It seems Aberhart was equally unsuspicious of progressivism, a much more subtle form of indoctrination, and missed the main point. He had great confidence in his fellow educators, he said, and lauded the province's new elementary school curriculum 'which has converted the classroom from a listening post to a hive of activity.'

Lincoln School, New York. Miss Baxter told the clubwomen how a class of 11-year-olds at Lincoln had pursued a Greek theme. The children viewed Greek sculpture and vases at the Metropolitan Museum (history), produced replicas of the vases in the school pottery shop (art), and put on a play of their own composition based on the Odyssey (English composition and literature, perhaps geography), with costumes they produced in the school sewing room (domestic science) and pillars for the stage set made in shops (industrial arts). Thus they learned about Greece, and a whole range of subjects, with much enthusiasm and no need for compulsion.

Miss Baxter was in Calgary that summer to help local teachers learn how to apply this technique, known as the Enterprise System. As at Lincoln School and elsewhere, Enterprise aimed to teach as much as was humanly possible in terms of one theme, with maximum pupil participation. For decades to come Alberta school children would produce in great profusion elaborate posters, murals, musical productions, charts illustrating such matters as rubber production, and

Here is Jack Beavers' report card for the 1932-33 school year. Such assessment criteria as class standing, comparisons of grades against a class average and value judgements with respect to students' behaviour were already becoming anathema to the pedagogic intellectual community.

Glenbow Archives, NA-2768-9

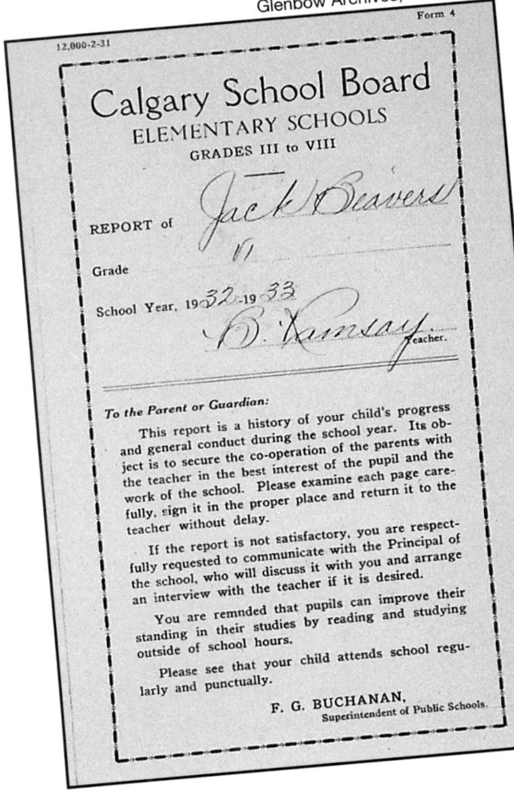

12,000-2-31 Form 4

Calgary School Board
ELEMENTARY SCHOOLS
GRADES III to VIII

REPORT of Jack Beavers

Grade VI

School Year, 1932-1933

B. Ramsay, Teacher.

To the Parent or Guardian:

This report is a history of your child's progress and general conduct during the school year. Its object is to secure the co-operation of the parents with the teacher in the best interest of the pupil and the work of the school. Please examine each page carefully, sign it in the proper place and return it to the teacher without delay.

If the report is not satisfactory, you are respectfully requested to communicate with the Principal of the school, who will discuss it with you and arrange an interview with the teacher if it is desired.

You are remnded that pupils can improve their standing in their studies by reading and studying outside of school hours.

Please see that your child attends school regularly and punctually.

F. G. BUCHANAN,
Superintendent of Public Schools.

Glenbow Archives, NA-2768-8

Name of Pupil Jack Beavers

ATTAINMENT IN SCHOOL SUBJECTS

The standing attained may be given by Symbol or in Numbers showing percentages.

METHOD OF GRADING

E.—Excellent (over 85%) F—Fair (50% to 59%)
V.G.—Very Good (70% to 85%) P—Poor (under 50%)
G—Good (60% to 69%)

Pupils are in danger of not being promoted whose Grading is below Good.

Term average

SUBJECTS	Sept.	Oct.	Nov.	Dec.	Jan.	Feb.	Mar.	Apr.	May	June
Literature and Memory Work	26	40	38	35	41	36	37	47	40	
Spelling	50	46	50	49	38	50	44	47	47	
Grammar										
Composition (Language)		38	37	38	40		40	37	42	
History and Civics									42	
Geography	33	39	36	36	40	45	35	37	48	
Arithmetic	46	34	33	35	42	30	40	40	26	
Accuracy	39	39	40	39	38	22	37	45	45	
Agric. or Nature Study	32			32						
Physiology and Hygiene			43	43					42	
Art					35	43	40			
Household or Manual Arts					29					
Reading, Oral	35	36	32	34	36	30	30	30	35	
Reading, Silent	?									
Writing	25	27	30	27	35	35	31	35	35	
Music							49	50		
This Pupil's Average	72	75	75	74	75	73	77	80	79	
Class Average	55	40	60		61	63	63	66	65	
Number in Class	42	40	41	41	39	37	41	45	45	
This Pupil's Standing	3	5	5	2	2	5	3		1	
Teacher's Initials	B.R.	B.R.	B.R.	B.R.	B.R.	B.R.	B.R.	B.R.	B.R.	

Note.—Attention is called to the trait opposite which an "X" is placed.

ATTITUDE TOWARDS SCHOOL WORK	Sept.	Oct.	Nov.	Dec.	Jan.	Feb.	Mar.	Apr.	May	June
Very Satisfactory		X					X	X		
Effort Good	X		X		X		X	X		
Work well prepared							X			
Shows improvement										
Becoming interested										
Capable of doing better										
Work carelessly done										
Lessons poorly prepared										
Gives up too easily										
Expects too much help										
Not interested — Gives few oral answers										
Making no effort										

CONDUCT

	Sept.	Oct.	Nov.	Dec.	Jan.	Feb.	Mar.	Apr.	May	June
Commendable							X	X		
Courteous, considerate	X	X			X		X	X		
Respectful, obedient	X	X					X	X		
Talkative										
Restless, inattentive										
Annoys others										
Inclined to rudeness										
Disobedient										

ATTENDANCE

	Sept.	Oct.	Nov.	Dec.	Jan.	Feb.	Mar.	Apr.	May	June
Days absent	1	0	0	0	0	½	0	0	0	0
Times late	0	1	0	0	0	0	0	0	0	0

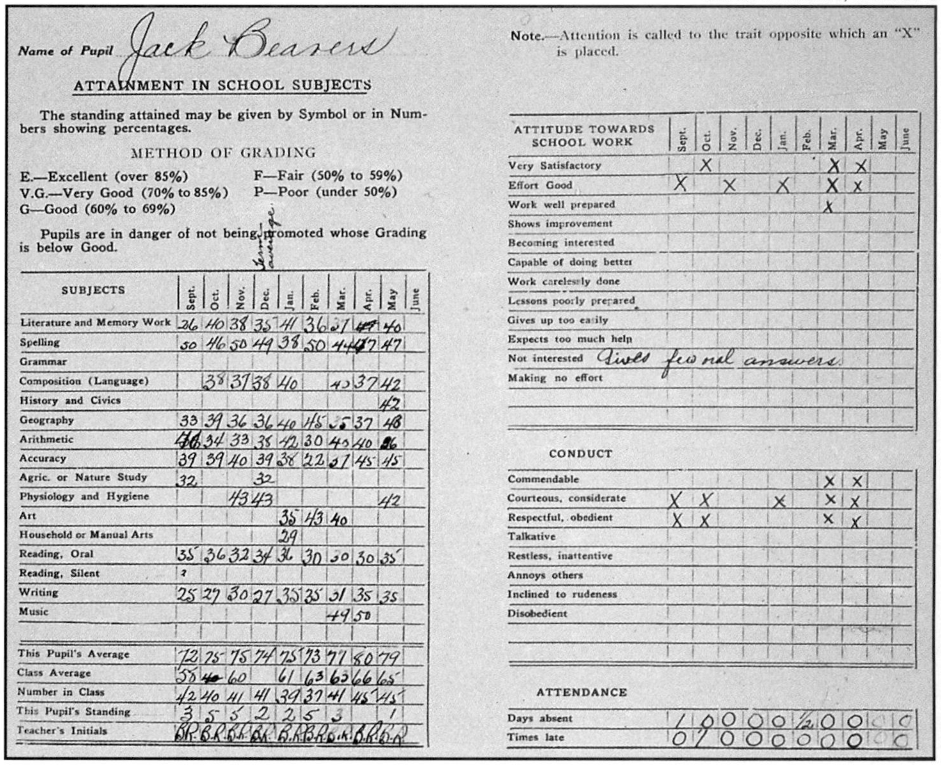

papier-mâché models of native villages. However, the Women's Club audience was assured, Alberta schools were following a "middle course," devoting only half the day to Enterprise and the other half to "straight reading, writing and arithmetic classes."

Such Progressivist mentors from the United States were in good supply. The 1939 ATA convention, attended by 1,550 delegates, heard from no fewer than five of them: Dr. Reginald Bell of Stanford University, Dr. Howard Lane of Northwestern, and Drs. Ralph W. Tyler, Hilda Taba and Wilfred Eberhart of the University of Chicago. Such powerful influence soon created tireless and eloquent disciples in Alberta. H.C. Newland, the provincial supervisor of schools, had explained in a speech reported the previous year by the *Calgary Herald* that the most important thing now was "education for democracy."

Some people, sensing dangerous change without being able to pinpoint it, fought back on issues like classroom reading of the Bible or the teaching of the theory of evolution. These efforts seldom got to the heart of the problem, however, and in any event seldom succeeded.

Whether or not Alberta children learned anything about Shakespeare, or a quadrant, or the cause of the Reformation. Newland declared, they must be trained to realize the ideals of democracy. But not by means of old-style teaching with its exacting standards, of course, because this "leads to a kind of learning that has no value." Superintendent Newland cited a California high school program that admitted any boy or girl, qualified or otherwise. Then the school just tried to find something each one "needed to know," and tried to teach him that.[7]

The fight to rid Alberta schools of "the dead hand of the past" gained a substantial foothold in the elementary schools and was beginning to make inroads at the high school level before the end of the 1930s. It was rudely interrupted by the exigencies and harsh realities of the Second World War which returned Canada to awareness of tradition, responsibility and self-sacrifice, slowing the march of progressive education for most of two decades. In the Sixties, however, it regained its momentum and became the largely unchallenged assumption of education until the last decade of the century. It was then discerned that, whatever the virtues of the "New Education," North American schools were lagging ever farther behind those of Asia and western Europe in academic performance and skills, a fact that to the Deweyist purist of the Thirties would hardly have mattered.

Deweyism was, after all, entirely in accord with the temper of an era when tradition of every sort — political, economic, philosophical and, most notably, religious — was being challenged. This challenge had its origins far back in western European history, of course; some would credit it to the Christian humanism that prefigured the 16th century Reformation. Certainly from the 1870s onward a major philosophical shift is evident in North American academic circles. Fascination with the power and possibilities of "scientific inquiry" became paramount; ethical idealism gave way to pragmatism and empiricism. The only dependable truth, it was argued, was physically measurable truth. "Naturalism" was in. "Supernaturalism" was out. Therefore theistic religion of any kind, including Christianity, was also out — no longer intellectually tenable.

Science was explaining more and more about the workings of the universe. The theories of Charles Darwin had supposedly eliminated any need for a supernatural creator, either for the world or its contents. "Progress" was the preoccupation of the 20th century, and science clearly led in that department. Faith and ethics appeared outmoded and downright stagnant by contrast to the wonders of modern technology; they seemed not to be progressing at all.

Typical of this intellectual atmosphere was Dewey himself. Raised a

Glenbow Archives, NA-2768-9

HOME WORK

[Regu]lar class homework assignments are not given below [Grade] VI.

[It] is advisable at times to ask a class below Grade VI to [obt]ain work at home, such as Memory Work, Reading [as]signed topic, or collecting Nature Study material. [Pup]ils who are behind may need to do come extra work [at hom]e, which could be suggested by the teacher. [Spe]cial requests from parents for home work will be [grant]ed by the teachers.

[The ti]me suggested for regular work at home is: [Grade V]I—30 minutes; Grade VII—45 minutes. [Grade V]III—60 minutes.

[Those wh]o are interested may find it useful to take a longer [time.]

[Work su]ggested for home study or reading in Grades [VII a]nd VIII are:

[Read]ation; Spelling; Supplementary Reading; History, [on] certain topics; Geography, collecting information; [comp]leting exercises; and occasional review exercises in [Arithmeti]c, Grammar and Composition.

[The ai]m is to develop in pupils the power of attacking [work] on their own initiative and securing information for [themselve]s. Home work should be used as an aid to this.

[SIGN]ATURE OF PARENT OR GUARDIAN

[CER]TIFICATE OF PROMOTION

[7]"What is involved in Alberta's educational philosophy?" was the question posed by H.B. Trout of the Provincial Normal School, Edmonton, in his essay in the June 1939 *A.T.A. Magazine*. "The answer is, in general outline, the democratic philosophy of John Dewey... It is common knowledge that the philosophy underlying Alberta's enterprise curriculum is to be found in Dewey's work *Democracy and Education*."

Revision of the educational system to emphasize character-building rather than passing examinations was advocated by Dr. S.R. Laycock of the University of Saskatchewan in an address in Saskatoon.

The present system, he said, was designed to meet the needs of the average child and the "under average" children were handicapped as a result. Parents should decide whether children should concentrate merely on efforts to pass examinations or give some time to training with a view to character development.

"Teachers should not be judged on their percentage of passes," Dr. Laycock said. In England, which he had visited a short time ago, emphasis was placed on character rather than on knowledge. Teachers were permitted to mould the character of their students.

"Constant emphasis on examinations makes matters difficult for the below-normal child," the speaker said. The mental effect of continuous failure caused the student to drift into undesirable channels and lose interest in school work.

Accurate diagnosis by the teacher was the only remedy. Parents were notoriously poor judges of their children's ability. Intelligence tests should be made to determine what studies the pupil was capable of assimilating.
—*Albertan*, February 29, 1936

THE REVOLUTIONARIES

The builders of 20th-century Alberta — early-on stage

These future farmers, soldiers, teachers, and homemakers all appear full of hope and promise despite the Depression. Grade 4 classes at [A] Clyde, about 1933, and [B] Calgary's King Edward School, 1931. [C] Diligence School District, Legal, May 19, 1930. Before consolidation, virtually every school outside the larger centres comprised a district. [D] Students at Craigmyle school in 1934 with their teacher, Katherine McAuliffe. [E] Brookside Public School, Warwick, 1937. [F] Students of the primary room, Smoky Lake School District, 1932-33.

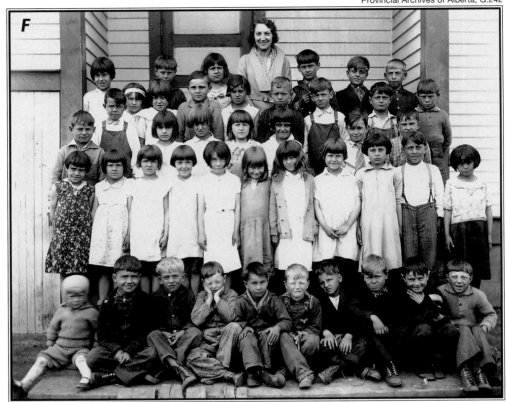

Protestant, he was still a professing Christian when he took up his first assistant professorship at the University of Michigan in the early 1880s, sustaining an uneasy combination of Protestant theology and Hegelian philosophy. But during the next decade he quietly shed his Christian beliefs, became a convinced exponent of the pragmatic school of philosophy, and began eliminating any tinge of "supernaturalism" from his thinking.

Dewey's acceptance of the Darwinian theory of organic Evolution through Natural Selection was typically enthusiastic and unqualified. (*The Origin of the Species*, incidentally, had been published in the year Dewey was born.) He believed Darwinism could entirely account for human physical and mental attributes. As for emergent social behaviour, he contended, ideas are conceived because of problems encountered. They are then acted upon, which eventually validates them, or demonstrates them to be either in need of adjustment or worthless, a kind of social Darwinism, the survival of the fittest idea.

Dealing with the thorny problem of "truth," Dewey preferred to speak instead of "values," a word destined to reach full flower in the 1960s. Values could be derived from human experience of desire and satisfaction, he contended. Admittedly, not every human desire could qualify as a worthy source of satisfaction, as he acknowledged in *The Quest for Certainty*. The desire of some for wealth, power, or physical satisfaction might have to have limits that could be determined by "reflective judgements." But this was no reason to presume some absolute standard allegedly derived from a source beyond human experience. A "desirable" desire could be distinguished by its personal and social consequences.[8]

Not surprisingly, such a philosophy was quite congenial to many if not most academics of the era, including members of theology departments, which by then were seething with modernist argumentation. But the puzzle to historians is this: Why in the 1930s was Progressivism, with its anti-theistic assumptions, so readily accepted not only by educators but by teachers and many parents? Most Albertans still cherished a robust, if largely unexamined, religious faith. Yet thousands of devout Christian teachers and parents cheerfully embraced Deweyist educational ideas that stood in flat contradiction of their declared beliefs.

The most likely explanation is this: Like so many other dubious propositions in the dawn of modernism, John Dewey's ideas came wrapped in a seeming utopian kindliness that was hard for ordinary well-intended people to argue with. There was no declared intention to revolutionize the schools, but merely to "improve" them. His avowed intent was to establish, through his philosophy, a kind of heaven on earth — or rather, a secular version thereof — by means of social science, educational technique and democratic government. Education could clearly become the primary instrument of social progress and reform. All this accorded very well with the Social Gospel that mainline Protestant churches had been preaching throughout the West since the turn of the century.

Furthermore, Dewey's style was soothingly moderate in an era of incendiary talk. On the central philosophical conflict between the assumptions of religion and those of scientism, he would explain mildly and rather ambiguously that actually there was no conflict. As Dewey biographer Alan Ryan puts it, he presented science and religion as "equal partners in the search for the 'meaning' of the experienced world." Besides, although Dewey might believe that God must go, for a long time he continued using the familiar religious language. In books like *The Quest for Certainty* and *A Common Faith*, he set about with missionary zeal to assert that the world could be just as meaningful from a secular viewpoint. Faith should be redirected to the principles of democracy, he declared, and he was apparently quite comfortable referring to his belief in democracy as a "religious" one.

All these reassurances were, to say the least, disingenuous. However sugary the presentation, the central claim of such a materialist philosophy is precisely that nothing can be regarded as reliably true unless it can be verified by the scientific method. Dewey's supposed reconciliation of

[8] Opponents were quick to spot the hole in Dewey's theory of values. If there is no standard apart from human experience, how are we to determine the difference between a "desirable" and "undesirable" social consequence? For instance, Robert M. Hutchins, the University of Chicago president best remembered for his *Great Books* program, argued that it might make sense to apply scientific method philosophically only if agreement already existed about what was to be achieved. Dewey could not, by means of his own philosophy, defend his own goals: "All he can do is say he is for them."

[9] Late in the century professional groups such as the American Association of Biology Teachers would formally reject Dewey's position. In 1997, the AABT eliminated from its teaching code a prohibition on the possibility that God could account for any natural phenomenon. This prohibition, it decided, was not founded on a scientific assumption, but a theological one. Sixty years after the event, critics commented, the teachers had finally figured out what Dewey was up to.

Provincial Archives of Alberta, A 13992

Superintendent of Schools H.C. Newland professed a strong belief in "education for democracy," which would apparently preclude such mainstays of the traditional school system as entrance requirements.

science and religion, therefore, required that the assumptions of the philosophy known as scientism be applied to religion, not vice versa. All issues, be they ethical, political or educational, must be judged at the bar of science. The world must be governed on a thoroughly "naturalist" basis, which he called "intelligent action." All truth (or values) must be judged by experience, meaning "rationally" discernible experience, not experience deriving from intuition or faith. Only science could truly ascertain fact, and all private intuitions about God would doubtless soon be scientifically explained by psychological research.[9]

The adoption of such presuppositions clearly rules out theistic assumptions in the classroom — Christian, Muslim or Jewish — and this over time was precisely the result of progressive education. Were Alberta's educators so overwhelmingly persuaded by this scientist philosophy that they were compelled by intellectual honesty to make the schools conform with it? Or were they merely carried along by the latest scholastic fashion imported from the United States, without perceiving its implications? Evidence can be found for the latter supposition. Thirty years later, for instance, in his *Schools of the Foothills Province* (University of Toronto Press, for ATA, 1967), education historian John W. Chalmers briefly evaluated Deweyism as it affected Alberta. Some critics, he noted, had argued that its rejection of authority, and its concept of truth as "that which works," were unchristian, even anti-religious. That may be. But the "more fundamental criticisms," in his view, were that progressivism made far more demands on the teacher, and required resource material which might not be available. In other words, where we were going didn't matter as much as the problems we encountered in getting there. Whatever the reasoning of the educators, however, popular opinion would gradually fall in line with them over the next half-century, as scientism took over the entire educational establishment.

Not everyone was entirely unaware at the time. Some people, sensing dangerous change without being able to pinpoint it, fought back on issues like classroom reading of the Bible or the teaching of the theory of evolution in high school. These efforts seldom got to the heart of the problem, however, and in any event seldom succeeded. There were exceptions. In 1928 the Edmonton Public School Board approved daily classroom Bible reading, for example. Although this resolution seems not to have been acted upon, board member F.C. Casselman was determined to get it off the books.

In May 1930 the *Edmonton Journal* reported that Casselman had once again moved that it be rescinded "in view of the fact that a very considerable number" of citizens were opposed to school Bible reading. Board lawyers advised that reading biblical passages without comment would be illegal, since it could not be defined as teaching. Reading with commentary would be religious instruction and therefore legal, but only in the last half-hour of the day.

He changed the schools and they changed society

Science was Dewey's morality and escape from the past his goal

The man whose ideas centrally directed the entire course of 20th century North American education with consequent changes in the moral and social attitudes of the succeeding generation was not, in fact, a teacher. Although closely associated with the educational establishments of the University of Chicago and of Columbia University, New York, John Dewey wrote philosophical treatises, not classroom manuals.

His *Democracy and Education*, for instance, which he seemingly intended as a textbook on his central theories, deals almost exclusively with the social implications of education, not with curricular details.

In Dewey's philosophy, however, can be clearly traced the religious, political and economic assumptions that informed his educational theories. Those theories would become the basis of education in Alberta for the last seven decades of the century, as they would the schools of Canada and the United States. Then, through the graduates of those schools, they would work dramatic changes in society itself.

As to religion, he replied unequivocally to the two most crucial questions of any age: Without a purposeful creator, can the world — and human lives — have purpose and meaning? Said Dewey: Yes. Without "supernatural" authority, can ethics in any meaningful sense survive? Again, yes.

He did not, however, provide reasons, feeling apparently no need to back up his contention or otherwise "explain" the universe. Science would in due time explain everything, from the distant nebula to the intricacies of the human soul, he believed.

Philosopher John Dewey in 1939.

He was a cosmic optimist, raised in the world's most optimistic nation at its most optimistic period. The world is what it is, he tells us. What you see is what you get. What he saw looked pretty good, so if we put our minds to the job we could use the discoveries of modern science to make the world better still. So we should just sort out our day-to-day lives and get on with things. There was, in short, no existential angst for this prosaic philosopher — but no sense either of any mystic power that might lie behind what he "saw."

To Dewey, religion was nice but unnecessary. Its positive aspects "can be had equally well, in the ordinary course of human experience, in our relations to the natural world and to one another as human beings," he wrote. However, religious attitudes, along with every other aspect of life, must be entirely freed from authoritarian holdovers from the past, and adapted to modern realities.

Not that he indulged very much, apart from recurrent controversy over parochial schools (which he condemned as divisive), in what he called "aggressive atheism." This, he observed in *Common Faith*, seemed to him "to have something in common with traditional supernaturalism" — which in Dewey's eyes automatically condemned it. But he firmly, sometimes savagely, rejected the Congregationalist faith of his youth.

Neither was he concerned that moral training of children on this liberal basis, i.e., without benefit of a Bible, a church or any other form of divine justification, might look unpleasantly like manipulation. Science justified all, and Dewey preferred to call his philosophy "instrumentalism" or, later on, "experimentalism." Critics naturally objected that experimentalism could not plausibly issue in moral principles. For instance, they demanded, on what philosophic grounds could it declare the democratic experiment to be preferable to the totalitarian experiment?

But Dewey's followers were not restrained by such questions. If progressivism had caused higher education to become somewhat confused in its aims, wrote Deweyist Boyd H. Bode, the remedy was emphatically not to return to "the intellectual ideals of Plato and Aristotle and St. Thomas Aquinas," promulgators of the philosophical absolutes to which mankind had for so many centuries been subjugated.

Modern science, declared Bode, which had already so enriched the world, had also opened the way to organize the whole of life on an entirely different basis. "Since it shuts the door on absolutes, it makes all truth subject to the same test. It brings truth, goodness and beauty down from the clouds and sets the stage for a reinterpretation of them in terms of a better associated or democratic living."

Preference for a democratic society was a central part of Dewey's instrumentalist/experimentalist philosophy. Education can have no meaning as a social process and function, he explained in *Democracy and Education*, "until we define the kind of society we have in mind." He considered democracy the best attempt to govern on an ethical basis, recognizing that each individual possesses intrinsic worth, and that the sole purpose of society is the good of its members.

The basis for these preferences ("values," as Dewey

called them) is not entirely clear. Be that as it may, however, he reasoned that education, in order to promote them, must deal with each child as an individual, not merely a member of a class or category. Also, since a democratic society should encourage diversity, different interest groups would develop and come into conflict.

Therefore schools must develop peaceful methods for resolving these conflicts, and be organized in such a way as to give children practice at this. (But an appeal to external authority or fixed standards was not to be considered, Dewey specified.) And finally, for the sake of both society and education, it was time to "employ science and technology for social instead of merely private ends," to replace the capitalist anarchy of economic competition with intelligent planning.

This sort of statement brought accusations that progressivists were socialist at best and maybe communist, and there probably was substance to such charges. But Dewey's own central vision seems to come down to a kind of communitarianism, based on the idea that the common faith of the common man, expressed in democratically ordered communities, will result in a beneficial and orderly life. This

personal experience, not from books (and omitting, we must assume, the ancestors' religious faith). Dewey categorized mind as a function of behaviour, which a child acquires as he absorbs the meanings embodied in the customs, traditions and techniques of his society. "Deliberate education" (schooling) could augment this process by providing pupils with appropriate situations. A situation of difficulty, for example, would inspire them to reflection, observation, the making of inferences, the gradual defining of its nature, a plan for dealing with it, and action that tests the plan.

Ideas only make sense as solutions to problems, Dewey theorized. Therefore, just as rural children experience life and work in terms of physical realities, city children must somehow be enabled to do the same. But the "realities" must be sufficiently convincing for them to experience life as meaningful (with no need for any appeal to religion), and to encourage each one to make his unique contribution to the community. A proper school "activity program," progressivists emphasized, must not be confused with mere motion, or busy work, or indulgence of childish whim.

Adulated by his followers, Dewey was indicted by critics

To Dewey, religion was nice but unnecessary. Any of its positive aspects 'can be had equally well, in the ordinary course of human experience, in our relations to the natural world and to one another as human beings,' he wrote.

---

does not mean he was a collectivist in the Communist sense, however. He was *not* among the many intellectuals who in the 1930s were taken in by the Soviet experiment. Politically Dewey was a liberal who believed in some degree of government welfare activity, and very much a democrat.

As for specific methods of achieving these philosophical ideals, Dewey biographer Alan Ryan suggests the master's own ideal school "might take many forms, but would be recognizably unlike the main alternatives. It would be secular, self-conscious, friendly to science, hostile to standardized tests and academic examinations, and a good deal more besides."

William H. Kilpatrick of Columbia University, Dewey's colleague, friend and follower, tried to explain all this in a little more detail. Dewey's contention, Kilpatrick wrote, was that education must start with the present interests of the child (the doctrine of interest) "and help him build himself into an ever more adequate personality, respecting himself and others" (the doctrine of democracy). As the child seeks to fulfil his wants, he learns naturally from experience (theory of knowledge). The good school will inspire him "to conceive finer and better things to do," and introduce him also to "the stored up results of race experience."

By the stored up results of race experience Kilpatrick seems to mean the accumulated wisdom and knowledge the child's ancestors acquired by the selfsame process, i.e., by

on many counts. He was accused of destroying discipline, of being against healthy competition, of emphasizing "socialization" at the expense of moral character, of being anti-intellectual, of advocating that children set their own agendas, and in general of turning schoolrooms into playrooms.

Dewey repudiated some of these claims (e.g., that children should not be guided by adults), and some were exaggerated. But there was some truth to all of them, and much truth to some of them. Furthermore, if the guru himself was not demonstrably guilty on all counts, some of his hordes of admirers definitely were — on the basis of their interpretation of his teachings.

One thing should be particularly noted in John Dewey's favour, however. Unlike Jean Jacques Rousseau, his fellow philosopher of education, who consigned all his own children to foundling homes, Dewey really seems to have liked children. He and his second wife even adopted two youngsters when they were quite elderly.

Still, good intentions are no guarantee of truth. He is depicted by his biographers as a man who hated anecdotes, wrote no memoirs, and seemed oblivious to introspection or the private person. Above all, he was dangerously unaware of the limits of "intelligence" alone in the ordering of society and its institutions — a shortcoming which, said his critics, would have devastating effects upon generations to come.

—*V.B.*

The following November, at its last pre-election meeting, instead of adopting Casselman's motion, the board formally ordered Bible readings to begin January 1, in the last ten minutes of the school day. It also decreed that parents could request exemption for their children, but refused a consultation request from the Alberta Teachers' Alliance. Edmonton teachers, who were on the other side of this controversy, met and declared that "religious instruction is an essential duty of home, school and church." Therefore they demanded Bible readings at the proper time of day: morning. Finally, on December 24, the newly elected board (even though Casselman had now become chairman), ordered a January go-ahead as planned.

Edmonton's mayor Joseph A. Clarke welcomed delegates to the Lamont Teachers' Convention by comparing teachers to stenographers, who ought to remember who they were working for (the taxpayers) and stay out of politics. ATA representative H.C. Clark described the mayor's remarks as 'a lot of hooey.'

The Bible-reading issue would be fought again and again before the century ended, with decreasing fervour. The matter of evolution theory was more problematic. Many progressive-minded people, teachers included, considered that the famous 1925 trial of Tennessee teacher John T. Scopes (for teaching that man evolved from lower forms) had discredited the idea of divine creation once and for all. Scopes had been found guilty and fined, but his skilled lawyer, Clarence Darrow, had so eloquently argued the modernist case as to make anyone who disbelieved in Natural Selection look like a complete ignoramus, utterly out of touch with enlightened thought.

Nonetheless, some Albertans were still willing to risk it. A contributor to the October 1930 *A.T.A. Magazine*, in an article headed "'Ware Evolution" and signed W.T.R., vehemently attacks Darwinism's scientific credentials. Leading evolutionary scientists, he asserts, no longer refer to it as a "principle" or even a "theory," but speak of it as "an act of faith." Meanwhile, W.T.R. adds, opponents refer to it as "scientific superstition" and he quotes many scientists on the fragmentary and incomplete nature of the supposed evidence. A year later, the Calgary *Albertan* reports that Mrs. Margaret B. Hughes has written to the Calgary School Board protesting against the teaching of evolution at Crescent Heights High School. In the opinion of the school management committee, the paper added, there is "no justification for the board taking any action."

Nor did Crescent Heights principal William Aberhart seem to detect any educational dangers in evolution and other manifestations of modernism, then or later. He and other Alberta politicians were fully aware of the efficacy of classroom indoctrination, of course. A *Calgary Herald* article describes an altercation at the 1934 convention of the United Farmers of Alberta, the government party, over a resolution submitted by the Didsbury local. It urged that struggle for private profit should be played down "through the entire curriculum," in favour of equity, justice, mutual aid and social well-being.

This was not a notion peculiar to the UFA. When the Social Credit government was elected in 1935, and 250 Edmonton ATA members staged a banquet at the Corona Hotel to welcome the new premier, he told them the whole Social Credit philosophy was educational and should be part of the school system. "Who among you will get busy and prepare a textbook," he asked, "even if it is only to be used as an elementary reader?"

Later in his first term, the premier declared: "We believe that until the child changes his outlook on life, there will be no peace among men, and we are consciously planning our school programs

On the whole, newspapers supported the revolution in education or, as in this Edmonton Bulletin *cartoon, found it amusing. Later in the century, as their readership reflected the general downward trend in literacy, they would see less humour in the situation.*

Edmonton Bulletin, January 10, 1935

SIDE GLANCES—By Geo. Clark

"I thought our modern school had gotten away from this sort of thing."

to bring about that change." He urged teachers at their 1935 southern Alberta convention to co-operate in instituting their province's "new social order." Thus, he said, "you will become so necessary that the government will be unable to get along without you." A year later, speaking at the province-wide ATA convention, he warned them "not to make themselves propagandists for the high financiers." Nor, he added, should they teach "atheism."

But on the subject of evolution Premier (and Minister of Education) Aberhart appears to have missed the main point. Preaching at his Prophetic Bible Institute in 1939, the *Calgary Herald* reported, he asserted that he had been accused of believing "the atheistic teaching that man was descended from a monkey simply because he thought that children should be taught a scientific evolutionary theory." He did not believe in descent from monkeys, he said. Furthermore, Alberta textbooks so far as he could see "in no way declare that the Bible story is wrong." Evolution theory, in other words, was simply science, and not a threat.

It seems Aberhart was equally unsuspicious of progressivism, a much more subtle form of indoctrination, and missed the main point here too. He had great confidence in his fellow educators, was much concerned about his government's school policies, and proud of its accomplishments. "Education is on the march throughout Canada, and nowhere is this more marked than in Alberta," he exclaimed in one speech. He then proceeded to laud the province's new elementary school curriculum "which has converted the classroom from a listening post to a hive of activity."

Thus, despite temporary frustrations and setbacks, the Alberta teaching profession undeniably did accomplish a great deal in the 1930s, aided by two potent factors. For inspiration they had John Dewey and his followers, preaching a genial liberal materialism, unlimited human potential, and a new age of scientific progress and social improvement. And the central facilitators of these wondrous developments, Dewey kept declaring, would be teachers. This was heady stuff! Then, for immediate support, they had a leader of government, very much in sympathy with them, telling them the same and backing them up with legislation.

Undoubtedly the Deweyist revolution was further abetted by Aberhart's massive consolidation of country school boards (see sidebar). Though consolidation unquestionably improved the lot of

A relatively young-looking William Aberhart poses with his staff when he was principal of Crescent Heights School in Calgary in the early 1920s. The preponderance of female teachers was the result of a staff revolt in 1919 against the future premier's heavy-handed leadership style, after which three male teachers were transferred to other schools. Aberhart's administration would pass the legislation that would bring Dewey's philosophy into Alberta classrooms.

the classroom teacher, its even greater effect, in the long run, was to increase exponentially the power and influence of the province's educational bureaucrats — the people who ran the ATA, the city school boards, the education department and (far from least) the teacher training institutions. These would soon be transformed from humble Normal Schools into university faculties. Efficient centralization made it easier to control what was taught, and how it was taught, than in the messy old days of local school boards and omnipresent parents.

In 1935 the *Edmonton Journal* interviewed Donalda Dickie, for more than two decades a leading lecturer in English and history at the province's three Normal Schools (Camrose, Calgary and Edmonton) and a prolific author of elementary school textbooks, who was in Edmonton to work

The whole Alberta system verges on collapse

Schools vanish, teacher pay slashed, pupils too ill-clad to attend

To keep Alberta's school system functioning through the Depression years took ingenuity, tenacity and sometimes a bit of larceny, played out against a chronic cash shortage.

As early as December 1930, Education Minister Perren Baker had to deny reports that rural schools were shutting down wholesale for lack of money. Country schools often closed in winter, he said, and no more than usual had yet done so this year. But several might have to close in January, he admitted. Local tax collection had been failing, and although the UFA government had established a fund to provide loans to cash-strapped country schools, all this money had already been spent. As the decade wore on, things kept getting worse.

Albertans by now had a considerable educational establishment to support. Total school enrolment in the calendar year 1929 was 164,850, with 19,433 in Grades 9 to 12, and 145,417 in Grades 1 to 8. The province's three Normal Schools had 827 teachers in training. High school teachers totalled 457, of whom 280 were university graduates. Some 2,023 students applied to the Institute of Technology at Calgary in 1929; the electricity, motor mechanics and tractor departments could not meet the demand. Also, according to

the annual Education Department report, the system had 120 "subnormal" children to look after.

In the cities, classroom space for a growing youth population was in short supply. Edmonton's school superintendent complained that sufficient space could not be found for all high school applicants. McDougall Commercial High School was running double shifts. Teachers and supervisors volunteered to run special evening classes for the unemployed, ranging from technical and commercial courses to physical training.

Volunteer efforts were very much in order. In December 1931, for instance, the Calgary *Albertan* reported that city school attendance had dropped because many children lacked warm clothes. A survey of the King Edward School district had found that in 22 of 40 households the family head was unemployed. School nurses were trying to round up clothing. Two years later, pupils of Calgary's Rosedale School were collecting clothes and books for Saskatchewan children at Loon River and Cando, who were even worse off — almost all their families were on relief.

In 1931 the Alberta Teachers' Alliance already had some 400 unemployed teachers on its rolls, in part because school boards could not afford to hire them. Trustees seemingly could not make ends meet, no matter how they tried. The Calgary School Board, for example, cut in half its equipment expenditure between September and December 1931, but still spent $18,440 more overall than it had in the same period of 1930. A slight increase in salaries was partly responsible, but increased debenture payments were the main cause. By 1932 the city's teachers had to accept an 11 per cent pay cut. Representatives of the Alberta Teachers' Alliance, ready to negotiate, caved in after board chairman F.E. Spooner opened discussions with the remark: "I don't know where we are going to get the money to pay your salaries for the next couple of months."

Desperate municipal and school officials would

Glenbow Archives, NA-4242-2

Moving the school at Del Bonita in 1939 in anticipation of consolidation.

on curriculum revision. "Asked whether any radical changes were being made," the *Journal* reporter wrote, "Dr. Dickie laughed. 'We think we are introducing radical changes, but in reality it is as old as Rousseau.'" It was a significant comment, if a curious one. Naturalist philosopher Jean Jacques Rousseau was, along with Dewey, the most revered figure in the progressivist pantheon. Her denial was, in other words, an affirmation.

By January 1936 deputy education minister Fred McNally was revealing details of what he called a "thoroughly modern curriculum suited to present-day needs." The emphasis in elementary school would be on pupil participation. Classrooms thereafter would feature sandboxes in which youngsters could create structures to illustrate everything from life on the farm to the Taj

entertain almost any proposal that might save cash, or acquire some. In southern Alberta the Raymond school board (emulated later by neighbouring Magrath) issued its own scrip and used it as part of teacher wages. This scrip was redeemable in taxes, and at least some merchants accepted it. Not so successful was a proposal made by Premier William Aberhart after Social Credit came to power in 1935. He told school boards that for any actual cash they remitted to the province, they could get back double the value in his innovative provincial government "prosperity certificates" to pay salaries. But even the desperate have a sticking point; he got few takers.

In mid-decade, however, Edmonton city councillors contemplated asking the school board to reduce the instruction week to four days. Calgary trustees briefly considered shortening the school day by one hour and revising the salary schedule accordingly, for an estimated saving of $155,655.

Students of Eye Hill School, south of Provost, in 1930. Some children stayed home from school in the winter because their families could not afford warm clothing.

Calgary also entertained the idea of charging fees for Grade 12. The Lethbridge board actually did institute partial Grade 12 fees, to deal with high school overcrowding. It decided that any student who took longer than five years to complete the four-year high school course must pay $15 a subject, or up to $100 annually, for the extra time.

strict accordance with the School Act, but that particular clause had never before been enforced in Calgary. So teachers found it very unsettling, especially since board officials, when pressed by an *Albertan* reporter, allowed that the intention was "to facilitate school reorganization." This sounded suspiciously like a prelude to wholesale layoff.

The good news was that Calgary staff was not being cut. The bad news was that salaries were being cut — right down the line. The affair caused a public uproar, and fourteen 'prominent local women' organized a meeting at the Grand Theatre to force the school board to cease and desist.

One curious Calgary cost-cutting move created a full-scale public hassle in 1935. Every June for the previous four years, the city's teachers had been required to sign a "waiver of contract" permitting salary reductions. At its meeting on Thursday, May 16, 1935, however, the board suddenly "terminated" all contracts. If they wanted to keep their jobs, every teacher must reapply forthwith. This was actually in

Among the employees affected was William Aberhart, principal of Crescent Heights High School, who was upset for two reasons. "I do not think I should be asked to apply for the position I have held for 25 years," he declared in his regular radio broadcast from the Prophetic Bible Institute the following Sunday. And secondly, "remarks" had been made about his having taken some days off to devote to Social

Mahal. Much plant life would appear, and veritable zoos of animal life. The key was flexibility — to let younger pupils proceed at their own individual pace, and in later years to accommodate "high school leavers" as well as university-bound students. The great showpiece, however, was the Enterprise System, to be used up to the Grade 6 level to teach written and oral English along with health, citizenship, drama, music and art.

Alberta wasn't leaving the process entirely up to chance or childish whim, however. An array of appropriate "enterprises" had been selected, McNally explained. Pupils and teachers would confer, and decide upon one or more that appealed to everybody. They would all discuss how the work should proceed, and then the children would organize themselves into committees and carry

Empty desks at Coaldale in 1928. The drought that drove thousands of people out of the South forced the closure of many schools.

This demonstration had no precisely discernible result, but in any event by late June only four contracts remained in doubt: those of Miss F. Todd, E.J. Thorlakson, C.A.L. Maberley and H.H. McKim. All were members of both the ATA and the Canadian Labour Party (Communist), and stood accused of "alleged political activities in school board affairs both inside and outside of school." But their contracts too were duly ratified after Superintendent F.G. Buchanan interviewed and cleared them, although the Trades and Labour Council registered a protest anyhow.

If city boards and teachers were troubled, distress in the countryside was acute. A 1931 editorial in the *A.T.A. Magazine* waxed indignant over a northeastern school board which was brazenly advertising for a teacher at $550 a year, ignoring the provincial minimum of $840. Two years later the Education Department reported that more than 600 rural teachers were below the minimum, and the Alberta School Trustees' Association was asking the government to reduce it to $600.

Credit planning. There apparently had even been reference at the board meeting to not "making a martyr" of him. So he wanted it clearly understood, he said, that he was grateful to the trustees for granting him those four days' leave without pay. What was more, he added, "I assure the public that I shall make up the time... in other ways, for the sake of the students."

That far more was at stake than Aberhart's four-day leave became clear within a week when the trustees revealed their latest stratagem. The good news was that staff was not being cut, as had been feared. The bad news was that salaries were being cut — right down the line. This was to take effect in September, but the cash shortage also made immediate *de facto* reductions necessary.

Meanwhile the whole affair had caused a public uproar, and fourteen "prominent local women" organized a meeting at the Grand Theatre to force the school board to cease and desist. Reporters estimated that some 1,500 people crowded into the theatre and seven hundred had to be turned away. In the course of the proceedings the original demand was enlarged to include the right to collective bargaining, equal pay, and freedom to engage in politics.

The ATA tried hard to hold the salary line, but it was an impossible task. At the 1937 convention, secretary John Barnett charged that spending reductions were producing sweatshop conditions" in Alberta schools, and hundreds of thousands of

Blanche McLean chopping wood. School boards sometimes paid teachers bonuses for doing janitorial work.

out the enterprise. Thus objectionable traits like excessive individualism, selfishness and laziness would give place to an enthusiastic group spirit, and learning would seem more like a game. It hardly needs be said, of course, that in this happy atmosphere the use of the strap, although it would officially be allowed for many years to come, was rapidly diminishing.[10]

Even the higher grades acquired an approximation to Enterprise, in the newly minted Social Studies program, a curious hybrid that incorporated bits of history, geography, civics and current events, with more than a touch of sociology. Such coherence as Social Studies possessed was seemingly derived from the notion of "themes," like the progressive Greek studies at Lincoln School. In 1939, three years after it was introduced, the *Lethbridge Herald* enthused about how

When Premier J.E. Brownlee announced the closure of the local Normal School in 1932, Camrose mayor James A. Code led a delegation of 300 to Edmonton to protest the move.

dollars remained owing to rural teachers because country boards were unable, or unwilling, to pay them. Polemics aside, nonpayment of rural salaries was mostly a case of "unable."▲

A request formulated by Alberta trustees at their 1937 convention was equally unlikely to succeed. They wanted the province to refinance the entire bonded debt of Alberta schools (amounting to about $10,500,000) and to finance current expenditures at lower interest. But the provincial government was broke too, and defaulting on its bonds. All it could do at that point was accede to the trustees' previous request, namely to lower the minimum salary. So the least a teacher could officially be paid now dropped to $620 per year.

A year later, in September 1938, provincial school super-visor H.C. Newland acknowledged that the shortage of rural teachers was "probably the worst in history." The Education Department knew of at least two dozen country schools unable to open, and the minuscule and chancy salaries were a prime cause. Not for many years to come would the Alberta school system again experience anything approaching prosperity. The impressive thing is that it survived at all, and would recover a decade later in remarkably good order.

—*V.B.*

▲The *Medicine Hat News* reported in the summer of 1937 that the parents of thirty pupils in Grades 8, 9 and 10 in nearby Winnifred could no longer afford to pay room and board so they could attend the high school in Foremost. These were "distressing times in Alberta, with the many crop failures," they explained. Therefore plans had been made to establish classes at Mrs. Joe Fisher's house.

Donalda J. Dickie, prolific writer and mainstay of the province's Normal Schools, denied the radicalism of the educational changes that were taking place.

much could be learned by taking up sugar, for example, and tracing its provenance, manufacture and marketing. This would touch on geography, customs of other lands, chemistry, agriculture "and practically every phase of learning."

The boys and girls were very pleased to be less dependent on textbooks, said the *Herald*. The new system was especially advantageous in the study of history, "a subject that has been changing from day to day with fast-moving events," thus making history books obsolete. Instead, Lethbridge students were actively compiling their own sources of knowledge by clipping magazines and newspapers.[11]

Parents soon began to see the changes. The twelve years of schooling, previously split into elementary and high schools, now featured three levels: elementary (Grades 1-6), intermediate (7-9), and high school (10-12). The purpose was to facilitate "flexibility." Edmonton and Calgary both established intermediate schools by the spring of 1936.

Another momentous change was to greatly reduce the number of formal examinations. When the decade opened, examinations were set for every class from Grade 3 on — by school boards in elementary school, by the province from Grade 8 upward. When the decade closed, most of these were gone; teachers decided whether their pupils should be promoted, on the basis of tests or the year's work. Only Grade 9 (high school entrance) and Grade 12 (matriculation) students must still write final exams handled by the department.

Examinations were bad for both teachers and students, progressive educators believed. "It is a most regrettable fact... that high school teachers should be judged, and judged almost solely, by the number of passes their students make at departmental examinations," declared a speaker at the 1933 High School Teachers' Convention, reported by the Calgary *Albertan*. Preparation for the exams forced teachers to do all their students' thinking for them, he said; no wonder these youngsters graduated without learning how to make important judgements. In similar vein, at a 1935 convention, University of Alberta president R.C. Wallace informed high school teachers that U of A entrance requirements were being made less "rigid" and "formal" in order to free teachers to express themselves individually.

Moreover, the remaining exams were now evaluated by letters, not percentages. Such reforms

[10] In May 1934 the Edmonton Public School Board's management committee recommended that trustees require detailed strapping reports every two months to keep teachers, in the words of the *Edmonton Journal* from "overdoing it." The paper listed some recent offenses: theft, smoking, rudeness to teachers, fighting, talking, throwing spitballs, copying during tests, swearing, exploding bullets in the classroom, spilling ink on another boy, forging notes, signing own report. The maximum punishment allowed in Edmonton was eight strokes across the palm. There were different sorts of excess, however. That August a country teacher who lined up and strapped fifteen of his seventeen pupils, and was thereupon fired by his school board, was appealing his dismissal.

Edmonton's inflammatory mayor Joseph A. Clarke welcomed delegates to the Lamont Teachers' Convention by comparing teachers to stenographers, who ought to remember who they were working for (the taxpayers) and stay out of politics. ATA representative H.C. Clark described the mayor's remarks as 'a lot of hooey.'

were intended to lessen competitiveness, it was explained, and reduce the incidence of both superiority and inferiority complexes. They also made it impossible, before the end of Grade 9, to gauge the relative efficiency of different school jurisdictions, schools or, for that matter, teachers.

The high school population meanwhile had grown by almost a third between 1930 and 1934, when it topped 30,000. After 1938 school divisions began to establish residences in the towns for high school students from the country, a not very satisfactory expedient. In the cities, secondary schools were able to provide a considerable choice of subjects, and a wide range of extracurricular activities. Calgary's Western Canada High, for instance, had a newspaper (*The Western Mirror*) and a yearbook (*The Acatec*), and an array of clubs that ranged from aeronautics to French.

In 1932 the Journal reported that Edmonton high schools, following the lead of Calgary and Winnipeg, would now drop voluntary cadet training because it was "militaristic," and therefore "brutalizing" to boyish minds. A special committee was named to consider an "extended physical education program" to replace it. This was not to consist of "a system of formal drill imposed by external authority and requiring automatic response to the word of command," however, "but rather a rich and varied program of opportunities for children to express themselves."

Industrial and commercial training, which already existed, now became widely available, as high school teachers' organizations campaigned vigorously to promote vocational training for "the non-scholastic." Complex schemes were developed to combine vocational and academic studies in the new "composite" high schools. Art, music and drama were burgeoning; previous generations of Albertans had considered these things very much optional extras, outside the strictly academic. Sixteen school music and drama festivals were held in 1932. These could be quite substantial; in May 1938 the *Medicine Hat News* reported that 1,200 children would be participating in the local

¶¶Newspapers and magazines, however, would not always remain unreserved supporters of the Deweyist reforms as they had been. By the 1980s steadily declining newspaper readership was widely attributed to an alarming increase in illiteracy — which, conservatives pointed out, could in turn be attributed to the New Education so lavishly supported by the newspapers themselves.

In the drybelt education was disappearing
BUILDINGS WERE ABANDONED AND SCHOOLYARDS RETURNED TO THE DESERT

"No rain: No crop: No taxes: No school: Why do parents put such a penalty on children as to keep them in this desert? What a world. What a people." So wrote the despairing secretary-treasurer of one hard-pressed central Alberta school district, in a letter to Lindsay A. Thurber, school inspector for the Berry Creek area east of Drumheller.[A]

The heartfelt plaint of Thurber's anonymous correspondent perfectly described the province's hardest-hit region: the south-central drylands. There drought and depopulation resulted in abandoned buildings, and overgrown schoolyards where tumbleweed rolled among placidly grazing cows.

"Impossibility of continuing on account of economic conditions and people moving out of the area has resulted in the closing of 65 school districts in the Berry Creek," reported the *Medicine Hat News* of July 6, 1933. (At the time, the province had more than 3,000 districts.)

Far from being able to pay school taxes, many citizens were on relief. In 1934, when an estimated 1,200 men in the Drumheller region were jobless, relief recipients at the village of Wayne actually went on strike. They wanted a 50 per cent increase in grocery vouchers, plus an allowance for rent, light and heat. Their children followed their example, incidentally, setting up school picket lines to protest a reduced milk allowance, but capitulated five days later.

Teacher layoffs became wholesale. In March 1933 the *Lethbridge Herald* claimed that 600 were unemployed throughout the province. Financial factors were not the only cause for dumping a teacher, of course; nor was incompetence. The local people just might not like his or her personality or lifestyle.

"We have no complaint," a parent acknowledged in another letter to School Inspector Thurber. "...The real cause of the dissatisfaction among others is that she would seldom

Glenbow Archives, NA-4359-3

Miss Murphy, the teacher at Braylake school in 1939 in the British Block, northwest of Medicine Hat, poses with her students, Terrence, Nellie, Robert and Mary Stevens. For many who stayed, opportunities for education dried up and blew away with the soil.

go to the Gospel Hall on Sundays and went to dances."

Pity indeed the lot of the hapless rural teacher. On one memorable occasion in 1938, however, just after the government lowered the minimum salary to $620 a year, some of them struck back. That fall, coincidentally or otherwise, fifteen teachers in the similarly stricken Sullivan Lake school district suddenly resigned — just before school was to open.

—*VB*

[A]Quoted by David Jones in his monograph *A Strange Heartland: The Alberta Dry Belt and the Schools in the Depression*, in *The Dirty Thirties in Prairie Canada*, R.D. Francis and F.H. Ganzevoort, eds. (Vancouver, Tantalus Press, 1981).

3,325 school boards were far too many

CONSOLIDATION MEANT BIGGER SCHOOLS AND A DIMINISHED PARENTAL ROLE

At the dawn of the Thirties there were 3,325 school boards in Alberta. Several, like those in Calgary, Edmonton and other larger towns, ran a system of schools. Most ran one school, a few ran two schools, and some ran no school at all, yet continued to function.

School "consolidation" was therefore the aim of the UFA government, but its Education minister couldn't get it through his own caucus. Rural members, reflecting determined rural opinion, did not want to forfeit local control of the local school, and not entirely for reasons educational. The citizenry feared bigger school districts would almost certainly mean higher taxes.

Teacher wages in the local school were often kept far below the specified provincial minimum of $840 a year. Some teachers were trying to live on $10 a week or less. Schools were routinely closed during harvesting and seeding time. Some didn't function in winter. To cut costs and keep tax rates stable, writes John W. Chalmers in *Schools of the Foothills Province* (University of Toronto Press, for ATA, 1967), some rural trustees would close the school and dismiss the teacher after 160 days — or even less. All this would change with consolidation, so school trustees, of whom there were some 10,000 in Alberta, determinedly opposed it.

UFA Education Minister Perren Baker argued in vain that consolidation would improve school administration, reduce costs and relieve, not penalize, local taxpayers. He was almost certainly right. Moreover, there were no high schools in the country; the best a local board might manage was Grade 9, if the current teacher was capable of it. Baker argued that consolidation of small local districts into larger "divisions" would cure these ills — a dubious proposition, however, since much of the trouble lay in sparse population, long distances and bad roads. In any event, although Perren Baker twice presented such a plan to the legislature, in 1928 and again in 1930, he was twice thwarted by the opposition of its farmer members.

The Social Credit government that took over in 1935 under the leadership of school principal William Aberhart was much more sympathetic. By then, as the Rev. Peter Dawson, MLA for Little Bow, observed during one debate, conditions endured by rural teachers were so unattractive that they usually pondered only two ambitions: to get out of teaching or get a job in town. Within a year Premier Aberhart, who also served as Education minster, proposed a plan whereby 43 to 45 divisions would "embrace" the existing country districts. In 1936 he argued the case before meetings of notably unenthusiastic trustees. When the premier confronted 500 southern Alberta school board members at the Palliser Hotel, the *Calgary Herald* described their mood as "militantly inquisitive."

Aberhart assured them that the divisional councils, composed of members elected by the local boards, would be pure-split administrative. (As things worked out, council members would actually be elected by delegates from subdivisions of the larger units.) Each division would have a superintendent (the education department's inspector now functioning in a dual role) who visited the districts. But there would be no interference with local autonomy, the premier promised: "If there's anything I stand for, it's decentralization of authority." The trustees voted non-support, almost unanimously.

Legislation to establish the scheme nevertheless got first reading a month later and, despite reluctance on the part of some government backbenchers, it passed. It provided that the new divisions — not the local boards — would hire the teachers and supervise the schools. The number of trustees in the province would incidentally be reduced from some 10,000 to a few hundred. The amalgamation process began in 1937, when seven hundred southern districts were melded into nine divisions. Forty-eight remote northern

Country Guide, April 15, 1930

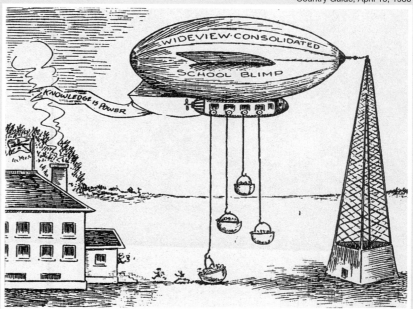

The Country Guide *took a lighthearted look at one of the problems of the consolidated schools, transportation. To parents who saw that their children were being taken out of their sphere of influence, the situation was alarming.*

A 1936 advertisement extols the benefits of consolidation — a variety of courses offered, organized athletics, and specialized teaching staff.

schools became Peace River School Division.

The *A.T.A. Magazine* expressed great approval. The editor's sole regret was that towns, villages and consolidated districts would not be included in the regional division unless they chose to be. As for the divisional superintendents, he wrote, they were sure to be men of such sagacity that "once the public in the areas become accustomed to the new set-up, it will receive endorsement and general support, proving of great advantage to all concerned — pupils, public, teachers and Department."

The legislation was likely necessary and inevitable, but it had a definite downside. Notwithstanding Premier Aberhart's assurances about decentralization, the big units shifted effective control of Alberta's rural schools from local residents to the divisional centres and to Edmonton. The lot of teachers was somewhat improved, but parents lost control of the boards — as had already happened in the cities.

School boards, as bitter trustees continued for some time to protest, were meant to enable local people to run their own schools, and particularly to decide "who can and can't teach our children." Now they had fallen largely under the professional influence of distant educational administrators

and the ATA. Another "professionalising" factor was that larger divisions made it more possible for teachers, ex-teachers and relatives of teachers to win seats as trustees. (This was true of cities as well.) The overall effect of the "big units" was to lessen parental and other local influence, and to centralize control of education in a variety of big units — all distant and all professional.

Administrative reform notwithstanding, however, money remained a serious problem. In February 1937 Aberhart had to admit that teacher salaries were a quarter of a million dollars in arrears. A delegation of rural teachers, headed by Raymond Shaul of Provost, told the legislature that salaries were commonly four months in arrears. Teachers had to beg for money from home to survive, and borrow enough to leave the district when they finally gave up. By December the new Peace River division was broke and its chairman, W.J. Williams of Brownvale, was appealing to the Department of Education: "This is not our baby, it's yours — are you going to let it starve?"

Sporadic but futile protests against consolidation continued for several years, to no avail. When Didsbury area ratepayers in 1938 voted strongly against having their seventeen schools included in Olds School Division No. 31, which would comprise 92 local boards in five subdivisions, the school secretaries were simply ordered to hand over their records by January 2, 1939, and that was that. The Didsbury boards ceased to exist.[A]

At the same time, Premier Aberhart warned a trustees' convention that his government would insist on a uniform curriculum throughout the province. "Individualistic teachings" by different districts would not be tolerated. "I believe in local autonomy and democracy," said he, "but where a child is concerned that is a different matter." Later on, the ratepayers of West Lethbridge Consolidated sued to keep from being absorbed by Lethbridge School Division No.7, and Aberhart as Education minister ended up on the stand, along with his deputy minister, G.F. McNally.

But nothing could stop the big units. By 1939 some 90 per cent of Alberta's rural schools were under the management of 44 divisions. That year C.E. Little, secretary of the Saskatchewan Trustees' Association, attended an Alberta trustees' convention to check out the situation. He returned home saying they seemed economically advisable, but the Alberta government had used "fascist" methods to launch them "in the face of strenuous opposition from a large body of their citizens," and without proper public consultation.

When reporters sought comment from Aberhart, he retorted that he could not understand how anyone could make such a charge "in connection with our progressive steps in education." Big units had been a plank in his 1935 election platform, he noted, when Social Credit won 56 out of 63 seats. If that wasn't endorsement, what was?

Teachers and the ATA were happy with consolidation, however, as promising somewhat better job security and more effective salary negotiations. Developments of even greater benefit were also becoming realities. One of the last acts of the UFA government, in the 1935 session of the legislature, was to pass a bill for which the ATA had lobbied hard and long. The Teaching Profession Act gave legal recognition to teaching as a profession, more or less similar to medicine or law. It also made a slight change in the name of the organization, which would henceforth be called the Alberta Teachers' *Association*.

This recognition was more a matter of principle than practice, however, largely because the legislation lacked one absolutely essential component. Recalcitrant UFA members, unwilling to make ATA membership compulsory, rejected this crucial clause. But the lack was rectified barely half a year later. In March 1936, after what the newspapers called "hectic" debate, the Aberhart government amended the Teaching Profession Act. By a vote of 32 to 16 it made ATA membership mandatory, and further decreed that school boards were to automatically deduct its annual fees from teachers' salaries.

One MLA who questioned this move, I.M. McCune (SC Gleichen), remarked that teachers now seemed to be "desirous of disciplining the trustees." The premier was reassuring, however; the department would allow nothing of this sort, he said. A.J. Hooke (SC Red Deer) said he felt it would do no harm if the teachers *did* have their innings for a change, but this was not the intention. "I suppose it is futile to oppose this bill when so many teachers are members of the House," remarked Liberal leader John J. Bowlen.

Still lacking was any provision for pensions, a less acrimonious proposition which even trustees tended to favour. In 1939 the Teachers' Retirement Fund Act provided such a plan, on a compulsory basis, to which teachers would have to contribute 3 per cent of their salaries. It was high time, editorialized the *Stettler Independent*. Anyhow, there would be little immediate expense, because the government was to match what the fund paid out, not what teachers paid in. Because most Alberta teachers were young, the costs would come later.

—*VB*

Glenbow Archives, NA-2196-12

High Prairie Consolidated High School: The result of a painful economic reality, consolidation of the rural schools was likely unavoidable and inevitable.

[A]With opinions on school administration running strong, provincial and school board politics occasionally became entangled. In December 1938, for example, according to a report in the *Ponoka Herald*, Premier Aberhart declared invalid the election of A.W. Huff as trustee in West Jasper District on Edmonton's western edge. In the October election Huff had defeated Mrs. Dan Mowbray, secretary of the local Social Credit group, by 53 votes; her supporters subsequently protested that seven unqualified voters had cast ballots, and a new vote was ordered. Resentful West Jasper voters thereupon doubled Huff's majority.

festival, then in its sixth year.

Even so, half a century later when observers looked back at the 1930s and those exciting early days of Progressive Education, and traced the results into the 1990s, many would be inclined to give Deweyism a very mixed report card. Some Deweyist ideas, such as providing industrial/commercial alternatives to a strictly academic high school curriculum, simply made good sense. Much Deweyist criticism of the old regime had likewise been well-founded. Doubtless there had been more "dull routine" than was strictly necessary, and more and tougher examinations than anybody really needed, and perhaps too much reliance on drill and the strap. Maybe the system had needed some shaking up.

But the real aim of progressivism was not mere improvement. It unquestionably was revolution. The central and openly avowed progressivist goal was to destroy the foundations on which the culture of the western world was built. Its leaders wanted to reconstitute society on an entirely different set of assumptions about the purpose of human life and how it should be conducted. And knowingly or unknowingly, Alberta's progressivist teachers absorbed, acted upon and disseminated John Dewey's basic philosophy.

Thus what began with classroom sandboxes would go on to eliminate phonics in reading, along with grammar and memory work of any sort, and to gradually oust classic English literature and coherent history courses. Within a generation "social studies" would have so absorbed and diluted any historical content as to render history barely recognizable. By the 1990s elementary school pupils might typically jump from the Canadian fur trade, to Tudor England, to the War of 1812, without the slightest hint of chronology or connection.

By the 1990s the development of pupil "self-esteem" would have become the declared goal of education — not self-esteem based on accomplishment, just self-esteem *per se*. This represented one major component of Deweyism — his "child-centred" model of education — carried to its logical conclusion. And since God had become a prescientific superstition, not fit for the classroom, any suggestion of objective moral truth would be supplanted by a steady indoctrination in sexuality, ecology and feminism.

Thus the progressivist educators, with Albertans well in the lead, had entirely transformed Canadian schools. In so doing, they were also transforming their society. By the end of the century, it would be the first in the entire history of mankind to overwhelmingly reject the supernatural — the first in which vast numbers of citizens acknowledged no supernatural power as authoritative, and none was in any real sense recognized by the state.

To attribute all this to one John Dewey is, of course, excessive. Dewey was pre-eminently a man of his times, and his philosophy was the product of his era. But he became a vital spokesman for it. He took hold of the philosophies dominant in academe in the late 19th century — pragmatism, humanism, scientism — and showed that they could be applied to education. Moreover, he was the first philosopher since his soulmate Rousseau to interest himself in elementary education. Once he had it all formulated, however muddily, he preached it as a religion: the religion of mental enlightenment, scientific advance, human development, material progress, societal improvement and all-round decency. How could anyone oppose all these fine things?

At the end of the century, notwithstanding many ominous consequences and sporadic attempts at reform, Alberta's educational establishment would remain solidly Deweyist, progressivist and relativist: schools, universities, bureaucracies and all, from the most modest kindergarten teacher to the most august professor. How could it be otherwise? Whatever teaching methods had preceded the great revolution of the 1930s would have long since been thoroughly discredited, or forgotten, or both.

Deputy Minister of Education Fred McNally played a key role in re-writing school curriculum during the first Social Credit administration.

It is unfortunate that the Hon. Perren Baker, minister of Education in the provincial Cabinet, has refused to consider the Calgary School Board's request for a provincial grant of $50 a year for every non-resident pupil enroled upon the attendance lists of city high schools... During the present time these students are finding it increasingly difficult to meet their education expenses and their number is augmented by students from the districts which have been forced to discontinue high school education, who are also in financial difficulties... Many [rural] students, especially girls, are attempting to work their way through high school by doing housework for their board and lodging, and the Calgary board is naturally unwilling to turn any of these applicants for education down.
—*Albertan*, October 9, 1931

THE REVOLUTIONARIES

Going away to school

Getting an education meant going further from their homes for more and more children as the decade wore on. [A] A horse at Plamondon pulling a heated caboose. [B] Even dogs helped solve the problem. [C] The school at Craigmyle provided this cart in 1935. [D] As early as 1919, Lomond Consolidated School was "busing in" students. [E] Audrey, Robert, Donna, Jean, Gerald and Melvin Kernaghan of Langdon rode Black Diamond to school. [F] More Langdon commuters. [G] Edmonton students took the streetcar home from Collège St-Jean. [H] By 1935, Lethbridge School Division No.7 boasted an impressive fleet of buses.

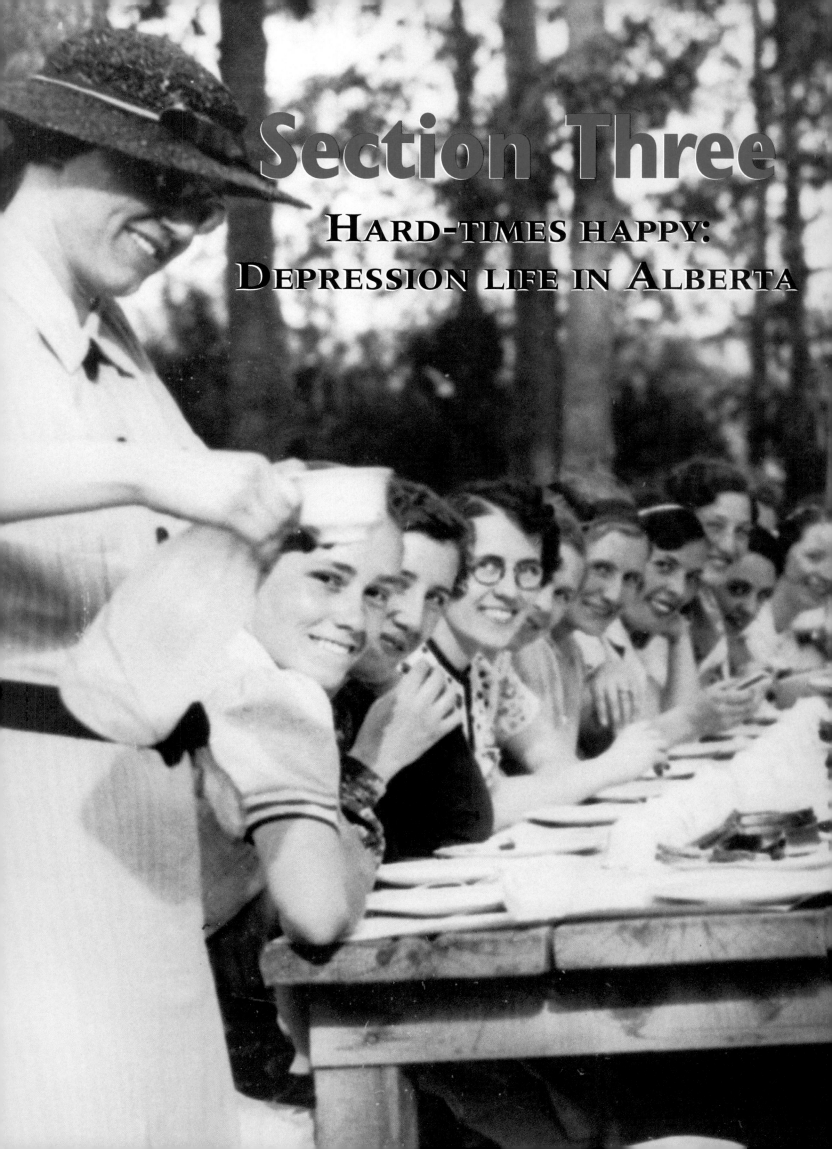

Section Three

HARD-TIMES HAPPY:
DEPRESSION LIFE IN ALBERTA

As the Great Depression spread its paralysis through the economy of Calgary and Edmonton, one effect was to reverse the trend towards spectator entertainment and restore to a degree the art of creating your own. While the movies certainly grew in popularity, so too did amateur theatre. Other activities like dancing, swimming, lawn bowling and just plain walking in the parks or reading in the library, which cost little or nothing, enjoyed a great renaissance. Likewise the communal picnic, typified by this unidentified church group here in Edmonton's Victoria Park in 1937.

CHAPTER ONE

The Edmonton boom seemed back at last when the big bust hit

SOME HURLED THEMSELVES OFF THE HIGH LEVEL BRIDGE,
SOME MARCHED, SOME LIVED IN RIVERBANK CAVES,
AND SOME ELECTED FIGHTING JOE CLARKE TO RUN THE TOWN

by RIC DOLPHIN

The big, black High Level Bridge, which eerily resembles an elongated scaffold, has since its completion in 1913 become Alberta's most popular public suicide site. Through the century more than a hundred despondent souls climbed the iron guardrail and flung themselves into the abyss. Dropping 150 feet, they hit the water hard at 105 mph and succumbed to what coroners call "deceleration injuries" as their organs were wrenched from their moorings, causing massive internal bleeding and not quite instantaneous death.

In no decade during the twentieth century did more people choose this final solution than in the 1930s. Leafing through newspapers from those bleak years, one is struck by the desperation that drove people to such an end in those days when suicide was still very much unthinkable.

The western Christian world has long considered suicide reason for banishment from Heaven. Death by suicide customarily means the victim is buried outside a consecrated graveyard. Before the government of Prime Minister Pierre Trudeau repealed the law in 1972, attempted suicide was a Criminal Code offence. To jump off the High Level Bridge in the Thirties required a great deal of resolve, and those who accomplished it were often curiously punctilious.[1]

One was Miriam W. Card, a 37-year-old woman on provincial relief, recently abandoned by her husband. In the early evening of September 27, 1935, she was seen walking back and forth along Whyte Avenue pushing a white wicker baby carriage containing her 2½-month-old son Johnny and a small stepladder. At 6:30 p.m. she parked the carriage on the sidewalk of the bridge, took her baby into her arms, climbed onto the ladder, and jumped. A passing motorist saw her go over, spotted the two bodies floating down the river, and telephoned the police from Steen's Drug Store.

Before her suicide, Mrs. Card had returned some milk tickets and food vouchers to the relief office with a note reading, "I shall not be needing the enclosed."

When she jumped, she left her coat and purse in the meticulously

---

> **Thinking he was a hobo, the Edmonton police grabbed a foreigner who was cooking himself a meal down by the railway yards. He was released when he pulled a roll of $903 out of his sock. It seems that the old lad was riding the bumpers to the Peace River to take up a homestead and was going north as cheaply as possible.**
> — *Medicine Hat News*, April 4, 1930

---

[1] Kenneth Blatchford, the air-minded former mayor (1924-26) and MP (1926-30) for whom the field was named, was one of the suicides recorded during the decade. In the early morning of April 23, 1933, Blatchford, who was in ill health, left his home at 7866 Jasper Avenue, walked down to the river by the Highlands Golf Course, waded in, and shot himself in the temple with a revolver.

As relief rolls mounted, taxpayers demanded what would later be known as "workfare." Manual labour was required in compensation for relief payments. Here an Edmonton crew unloads snow from a wagon at an empty lot at 103rd Avenue and 100th Street. The date is December 12, 1935. The old provincial clinic is visible in the background.

"Be it ever so humble" took on a new meaning to scores of Edmontonians who at the depth of the Depression called Grierson Hill dump home. For better or worse, they had only to raise their eyes and perceive that things weren't all that bad for some people. The Hotel Macdonald is above them.

[2]Edmonton's bank clearings totalled $358,961,731 in 1929 compared with $351,325,045 in 1928. Clearing house officials attributed the increase solely to expanding volume of business and not to an extraordinary circumstance such as occurred in 1928 when Canadian National Railways cleared an enormous sum to purchase the northern railways from the Alberta government.

clean carriage. Inside her purse was a suicide note: "Will anyone seeing my act please notify the police as I should like verification of my death. The carriage and the coat will be taken to the relief dept., I think, if someone is notified." A newspaper reported that the note was "written in pencil and in a firm hand."

In the 1930s, such tragedies were a constant reminder of how grim things had become for the quarter of the population that was out of work. Edmonton's problems seemed even worse because the city's hopes had been so recently dashed. Since its early boom ended just before the Great War, Edmonton had struggled back and forth between times of gain and setback, but rarely lost the youthful optimism that foresaw prosperity just around the corner. Edmontonians remembered that incredible era between 1901 and 1913 when the population increased from 4,200 to 70,000.

By the 1920s cautious optimism seemed justified, even though the war and postwar recession had reduced the city's population from 72,000 in 1914 to less than 59,000 in 1921. Around mid-decade grain prices strengthened, Alberta croplands increased from 28 million acres to 35 million — most of the new ones were in the north — and Edmonton's agriculturally driven economy promised to boom again. With more jobs available, Edmonton boasted 75,000 inhabitants in 1929.

By then it seemed that the Roaring Twenties had at last reached Edmonton. The city's publicly owned telephones, electricity companies and street railway system were profitable; municipal taxes were reduced; one year, civic employees even received a 10 per cent raise. Enrolment at the University of Alberta rose from 700 in 1920 to close to 1,600 by 1929. A zoo, a river valley park system, and several golf courses had been established. Blatchford Field, the municipal airfield named by Mayor James Douglas for his mid-decade predecessor Kenneth Blatchford, was expanded, and given lights and a new hangar. The airstrip became a symbol of the citizens' confidence that Edmonton was truly the gateway to the north.

There were of course dire prognostications emanating from the stock market collapse of October 1929, but as 1929 turned into 1930 things had rarely looked better for Edmonton: record bank clearings ($7 million over 1928),[2] near-record construction ($5.7 million, the highest since the boom year of 1913), near-record sales of city property acquired during the previous recession (up 20% over the previous year), and record filings for homestead land in the district (up 25%). For the northern city, 1929 was *the* Roaring Twenty.

No surprise then that there was little thought of suicides, soup kitchens, hobo jungles or civic bankruptcy as the New Year of 1930 was ushered in on a mild Tuesday night at Edmonton's Hotel Macdonald. Five hundred people attended a party fulsomely described by the *Journal* as possessing "scenes of hilarity and gaiety almost without parallel in the history of an institution famous for the excellence of its various celebrations":

> Over the orchestra stand was the figure of a huge clock face, its hands pointing close to the midnight hour. Higher and higher rose the uproar until it almost deafened — the Old Year was passing, the New Year was coming.
>
> Out went the lights — then in the weird light of a single powerful ray, the feeble, hoary-headed figure of the Old Year, as typified by Father Time, held his lantern in shaking hands against the face of the big clock.
>
> Two minutes to midnight — "Goodbye, Old Year!" blared the noise-makers — and then the clock face was torn apart by a vision of dazzling child beauty — the fair and innocent New Year in the person of dainty little Miss Betty Flavin, dancing pupil of Miss Dorothy Kinney — in modish top hat and swagger cane, bowing to the cheering, enthusiasm-maddened crowd.

Such enthusiasm continued into the New Year, encouraged by even more cheerful statistics.

In April, for example, Edmonton posted the fifth highest building total in Canada: $922,480 for the month compared with Calgary's $847,888, and moving Edmonton up from fifteenth place in April 1929. By May 16,601 telephones were in service, up from 15,899 a year earlier. And in April the homestead filings at the Edmonton branch of the Dominion Lands Office broke the records and exceeded the previous April's total by 527 to 349. Similar gains in filings were reported in Grande Prairie and Peace River, towns much serviced by Edmonton.

As late as October 1930, Alderman J.T.J. Collison could still sound bullish. "There is a world depression, we can not get around that, but Edmonton, Alberta and Canada are suffering least of all," Collison told an inaugural gathering of something called "Prosperity Week" "... What is needed is to move away from the depression idea. There are men here and all over Canada who could go ahead with development schemes but, through fear, are not doing it. Alberta has just had her natural resources returned to her and there is a grand opportunity now to go ahead with development work."

Either Collison was as ingenuous as little Betty Flavin or he was putting the bravest face on what, even by October of 1930, was shaping up to be an unmitigated disaster. It must, after all, have been hard to relinquish the reprieve; hard to believe that many of those in possession of the sorts of resources necessary to accomplish that "development work" were now contemplating leaps from high structures in other cities. But believe it the Collisons soon had to do, as the miserable realities of the Dirty Thirties started to arrive by the boxcar load.

Between 1929 and 1936 the city's population increased from 75,000 to 85,000, with more than half that increase caused by the influx of easterners who had lost their labouring jobs, and prairie farmers and hired hands rendered destitute by ludicrous prices. (Between January 1930 and January 1931, the price of a bushel of No.1 Northern wheat fell from $1.11 to 34 cents.) In the darkest years of the Depression — 1930 through 1936 — an average of 15,000 people were claiming relief. Between 1931 and 1938, the tax assessment on Edmonton properties dropped from $66.5 million to $53.5 million, and the value of building permits, which had been $5.7 million in 1929, declined steadily, bottoming out at $428,000 in 1938.

At 6:30 p.m. on September 27, 1935, Miriam Card parked her baby carriage on the sidewalk, took her 2½-month-old son Johnny in her arms, and jumped off the High Level Bridge.

Add to this dismaying situation a steady flow of homeowners and businesses defaulting on their taxes (tax arrears went from $465,000 in 1929 to $1.2 million in 1934), and a resulting stockpile of forfeited properties on which the city now had to make mortgage payments to the banks, and it might seem miraculous that Edmonton did not go bankrupt — miraculous until one takes into account the fact that just about every other city in North America was suffering similar debt crises, and the banks could hardly gain from taking over assets that were worth next to nothing and had no market.

By the 1930s Edmonton's social character had already established itself. The northern capital was predominantly a working-class town full of railway workers, meat packers and miners who lived in unpretentious neighbourhoods like Calder, Norwood, suburban Beverly and Parkdale. A majority of these workers belonged to American-affiliated unions that were becoming inclined to socialism, communism and other anti-capitalist notions.

As early as 1924, the Communist Party of Canada had been active in Edmonton. That year it

The Bennett Buggy, meaning the family car now pulled by a horse because buying gasoline was out of the question, was far more familiar in the country than the city. The odd one, however, made it into town.

It was a case of taking a thrashing or going to jail for Edward Grant, 17, John Scott, 19, and James Hebden, 17, when they appeared before Magistrate P.C.H. Primrose in the city police court Monday afternoon on charges of stealing a car. The boys took the thrashing, which was administered in the cell at the police station before they left. The fathers administered the punishment in the cases of Scott and Grant, while an older brother took care of James Hebden.

"Which would you rather have: a first-class thrashing or go to jail?" Magistrate Primrose asked the trio.

"Jail," the three responded in unison.

"Well, I'm afraid you will have no choice in the matter," they were told.
—*Edmonton Journal,* January 7, 1930

Advances in photo technology made possible night photography, which this cameraman used to secure glimpses of Edmonton's 1930s night life. While most people did what entertaining they could at home, downtown streets remained busy after dark. Right, Jasper Avenue, 1930, looking east from 102nd Street. (Opposite page) Another view of Jasper Avenue, 1939.

City of Edmonton Archives, EA-10-226

[3]Margaret Crang was elected for the first time in 1933 at the age of 23, then re-elected in 1935. In 1936 she attended the world peace conference in Brussels as a delegate of the local branch of the League Against War and Fascism, and toured the main rebellion battlefronts of the Spanish Civil War. On her return, the *Edmonton Bulletin* (October 21) asked her to confirm reports that she had taken up arms in defence of the Spanish government; she responded that she had "merely tried the feel of a gun, firing in the general direction of the rebel lines." She ran unsuccessfully for the provincial legislature three times between 1936 and 1940. Crang became a reporter for the *Montreal Gazette*, and spent much of her later life searching for a cure for Cushing's disease, with which she was afflicted, and died in Vancouver in 1992.

[4]Hon. Frank Oliver, founder of the *Bulletin* in 1880, minister of the interior in the Laurier government, and the man whose political manipulations made Edmonton the provincial capital, thereby permanently establishing the city as an enduring rival to Calgary, died on Friday, March 31, 1933, at the age of 80. He was then in Ottawa, acting as a special officer on grade separation for the board of railway commissioners. His son John, a musician and a legislative reporter for the paper his father founded, was in the press gallery when Premier Brownlee stood up and announced, "It is my sad duty to inform the House that word has just been received of the death of a man whose name is a household one in Alberta, particularly Northern Alberta. The Hon. Frank Oliver has just died in Ottawa."

had held a meeting at the Rialto Theatre, prompting the provincial government to assign Alberta Provincial Police spies. The Department of National Defence increased the military guard around the armouries during the May Day parades that became an annual event in 1925 and grew steadily during the Depression years, bolstered by the newly recruited armies of the unemployed.

Edmonton was also by now well established as a university and government town employing middle-class professionals, a vocal minority of whom were sympathetic to the fashionable leftist ideas gaining currency in their British motherland. These middle-class "progressives," who included socialists like the "girl lawyer" and mid-decade alderman Margaret Crang (who, at the age of 24, topped the aldermanic polls in 1935)[3] and Canadian Labour party leader and business-

---

There was little thought of suicides, soup kitchens, hobo jungles or civic bankruptcy as the New Year of 1930 was ushered in by 500 party-goers at the Hotel Macdonald, celebrating amid 'scenes of hilarity and gaiety almost without parallel.'

---

man Elmer Roper, were electorally aligned with the workers. So, to a degree, was the *Edmonton Bulletin*, the province's oldest paper, which supported the Liberals.[4]

Meanwhile the founders and rulers of the city, those with the Scottish names for whom most of the landmarks had been named a quarter century earlier, grew less influential in the civic democracy, entrenched in their enclaves of Garneau, Groat and Glenora, staunchly supporting the fiscally responsible elements of council that, for the moment, were on the descendent. For as James MacGregor, in his book *Edmonton: a History* (Edmonton, Hurtig, 1975) pointed out, "No government pursuing orthodox politics could stand the strain of the depression."

The organ of the establishment was the *Edmonton Journal*, a Tory newspaper. On the eve of the 1931 municipal elections its editorial sounded like a voice in the wilderness:

It can be truthfully said that no city in Canada has weathered the stress of the last two years better than Edmonton. Its credit is unshaken, its finances in order, its improvement program has gone steadily forward, its services are being maintained as usual. In fairness a large share of the credit for this favourable position of the municipal affairs must be given to the man who has discharged the dual functions of chief executive and presiding officer of the city council.

The man the paper was endorsing was incumbent Mayor James M. Douglas.[5] Former

CLEAN HEAT GAS

CAPITOL

McNEILL'S TRANSFER TAXI

GREER & CROKEN

"THE STAR MAKER"
CAVALCADE of OLD & NEW SONGS

BILLIARDS

STORAGE

VICTOR CAFE

Swift's
Premium Ham & Bacon

GAINERS
Super

[5]James McCrie Douglas was born February 5, 1867, at Middleville, in what later became Ontario. He moved to Edmonton in 1894 and was elected as a Liberal in the 1909 Strathcona by-election. He was re-elected in 1911 and 1917 but was defeated in 1921 as a Conservative.

[6]On March 7, 1930, an estimated 400 single men marched on the Legislature, carrying red banners and shouting "Long Live the Revolution." Police kept them from entering the building. "Orators in English, German and Russian poured forth their vials of wrath on everything not of the Commune," the *Journal* reported, "while indoors...legislators went about their accustomed business in the decorum of the velvet-hung pillared chamber."

Two things the Depression couldn't take away from the people of Edmonton — the freedom to read, and the beauty of their city. During the Thirties, the Edmonton Public Library almost matched the level of circulation of the Toronto system, a city more than three times as populous.

merchant, farmer and police magistrate for the Northwest Territories, Douglas had been a three-term MP for the old city of Strathcona, and was now trying for his third one-year term as mayor of Edmonton. A business and development promoter by inclination, he had been elected by a substantial majority in the dying months of Edmonton's Roaring Twenty when all the statistics had been bullish and the Depression was something that was happening in the East.

A month and half after his election 100 single men had staged an unemployment march on city hall — the first and smallest of what would be many in the years to come. They were put to work clearing bush. Similar expedients were employed through the remainder of Douglas's first term as the number and strength of such delegations grew. Through that first year of the Depression, however, the growing Communist agitation was directed more at the provincial Legislature than at city hall.[6] The civic government paid unemployed married men $2 a day for four days a week of clearing parks. "We cannot allow our people to starve," said the mayor, "even if it means an increase in the tax rate."

In 1931 the city works department had to padlock the entrance to the giant storm sewer near the Low Level Bridge to prevent what the *Journal* called homeless wanderers from bunking there.

In October, before the November election, a $358,000 unemployment relief program was inaugurated and Douglas was reinstated by acclamation to a second term. By early 1931, though, there were 5,171 unemployed men in the city and the rate was growing at between 300 and 400 every week. Crimes like armed robbery and assault were seemingly on the increase.[7] The city works department had to padlock the entrance to the giant storm sewer near the Low Level Bridge to prevent what the *Journal* called "homeless wanderers" from bunking there.

It was these wanderers — most of them single, male, unskilled immigrants — who complicated the dispersal of relief funds. A *Journal* reporter spent a day and a half incognito at Immigration Hall, a combination soup kitchen and flophouse into which 150 men were crammed when they weren't visiting the relief office at the old Canada Dry Building. The reporter wrote in December of 1930, "I found that conditions were bad, the men were verminous and the food

alternately good and almost uneatable. I also found that many drifters, who would not accept the work offered to them, are included in the ranks of the legitimate unemployed. These men are getting relief from Edmonton to which they are not entitled."

One of the transients told the reporter, "My chum in Vancouver told me they had good relief here, so I hopped a freight. But I'm going to blow right back! Yesterday they offered me another meal ticket if I would sweep the hall. Just catch me working in that lousy place for the price of a meal. I can get fifty cents or a dollar easier by panhandling."

Another complained about being made to attend the relief office twice a day, which cut into his "bumming" time. A colleague "of German extraction" put in, "That is the capitalist system. They won't give you time to parade."

For contrast, the same issue of the paper, in promoting its charitable "Sunshine Fund," included the story of Nona, a three-year-old girl with "silkily golden hair and big blue eyes" who wanted a "dolly" for Christmas, but doubted Santa would oblige. Her father could find no work, and her younger sister was malnourished and crippled from rickets. "We'll be all right as soon as my husband finds work," Nona's mother told the Sunshine reporter. "Don't you bother about us. There are so many people in worse circumstances."

In the summer of 1931, it wasn't the suffering families, but the unemployed single men, led by Communist instigators, who were making trouble. Demonstrations in the market square

Edmonton voters voiced their dissatisfaction with the status quo by repeatedly ousting the mayor. (Left) Reforming Mayor Dan K. Knott buys a poppy from war veteran Wilfrid T. Rice. (Right) Fighting Joe Clarke prepares for his triumphant inaugural speech. (Below) Alderman Margaret Crang, known as "the girl lawyer," stood stalwartly for the leftwing liberal view.

[7] **Statistically, Edmonton crime varied little with the onset of the Depression. But the recurrence of highly publicized crimes but created the impression that the city was suffering from a "crime wave." So accepted did this perception become that the police department and Chief Anthony G. Shute, was accused by politicians and press of both incompetence and corruption. Shortly after his acclamation as mayor, James Douglas announced the appointment of Maj.-Gen. William Griesbach, as head of the inquiry. In late January of 1931 Griesbach released a report that dismissed most of the allegations against the force.**

The years when a new building was a major triumph

BY 1933 EDMONTON CONSTRUCTION WAS DOWN MORE THAN 90% FROM 1929

In the 1930s Edmonton saw so little development that the appearance of the city changed less than in any other decade of the 20th century. Despite a population increase to 85,000 from 75,000, the distance of paved streets only grew from 56 to 62 miles, the extent of sewers from 200 to 210 miles. The value of building permits declined from a high of $5.7 million in 1929 to a low of $428,000 in 1933, a drop of more than 90 per cent. It then rose slowly until the back of the Depression began to break in 1937.

As historian James MacGregor noted in *Edmonton: a History* (Hurtig, 1967), the significant buildings

constructed could be counted on one hand. "Except for a slight increase in population and a further descent into dowdiness, Edmonton did not change during the Thirties. Building-wise and street-wise, it was still the same city it had been when the 1913 boom-time carpenters took off their aprons."

The structures completed in the early part of the decade were an aftermath of the short-lived prosperity of the final years of the 1920s, but their achievement, coming at a time when any hope of further development seemed a pipe-dream, was always celebrated.

In 1930, $350,000 wings were completed on both the Royal Alexandra and University of Alberta Hospitals, increasing the capacity of each by 100 beds and including x-ray facilities and several sun parlours for the recuperation of tuberculosis victims. "In constructing and equipping the

building," enthused the *Edmonton Bulletin* of the latter wing, "the government spared neither effort nor expense in making it worthy to stand alongside the best in the world."

Meanwhile the completion of the four-storey, $500,000 Birks Building provided state-of-the-art office space for dentists and doctors, as well as for the ground-floor jewellery store from which it took its name. "With construction and style as near perfect as builders and architects could make it," said the *Edmonton Journal*, "the new Birks building at 104 St. and Jasper is the most modern building in Edmonton, and is patterned after the latest in construction methods

Though the city was not significantly growing, the number of automobiles was, which made necessary a new crossing over this ravine on 102nd Avenue at 132nd Street which would become known as the Wellington Bridge and would survive for the rest of the century.

adopted in skyscrapers in the east."

That same year saw the building of a $10,000 underpass to the railway tracks on 97th Street, a new regional office on 103rd Street for the Hudson's Bay Company, and a large factory for the manufacture of Canada Dry ginger ale. The $100,000 soda pop facility — "an exact model of the company's Chicago plant," according to the *Journal* — would use the very latest technology to produce ten million bottles a month of the "champagne of ginger ales."

After the opening of the new Canada Dry plant (the old one in the downtown core was taken over by the city and later used as a relief office) pickings were slim in Edmonton development for the next few years. The paving and opening of a two-mile stretch of Calgary Trail South in 1931 rated a headline in the *Bulletin*: "Gleaming Paved Road Now Follows

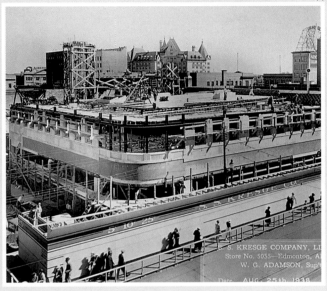

In a decade when every construction project attracted great interest because there were so few of them, much was made of the new Kresge's store under construction (left) at 101st Street and Jasper Avenue, Edmonton's busiest intersection. The Depression, understandably, proved boom times for "five-and-ten" stores, five cents or ten cents being the price of much of their merchandise. This store (above) was built in 1938.

Trail Where Not Long Ago Bullock Carts Wallowed Through Mud." A 600-lamp sign was erected outside the Strand movie theatre that same year, and in 1935 the new Masonic Hall was opened on 100th Avenue.

The most significant development during the lean years was the opening of Canada Packers' $2-million plant in northeast Edmonton in the fall of 1936. This abattoir not only provided employment for more than 200 men, it gave northern Alberta hog farmers the opportunity to sell more hogs. The mayor and the premier were on hand for the grand opening, a 17-piece orchestra played, and the inaugural tour was broadcast over radio.

"I am satisfied that the foresight and initiative exhibited by Canada Packers on this occasion will be more than justified as time goes on," said Premier Aberhart. "The development of our vast resources in the northern part of our province is only in its initial stages. I feel assured that we may look forward with confidence to a very rapid progress and an encouraging expansion in meat production in the near future. In fact I do not hesitate to believe that Alberta will become the greatest meat producing province in the Dominion."

In 1937 the Depression began to abate and large-scale development recommenced. Construction during the remainder of the decade included more than $100,000 worth of improvements to the Blatchford Field airport, a $35,000 renovation of the 820-seat Empress movie theatre, and the creation of two $1 million department stores: the streamlined, granite-clad T. Eaton Company store on 102nd Avenue and 101st Street, and the Hudson's Bay Company store on Jasper Avenue. Both were equipped with the most up-to-date fluorescent lighting,

plate glass windows and escalators.

The city could breathe more easily. As the *Journal* wrote of the Bay store, "The faith in Edmonton's future that is displayed by the decision to proceed with the project counts for all the more because the company has been established here for so long and thus has exceptional opportunities for appraising properly the possibilities of the city and its surrounding territory... Such a construction program must mean a great deal to the city during the coming year, which will be faced with much additional confidence as a consequence."

— R.D.

Whenever a new project was begun, this became an opportune occasion for political sod-turnings and ribbon-cuttings. Thus Mayor Joe Clarke did this honor for the Canada Packers plant, March 16, 1936. (Left to right): A.G. Shute, chief of police; P.W. Abbott; W.J. Greenfield, general superintendent of Bird Construction Company; Mayor Joe Clarke; H.J. Bird, company president; Alderman J.T. McCreath; city engineer A.W. Haddow; L.T. Attwood, livestock buyer for Canada Packers, and Joe Harris, representative of Canada Packers Ltd., Winnipeg.

Before most people in Edmonton knew the meaning of the word "entrepreneur," Harold "Goofy" McMasters developed his own job creation program based on his ability to work hard and his apparent inability to feel embarrassment. This was likely one of his easier gigs (see sidebar), as Edmontonians didn't need to be prodded to the movies. That's Goofy in the Spanish outfit (foreground).

and outside city hall became riotous, with stones being thrown and blows being exchanged between police and demonstrators, as well as between ex-servicemen and those who were consid-ered the less worthy welfare claimants (immigrants, transients, Communists). Arrests were made, firearms seized, and the city and provincial governments, fearful of the more extreme riots in cities like Winnipeg and Regina, bolstered the police force with cavalry units. In early 1931, the mayor prohibited the unemployed from holding parades. The Labourites made much hay from these shows of force, declaring Mayor Douglas to be a tool of the sinister Eastern forces that sought to trample the poor working man.

To help defuse what at times threatened to become an anarchic situation, 12½-cent food tick-ets were handed out to single men, even when they could not prove they had been in the city the required six months. This further strained the already over-taxed city treasury.

No council meeting went by without some new permutation of the organized unemployed — from the Unemployed United Empire Loyalists to the "youth" wing of the National Unemployed Association — making representation to council, declaring itself more worthy than others of aid. They were summarily referred to the unemployment committee, which handed out food tickets or dispatched them to one of the work camps, clearing bush outside city limits for 75 cents a day plus room and board.

By the next civic election, in November 1931, Mayor Douglas and his partisan Civic Government Association, the CGA, were increasingly seen by the panacea-hungry voters as a spent force, unnecessarily antagonistic to the strengthening militancy of the politicized unem-ployed. Even the Ku Klux Klan, which supported a tougher stand against the "undesirable aliens" (immigrant relief workers who were not British subjects), urged in a paper that "citizens unite in defeating Mayor Douglas."

And so began a six-year experiment with more "progressive" mayors, beginning with the elec-tion of Labour party Mayor Daniel K. Knott, a six-year veteran alderman who received 13,014 votes to Douglas's 9,569 in the largest voter turnout in Edmonton history. Four of the twelve aldermen elected were also from the Labour party.

"Figures from the polls," wrote the *Bulletin*, "revealed that D.K. Knott secured a tremendous turn-over in all districts of the city save in the Garneau on the South Side, and in the west end, mainly in the Groat section... The tremendous interest taken in various matters discussed during the campaign, particularly the question of unemployment and the handling of relief work, are the

reasons given for the result of the mayoralty election and also the number of the Labour candidates elected to council."

The Canadian Labour Party, the CLP, to which five members of council now adhered, had as one of its more outspoken local representatives Elmer Roper, who was elected president of the Alberta branches of the CLP in 1933. Described by the *Journal* as "the lean wiry type," Roper was a former Calgary newspaper printer who now ran a printing business in Edmonton, belonged to the Rotary Club, and yet believed in the complete socialization of production and distribution. A sometime candidate for mayor, he would eventually be elected to the post in the late 1950s after William Hawrelak was kicked out for ostensible corruption. (Hawrelak was later exonerated by the courts.)

"I am in the position now to realize more than before the enormous stupidity of the existing economic system," he told the *Journal*. "I am convinced that what is required is a system based on the principle of production for use instead of for individual profit."

Asked why his favourite recreation was golf, Roper joshed: "The game is ideal for a labour man as its exasperations constitute excellent training for patience and persistency."

Certainly aldermen of every political stripe would need these virtues and more in the six hard years to come. City councils were riven ideologically as they strove to remedy a problem well beyond their control. Relief payments continued to soar, businesses continued to go broke, the tax base shrank and the deficits and the debt mounted. Those in the labour camp appealed for more relief to the needy; those of the capitalist CGA wanted taxes lowered to encourage job creation, arguing that prosperity was still just around the next corner. But both sides agreed that now was not the time to be balancing the budget.

Yet no matter the degree of spending, the problem just didn't seem to want to go away. Through his three years in office Knott grew just as exasperated with the continuing clamour from the unemployed as his predecessor had become. The man who had come to office on a promise of

A university education in the Thirties was generally the preserve of the affluent, as this (upper) photograph evidences. It's the junior prom at the University of Alberta, December 8, 1933, strictly a black tie and evening gown affair. (Lower photo) Prohibition was definitely over, as this well-stocked bar at a similar function later in the decade demonstrates.

reasonably sorting things out was dispatching billy-club-wielding police to quell unruly demonstrations just as readily as Douglas had.

"Edmonton has the highest relief scale in Canada," Knott declared at a council meeting towards the end of his third term in 1934. "We treat the unemployed square and all we ask is that they treat us decently in return. With this group all I get is abuse and plenty of it. I have completely lost my patience. They ask one thing and when we give it to them they want something else, and when they get that they still want something more. The idea is to agitate, agitate, agitate."

Knott wasn't the only frustrated one. By the time of the 1934 election, the three-quarters of

Most fun was home-grown and low-cost

THE DEPRESSION CLAIMED THE SYMPHONY AND BORDEN PARK'S 'FUNLAND,' BUT NEW DIVERSIONS AROSE INSTEAD, LED BY LOCALLY-PRODUCED RADIO

Some of Edmonton's recreations were temporarily eclipsed by the Depression. Alberta's capital lost its professional football and hockey teams, the Edmonton Symphony Orchestra was disbanded in 1932, live theatre venues fell into disrepair, and the Borden Park "Funland" with its "Green Rattler" roller coaster and "Tunnel of Love" was demolished in 1935.

Yet the city's pleasures did not disappear, but became diversified in less ambitious — and often more ingenious — directions. When the city ran out of money to build swimming pools, the youngsters of Mill Creek devised a system of dams to create a 150-yard-long swimming hole. There was no funding to build theatres or galleries, but small musical and theatrical groups mounted their productions in places such as the Normal School auditorium or the Palm Court at the Hotel Macdonald.

Vernon Barford's choir at All Saints' Cathedral had long developed a solid coterie of followers (Vol.2, pp.63 & 319). The Women's Musical Club evolved into the Edmonton Civic Opera, funded by lumberman and stern-wheeler manufacturer John Walter (for whom the Walterdale Bridge is named), and managed to bring in classical celebrities such as British cellist Beatrice Harrison in 1931. Productions of the newly formed Edmonton Little

Theatre, the Dickens Society and the University Dramatic Society were regularly broadcast on CKUA.

Radio was then the great entertainment, free once you'd bought the set and paid $2 for a federal licence to own it. Listeners could hear of the progress of the northern bush pilots, or Graydon Tipp and his High-Class Orchestra at the Capitol Theatre, or the plays of up-and-coming Edmonton playwright Gwen Pharis Ringwood who, for $5 a script, wrote works on everything from Socrates's wife to the *New Lamps for Old* series, which cheerfully dramatized the family life of the pioneers.

For some Edmontonians, day trips to neighbouring lakes provided relief from the summer heat. For city children the country could excite dreams and wonders of things wholly unknown to them. What romantic vision of the deep sea might shine in the mind of this youngster (left) contemplating sailboats on Cooking Lake one can only imagine. This photo was taken August 4, 1935. (Above) At night, Edmonton reaches for a touch of Hollywood glamour in this band and dance review at the Strand Theatre, Jasper Avenue and 102nd Street, March 5, 1935.

Then there were the movies. With the advent of the talkies in 1928, cinema became one of the few growth industries of the next decade. Edmonton's Pantages vaudeville house, conthe population still working and paying municipal taxes were becoming tired of the burden they had to bear. The mill rate, less than 40 in 1929 had climbed to 64.[7] This last development came as a result of threatening noises from the banks to which Edmonton owed $2.4 million in 1934.

To the plethora of groups with grievances was added a new and different one: an association of ratepayers dissatisfied with the financial management of the city. At a meeting in the late summer of 1934, they threatened a tax revolt unless council complied with their demands. The group, consisting mainly of business owners and professionals from the well-treed areas of town, called for a full investigation of city finances. Taxpayers should have first rights to temporary city

[7]A mill is a thousandth part of a dollar, or a tenth of one cent. It is applied to the "assessed" value which the city places on every taxable property. Thus a mill rate of 40 applied against a property assessed at $2,000 in the Thirties would result in taxes of $80 for the year. When the rate was increased to 64, the taxes would rise to $128.

verted into a movie house in 1929, became one of several such facilities — including the Dreamland and the Rialto — that provided a low-priced escape from the grimness of the day. None was salubrious until renovations — notably a $30,000 overhaul of the 820-seat Empress in which *The Wizard of Oz* was shown on December 23, 1939 — could be afforded late in the decade. But threadbare seats couldn't detract from time-filling cinematic escapes.

"Chalk this up on your calendar!" wrote the *Journal*, reflecting the general enthusiasm for film in early 1930. "*Dynamite*, Cecil B. De Mille's first talking picture, is coming to the Rialto theatre Monday and will be shown for one complete week. The picture, decked with beautiful gowns, pretty girls, thrills, a glass bathtub, and spectacular mine explosion,

Provincial Archives of Alberta, A 12130

Not everyone, however, was penniless and the Edmonton Golf and Country Club, a good half-hour drive southwest from downtown, continued busy through the decade. On August 16, 1933, these duffers cross the club's suspension bridge that would remain through the decades.

concern that cinema was a corrupting influence, the psychologist noted that a quarter of the boys said that movies taught them how to do wrong without being caught.

Gambling, that favourite vice of older boys, didn't suffer from the Depression either. The parimutuel windows at Exhibition Park, for example, prospered through the decade; one six-day period of thoroughbred racing in 1931 netted $187,000.

The Northlands Exhibition, one of North America's Class A fairs, was

City of Edmonton Archives, Hollingsworth Collection, EA-160-366

Professional sports waned, but Edmontonians found leisure according to their means. Though a good bicycle could set you back as much as $20. they were certainly cheaper than cars. Hence there were entries aplenty for this bicycle race, at a south side athletic park in August 1938.

returns the producer to the highly-coloured type of story with which he made his earlier triumphs."

Young people loved the movies. In 1933, a University of Alberta graduate student in psychology, surveying Grade 6 to Grade 10 students in Edmonton and Calgary, found that 45 per cent attended the movies at least once a week, a further 20 per cent twice a month. Sensitive to the growing

Fish still abounded in the North Saskatchewan, even as large as the whopping sturgeon, held by Matthew Waite and Robert Smith (below) and caught in the river in 1934 at what would later become Rundle Park.

City of Edmonton Archives, Hollingsworth Collection, EA-160-329

initially hard hit and lost $14,800.22 in 1931. But under the managership of lawyer Percy Abbott, who recruited the city's service clubs to sell tickets, enlarged the parade, instigated a free-admission "unemployed day," and arranged popular

jobs, they argued. And they wanted sharp cuts in the mill rate and the city's departments, its borrowing, and its spending increases that in 1934 amounted to $333,000 over the previous year, raising municipal debt to $35 million compared to assets of $25 million.

Council members dismissed the suggestion that a tax revolt might tip the city over the edge into receivership. "The cry that our credit rating would be ruined is not to be taken seriously," said Dr. Robert Colwill. "On the contrary, our credit has ruined us. If we had not been accorded credit so generously in the past, we would not find ourselves in this predicament now."

The tax revolt never materialized, but the influential group succeeded in bringing their con-

---

attractions such as an appearance by Boy Scout founder Lord Baden-Powell in 1932, the fair rallied, making annual profits of $10,000 or more. By the end of the decade attendance was soaring — 132,031 for the first five days of the 1938 exhibition, compared with 87,566 for the same period the year before. Profits paid for a new starting gate and an "eye in the sky" photo-finish camera at its racetrack. The installation of artificial ice in its arena (known as "the barn") allowed it to play host to the re-formed professional hockey team, the Eskimos, starring sharpshooting centre Eddie O'Keefe.

Spectator sports, though no longer major attractions, retained loyal fans. The Edmonton Grads women's basketball team, who won the summer Olympics in both Los Angeles (1932) and Berlin (1936), were still undoubtedly Edmonton's champion athletes (Vol.5, Sect.5, ch.4). The last thing the famous feminist magistrate Emily Murphy (Vol.5, Sect.3, ch.1) did before she went to bed on October 25, 1933, was to ask the score of the Grads' basketball game. That night, at the age of 65, she died in her sleep.

More typical sports were local events. The best was the Edmonton Athletic Association men's hockey team which often packed the 7,500-seat "barn." The worst was heavyweight boxer "Goofy" McMasters, a sometime advertising man and notorious drunk, who lived in Salvation Army residences. McMasters lost 95 of his 96 fights; during one of his bouts at the Empire Theatre, he fell head first into the water bucket.▲

In summers, first Diamond Park, then Renfrew Park (its construction was bankrolled by printer Henry Roche) were venues for the hotly contested baseball games between the

amateur teams sponsored by such local businesses as Frank Wolfe's Edmonton Motors, Chris Shasta's Shasta Cafe and Harry Cohen's Army & Navy store. The games were famous for their city-country rivalry. Insurance man Bill Matthews and his cronies, for example, would gather in the right-field bleachers and heckle Wetaskiwin's farm boy pitcher Elmer Randall with, "Hey, Randall, it's time to feed the pigs!"

Dining out was appropriately frugal. Topping the restaurant list were five Rite Spots, three on Jasper Avenue, which

Glenbow Archives, McDermid Collection, ND-3-7170   Glenbow Archives, McDermid Collection, ND-3-7134 (a)

Once you had scraped together the money for the set and the licence, radio was cheap entertainment. If you had the savvy to put together a bootleg crystal set, it was free. Network shows like Fibber Magee and Molly were the rage, but there was still room for the local celebrities, like announcer Dorothy Horrocks (above) and singer Ruth Morgan at CJCA.

served hamburgers crafted by Mr. and Mrs. Clarence Morris. Doughnuts produced by the new machine at the Metropolitan store also acquired an enthusiastic following.

Those making their own meals often shopped at the City Market. By the early Thirties it boasted fourteen permanent retail businesses, and up to a hundred farmers' stalls selling fresh produce and meat. Opened during that decade, Bre-Win's Meat, run by English butcher Howard Brewin, and Virginia Park Greenhouses, owned by the Danish bulb and flower specialists Marius and Pete Granstrom, survived the Depression years and beyond.

But when times were toughest most people stayed home. Beer parlours, such as the one in the Cecil Hotel, still

cerns to the forefront in the ensuing election, which saw their CGA candidate, lawyer James Ogilvie, pitted against Knott and an even more prominent candidate. This was former mayor Joseph Arthur Clarke (Vols.3 and 5) whose tumultuous political career went back to the prewar boom and who now emerged as the representative of something called the Independent Labour Party. One-time Klondiker and varsity footballer, second-generation Irishman and ostensible pal of former and future prime minister Mackenzie King, Fighting Joe Clarke beat Ogilvie by a narrow margin of 9,865 votes to 9,443. Knott got only 5,920 votes.[9]

Clarke won on the strength of his appeal to both workers and unemployed, and by making fis-

[9]After leaving politics in 1934, Knott returned to his job as a lino-type operator at the *Edmonton Journal*. He was 80 years old when he died in November 1969.

City of Edmonton Archives, Hollingsworth Collection, EA-160-1588

attracted customers, mostly single men. On Saturday night party goers were more likely to gather at a friend's house, where the rugs would be rolled back for dancing to the gramophone or piano.

The treasure hunt, in which party-goers searched for prizes while following clues devised by the hostess, also became a fad.

A soap box derby in which children, some of them well into adulthood, raced their home-made peddle cars, could draw an enormous crowd, like this one that lines McDougall Hill in 1937.

City of Edmonton Archives, Hollingsworth Collection, EA-160-1000

Though by the 1990s Edmonton would spend many millions trying to build, launch, and operate a workable excursion vessel on the North Saskatchewan, very few thousands were spent hammering this one together which plied between the city and Fort Saskatchewan, twenty miles (by river) downstream. The photo was taken on Dominion Day (later Canada Day) 1937.

Edmonton's younger set, the *Journal* reported, played an outdoor version that was really a glorified hike: "Someone must go out ahead and bury the 'treasure' which may be rolls and weiners or bacon and potatoes for roasting. The party sets out with the aid of a chart and finally finds the spot where the 'arrow points' to the 'pirate's chest'. The party then ends in the usual campfire meal and sing-song. Such treasure hunts may be carried out by moonlight, too."

The public library also provided strapped citizens with cheap entertainment; this was the decade in which Edmontonians established themselves as Canada's leading borrowers of books. Between 1931 and 1932 alone the circulation at the city's libraries rose from 643,821 to 724,788. The *Journal* noted that Edmonton's main library on the north side loaned 481,252 books, almost as many as the 487,490 loaned by Toronto's Central Library which was twice as big.

Shows and exhibitions drew crowds, even though few could buy things on display. The

cal promises that on the surface sounded both Rooseveltian and common-sensical. "I intend to give every citizen a square deal and I think the first fellow who should benefit by a square deal is the fellow down at the bottom of the ladder," he declared. He promised that demonstrators would suffer "no clubbing by a bunch of police," that he would appoint special liaisons between council and the grievance groups, and that he would reduce the mill rate to 40. This he would accomplish by cutting interest rates paid on city bonds, suspending payments into the city's sinking fund, and persuading the provincial and federal governments to pick up a bigger share of the relief bill.

Partly because of the enduring ideological split on council, Clarke achieved none of this, even

A

B

C

automobiles got bigger and sported fancier gadgets. Describing the new Studebakers, the *Journal* mentioned their larger wheelbases, vastly increased body dimensions, new "aircurve" design, and automatic features such as starters, ride control and spark control.

But the most characteristic divertissements of the 1930s in Edmonton were the seemingly trivial events that passed the time or raised a smile. There were the model airplane contests that captivated youngsters, the black-faced minstrel shows at which Rotarians pretended to be what they then called Negroes, the various pronouncements and predictions of the "astrologists," the stunts at which a "human fly" climbed the Northern Investors' Building or snowplane racers sped along the frozen North Saskatchewan, the bowling and miniature golf fads, and the yo-yo craze.

"Each passing day sees an increase in the number of youngsters who are becoming Yo-Yo addicts," wrote the *Edmonton Bulletin* in promoting its April 1931 competition at the Empire Theatre. "Retail stores handling the Duncan 77 Yo-Yo announce that thousands have been sold during the past two weeks. The popularity of the Filipino toy has spread like wild-fire. Old folks and young folks alike have discovered that the Yo-Yo provides something a little different. It provides relaxation and requires skill in handling and each Yo-Yo fan feels a personal satisfaction in being able to keep the little wooden wheel spinning without tangling."

— *R.D.*

ᴬHarold McMasters may not have been the best boxer in Edmonton, but during the Depression, he was the only one who made a decent living.

Homemakers' Convention held in the Empire Theatre in 1933 attracted thousands of housewives with its array of up-to-date kitchen appliances including that relatively new invention, the refrigerator (almost all Edmontonians still cooled their food with ice hewn from the North Saskatchewan River).

The annual Edmonton Auto Show, inaugurated in 1932, donated its 25-cent gate proceeds to aid the unemployed, but Mayor Knott declared that the public's enthusiasm for the new cars suggested "that we have got over the 'hump' of the Depression." He was wrong, but at least the shiny vehicles were cheerier than the Bennett Buggies passing through town in rising numbers. Paradoxically, during the Depression

though he stayed in office three years by aligning himself with both the working man and the Social Credit provincial government. By now Edmonton's civic representatives had succumbed to a sort of mournful defeatism. Perhaps they recognized that mere municipalities couldn't really do much with finances so completely at the mercy of the shambled world economy. Or perhaps they simply hoped — and history would justify their faith — that the Depression would some day end.

At a council meeting soon after Clarke's election, the question of cancelling payments to the sinking fund was raised. Alderman James East said, "It is not necessary for us, excepting on legal grounds, to lay aside money or bonds to take care of a liability occurring ten years from now. In

He was allowed in the ring because he put on a great show and he promoted his own fights, once by being wheeled down Jasper Avenue while taking a bath in a steaming tub of water. Emile Van Velzen of Edmonton describes one fight with McMasters where they came running out of their corners, McMasters ran into Van Velzen's chin and

McMasters went down for the count. Van Volzen didn't like it. The crowds did.

When McMaster wasn't fighting or working at the shoe-shine shops on Jasper, he played poker to augment his income. The last Van Velzen heard, he had joined the army and gone overseas to fight.

Apart from Christmas, the most exciting time for many locals was the annual Edmonton Exhibition and above all the "midway" produced by Royal American Shows, whose four-turnstyle entrance is shown in Photo A. There were big thrills, like the six men [B] who bet their lives that this motorcyclists would clear them all, and the diving horse [D]. Lots of great clowns too [C]. The 'Ex' began with a parade down Jasper Avenue [E]. Then out at the park, there were make-believe horses [F] for young Jocelyn and Terry (children of politician Gerald O'Connor) and make-believe sea monsters for children of, well, anything up to 70 or 80 [G].

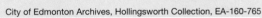

ten years from now sinking fund payments will pass into the ash can of history." To which Fighting Joe Clarke could only add, "Hear! Hear!"

Edmonton, councillors reasoned, would weather the difficulties just as surely as the High Level Bridge would continue to stand. For, like the local economy, the fall of the half-mile steel span crossing the North Saskatchewan River had been predicted for a date less than two weeks before Mayor Clarke's election. Werner Mueller, a man described by one of the papers as a "self-styled astrologist," had said that the stars had told him the span would drop at 6:53 p.m. on November 2, 1934. Four policemen were on hand for the event, which drew about 600 spectators. "Some gingerly stood at the mouth of the bridge," reported the *Medicine Hat News*, "while youths gleefully walked right on it. Motorists or street car motormen didn't worry. They didn't stop."

As Edmonton waited out an economic storm that had become a seemingly monotonous grey winter, Clarke provided a measure of reassurance and entertainment. His strident pronouncements, though largely ineffectual, sounded like the voice of a never-say-die coach to a football team at the bottom of its league. There he was, in the gallery of the legislature, calling UFA cabinet minister Oran L. McPherson a liar, and being escorted from the House.[9] There he was again, cheerfully dismissing a death threat he'd received in the mail and joking about subsequent calls he'd received from life insurance salesmen. And there was the mayor of Edmonton accusing the mayor of Calgary of being in the pocket of "the moneyed interests of eastern Canada." Calgary Mayor Andrew Davison deemed Clarke to be suffering from "hallucinations."

Top photo: The Thirties welcomed the era of the trolley bus, enabling the city to begin tearing up some of its old streetcar tracks. Drivers in those days called out the stops — "Jasper Avenue!" this driver would cry, awakening possible dozers and dreamers. The bus is shown running south on 102nd Street at Jasper Avenue. Stoney's White House Lunch (Olive Stoney, prop.) is just across the street. Lower photo. (Bottom) Also in the Thirties the gas station came into its own, like Loveseth's formidable establishment at Jasper Avenue and 106th Street.

There again was His Worship in council chambers telling his colleagues to sit down and shut up, or announcing, after his first term, that he had not taken a holiday because he considered none of the aldermen capable of serving as deputy mayor in his absence.

And there was Fighting Joe back on the stump, dismissing former mayor James Douglas (who returned to represent a new balanced-budget party called the Citizens' Committee in the 1936 election) as an agent for Big Money attempting to keep Edmontonians in "financial slavery" through high interest rates.

"The question is," Clarke asked, in a long adulatory interview with the *Edmonton Bulletin*, "will Edmonton taxpayers be suckers again? I don't think so. I think their eyes have been opened as to this 'sound money' racket in the last year or two, and if they haven't, one look at that platform and that slate and a running back over the records of some of those on it, should convince them that there's another nigger in the woodpile that needs to be smoked out."

Again it was a close one (Clarke's 12,992 to Douglas's 12,417), but in 1936 Clarke was elected mayor for a record fifth term (counting 1919 and 1920). "Not since he first ascended the mayoral chair has His Worship been the centre of a more spontaneous outburst of popularity than when his election became assured," said the *Bulletin*.

And all this despite the fact that the city comptroller had, just months before, declared Edmonton to have the highest *per capita* debt of any city in the world, and that the provincial capital was "perilously close to financial collapse."

But this time Clarke with his bare majority

[10]John W. Fry was born in
December 1876 near Woodstock,
Ontario. After graduating from
Normal School, he taught for three
years at Gainsborough,
Saskatchewan before marrying and
deciding to homestead near
Lloydminster. In 1911 he moved
from the farm to Edmonton and
began work as a real estate operator.

*The Depression saw the end of
many small retailers in downtown
Edmonton as the Woodwards,
Eatons and the Hudson's Bay
Company firmly established the
department store era. Hence the
massive structures on the east
side of 101st Street looking south
from 103rd Avenue (above).
Doomed were little shops like this
little ice cream parlour on Jasper
Avenue at 103rd Street (below).*

faced the entire slate of five aldermanic Citizens' Committee candidates who were elected. The
rest of the council consisted of three Social Credit, one Civic Youth Leaguer, and a single
Labourite. Mayor Clarke too was now a spent force.

But so too, everyone hoped, was the Depression itself. By 1937, the economy was at last on
the rise. That November Edmonton elected as its mayor John Wesley Fry,[10] five-time alderman
and Garneau resident, who beat Clarke by a decisive 3,419 votes. Fry came to power with a full
slate of six Citizens' Committee aldermen.

"Mr. Fry lost to Mr. Clarke in 21 out of the 40 polls," recounted the *Journal*, "but in the other
half he piled up such thumping majorities that there was little doubt half an hour after the returns
began to come in that the Citizens' candidate would be elected." Clarke, it added, "would make no
admission of defeat even when the last of the
unofficial returns had been compiled."

The *Bulletin* devoted more space to its
defeated candidate, pointing out that Fry had
won a minority of the total votes, and that
the "progressive" vote had been split among
Clarke and two other candidates, J.S. Cowper
and Guy Patterson. Although defeated, the
paper reported, "Mayor Clarke took the result
of the polling with a smile."

"I've still got more friends than the other
fellow," he said as he was greeted with a
cheer at his campaign headquarters after con-
ceding his defeat. "It took three of them to
lick you," shouted a member of the crowd
and again the cheers broke out.

"You mean it took three of them to split

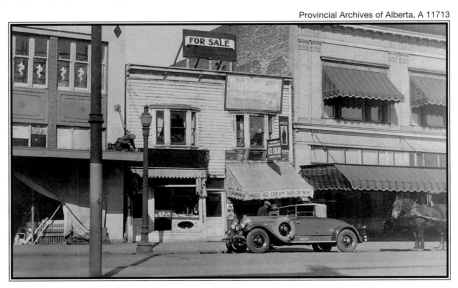

One big fire produces one big lawsuit

AN INFERNO AT THE CORONA HOTEL, HABITAT AND TAVERN TO POLITICOS, DRIVES THEM OUT IN THEIR PYJAMAS AND CREATES A BONANZA FOR LAWYERS

by TED BYFIELD

City of Edmonton Archives, EA-157-385

The fire that destroyed Edmonton's 122-room Corona Hotel on the night of Sunday, February 21, 1932, was not only Edmonton's biggest-ever fire up to that date, but also led to what in the Thirties was one of Alberta's biggest-ever lawsuits.

The hotel was on the south side of Jasper Avenue between 106 and 107 Streets. The favoured habitat of provincial politicians, it would be rebuilt rapidly and figure prominently in the great caucus rebellion against Premier William Aberhart five years after the fire.

About 150 people fled the building, including the UFA cabinet minister Irene Parlby in her nightclothes and eleven other members of the legislature. About a thousand spectators watched the wind-lashed flames shoot high into the air, damaging buildings across the street and threatening the whole block. The loss was finally assessed at $300,000.

The only serious injury was sustained by night engineer James Christie, who suffered severe burns. The fire started when Christie heard a hissing sound in the furnace, lit a match to investigate, and set off a "blinding blast."

The gas, said city fire marshal John Booth, had seeped into the hotel from a gas leak in the lane. That set off the lawsuit. On May 15 the Edmonton law firm of Woods, Craig, Field & Hyndman filed a statement of claim on behalf of 41 insurance companies

Glenbow Archives, McDermid Collection, ND-3-6025(a)

Glenbow Archives, McDermid Collection, ND-3-6025(l)

A leaky gas pipe sent MLA Irene Parlby fleeing into the street in her nightdress and destroyed the venerable Corona Hotel, shown before, during and after the 1932 blaze.

against Northwestern Utilities.

Northwestern, Edmonton's natural gas supplier since 1923, when it tapped into wells at Viking, 75 miles (120 km) east of the city, had that winter laid a twelve-inch main behind the hotel. The failure of the subsoil under it caused the break. So the question arose: Why did the subsoil fail?

Northwestern blamed negligent work by City of Edmonton workmen a year earlier when they were laying a storm sewer. The gas company said the city had not informed them of the previous ground disturbance when they laid their main above it. The city argued it did not have such an obligation. The trial the following February before Mr. Justice Frank Ford lasted an unusual three weeks and provided a showcase assembly of the Alberta legal profession.▲

Mr. Justice Ford laid all the blame on the city. The Appeal Court, in a 3-2 decision, said Northwestern had an over-riding responsibility for the ensuing explosion and fire because it "failed to inspect city operations which might affect the security of its pipes." The gas company took the case to the judicial committee of the Privy Council in Great Britain, then Canada's final court of appeal, which decided that the company's failure to know about the prior city work "was not consistent with due care on its part in the interests of the public."

The Corona case was an expensive and bitter loss for Northwestern. It had to pay not only the fire losses, but meet the claims of some ninety hotel guests plus the legal fees. Thereafter the company began odouring its product and developed new safeguards to detect escaping gas. The case remained an authoritative precedent in the annals of the law of liability for the escape of dangerous substances. It would remain particularly relevant to the province's hydrocarbon and petrochemical industries.

Edmonton architect James Edward Wize had built the Corona as an apartment block in 1908, then converted it into a hotel in 1912. His son, Leonard E. Wize, used the same plans to reconstruct the building after the fire so that the new Corona was much like the old. With the Macdonald, the King Edward and the Windsor it was one of Edmonton's "quality" hotels until the Second World War, after which it gradually declined. Wize sold it to a syndicate of Edmonton businessmen in 1959. It was demolished in 1981 over the objections of history-conscious citizens who wanted it preserved. It was replaced by First Edmonton Place. A local LRT station preserved the name.

AThe insurers of the hotel guests hired J.E. "Jim" Wallbridge, Lawrence Cairns and George B. O'Connor, later chief justice of Alberta. The city was represented by Sydney B. Woods, a former deputy attorney-general, S.W. Field, and Harry Friedman, KC. Northwestern countered with A.L. (Art) Smith, KC, from Calgary, H.R. Milner, KC, Stanley Kerr, KC, later chief justice of the District Court of Northern Alberta, and the emerging Ronald Martland, who would serve on the Supreme Court of Canada for 24 years.

Edmonton suffered many losses to fire during the dry decade of the '30s. (Above) The blaze at McNeill's Garage, near 102nd Street, drew a crowd on June 11, 1931. (Right) Metropolitan Stores at 10157 - 101 Street, burned in 1938. (Below) The racetrack barns went up in smoke in the 1930s as well.

The automobile as killer

Despite the Depression, there were more vehicles on the road in the Thirties, and they were much faster. Hence the automobile, hailed as a great boon back in the teens, was increasingly showing the other side of its nature. Its encounter with streetcars was becoming a grave problem for traffic planners, and the wreck above (whose location is not recorded) shows why. The one at right occurred at Jasper Avenue and 109th Street on December 6, 1930, at 6:30 in the morning, claiming the life of streetcar motorman Clarence Ostrander. (Below) Cars line up for a safety check on 100th Street on June 1, 1931.

Provincial Archives of Alberta, PA-10069

Glenbow-Alberta Archives, McDermid Collection, ND-3-6318 (b)

the vote to make sure I was defeated, but they haven't licked me yet," the mayor replied, and another yell of 'Good old Fighting Joe' split the air."

Clarke, who died in 1941, would not return as a force in municipal politics. For the time being, the progressive trend was over. Business mayors and business aldermen would predominate in the era just dawning, an age of prosperity that began with the Second World War and continued with the oil boom of the Fifties, Sixties and Seventies.

This era came slowly into being during the last years of the 1930s, with slight but incremental reductions in the relief rolls and a strengthening in the farm economy driven by a return to 1929-level wheat prices. Other significant advances included the expansion of Blatchford Field, the construction of two department stores (see sidebar), the inauguration of a new rail service between Edmonton and Calgary, and the Trans-Canada Air Lines connection to the East and the coast.

Although Joe Clarke was not a direct architect of this period of rebirth, his name was prominent in 1938 when Edmonton's new 3,000-seat football stadium was completed. Clarke had negotiated (some said finagled) with the federal government in the Twenties to have land formerly used as the penitentiary farm turned over to the city for a stadium. When at last the money was found to build it, and professional football returned to Edmonton after a seven-year absence, the facility was named Clarke Stadium in honour of Fighting Joe.

The year the stadium opened, there was another indication that prosperity was, this time, really just around the corner. The city's shantytown, a collection of shacks at the foot of Grierson Hill below the Hotel Macdonald, home to about 65 residents, was starting to feel the pinch of the economic recovery.

One-eyed Tim Lane, an Irish-born long-time resident, griped to a *Bulletin* reporter, "Those uptown can now afford to buy more expensive parts for their autos and things. Two or three years ago, we used to earn a fair decent living selling odd parts we could salvage from the dump. You'd be surprised at the class of people who used to drive down in their big cars to see if they could pick up a fourth-hand part cheap. But now they're better off, it's us fellows that are taking the beating."

It was a portent all right. If the junk business was on the decline, things must be looking up.

In April 1933, the people of Edmonton gathered to pay their last respects to the man who more than any other rescued their city from impending obscurity and made it the capital of Alberta (See Vol.2, Sec.1, ch.4). The funeral at First Presbyterian Church on 105th Street is that of Frank Oliver (left), founder of the Edmonton Bulletin. As federal minister of the Interior when Alberta became a province, his manipulations outraged Calgarians and set the two cities at war for the rest of the century. Members of clergy and pallbearers are: (left line, front to back) Rev. Dr. Andrew R. Osborn; Chief Justice Horace Harvey; John Howey (Bulletin editor and writer); William R. West; Joseph J. Duggan (real estate agent); (centre) W. McBride; (right line, front to back): J.E. Brownlee; James A. McCool (AGT); Kenneth A. McLeod; Angus MacDonnell.

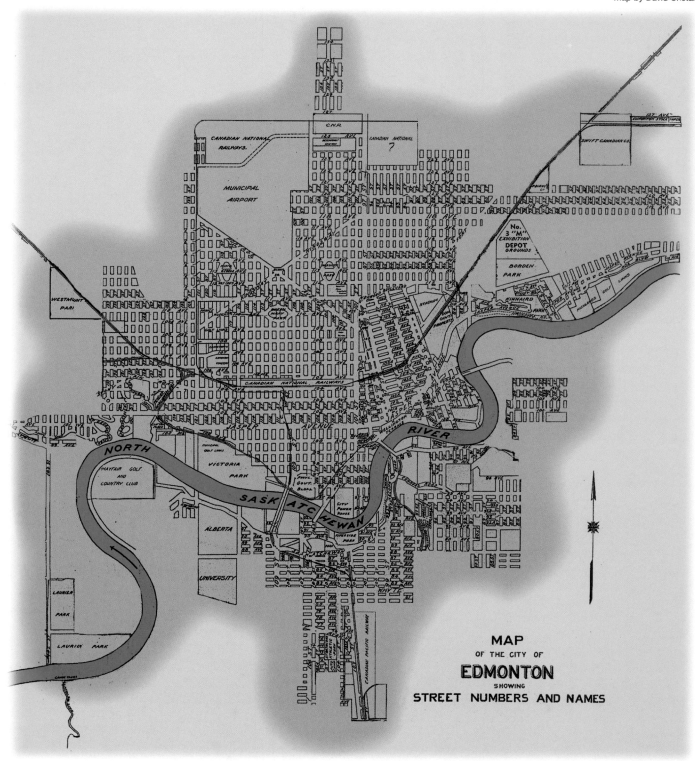

MAP
OF THE CITY OF
EDMONTON
SHOWING
STREET NUMBERS AND NAMES

Edmonton
in the Thirties

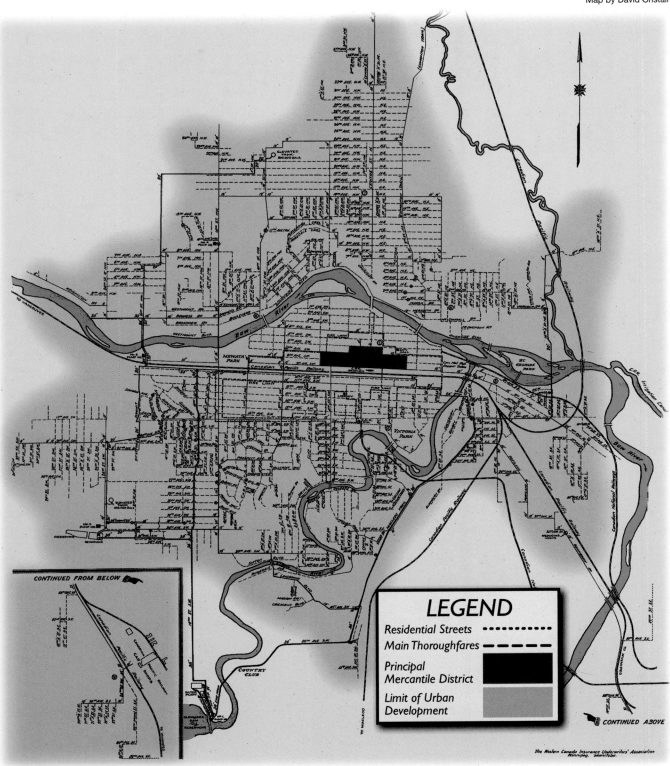

Calgary
in the Thirties

CHAPTER TWO

Mobs of jobless young men make Calgary a city of painful turmoil

As his boom town becomes a bust town, Mayor Andy Davison battles banks, Reds and governments and beats them all

by HUGH DEMPSEY

In 1934, Peter and Mary Henderson of Calgary were out of work for the first time since their arrival from England in 1911. He had earned a good living as a carpenter, and she had worked as a maid while they raised four children. The Depression forced them to go on relief. It killed their marriage, and it killed Peter.

On June 22 they walked from their rooms at 622 4th Avenue SW to the city relief office where they received a rent voucher for $13.75 and a grocery voucher for $14. On the way home, Peter picked up $6 cash owed him for carpentry work. When they stopped for a glass of beer, he sent his wife into the liquor store with $2.75 to buy a quart of rye whiskey. At a meat market, Mary paid fifty cents from the food voucher for a meaty chunk of bone for stew. Their landlady was waiting for them at the front door, her hand out for the rent voucher.

That evening Peter opened the rye, gave his wife an eggcup full, and poured a drink for himself. When he was out of the room, Mary pitched the rest of the whiskey down the sink so he wouldn't get drunk and abusive. When Peter found out, she said, he slapped her face and made a move to hit her with a chair, saying he would "finish her right now."

Often beaten before, Mary managed to pacify him, and began making the stew, using a hatchet to chip the meat from the bone. When she discovered she had no vegetables for the stew, something in her snapped. As her husband stood lighting his pipe, she grabbed the hatchet and smashed him in the back of the skull. "Oh God," he cried, and fell to the floor. Then, she said, her mind went blank. Evidence showed she hit him thirteen more times. Charged with first-degree murder, she was found not guilty by reason of insanity, and sent to the mental hospital at Ponoka.

In the depths of the Depression, such tragedies had become, if not commonplace, altogether understandable. Behind the statistics, beyond the protest marches and strikes, lay an interminable agony that beset the lives and challenged the sanity of tens of thousands of people. Some like Mary Henderson couldn't, or anyway didn't, meet the challenge.

Five years earlier, Calgarians would have been horrified at the idea that poverty could precipitate murder. In 1929 optimism was running high. Land sales had almost doubled within two years, setting a new record at $830,000. Oil drilling footage marked another record high, and the opening of the Red Coulee field near the Montana border spelled more prosperity for the foothills city. Tax collections reached almost $3.5 million while new construction and retail and livestock sales rose steadily.

Andrew Jackson Davison, the city's outspoken and controversial incoming mayor, expected to preside over a buoyant economy. Success was his trademark; every time he ran for civic office he won by acclamation or with a comfortable majority. Since coming from Ireland to Alberta with his family in 1885, when he was ten, he had worked as a printer, served overseas with the Canadian Army pay corps during the Great War, edited the *Alberta Veteran* and joined the *Calgary Herald* as a linotype operator. Elected as a labour alderman in 1921, eight years later he gained the mayoralty by acclamation, and retained it for an unprecedented fifteen years. Throughout the Depression he battled the unemployed, Communists, banks, federal politicians, Social Crediters, and members of his own council, and defeated them all.

[1] In *Days Gone By* (Saskatoon, Fifth House, 1993) Jack Peach tells how Greyhound traffic manager Gerry Brown talked H.K. "Pat" Williams, an unemployed railway bridge engineer, into becoming a driver even though he had never handled a truck, let alone a bus. "I have a taxi outside, and there are 35 passengers waiting down at the depot," Brown said. Harold Olson, one of Greyhound's owners, gave Williams a quick driving lesson, then took him to the depot, showed him a big vehicle and said, "Take her to Lethbridge!" Williams had no idea of the route, but a helpful passenger gave him directions and told him where to stop in each small town. After driving for a few months Williams began designing steel-bodied buses to replace the original wooden ones. He went on to plan and build 45 garages and depots, and was assistant to the president when he retired in 1973 after forty years with Greyhound.

When he took office in January 1930, Davison saw a very different Calgary, with rising unemployment, plunging stock markets and a drastic drop in grain prices as temporary setbacks. Though no federal scheme to help the unemployed had yet been proposed, he immediately announced that the city would hire all single unemployed men for the rest of the winter at a dollar for a four-hour day; married men would get relief without working. The city would pay half the costs, the provincial government the rest. Davison estimated that some 800 single men would qualify for assistance, using city equipment for grading streets and other public works. The thinking was they could easily survive by sharing a furnished room at 75 cents a day and living on hamburger (25 cents for three pounds), buttermilk (15 cents a gallon) and day-old bread (5 cents a loaf).

At that first 1930 meeting, council rejected its earlier plan of building low-cost houses to be sold to working citizens under a time-payment scheme. Since forty per cent of Calgary's houses were already at least thirty years old, and only 6,055 were built between 1911 and 1941, this myopic decision subjected the city to a chronic housing shortage. By April it was issuing $2 permits to destitute families camping in the Bow Bend area west of the railway tracks. Within three weeks the tent city reached its allowable limit of sixty people living in twelve tents. By June squatters had moved in, and nearby householders wanted the place torn down.

In February, indignant because at least a quarter of relief recipients were "foreigners," by which he meant all post-war immigrants including British,

Andrew Davison was first elected mayor of Calgary in 1929. He would stay on to see the city through the Depression and into the ensuing war years.

Davison went to Ottawa demanding aid, which wasn't forthcoming until Conservative R.B. Bennett's government succeeded that of Liberal Mackenzie King in July.

All through the Depression, Davison pursued a single-minded policy of supporting poverty-stricken Calgarians while fending off an invasion of jobless men from across Canada. It didn't work. As a railway junction, Calgary was peculiarly vulnerable to the ravages of the Depression and by spring 1930 it was besieged by transients applying for relief. They mustn't get it, said Davison, who ran notices in Canadian newspapers on May 16 warning them to stay away. Relief was suspended and single men were encouraged to work in provincial relief camps (Sect.2, ch.1).

Termination of city aid became a clarion call for the communists, who considered themselves spokesmen for the unemployed. During the May Day parade, one yelled, "Comrades and fellow workers. This is your day! Fight for it!" until someone hit him over the head with a banner pole. In the ensuing melee, baton-wielding police arrested five men and two women. When sixty

Refugees of the southern drought poured into Calgary during the late 1920s, swelling the number of people who depended on a salary for survival (see chart below). When the Depression hit and those wages vanished, the city tried valiantly to provide for the destitute, and by 1930 a work-relief program was in place for unmarried men. This group (above) toiled in the Bankview area in 1931 as part of a program funded by three levels of government. Only those who could prove residency in Calgary could receive assistance, and the population decrease between 1931 and 1936 (opposite page) may have been caused by some short-timers being forced to go elsewhere or to labour camps.

Communist protesters threatened the council meeting on May 11, Davison subdued them by calling a police squad under Chief David Ritchie.

Davison soon found himself vilified by both right and left. He was criticized by the Calgary Ratepayers' Association for helping the unemployed, and vilified by labour groups for selling out to Calgary business interests. He came down hard on Communists, whom he saw as professional agitators. Claiming that one man, F.L. Farbey, was in the pay of a Moscow newspaper, he invited Communists to apply to his office for deportation. To his surprise, 57 families turned up. Doubtless some of them did wind up among the 2,500 people deported from Alberta during the Depression.

Sympathetic to local need — an average of fifty people a day visited his office — Davison saw as many as possible and sent the rest to Commissioner A.G. Graves. This open-door policy became known as Davison's "private employment bureau." Meanwhile, other Calgarians helped the unemployed: some downtown merchants provided hot porridge, the Kiwanis Club and Boy Scouts collected clothing, and the *Calgary Herald*'s Sunshine Club found stoves and heaters. The main library provided free daylong shelter, recreation and information; most in demand were do-it-yourself manuals and books on political theory.

By November city files held more than 1,200 applications for work and 1,600 from single men wanting direct relief. Most were farm labourers and drifters, and Davison notified all Alberta municipalities that Calgary would bill them for relief payments to their citizens. Unemployed men were barred from liquor stores and beer halls.

Astonishingly, at the end of 1930 Calgary was financially better off than any other big Western city, with a balanced budget and $4-million revenue from taxes and utilities. In January Canadian Greyhound Coaches Limited began running locally-built buses between Alberta, Vancouver and Spokane.[1] The Hudson's Bay store still dominated retail trade but Eaton's, a relative upstart, was thriving in a $1-million store opened at 8th Avenue and 4th Street West in 1929. Jen-kins' Groceteria, a Calgary family firm that in 1918 opened the first cash-and-carry, self-service food store in the Canadian West, was now rivalled by Safeway Stores Ltd. and Piggly Wiggly. The *Albertan* plant, Birks building, shops, apartments and 400 houses had been built. Two hotels, the Wales and York were about to open.[2] The Glenmore Dam, a new post office, the Bank of Montreal building, and Kresge's chain store were under construction. Davison and other officials saw prosperity ahead.

Events proved otherwise. Over the winter the city spent $54,000, plus a matching sum from the provincial government, to support more than 3,000 men. While some other cities cut off the unemployed in spring,[3] city council finally decided to give men food and lodging tickets worth $3.50 for working one eight-hour day a week. Provincial officials suggested helping only those registered during the winter, but Davison insisted on including men who had scraped by but could no longer support

Population in Calgary

as a % of 1946 population

Population as % of 1946

YEAR

(graph x-axis: 1890, 1900, 1910, 1920, 1930, 1940, 1950)
(graph y-axis: 0, 20, 40, 60, 80, 100)

themselves. He said there was "no possibility" that outsiders would be placed on the relief list.

How wrong he was. Next spring, hundreds of drought-stricken southern Albertans and freight-car loads of jobless men were still pouring into the "Transportation City of the West." By June 24, 1,560 people had applied for relief. Only 17 per cent were born in Canada; by Davison's definition, the rest were foreigners. Shocked by the influx, Davison closed down the registration office even as trains were unloading transients from British Columbia. Before the end of the year, 4,719 unemployed single men had qualified for relief. Without enough money to pay the massive

The Depression forced a middle-aged Calgary couple, Peter and Mary Henderson, to go on relief. That killed their marriage, and Mary killed Peter.

costs, even with help from the province, the city was compelled to borrow $450,000 through the Bank of Montreal to keep operating, and tried to discourage malingerers by doubling the work requirement to two days. This put Davison on a collision course with local Communists and their National Unemployed Workers Association, resulting in a series of brawls that broke out at both Calgary and Edmonton (described in Sect.2, ch.2).

In mid-October, the Communist Party of Canada announced that it would field two candidates in the upcoming civic election: for council, John O'Sullivan, and for city commisioner, Phil Luck. Both had been arrested in the riots and both were still under indictment.

A week before the election, a public forum attracted a crowd that packed Paget Hall and spread out onto the street; reporters estimated that three-quarters were Communists. Luck had been speaking for forty minutes when Davison arrived. Booed and heckled, the mayor declared the city had already spent $180,000 for relief that year, more than any other city in Canada. He refused "to be stampeded into spending ratepayers' money recklessly for the relief of every transient man who happened to drift into Calgary." As he left, someone yelled, "Good for you, Andy! Give 'em hell!" and the meeting broke up in confusion.

On November 18 Davison swept the polls with 17,243 votes, and O'Sullivan, with 458 votes, didn't make council. A week later, Luck was found not guilty for his role in the riots while O'Sullivan received a one-year jail term.

By the end of 1931, Calgary's finances were precarious, with only about half of property taxes collected and the transit system losing $9,000 a month. Having paid out almost $243,000 in relief, the city was more than $70,000 over budget. Wages of civic employees and school teachers were cut four per cent, those of department heads twelve per cent, street-car service was reduced, some schools closed, and destitute homeowners given the option of working off back taxes. Instead of giving unemployed men 25-cent meal tickets, the city saved $250 a day by opening Canada's largest soup

Data provided by Barry Hepp. Graph by Dave Stevens

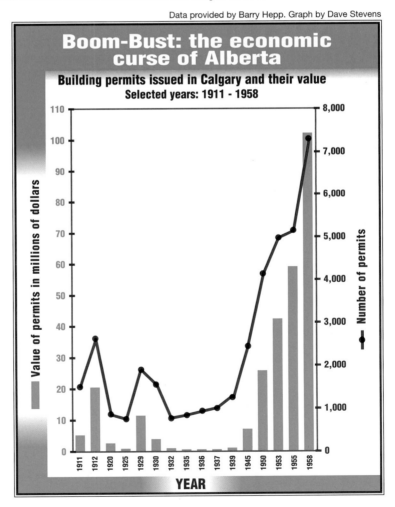

Boom-Bust: the economic curse of Alberta

Building permits issued in Calgary and their value
Selected years: 1911 - 1958

YEAR

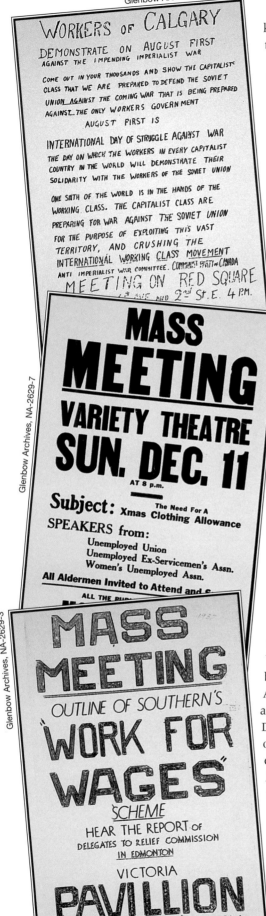

kitchen in Victoria Park, feeding more than 2,000 a day and staffed by the unemployed themselves.[4]

By February 1932 Calgary was providing relief for almost 3,000 single men and women and 2,700 families, a total of 13,500 people in a city of 83,000. Contrary to popular belief that many were out-of-towners or layabouts, a *Herald* reporter found merchants, tradesmen and professionals forced to resort to the dole.

One was a professor of music whose piano lessons became luxuries with the advent of radio and phonograph. A minister who had fitted his church basement with beds for the unemployed and resigned to work with the poor went on relief when he couldn't return to his pastorate. A lawyer had gone broke playing the market at the onset of the Depression. A newspaperman who had crossed Canada vainly seeking a job brought his family to Calgary because its relief payments were generous. A man who worked 22 years for a well-known Canadian firm put his savings into a partnership, and sold out for $30 when the Depression crippled the business. After paying a month's rent in advance, he had only $2.50, and his children would have gone to school hungry if the landlady hadn't provided breakfast. An architect who couldn't get work even as a draughtsman lost his home to taxes and moved to a rooming house. Overcrowding was common; a four-room house held a family of four and five roomers, and a couple with three children occupied a five-room house with eight boarders.

Hundreds of drought-stricken southern Albertans and freight-car loads of jobless men poured into the 'Transportation City of the West' in the spring of 1931. Within a year Calgary was providing relief for 13,500 people.

For many Calgarians, relief had become a normal way of life. While her children were playing "house," a mother overheard her daughter, as hostess, asking a little guest to return on Tuesday. The child replied, "Sorry, that's the day I get my relief tickets." Even in July 1932, when the city cut off relief to single men who refused to go to bush camps, 344 chose to stay in town waiting for harvest work and were struck from the list.

Meanwhile Davison struggled with municipal debt. With only $887,000 in its sinking fund, Calgary had to pay off debentures of $1.8 million. Davison met commitments to Canadian bankers by persuading the Bank of Montreal to extend its line of credit, but a loan from a New York financial house, due in July, carried a premium of $43,000 because it was payable in either gold or U.S. funds, and a further $2-million worth of American debentures were due early in 1933. To avoid huge exchange rates, Davison asked the federal government to trade Calgary dollars for gold. When Ottawa demurred, Davison announced that the city would meet the debentures, payable in either Toronto or New York, by sending Canadian money to Toronto. His decision angered bondholders, who feared other municipalities would follow Calgary's example. The Bank of Montreal threatened to suspend Calgary's line of credit; Davison responded defiantly that if this occurred all city business and services would be halted.

On January 2, 1933, Calgary paid the loan in Canadian funds, ignoring the $350,000 premium for U.S. dollars, and leaving its treasury almost empty. One resident offered to lend the city $100,000 at five per cent for a year, if nine others would do likewise. Businessmen began a campaign to boycott the Bank of Montreal. Since Davison would not back down, the bank reluctantly extended a $1.8-million line of credit to the city, "to prevent hardship and suffering to citizens, and to prevent shutdown of city services and schools."[5] But some schools closed because they couldn't be adequately heated, and many children stayed home for lack of shoes and warm clothes. With more than 7,000 workers unemployed, stores offered not seasonal treats but boiling beef at five cents a pound and three tins of soup for 25 cents.

Within three years Calgary's manufacturing output had dropped from $39 million to $19 million, and its financial situation worsened as Eastern bond dealers discounted the value of its new debentures below those of Canadian cities that paid the American premium. As relief payments soared and tax collections dropped, the city faced bankruptcy. To meet the crisis, police wages were cut five per cent, firemen eight per cent, three firehalls were closed, the city work week reduced to five days, and garbage collection cut to twice monthly. These measures reduced expenditures by almost $100,000 but Calgary was still broke, partly because it had the

most generous relief program in Alberta, paying $1.38 a day per capita compared to Edmonton's 99 cents, Lethbridge's 82 cents and Medicine Hat's 54 cents. That spring, city council voted on a motion to cut back to Edmonton's relief schedule. With Civic Government Association aldermen in favour and left-wing councillors opposed, ending in a 6 - 6 tie, Davison cast the deciding vote against reducing welfare. He proposed starting it a month earlier but, as a sop to the defeated right wing, requiring married unemployed men to work two days a week.

That decision triggered a long, bitter strike led by the Central Council of Unemployed Associations and supported by the Ex-Service Unemployed Association, the Unemployed Married Men's Association, Single Unemployed Girls' Association, and the Workers' United Front Council. Four thousand members attended a protest meeting at Victoria Park, and 500 married men failed to report for work on April 3. Convinced that the confrontation was organized by Communists, Davison threatened to slash their relief by twenty-five per cent if they didn't show up in two days. When ninety men remained on strike, he cut their allowance accordingly. Every day more men refused to work; by mid-month, more than the original 500 had joined the walkout.

On April 24 in Victoria Park, at the largest mass rally in the city's history, organizers harangued the crowd, then led a parade to city hall where the strikers presented the mayor with their demands. These included a return to winter rates, refunding money lost by strikers, relief increased to $5 a week, a clothing allowance, and a promise not to deport any foreign-born strikers. Without rejecting their demands outright, the mayor promised only to call a special council meeting to discuss them.

Next day, the strike turned violent. Fifteen hundred men and women led by Fred Nutt of the Central Workers' Council and James Newall and Eric Poole of the Unemployed Married Men's Association descended on unemployed workers on Mission Hill, demanding that they lay down their tools. When they refused, the strikers attacked, using shovels and pick handles against the batons of police guarding the site. When the riot was quelled, two policemen had been injured, two strikers arrested for assault, and several ringleaders taken into custody.

Davison prepared for further demonstrations by calling the RCMP, who brought in sixty men from Edmonton, Lethbridge, and Regina. Perhaps because of their presence, the May Day parade a week later was peaceful, as more than

As governments scrambled to develop programs for the unemployed, the established charities, many religiously based, providing for the needy on a larger scale than ever before. (Above) The Calgary Herald's Sunshine Society sponsored a toy shop run by local boy scouts and girl guides, (Below) The YMCA ran wrestling classes for unemployed men. (Opposite page) Scores of advocacy groups for the unemployed sprang up.

4The soup kitchen used daily 600 loaves of bread, 170 pounds of butter, 1,100 pounds of beef, a ton of potatoes, 200 pounds of sugar, 140 gallons of of milk, and huge quantities of tea, coffee, and porridge. Within a year it needed even more. On November 23, 1932, supper for 3,000 used 1,190 pounds of beef, a ton of potatoes, half a ton of cabbage, 800 loaves of bread, 310 gallons of soup, 400 gallons of tea and 32 gallons of milk.

3,000 men, women and children marched to Mewata Park, singing *The Internationale* and *The Red Flag*. Then, at the request of the Calgary Ministerial Association, the dissidents agreed to suspend the strike during a week of negotiation with city council. After several hours of discussion, the mayor and aldermen agreed to rescind the 25 per cent penalty and pay winter rates for utilities during April if the men returned to work. The delegates accepted and on May 15 the six-week strike was over.

That summer, after three years of falling attendance and deficit returns, the Stampede made an astonishing comeback. Guy Weadick had been fired as Stampede manager the previous year, and now Jack Dillon, as arena director, took over its organization. Backed by Jim Cross, chairman

of the Stampede committee (and eldest son of rancher A.E. Cross), he cut imported stage acts in favour of competitive events. Chuckwagon races, until now relatively tame affairs, became exciting contests for cash prizes; Dick Cosgrave's flawless performance beat Clem Gardner's hell-for-leather ride, and dominated the sport through the Thirties.

Though 31 Americans competed in the rodeo, Canadians won all the events. In a week of fine weather, the parade and carnival drew record entries, the livestock exhibits were first-class, attendance increased by 14,000, gate receipts rose even though admission was halved to 25 cents, and the Stampede made a profit of $1,064. Next year it drew 214,000 people, the third-highest number in its history, and attracted Indian competitors and corporate sponsors who would guarantee its success throughout the Depression.

Dillon ensured a supply of champions for future Stampedes by forming the Alberta Stampede Directors' Association, with more than twenty members who ran local stampedes where ranch hands learned the skills that equipped them for top competition. He helped many to cover entrance fees by giving them jobs during Stampede week, at wages ranging from $3.50 a day for unskilled labour to $8 for pickup men, who had to bring two horses to the bucking contests. With some 300 cowboys entering events, few made the finals, but those who did earned up to $200 for a week's work.

Calgary's new zoo survived the Depression, thanks to the diligence of curator Tom Baines, its only full-time employee, and the generosity of local industries and individuals. Lars Willumsen's construction company offered men and equipment to build animal pens, lumber firms gave building materials, Trotter and Morton supplied free plumbing, and veterinarian Gordon Anderson donated his services. Baines' allowance of $1 a day to feed 350 animals and birds was supplemented by 100 pounds of meat a week from Pat Burns, grain from milling companies, vegetables from Safeway Ltd., stale bread from bakeries, and various foods from other donors.

Over the next year, the city tried ways to help the unemployed without going further into debt. One such scheme provided vacant lots and seeds to grow vegetables; more than 500 gardens were cultivated in 1933, and at least 1,000 in 1934. Plenty of lots were available, since more than a third of Calgary's land area had reverted to the city for nonpayment of taxes. Three property owners had destroyed buildings to avoid being taxed for improvements. At a sale in the spring of 1934, more than 1,400 parcels of land were offered but only five were sold.

That summer Calgary's debt mounted when both federal and provincial governments reduced

(Above) When this panorcmic photo was taken from the Palliser Hotel in 1929, Calgary's burgeoning populace was anticipating a time of corresponding physical growth. The Hudson's Bay Company store (left) was putting the finishing touches on an addition, and the York Hotel was under construction (centre) The newly-built Ycle Hotel can be seen at the far right. This looked-for prosperity was not to be. Calgary's skyline, which Harry Pollard photographed in the 1930s (below, opposite pcge), remained virtually unchanged throughout the Thirties.

[5]The fight over Calgary's near default was not over. The city was served with legal papers from the Malden Kennedy Trust Company of Massachusetts, demanding payment of $5,000 in gold. Davison persuaded Ottawa to provide it, a canny move, since Canadian law prohibited the export of gold. The city's solicitor delivered the coins to the bondholder's agent, who refused them. Malden Kennedy realized that it would have to sell the gold in Canada and thus receive payment in Canadian funds, just as Davison had offered. The coins sat in a Calgary bank vault for more than a year until Malden Kennedy, facing its own financial crisis, reluctantly accepted them.

Pat Burns turns 75 and 15,000 share in a gigantic birthday cake

CALGARY'S GRAND OLD MAN BESTOWS A FIVE-POUND ROAST OF BEEF TO EVERY FAMILY ON RELIEF

One of the grand old men of Calgary during the 1930s was Patrick Burns, cattle dealer, meat packer and philanthropist. Unlike most multimillionaires, Burns never lost touch with the people around him. He was a popular employer and an active supporter of civic causes. "No man in the West has a kinder heart," wrote Elizabeth Bailey Price, praising Burns's help "to the fatherless, to the crippled, to ambitious students, in fact to every charitable cause."

In 1930, when friends learned that Burns' 75th birthday was July 6, 1931, the opening day of the Stampede, they planned a gala celebration. Over the next year leading Calgarians and many others who wanted to repay Burns for his friendship and support organized events to honour him, and the entire 1931 Stampede was declared Pat Burns Week.

The Canadian Bakery was commissioned to make "Canada's biggest birthday cake." It weighed one and a half tons, and measured eight feet square and seven and a half feet high in three tiers. It absorbed more than 4,500 eggs, 285 pounds of sugar, 304 pounds of butter, 380 pounds of flour, twelve pounds of spices, 115 pounds of raisins, 290 pounds of currants, 190 pounds each of mixed peel and cherries, eighty pounds each of almonds and walnuts, 120 pounds of dates, sixty pounds of candied pineapple, 160 pounds of icing sugar, 300 sugar roses, and 500 sugar lilies. Topped by 75 candles, the cake was loaded on a truck with a derrick to serve as a star attraction in the Stampede parade, where it received thunderous applause from the crowds lining the streets.

That evening, Burns's birthday banquet was held in the Palliser Hotel. Seven hundred and fifty guests jammed the dining room and many others had to be turned away. At the head table were lieutenant-governors of the three prairie provinces, the premiers of Alberta and British Columbia, Catholic and Anglican bishops, and old friends like A.E. Cross and Archdeacon J.W. Tims. Master of ceremonies was J.H. Woods, publisher of the *Calgary Herald*.

At the beginning of the dinner, Woods exhibited more than 150 letters and telegrams from well-wishers, including the Prince of Wales, Governor-General Lord Bessborough, Prime Minister R.B. Bennett, CPR president Edward W. Beatty, CNR president Sir Henry Thornton, federal Minister

Pat Burns observed his 75th birthday by giving to Calgary's poor. Others celebrated by heaping honours on the venerable Alberta stockman.

of Agriculture Robert Weir, and Bank of Montreal director Sir Frederick Williams-Taylor. Then Woods made a sad announcement: suffering a slight indisposition, the guest of honour would not be able to attend the party.

But Burns was not to be denied this chance to be with old friends. Later in the evening, the audience was excited to learn that he had recovered from fatigue and would soon appear. At last he arrived and "three deafening cheers and three more greeted the guest of honour when he entered the crowded dining room, and three more after that."

The first speaker was Premier John Brownlee, who described Burns as "a grand old pioneer, a true Canadian gentleman, a philanthropist, and a prince of good fellows,"

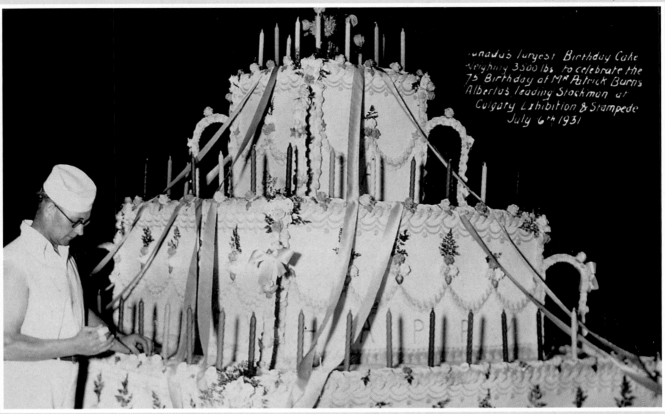

Canada's largest Birthday Cake weighing 3500 lbs. to celebrate the 75 Birthday of Mr Patrick Burns Alberta's leading Stockman at Calgary Exhibition & Stampede July 6th 1931

Pat Burns's "world's largest" birthday cake was a featured attraction at the 1931 Calgary Stampede.

and unveiled the province's gift, an oil portrait of Burns by Kenneth Forbes, RCA. Next, J.D. McGregor, lieutenant-governor of Manitoba, recalled their long friendship, remarking that Burns bought his first carload of cattle from McGregor's father in the 1870s. "A year or two later," said McGregor, "I saw him breaking the first prairie sod in the Brandon district with a walking plow, and he was doing a good job."

The highlight of the evening came when Woods read a telegram from Ottawa: "His Excellency the Governor General, on the recommendation of the prime minister, has been pleased this day to summon to the Senate of Canada, Patrick Burns, Esquire, of the city of Calgary, in the province of Alberta."

Clearly moved by the demonstrations of good will, Burns explained that this was the first time in his life that he had ever spoken into a microphone. "You have all been so kind to me, an old cattleman," he said. "This senatorship — I do not deserve it." The crowd thought otherwise and cheered themselves hoarse for Canada's newest senator.

Since Burns wasn't well enough to attend the ceremonies at the Stampede grounds, he asked his nephew, John Burns, to act in his stead. Standing in front of a grandstand filled to capacity, on his uncle's behalf he accepted a scroll from Mayor Andy Davison praising Calgary's "best-loved citizen," and a bronze sculpture of a buffalo, a reminder of Burns's pioneer days. The huge birthday cake

was cut into 15,000 pieces; the first ones were presented to the platform party, each in a suitably inscribed box, and the rest handed out to the crowd.

Pat Burns had his own plans for the celebration. Rather than receiving honours, he preferred to mark his birthday by sharing it with those less fortunate than himself. He announced that he was giving a five-pound roast of beef to each of the 2,000 Calgary families on relief, and a 50-cent voucher, good at any of the city's restaurants or grocery stores, to each of Calgary's 4,000 unemployed single men. The vouchers were inscribed, "Given on the occasion of P. Burns' 75th birthday, July 6, 1931." During Stampede week, tickets for the beef and the single men's vouchers were available at the welfare office on 3rd Street East. The following week, two thousand roasts, each wrapped by Burns & Co., were ready to be picked up at the old City Market.

Pat Burns was active until a few months before his death on February 24, 1937. On his eightieth birthday in 1936, the *Herald* published an interview written in May, just before he fell ill. Still fully occupied with his business, he gave the reporter his advice to Depression-ridden Calgarians: "When I was a young man I took work whether or not I liked it. The man who takes what he can get today and does his best with it is the man who will come out of the Depression with flying colours."

— H.D.

7Deserted wives were a major problem for relief officials. After eliminating couples who had faked claims, they required the wife to issue a warrant for her husband, who could seldom be found, or was out of work and incapable of supporting a family. Women with young children were usually given relief because it cost less than sending them out to work and putting the children in a home. Those without children were allowed relief if they couldn't find work. A surprising number of deserted wives registered at the labour bureau, willing to work because they could leave older children during the day, or arrange private care for little ones.

Calgarians suffered many setbacks in the 1930s, but they didn't lose their heroes, the cowboys. At the height of the Depression, attendance at the Stampede actually increased. Shown here are some of the big names (L-R): Jack Dillon, Herman Linder, Sykes Robinson, Jack Wade, Cecil Bedford, Charlie Ivens, Dick Cosgrave.

relief funding to municipalities. City councillors unanimously rejected the Alberta government's advice to cut relief rates. Within weeks, Calgary was in another financial crisis. The Bank of Montreal warned city council that inability to collect taxes had created a deficit of $275,000 for the first half of the year, and relief spending was already $150,000 over estimate. Council again refused to cut relief payments, and the bank reduced its line of credit.[6]

Meanwhile doctors, who estimated that they were delivering $250,000 worth of services free to the unemployed annually — $1,000,000 over four years — asked the city to pay at least a fifth of this cost. Until 1929, they had treated 20 per cent to 35 per cent of patients without charge. Now one doctor, spending 75 per cent of his time on unpaid relief work, had lost his practice; others reported that they were rarely paid for maternity cases. Ottawa refused to cover medical care. That autumn all but ten of the 97 members of the Calgary Medical Society signed an agreement to treat the unemployed for a lump sum of $8,000 a year.

Contrary to popular belief that most relief recipients were out-of-towners or layabouts, a *Herald* reporter found merchants, tradesmen and professionals forced to resort to the dole.

In August the *Albertan* launched a campaign to expose people who abused the relief system. Its reports alleged that some took advantage of legal loopholes: the provincial Maintenance Order Act of 1922 required those who could afford it, to support relatives if they couldn't work because of age or infirmity, but not if they couldn't get jobs. The newspaper found salaried sons and daughters whose wages weren't being deducted from their parents' relief; when their scams were discovered, they avoided liability by moving out. Others included country folk who moved to Calgary to qualify for relief, and women who falsely claimed that their husbands had left them.[7]

The worst offenders, the paper claimed, were using their influence with city officials to get welfare to which they weren't entitled. When the city put a sewer through vacant lots without the owner's permission, the owner sued and collected some $800 after paying his lawyer. Two months later, the same man's request for relief was initially refused, but granted after he appealed the decision. Another man who owned three rent-paying houses, and whose wife earned $500 a year, drew $1,275 in relief over two years; his relief was stopped but, unlike less well-connected shysters, he wasn't prosecuted. A young couple, both unemployed and supported by the wife's father, collected $28 a month for rent and food.

The *Albertan* charged that the relief system was riddled with abuses, that certain aldermen were shielding relief recipients, and that relief officials were continually overruled by those higher

up. The newspaper's findings sparked a city inquiry under Police Magistrate H.G. Scott, which addressed the specific charges as well as general relief administration. Relief superintendent George Thompson filed a list of his six full-time and one part-time investigators and all his employees for the past few years. One was *Albertan* reporter P.H. Dunne, who testified that several applicants he rejected had been allowed relief after Mayor Davison sent notes to Thompson.

Questioned by *Albertan* acting news editor D.E.C. Campbell, Davison said that he had written to Thompson after getting a telephone call from a friend who wanted his father to get relief. Next day, both Davison and Commissioner T.B. Riley admitted that they had each once prevented the prosecution of people who had allegedly obtained relief though fraud. But in general the evidence

A bitter *adios*: why the Stampede fired Guy Weadick

AS THE AMAZINGLY SUCCESSFUL '32 SHOW ENDED, THE FOUNDER BLEW HIS CORK

by Ted Byfield

Guy Weadick, envisioner, creator and chief promoter of the Calgary Stampede (Vol.3, p.115), was not a man for depressions. Not economic ones, anyway, and when the Great Depression hit the Calgary Stampede it proved more than he was able to, or cared to, cope with. The result was the embarrassing incident that attended the Stampede in 1932 after which Weadick was ignominiously fired.

This at least is the explanation for Weadick's ouster convincingly offered by his biographer Donna Livingstone (*The Cowboy Spirit: Guy Weadick and the Calgary Stampede*, Greystone) published nearly sixty-five years later. The Depression hit the Calgary Stampede in 1930, she writes. Attendance dropped by an enormous 56,000 and receipts by $57,000. The following year, the loss hit $16,000 and the board cut Weadick's salary and that of general manager Ernie L. Richardson by ten per cent.

What bothered Weadick most, however, was what he considered the parsimonious attitude of the board in planning the 1932 Stampede. To Weadick, the secret of the Stampede was biggest and best. You hired the most highly publicized and best received shows on the continent whatever the cost — an impossibility now expense cuts of 25 per cent were being insisted on.

Worse still, they were cutting the rodeo prize-money by a whopping sixty per cent. Cowboys wouldn't risk their necks for such a niggardly purse, he repeatedly warned Richardson as they acrimoniously planned the 1932 show.

Things became ever more bitter. Weadick wanted, demanded and got a contract giving him a copyright on the term "Stampede," agreeing he wouldn't stage one at any other western Canadian site. But nothing satisfied him. He predicted the 1932 Stampede would be a disaster. He threatened to put on a bigger and better Stampede at Great Falls, Montana. He began drinking heavily, missing meetings, not showing up at the office.

But Weadick had created better than he knew. The cowboys did not boycott the 1932 Stampede, but put on a better performance than they ever had before. The crowds held and the Stampede survived. Weadick had misjudged what biogra-

Guy and Florence Weadick.

pher Livingstone calls "the Cowboy Spirit." The explanation can only be guessed at. Despite the reversals of the Depression, Weadick and his wife, Florence, lived comfortably. They wintered on his ranch, wrote articles and columns for cattle and entertainment magazines. The agony that the whole West was undergoing they didn't quite share. The cowboys did; they expected cutbacks. Weadick didn't know this.

When events proved him wrong, his bitterness overcame him. Drinking heavily on the last night of the 1932 show, he lurched towards the platform. "I'm going to tell them they can take this show and keep it," he said. "I'm through after tonight." Efforts to restrain him failed and he took over as master of ceremonies, awarding the prizes himself that special guests had been designated to confer. Finally, he shouted, "I've put on your first Stampede and I've just put on your last." But few heard him. Somebody had cut off the microphone.

A month later a brief announcement appeared in the *Calgary Herald* that his services had been "dispensed with."

Weadick sued for wrongful dismissal and breach of contract and three years later Mr. Justice William Ives (known behind his back as "Cowboy Billy") handed down an astonishing judgment. The Stampede had, immediately before trial, switched its defence. Weadick's drinking, it argued, had made him incapable of doing the job.

Nonsense, Ives in effect replied. Drinking was an indispensable part of Weadick's job, and if the Stampede board didn't know it, they should have. He awarded the jubilant Weadick six months' salary ($2,700) and legal costs of $1,700. The Stampede had grounds to appeal but didn't.

For the next twenty years Weadick shunned the Stampede, ignoring it in everything he wrote and staging similar, usually successful, stampedes in smaller centres. In 1946 his wife and lifetime partner, Florence, died, leaving him in a desolation he sought to solve with a second marriage that soon ended.

Finally, in 1952, he was invited home and in a tearful reunion on its 40th anniversary the Stampede was reconciled with its founder. He died suddenly at High River on December 15, 1953.

The cowboys come to the rescue

Stampede organizers changed the direction of the exhibition in 1932, emphasizing the local rodeo competitions and downplaying the imported spectacles. This decision brought it out of the slump that had started with the onset of the Depression, and created a gallery of local heroes. [A] Johnny Jordan on Little Sweat. [B] Bareback rider Bert Armstrong of Turner Valley, 1935. [C] Jimmy Shaw of Midnapore competing in steer riding. [D] High River's Clarence "Slim" Watrin, in the saddle bronc event. [E] Lloyd Meyers of Wainwright on Thunder in the saddle bronc event. [F] Harry Knight of Banff riding Good Enough in the saddle bronc event. [G] Chuckwagon races became a main attraction in the 1930s. [H] A pancake breakfast in front of the St. Regis Hotel 1931. [I] The 1938 Stampede parade.

G

I

H

The birth of serious bus travel dooms the streetcar

Relief-built roads and reliefers who couldn't afford to run cars any more meant a demand for inexpensive bus service. (Left) Driver Ken Gush poses proudly with the first bus in Calgary's transit system in 1935. (Above) An Edmonton-bound bus waits at the depot in front of the Southam building at 7th Avenue and 1st Street in 1939.

showed that, if officials occasionally erred on the side of leniency, everyone responsible for welfare was doing his best in a tough job. To the chagrin of the *Albertan*, on October 1 Magistrate Scott issued a report that exonerated elected officials and employees of the relief department, and sharply criticized the paper for publishing unfounded accusations.

Beleaguered by the press, the doctors and the banks, Calgary appealed to Ottawa and Edmonton for interim funding. After both governments refused the request, city council reluctantly agreed to order reregistration and rechecking of all relief recipients, and cut relief payments to match federal and provincial reductions. Even then, Calgary still paid the highest rates of any Canadian city: $42.58 a month for families and $10 for individuals (Edmonton was second with $35.75 and $8.25). The reaction was predictable: 3,000 relief workers went on strike and a hundred RCMP had to be called in to prevent rioting. With a $250,000 loan from the Alberta government, the city carried on.

The civic election of November 1934 became a heated battle between labour and Civic Government Association candidates. Communists and strikers were unwelcome but vocal supporters of labour; once they shouted down CGA speakers so rudely that the mayor cancelled the meeting. When the election was held, the council was evenly divided between labour and the CGA, with Davison easily retaining the mayoralty as an independent. Its first meeting, to deal with the strike, sparked an acrimonious exchange between labour members, who wanted relief allowances increased, and CGA supporters determined to keep the city solvent. Two aldermen came so close to fisticuffs that they had to be hauled apart and restrained from settling the argument outside. But what politics could not settle, the weather did. When Calgary plunged into one of its coldest winters in history, that of 1934-35, the strikers reluctantly returned to work.

Next June, 1935, when 1,000 well-behaved On-to-Ottawa protesters passed through, the city gave them 5,000 15-cent meal tickets, citizens cheered them off, and about 220 young Calgarians and eighty Edmontonians joined the trek. Times were getting worse, even for those with jobs. Teenage shoe salesman Carl Nickle, son of oilman Sam Nickle, got his $14-a-week salary cut to $12 for both selling and shoe-shining. Frank Wilkins was glad to keep his job at Swift's Meats even though his weekly pay was knocked down to $20. But when his boss told him another man would work for $10, Wilkins asked, "Does he know anything about smoking meat? You've got 4,000 pounds of meat in them smokehouses. How long will it take to spoil?" The boss said, "Okay, forget it."

(Below) By the early 1930s, when this picture was taken looking east on First Street West, the days of the streetcar in Calgary were already numbered. (Above) A work crew tears up streetcar tracks, as an era fades away.

When Social Credit swept into power in Alberta in 1935, local supporters decided to contest the autumn civic elections. They vied for the mayoralty, city council, and school boards seats in a hotly contested election. Davison narrowly defeated Social Crediter W.H. Herbert, but only one labour alderman was left on a council dominated by CGA and Social Credit representatives. A February by-election, in which a Social Credit candidate replaced a CGA alderman, gave the party a majority on council. This left only Mayor Davison and labour alderman W.G. Southern openly sympathetic to the unemployed, and meant that people who shared William Aberhart's monetary theories now had a significant voice in municipal politics. They immediately demonstrated their contempt for the banking system by forcing a resolution through council to reduce the interest on debentures to 2.75 per cent, regardless of the agreed rates. When a number of debentures came up for retirement in the summer of 1936, they voted to default and to pay only a token amount. For the first time, the city actually went into default.

However, an appeal to local courts by city debenture-holders determined that the action contravened the city's charter, so the council approached the Bank of Montreal and received a loan of $186,000 to meet the debenture issue.

The decline and fall of elegance

Life in the sumptuous grand style of Calgary's early tycoons pretty much came to an end in the Thirties. Some of their great homes were demolished, some sold for taxes, some preserved as museum pieces. [A] The home built by Hon. Charles R. Rouleau at 342 19th Avenue SW was sold in 1896 to Judge W. Roland Winter whose family occupied it until 1939. It was torn down in 1939 to make room for an apartment block. [B] The great sunken garden and pond at John Burns's house, 930 Prospect Avenue, survived until the 1940s. Burns was the nephew of the great Pat Burns and ran the meat-packing company. [C] Senator James Lougheed's home, Beaulieu, 707 13th Avenue SW, was seized for city taxes in the Thirties and the furniture auctioned. It was preserved as an historic site. The home of natural gas developer Eugene Coste, 2208 Amherst Street SW [D], was seized by the city for taxes in 1935. [E] Patrick Burns "Manor House" at 510 13th Avenue SW stood empty after Burns' death in 1937 and was demolished in 1956 to make room for an expanded Colonel Belcher Hospital. [F] William Pearce's house, known as Bow Bend Shack at 2014 17th Avenue East, survived the Thirties unseized, but was demolished in 1957 to make room for a warehouse.

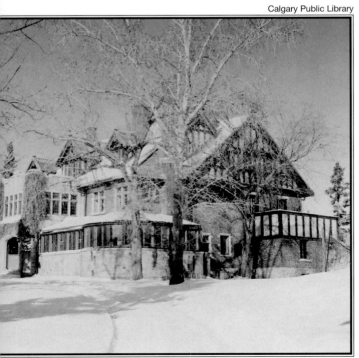

The well-heeled and well-known kept on working and playing

(Above, left to right) [A] An aerial view of the Calgary Golf and Country Club in the late Thirties. [B] Laurie Johnson competes in a polo tournament. [C] Tom Baines and the zoo were both Calgary institutions. [D] Radio pioneer W.W. Grant enjoys a canoe ride, possibly at Bowness Park. (E) Josef Csavossy (left) entertaining friends at his Bow River ranch, near Cochrane. The woman is identified as Doris Rooney.

Since by then the province itself was defaulting on bond issues, Calgary's fidelity was implicitly incompatible with the non-fidelity of the Social Credit government in Alberta. This helped place Davison in direct conflict with Premier Aberhart. So too did Davison's refusal to accept Aberhart's newly created prosperity certificates as payment for the provincial share of relief costs. Davison contended the certificates were neither actuarially sound nor acceptable by wholesalers, retailers and the public in place of legal currency. The provincial government responded by cutting back on Calgary's funding for unemployed single men, and another strike ensued.

Convinced that Calgary was being punished for refusing "funny money," Davison charged that the province offered no solution beyond augmenting local police with provincial units to control strikers. "These men are crying for bread," he lamented, "but Mr. Aberhart and his colleagues seem firmly convinced that we should feed them a diet of bullets." Even the Social Crediters on Calgary's council were appalled at Aberhart's treatment of the city and its unemployed, and late in 1936 three of them opposed the province and were summarily expelled from the Social Credit party.

Then came the big fires of 1936. On November 19, bush fires raged though ranches and farm-lands south of Cochrane, laying waste a strip thirty-five miles long and six miles wide along the south bank of the Bow River and threatening Calgary's west end. Power lines from Kananaskis burned through, leaving Calgary residents in darkness and streetcars stalled in their tracks. Within the city a hundred light standards and more than sixty telephone poles were levelled by high winds. The roof of Crescent Heights School was badly damaged, and six other schools suffered lesser losses.

[T]he Chinese weren't recognized as human beings in [Calgary] unless they had money. There was no relief for them... nothing. And they came to us [in 1937]... we decided we had to do something drastic. And we organized them and some others and we marched them down to 8th Avenue and 1st Street West... There we put them down, right across the car tracks. We tied up the machinery... This immediately brought the whole question to the attention of the people and the city council was forced to put them on relief.

—Pat Lenihan, in an interview with Warren Caragata preserved in the Provincial Archives of Alberta (Acc.No.80.218)

Started too late to stop, the Glenmore Dam provided a Thirties megaproject

THE HORRIFIED ALDERMEN WATCHED AS THE COSTS SKYROCKETED, BUT RELIEF LABOUR FINISHED THE JOB

When Calgary entered the Depression, the only major capital project on its books was the projected obstruction of the Elbow River on the city's southwestern outskirts to improve the city's water supply. It would be known as the Glenmore Dam. In November 1929, before the euphoria of boosterism and prosperity had been dampened by the stock market crash and the drop in grain prices, electors voted 4,279 to 1,679 in favour of spending $3,770,000 to solve their drinking water problem.

And it was a problem. In 1907 Alderman John Watson had convinced Calgarians that water could be diverted from the Elbow River and carried by a gravity system into the city, a proposal that won him enduring renown as "Gravity Watson."

But soon it was apparent that the lines couldn't supply enough water for the city's booming population, and the river water was often dirty. Historian Jack Peach recalls filling two glass pitchers with murky water, then letting them sit. "By noon," he said, "a most intriguing assortment of 'things' lolled on each pitcher bottom. Visible to the naked eye were grains of sand, tiny plant bits and things reluctant to lie still."

Even after a water tower, pumping station, and reservoir were added to the water systems, household taps sometimes ran dry in summer. During the spring runoff, the water was often so filthy and smelled so much like rotten vegetation that it was almost undrinkable. Then in the autumn of 1928 another disability evidenced itself. The Bow and Elbow rivers became blocked with ice, disrupting the drinking water supply further. Though the system was patched up, it was clearly obsolete. It had no treatment plant, no filters, and was designed for a population of 30,000 while Calgary's had reached 80,000. Little wonder that the majority of residents wanted a dam and new waterworks.

For its day it was a mammoth undertaking. It consisted of four units: a dam across the Elbow with an earth embankment on the east side of the river about a mile and a half south of the dam; a pumping station; a water purification plant; and 270 miles of water mains for carrying the supply to the city. The dam itself was seventy feet thick at the bottom, sixty feet high and extended a further thirty feet into the river bed.

The sod-turning ceremonies took place in July 1930, with the overall project management awarded to Gore, Naismith & Storrie of Toronto. Much of the substructure and pumping station were built by Bennett & White of Calgary, and the superstructure by J. McDiarmid Company.

As work progressed through 1930 and 1931, costs began to rise astronomically in spite of the Depression's devaluations. The mayor and council learned that the water turbines and other pumps would cost more than the dam itself, while other expenses ran far above estimates. To save money, the dam was added to the list of make-work projects for the unemployed, and at times more than a thousand men were engaged at the site. But expenditures continued to soar and the project was $196,000 over budget by the spring of 1932. When it was finished, the price had exceeded the original plebiscite figure by $315,000. This had to be financed by a separate debenture.

Engineers determined that the reservoir behind the dam would encompass some

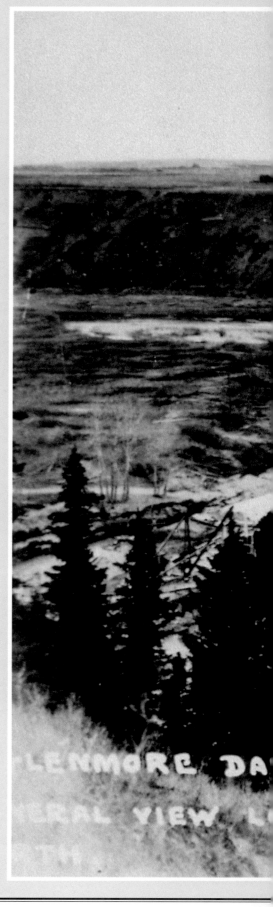

Recurrent flooding of the Elbow River and chronically undrinkable water led Calgary to embark on the Glenmore Dam project, which would see spiralling costs collide with the Depression. The dam is shown here under construction.

Started as a megaproject, the Glenmore Dam was finished with relief labour. (Top left) Field engineer R.T. Hollies poses with his wife, Amy, in the pool below the dam, under construction in August 1931. (Top right) Bill Robinson in front of a retaining wall taking shape a month later. (Above) This view of the completed mega-relief project was captured by botanist William Copeland McCalla.

900 acres of land, of which about a third was on the Sarcee Reserve. Early in 1933 the city began negotiating with the tribe, whose chief, Joe Big Plume, demanded $100 an acre. City solicitor Leonard Brockington ridiculed this figure: "The citizens would hang this committee to the nearest lamp post if we paid that much for it."

"Well, maybe that wouldn't be much of a loss," replied Sarcee David One Spot.

The Sarcees finally settled for $50 an acre, and later they must have reflected on One Spot's comments when they learned that Calgary paid other property owners, such as Dr. Stewart Mackid and J.H. Goodman, up to $400 an acre for the reservoir land.

As the dam neared completion, there were rumours that certain local individuals had personally profited from it. A judicial inquiry was launched but an examination of accounts by an Alberta supreme court judge revealed no payoffs to politicians or others.

Similarly, when concerns were expressed that the dam was unsafe, an engineering study indicated that it was much more substantial than required. This was confirmed late in 1932 when the dam was struck by a huge flood. Water normally flowed along the river at some 40 cubic meters a second, but during the violent storm, 726 cubic meters cascaded down the stream. Though not intended for flood control, the dam admirably served that purpose. The reservoir, scheduled to be supplied with water over a period of several weeks, filled up in just three days during the flood. As Peach noted, "The brand-new dam held stoutly and the water deepened. Downstream, basements remained dry, but above the Glenmore Dam and up to its rim was a new lake that has graced our community ever since."

Officially opened in January 1933, the dam met Calgary's water needs until the construction of the Bearspaw Dam on the Bow River in 1972.

— *H.D.*

After the school at Brushy Ridge, south of Cochrane, was razed by the fire, teacher Grace Davis of Canmore and three pupils were believed dead. As ashes suddenly fell in the schoolyard, and the classroom filled with smoke, rancher Ted Calloway drove fourteen children to Cochrane through a wall of flame on each side of the road. Miss Davis and the three other students skirted the south side of the fire and walked east to seek shelter with W.H. Edge, whose house had been spared when the flames leapt over and consumed his stock and barns. Fought by some 300 volunteers, the blaze was stopped about eight miles west of Bowness. It destroyed the homes, barns, livestock and feed of six families, and a dozen others lost everything but their houses. Ranchers and farmers estimated their total loss at $200,000. Next day they began the sad task of rounding up surviving cattle.

In 1937, Davison finally settled Calgary's financing problem by proposing a radical procedure known as the Fortin plan, which allowed the city to shift its total debt of $17 million from short-term debentures into a long-term debenture to be repaid over 25 years. Spreading the debt over a longer period would avoid heavy payments during the Depression and allow the city to undertake public works whose costs would be partly carried by the future residents who benefited from them. A plebiscite held in March, opposed by only one labour alderman, received resounding approval from the Calgary electorate.

Meanwhile, Davison continued his attack on Aberhart and his niggardly treatment of the unemployed. When Liberals and Conservatives joined forces to organize an anti-Social Credit rally in the summer of 1937, Davison was chairman. Before an audience of more than 8,000 people, he accused the premier of "sanctified stupidity and pompous piety." In the 1937 fall election, Social Crediters united with labour candidates in an effort to unseat him but failed dismally. Davison was

---

Davison soon found himself vilified by both right and left. He was criticized by the Calgary Ratepayers' Association for helping the unemployed, and castigated by the unemployed for selling out to the business interests.

---

returned with a healthy majority and the Social Credit/Labour candidates were all but wiped out when the CGA, now known as the Civic Government and Taxpayers Association, swept the polls.

Finally, by 1938, the Depression began to ease, thanks chiefly to a good harvest and increased oil production at Turner Valley. It was none too soon. The city had spent $10 million on relief since 1929. By the fall of 1938, only 2,034 families were still on relief, the lowest number since 1932. The usual spring strike by the unemployed petered out, and the city dropped charges against those arrested. The Stampede drew its largest attendance since 1929, with 60,000 turning out for the opening parade. Ratepayers approved a plebiscite to permit construction of a $1.2-million British American Oil refinery in southeast Calgary, and construction started on a new municipal airport. By the end of the year, the city had put more property back on the tax rolls than in any year since the Depression began.[8]

By 1939, talk in Calgary shifted from unemployment to war. The local Canadian Legion charged that alleged Nazi agents were encouraging German residents of military age to return to their homeland. Calgarians turned out by the thousands to greet King George VI and Queen Elizabeth during their royal tour of 1939. By September, when the war began, the hobo jungles on the banks of the Bow River that once housed hundreds of jobless men were reduced to a few shacks. Stores reported that customers were flashing $100 bills, and even paying accounts long deemed uncollectible.

By now Andy Davison had defeated most of his enemies. As the ranks of the unemployed shrank, the Communists lost the base of their support. The eastern banks had been mollified, and though he was still battling Aberhart over financial aid to the city, the Social Credit party had given up opposing him at the polls. So he ended the decade as he started it, winning the mayoralty by acclamation. Davison was by now a card-carrying Conservative, but one with a notable distinction. Chiefly through his efforts, no city in Canada had given men on relief more than Andy Davison's Calgary.

In A Brand of its Own (Saskatoon, Western Producer Prairie Books, 1985) James Gray writes, "Pete Knight of Crossfield won both the Canadian and North American open saddle bronc competitions. Pat Burton of Claresholm beat three American finalists in the calf roping contest. Frank Sharp of Black Diamond won the Brahma bull riding, and Herman Linder was the best all around cowboy for the third year in a row." Knight won $890 in prize money and $300 worth of merchandise. By the time he was 33, in 1937, he had four times been named world's champion bronc rider by the Rodeo Association of America, and was considered the best roughrider in Canadian history. That year, riding in Hayward, California, on May 23, he was thrown and trampled to death by a wild black horse named Duster.

[8] By 1938 even the renowned Lougheed family had fallen on hard times. Sir James's mansion, Beaulieu, at 707 13th Avenue SW was seized by the city for non-payment of property taxes. Before the family auctioned the contents in August, ten-year-old Peter, the future premier of Alberta, crept in through a cellar entrance to explore his grandfather's house. At the sale, the dining room suite fetched $200, but other furniture was knocked down for prices ranging from $2 for an oak table to $45 for a mahogany desk and bookcase. Bids on oil paintings valued at up to $2,000 reached only $45 to $125. Beaulieu passed through many owners until 1979, when it was bought by the Alberta government. It had been declared a Provincial Historic Resource in 1977, and in 1995 was declared a National Historic Site.

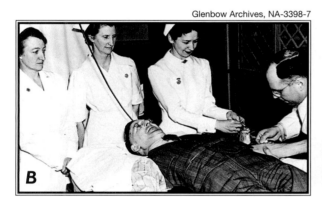

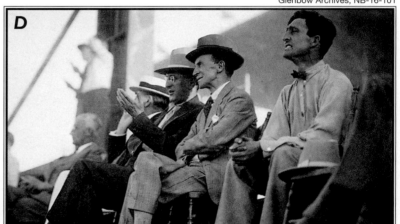

The indefatigable Andy Davison, Calgary's longest-serving mayor with the worst problems ever

One Calgarian had steady employment throughout the Depression, and that was Mayor Andrew Davison. Obviously not blamed for the city's woes by the citizenry, Davison was a tireless advocate for all sectors of Calgary society. [A] R.B. Bennett was feted as the new prime minister of Canada in 1930 with fellow Calgarian Davison in attendance. [B] The mayor setting a wartime example for his constituency by giving blood. [C] Alderman Ernest A. McCullough (left) and Mayor Davison open the city's first municipal pool. [D] The man who gave Calgary among the highest relief rates in Canada, Davison was equally at ease with such people as the Governor-General Lord Tweedsmuir. They are shown here at the 1936 Stampede. [E] On July 26, 1930, the sod was turned for the Glenmore Dam. For this occasion, Davison availed himself of a gold-plated shovel. [F] The mayor who saw Calgary through the Depression stayed on through wartime. Here he greets the Earl of Athlone, Governor-General of Canada, in 1944. [G] Davison and Chief of Police David Ritchie were photographed during the 1939 royal visit.

There was the ski jump, the Tea Kettle Inn and the Calgary Hillbillies...

Throughout the bleakest times, Calgarians found fun to suit their interests and pocketbooks, with help from local terrain and talent. [A] A motorcycle hill climbing contest at Cochrane drew an impressive crowd in 1938. [B] The venerable Tea Kettle Inn, opened on 7th Avenue W. in 1921 by Mrs. J.D. Watson and bought by Horace King in the late 1920s, was a popular eatery for the next 30 years. [C] "Ma" Trainor and her Calgary Hillbillies perform at CJCJ's studio. Announcer Don Mackay is standing behind Mrs. Trainor. [D] The bandstand at St. George's Island hosted live concerts from 1910 until it was demolished in 1949. [E] A crowd gathers to witness athletic performances at the ski jump at Elbow Park, developed jointly by the city and the local ski club.

...to say nothing of Bowness Pool and the world of the movies

[A] The movies were a popular escape from the Depression. [B] No record remains of what happened to the cigarette when this man butted out before diving into the Glenmore Reservoir. [C] Picnickers at Bowness Park were serenaded by a phonograph in the lagoon house. [D] Swimming in the Elbow River was fun and free for children on the hot summer days. [E] Sizeable pike and trout, caught by Walter Boote of Ogden for the provincial government, served to demonstrate the potential of the Glenmore Dam. [F] The Calgary Light Opera Society presented "The Rebel Maid" in 1930 at the Grand Theatre. [G] Admission to Bowness Park was five cents, making it an affordable summer treat for many families.

CHAPTER THREE

Cold, rain and summer snow often ruined the promise of the Peace

BROWNLEE'S VISION OF A MILLION SETTLERS DIDN'T HAPPEN, BUT THOSE WHO ENDURED HAVE FOND MEMORIES OF A GREAT CHALLENGE WELL MET

by **JANICE TYRWHITT**

The drought had turned much of their southern prairies into a dust bowl, the hungry unemployed were marching in their cities, labour strife was besetting their coal mining towns, and grain prices had fallen so low that even farmers beyond the dry lands could scarcely afford seed. In these desperate days, the eyes of many Albertans turned northward to the high plains of the Peace River country. Here, they reasoned, lay promise. Here lay hope. Here lay the last great agricultural frontier where the boom times of yesteryear could be lived all over again.

They were, of course, dead wrong. Though millions of acres were still unstaked in the 93,000-square-mile tract of the Peace River region, spilling over into the only section of British Columbia that lay east of the Rockies, many pioneers had already failed to wrest a living from it. In the recession of the early Twenties more than a thousand abandoned their homesteads.

Those who left were defeated less by their own ineptitude than by the hazards of travelling to, and through, inaccessible terrain. The Peace River country was cut off from Edmonton by the muskeg and forest of the Athabasca River basin, and from Vancouver by the Rocky Mountains. Steam-driven river boats and railways provided the only regular transportation. Beyond Peace River and Grande Prairie, the rail heads north and south of the Peace, journeying overland meant following dirt wagon roads or pack trails through woods and marshes. From 1924 until after the Second World War, only one impractical road connected Peace River communities. A winding combination of trails, mud roads and ferry crossings, it wandered north from High Prairie though Peace River and back south through Dunvegan to Spirit River, Grande Prairie and Beaverlodge, where a trail led to the B.C. block (see Vol.4, Sect.4, ch.1).

Within the district settlers were further cut off, because they were naturally drawn to six stretches of prairie — only about one-fifth of the total area — widely separated by vast tracts of bush and swamp. In his admirable doctoral

Throughout the Twenties and Thirties, settlers came to the Peace looking for refuge from the southern drought and a chance to start over. For many it was not the first such pilgrimage. They had come to southern Alberta and Saskatchewan from the United States or Europe, but were driven north in their quest for arable land. Those who came as part of a group, such as these Lutherans who would form the Northmark community, eighteen miles southwest of Spirit River, had a better chance of making it than those who faced the long winters and isolation alone.

thesis on the Peace River country, *The Emergence of Regional Identity* (University of Alberta 1995), Robert Scott Irwin describes how communities developed as "a series of islands isolated from one another by kilometres of unproductive forest land." When the fertile black-soiled grasslands around Grande Prairie filled up, newcomers went to open country far beyond the end of steel, in the Clear Hills west of Peace River, and the Pouce Coupé district across the border in British Columbia. Even after the two rail heads reached Fairview and Hythe in 1926, four out of five farms were from 25 to 100 miles from rail.[1] By 1929, most homesteaders had to stake their claims in the backwoods, repeating the laborious process of earlier settlement in eastern Canada. Though they had timber to build log cabins, they had to spend a season clearing land before they could sow their first crops, breaking grey-wooded soil that often proved too poor to grow grain.

Yet the Peace River country *was* Canada's last unclaimed farmland, and in 1929 the UFA

[1] The Edmonton Dunvegan & British Columbia Railway decided in 1928 to bypass the existing locality of Waterhole and the railway named its siding at Mile 365.8 Fairview. Most buildings at Waterhole were moved 4 miles north to that site.

Newspapers all over Alberta trumpeted stories of the prize-winning grain being grown in the North. To southern farmers, whose children were growing up without ever having seen a rainfall, the Peace became the promised land. Shown here is the oat crop of Berger Bolan of the Rio Grande area, 1930.

government launched a vigorous campaign to develop it. In July, Attorney-General J.F. Lymburn extolled its attractions for British emigrants before a committee of the Empire Parliamentary Association in London. That summer, Premier Brownlee toured the north by river, rail, road and airplane, travelling 3,000 miles from Edmonton to Great Slave Lake. *Edmonton Journal* managing director John M. Imrie went along to promote Brownlee's vision: "Farm homes for a million people — agricultural production exceeding that of all western Canada today — and both accomplished facts within his own lifetime." In 1927 the drylanders had begun their great exodus to a region where water and wood were plentiful, hailstorms, grasshoppers and cereal rust unusual — and gophers unknown. There were no weeds until the settlers brought them in.[2] Since then, the population had doubled to 60,000 with the arrival of 10,000 families who settled on 1.6 million acres of land, which Imrie equated to a strip 14 miles wide from Edmonton to Calgary.

[2]**Robert Irwin quotes the *Block News* of July 21, 1931, "Do you want to be driven from the Peace River Block? If not then keep the Peace River Block free from weeds."**

[3]Land offices in Grande Prairie and Peace River registered more than 800 new settlers in May 1931.

[4]The Hudson's Bay flagship, the *D.A. Thomas*, boasted a formal dining salon and staterooms with electricity and hot and cold running water. With two 200-hp engines, she burned so much fuel that she had to put in at woodpiles all along the river. Damaged by a series of mishaps, she was scrapped in 1930.

World championships in wheat and oats, won by Herman Trelle of Wembley (Vol.5, Sect.1, ch.2), proved the quality of crops, at least in the Grande Prairie district. Spectacular harvests of 1926 and 1927 saw some farmers threshing more than 70 bushels of wheat an acre, and oats exceeding 100 bushels. Imrie predicted, "This year [the Peace River country's] average yield in wheat will be more than double that of the prairie provinces as a whole... Already Peace River is producing more than all Alberta did 24 years ago. In this year of below-average crops elsewhere, Peace River will contribute one-tenth of Alberta's total wheat."

Even the most fervent boosters understood the need for planned development, rather than the unrestricted immigration allowed by the federal government, which controlled land and resources until October 1930. Imrie wanted to open up the entire region by providing telegraph and telephone communication, roads, branch railways, and above all a direct outlet to the west

coast. The UFA supported the pragmatic policy long urged by W.D. Albright, an experienced settler who managed the Dominion Experimental Station at Beaverlodge.

On January 23, 1930, Brownlee announced that the province would discourage isolated settlement by developing areas close to railways, schools and communication systems; he stopped short of endorsing Albright's proposal that government fund the substantial cost of clearing bush land. In March, a redistribution of ridings gave Peace River two seats in the legislature, and Northern Alberta Railways pledged almost $4.5 million to upgrade service.[3] By June, faster trains ran from Edmonton to Hythe and Fairview three times a week, and the two lines were stretching westward. On the Peace River, the big steam-powered sternwheelers were replaced by Hudson's Bay motorboats running between Fort Vermilion and Hudson's Hope from May to September.[4]

Through the Thirties, the river itself was still the thoroughfare that linked the communities of

To the outdoor enthusiast, the beauty of the Peace beckoned as a wilderness to be explored before development encroached too far. Laurence Blades is shown here on a hill at the confluence of the Peace and Smoky Rivers. Blades kept a detailed diary of this trip, made with his friend Harold Casselman in 1933. It's preserved in the Glenbow Archives.

[5]Unemployed applicants were assigned to road crews by the provincial police. In January 1931, nearly 1,000 were cutting timber on a proposed highway from High Prairie to Sturgeon Lake. Local residents repaid their monthly relief grants — from $4 for a single man up to $8 for a family of four — with summer road work.

Those homesteaders who had moved to the Peace from the bone-dry South in search of water got more than they bargained for in the Thirties. (Opposite page, top) This young boy in a cattle-trough canoe paddles through the 1934 flood on the Sheridan Lawrence Ranch in Fort Vermilion. (Opposite page, bottom) No amount of gasoline from the filling station in Peace River is going to help the owner of this car one day in 1935. (Below) Also in 1935, Peace River residents make their way through town.

the Peace. Most provincial funds available for roads were spent on highways designed to attract tourists to Banff and Jasper. Road work by men in northern relief camps progressed slowly.[5] Existing mud roads washed out in spring and remained execrable year round.

For Ernest Glasier and his family, who moved from the dry plains of Consort to a homestead north of Peace River in 1931, the river was a lifeline. In winter Glasier hauled his grain upstream, guiding his team and sleigh to avoid spots where the ice was undercut by fast water, creek mouths or underground springs. After school on Fridays, his children skated home from Peace River. In summer they built rafts to float downstream, or to cross the half-mile-wide river and tend stock on the other side. Like other Peace River families, the Glasiers relied on fish, game and wild berries to augment their home-grown meat and vegetables.

Occasionally the Peace turned from ally to enemy. Late in April 1934, spring breakup caused a calamitous flood at Fort Vermilion. After a winter of heavy snow and temperatures ranging from

'The whole town was under water,' wrote Melinda Satre. 'They served meals in a tent on top of the hotel kitchen, and if you rowed into the beer parlour in a small boat you were served beer.'

above zero to -72°F, alternate freezing and thawing had built up an ice jam east of the town. From a tent on high ground, Carl and Rose Sanderson and their five children saw the rising torrent tear their log house from its foundation; sixty miles downstream at Little Red River, Bobby and Valle Gray watched it sailing by. Well before their own house was surrounded by water, the Grays had moved in with a neighbour up the hill. The flood swept away seventeen buildings, and left low-lying houses all down the river filled with mud and chunks of ice. At Carcajou, Mennonites had built log cabins for a party of fellow settlers coming down the Peace; by the time they arrived, the houses were either floating or submerged.

The great flood of July 1935 isolated the entire region when high water smashed the railway

Sir Alexander Mackenzie Historical Society

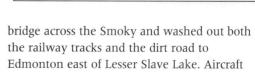

[6]Jacob wanted to turn for home, but Peter talked him out of it. They hitched rides to Peace River, spent four days floating down the Peace on a raft, and found their uncle's farm. Each eventually married, had seven children, and settled near La Crete.

Homesteaders succeeded in the Peace because they worked together, recalled Alex Batt, shown here with his wife, Katy.

Fort Vermilion Archives, FVA 1259

bridge across the Smoky and washed out both the railway tracks and the dirt road to Edmonton east of Lesser Slave Lake. Aircraft flew in emergency supplies, such as yeast for bakeries. Mail from Edmonton was put aboard a seaplane, which landed on Bear Lake, and then transferred first to a rowboat and later to a truck for delivery to Grande Prairie.

That summer young Jacob and Peter Friesen were swiping rides on freight cars from Osler, Saskatchewan, to go trapping with their uncle in Carcajou. When the flood stopped the train at Mitsue, they walked on the swamped tracks until the water reached their shoulders, then made a raft from three railway ties. Peter climbed on the raft with their packsack and bedroll and Jake pushed it for half a mile until the tracks resurfaced.[6]

Martin and Melinda Satre set out for Hines Creek from southern Alberta with their five small sons, eight horses, a home made covered wagon and two open wagons. Before they reached Slave Lake, like the Friesens, they were faced by a sheet of open water. A scow was taking travellers across to the town of Old Slave Lake. The Satres set up camp and waited more than a week for their turn to board the scow. Their horses would swim behind it. "The whole town was under water," wrote Melinda Satre. "They served meals in a tent on top of the hotel kitchen, and if you rowed into the beer parlour in a small boat you were served beer. Oddly, this hotel burned to the water while we were there."

Peace River was hit by floods on both the Peace and the Smoky. Though a volunteer crew protected the power plant, fire hall, hotel and stores on Main Street with sandbags, several feet of water poured through the buildings. Clara O'Neill, a widow who had come from Red Deer with her two children in 1933, had a dress shop beside the fire hall. She and her daughter Stella spent that night perched on the counter waiting to be rescued. Next evening, Mrs. O'Neill and Bea Bailey, who owned a Main Street restaurant, waded waist deep across a creek to a July 1 dance. "We enjoyed our night out," she wrote, "but after the flood countless days were spent in overalls and gumboots."

By then the diverse, independent character of the Peace River country had been established. There, wrote pioneer rancher and author R. D. Symons, "the ordinary norms of community life did not appear to exist. Only years of living together would make ancient history of the petty feuds that divided people of different backgrounds, cultures and motivation, who were thrown together by chance. The majority of settlers came because they were seeking a freedom based on elbow room, and the opportunity to tell others to go to hell. But in times of real need — and on the frontier that is often — animosities were laid aside and misunderstanding forgotten."

Courtesy of Jacob Friesen

Courtesy of Jacob Friesen

Peace River faces: Wherever they came from, the Peace left its mark on the visages of the people who learned to live there and prosper. [1] Robert Jones (right), director of the Dominion Experimental Station at Fort Vermilion, met John E. Brownlee in 1929, when the premier toured the Peace with Edmonton Journal editor John Imrie. Brownlee was keenly aware of the untapped resources of northern Alberta. [2] Shop-keeper Clara O'Neill honoured by the town in the 1960s. She and her daughter spent a night on her shop-counter during the 1935 flood. [3] Peter and [4] Jacob Friesen hitch-hiked from Saskatchewan to join their uncle in Carcajou; each is shown here in front of their uncle's cabin.

Between 1921 and 1931, as settlers swarmed in from the dry lands of Saskatchewan and the U.S. Midwest, the population of the Peace country had grown from 21,000 to more than 76,000. "Truly, the Peace is the promised land, where drought is little known," wrote George M. Murray in the *Vancouver Province*. "When the south land is parched, the new North is one great field of green."[7] And so it appeared to families from the Palliser Triangle. Muriel Oslie and her husband Oliver "Twist" Oslie left Trossachs, Saskatchewan, to join Twist's brother in Three Creeks, near Peace River. Her sister-in-law, May, offered her seeds and a space in her garden. Muriel was sure that nothing would grow: "I buried a bunch of seeds in the dirt, and forgot about them. One day

'The ordinary norms of community life did not appear to exist,' wrote pioneer rancher and author R. D. Symons. 'The majority of settlers came because they were seeking a freedom based on elbow room, and the opportunity to tell others to go to hell.'

May told me that my garden was up. Then I realized what five years of gardening in the dust bowl had done to me."

In 1928 Lorraine Olstad's parents moved from Bittern Lake in Saskatchewan to Hines Creek. As a child she saw the north banks of the Peace covered with spring crocuses in bloom; in mid-summer tiger lilies flamed across the hills. She and her sister were taught by their mother until their father built the first school in 1931. Years later she would recall: "I was very lucky to live in the Peace River country. We had no running water, electricity or telephones. But we had a piano, a gramophone, enough books to fill bookshelves four by eight feet, and when we got a radio in 1932 everybody came to listen to it. We had some grassland — my father could plough 40 acres without cutting a tree — and we grew lots of food and raised dairy cattle. But it *was* hard in those years; even if you had a good crop you couldn't sell it. Once Dad shipped a cow to a packer in Edmonton, and didn't get enough for it to pay the freight. It was very difficult for the men who came on their own. Some, who couldn't handle the loneliness, went crazy and had to be taken out in straitjackets. We were fortunate... Like every town, we had a hockey team. We raised money to buy matched rocks for our curling team, and Dad and his brothers got together a baseball team. Every player was an Olstad."

From her house on a knoll, Lorraine Olstad watched Ukrainian settlers trudging along the Fort St. John trail blazed by the Klondikers of '98, carrying all their possessions. "The poverty of those families was pitiful," she says. "A few had a horse and

[7] In 1943 newspaperman and politician Murray and his wife Margaret, the indomitable "Ma" Murray, moved to Fort St. John where they founded the *Alaska Highway News*.

In the same way that their parents learned the value of community, children in the Peace found that the daily chores — and there were a lot of them — went faster and were more fun when the work was shared. Here Fern Alm, Billie Oslie and Buddy Hughes of Three Creeks, near Peace River, are carrying water from a nearby stream.

Sir Alexander Mackenzie Historical Society

wagon, perhaps a cow, but they all walked. Sometimes the children didn't come to school in winter because they had no warm clothes. They lived in log houses with dirt floors, and the women must have been terribly lonely."

Ukrainians who settled near Fort Vermilion, an historic trading post that became an early exemplar of northern agriculture, ensured companionship by migrating in groups. Harry and Katarina Batt began moving their seven sons from Jasmin, Saskatchewan, in July 1930. As the young men filed land claims, married and raised families, they established a community that became known as the Batt Settlement. It succeeded because, as Alex Batt remembered, "We all worked together. When we came the 'Fort' was very small and the few people there were mostly natives and trappers. Many people who came to homestead and didn't have families to help them didn't stay."[8]

Mike Raychyba's plan to set up a co-operative colony with its own school and church in Fort Vermilion was equally successful. Leaving his wife, son and eight daughters to manage their farm

Whether erecting a barn or taking care of a bothersome bear, neighbour helped neighbour in the Peace. Here George Pengelly and William Zwick show off the bear they shot near Hines Creek in 1934.

Provincial Archives of Alberta, A5932

in Prelate, Saskatchewan, 41-year-old Raychyba set out in April 1930 with a party of twelve young Ukrainians and a Greek Orthodox priest, Father Mayba. Two newly married couples drove a half-ton truck filled with furniture, while single men went in a freight car with four horses, two cows, chickens and farm machinery. At Peace River they bought lumber and built a cumbersome but commodious scow fitted with a motor between two paddle wheels. As they loaded their truck, livestock and belongings, a local reporter dubbed the boat "the Russian Navy." On May 5 the settlers boarded the scow and knelt to pray for safe passage down the swift, shallow Peace.

From Fort Vermilion they travelled west some thirty miles to a 5,000-acre stretch of grassland, where they pitched tents and began breaking land and planting oats and vegetables. By September they built two log houses for the married couples, who shared them with the bachelors. Raychyba went home to harvest his farm. That winter the brides cooked potatoes and rabbit stew, while the men found jobs freighting groceries north to Hay River or working for neighbours. Andrew Sarapuk hauled cattle feed for Fort Vermilion pioneer Sheridan Lawrence (Vol.4, Sect.4, ch.1), earning a dollar a day in

---

Muriel Oslie's sister-in-law offered her seeds and a space in her garden. Muriel was sure nothing would grow: 'I buried a bunch of seeds in the dirt, and forgot about them. One day my garden was up. Then I realized what five years in the dust bowl had done to me.'

---

[8]Batt marriages are a testament to compatibility. Fred, Nick and Bill Batt married three daughters of Peter Sokoloski, whose two sons had come north with them in 1931. Katy and Katie Bancarz, who married Alex and Metro Batt, were more distantly related.

[9]The commands the dogs obeyed were "yew" for right, "chaw" for left and "how" for mush ahead.

[10]On May 11, 1932, when 42,000 acres of crown land were opened for filing in the Lac La Biche district, which like the Peace country lured settlers northward, fifty homesteads were taken by noon.

goods from Lawrence's store. "It was tough for young people in this isolated country," he wrote. "I had only $3 in my pocket after I paid my $10 homestead fee."

"Money was the only thing we didn't have," says Jean Campbell, who was six when her family moved from Saskatchewan to Buffalo Head Hills in 1931. "After we got here we never felt poor. We had a couple of cows, a pig and chickens, and Mother canned vegetables, jams and jellies from her garden. Dad got around in a sleigh with a team of horses, and we kids drove a dog team trained by Indians, so the dogs spoke Cree."[9] But the Campbells had no access to roads or railways and their nearest river port was Fort Vermilion, a 35-mile daylong journey by wagon trail. Two years later, Alex Campbell gave up his homestead and moved to Fort Vermilion.

Under the UFA's new settlement policy new homesteaders were restricted to areas near Grande Prairie and Peace River, and only Alberta residents were eligible. The age limit was lowered from 18 to 17, filing privileges were extended from widows to wives and mothers, time spent on the homestead was reduced from six to four months a year for five years, and a three-way agreement among the railways and Dominion and provincial governments provided free transport for settlers and their livestock and equipment. By year's end, 422 families moved from southeast Alberta.[10]

To start from scratch on unbroken land, settlers beaten penniless by the Depression needed

The land where long days offset a short season

Newcomers to the Peace were amazed at what long summer days and abundant rain could produce. [A] Watermelon, that staple of the South, grew abundantly in the garden of J.B. Early of Peace River in the 1930s. [B] Florence Boire, later Sutherland, in 1937 on the family's Ponton River homestead; the garden produced sauerkraut for the winter. [C] The Dominion experimental farm at Beaverlodge demonstrated which flowers, as well as vegetables, could survive in the Peace. [D] A cabbage patch flourishes on the Craig Brothers' farm in the Wembley area.

HARD-TIMES HAPPY

Getting around in the Peace

During the Depression, the government had little money to spend on northern roads. That didn't stop people from getting to where they had to go: [A] Nick (right) and Alex (left, seated) Batt posed proudly with their boat in 1937. [B] Steve Slyshak used a handcart at Hines Creek in 1932. [C] This snowmobile, complete with heated cabin, was built for Dr. Harold Hamman. [D] The D.A. Thomas plied the Peace for many years. [E] This pioneer trusted all he owned to his own carpentry skills, as he headed to Fort Vermilion on a covered raft in 1931. [F] Using volunteer labour and donated materials, construction of the Monkman Pass Highway went on from 1937 until 1939. [G] Mobile clinics that served the North learned to adapt to the local conditions; many found it an adventure.

more than transportation. What they wanted, as a delegation of unemployed men told Medicine Hat MLA Hector Lang, was not part-time city relief work but a small grubstake to plant their roots in Peace River country. A one-time investment to plug a continuing drain on the public purse made sense. Therefore in April 1932, the federal government announced a plan to divert relief funds to help the jobless resettle. The amount allotted to Alberta, $172,000, would be matched by the province and municipalities for a total of $516,000, to offer 860 homesteaders $600 each.

Alberta got off to a slow start. Edmonton was the only city that agreed to ante up its share. ¹¹ Applicants who didn't own land had to pay the usual $10 homestead fee; many couldn't. By the

The medical angel of the Peace country
BY HORSE, BOAT, DOGSLED AND MUD TRAIL, DR. MARY PERCY SERVED THE NORTH

In July 1929 Dr. Mary Percy, a 25-year-old medical graduate of Birmingham University in England, took the sternwheeler *D.A. Thomas* north from Peace River with Kate Brighty, provincial superintendent of public health nursing, who would introduce her as the new government doctor sent to Battle River Prairie. When they disembarked a hundred miles downstream, pioneer Sheridan Lawrence and a fur trader, Frank Jackson, transferred Dr. Percy's supplies to a Cree driver's wagon. In blazing heat, plagued by swarms of mosquitoes, the two women spent eleven hours on the eighteen-mile journey to Dr. Percy's designated headquarters, a filthy fourteen-by-twenty-foot shack on the Notikewin River.

Next day, Superintendent Brighty summoned the surrounding settlers, who were expected to supply Dr. Percy with food, firewood, water and a horse. They passed a hat, collected $31, and bought her a sturdy gelding called Daniel. The following morning, Miss Brighty left for Edmonton. Mary Percy was on her own. She loved it. Years later she told Janice Dickin McGinnis, who edited her letters, "By the end of a month's time when I *could* have got out, wild horses wouldn't have dragged me away."

Dr. Percy owed her posting to a campaign launched by the UFA government to encourage settlement north of the railhead that now reached Peace River. The need for medical services was urgent. Health minister George Hoadley wanted women doctors, who could double as nurses and, at $160 a month, came cheaper than men. The Fellowship of the Maple Leaf, founded by the Rev. G.E. Lloyd of the Barr colony, provided travel funds for British physicians.

Dr. Percy spent the next two years serving a district so far north that it wasn't shown on government maps, officially 250 square miles but actually much bigger, without roads or

She wanted to practice medicine and ride a horse, so Dr. Mary Percy came to northern Alberta. She often got more than she had bargained for, she would say later.

electricity, let alone telephones. She travelled on horseback and by boat, car, wagon, sleigh and dogteam. She pulled teeth, delivered babies, patched up accident victims and battled infectious diseases such as tuberculosis, which ravaged the Métis community. In emergencies she took patients to the Irene Cottage Hospital, sixty miles away in Peace River.

In April 1930 one of her busiest weeks was made tougher by foul weather. She got home after midnight on Wednesday to find a man waiting to take her to a hemorrhaging patient. On horseback they followed a trail, much of which was under water, and swam two creeks. Eighteen miles on, they were met by another man, who asked the doctor to hurry.

"I did the last two miles of a 45-mile day at a dead gallop," she wrote. "Found the lady pulseless, cold and clammy, so it was a darned good job we hurried." After getting home at ten Thursday night, she was wakened at 1 a.m. by a man whose wife had appendicitis. She dressed, packed her bags, saddled Daniel and rode off down another trail.

As she was arranging to get her patient to hospital, she was summoned by another settler, whose wife was in labour. On Friday, she delivered the baby; on Saturday, she revisited the woman recovering from hemorrhage; on Monday, she rode 35 miles over the prairie in a blizzard to see another woman with acute appendicitis; on Tuesday, she gave her patient a stiff dose of morphine and took her to Peace River on a sleigh pulled by a noisy crawler tractor; on Wednesday she administered the anesthetic before Dr. F.H. Sutherland removed the woman's appendix.▲ Thriving on adventure, she wrote her parents, "I know I'm doing the right job."

She gave up that job in March 1931 to marry Frank

time the first 29 applicants were chosen in August, Nova Scotia and Ontario had already approved more than 200, Manitoba and Saskatchewan had placed 420 families on the land, and Quebec, which had previously resettled thousands without federal funding, planned to move up to 10,000 more under the joint scheme. Only 51 Albertans were approved by mid-September, the latest date considered feasible for northern homesteading. By 1934, after Calgary, Medicine Hat and Lethbridge signed up, a further 300 families had been set up on new farms.

Many more took advantage of free transport: 567 in 1933 alone. These were southeastern Albertans who had stubbornly hung on through the Twenties, when thousands fled the combined

Jackson of Keg River, the trader who had helped unload her supplies when she arrived. When she next met him he was a widower; his wife had died in childbirth after Wop May had flown her to hospital in Edmonton.

Jackson came to Mary Percy with a blood-poisoned hand and, since there were no antibiotics then, stayed with a neighbours while she treated it for several days. Their friendship grew; he visited her more and more often. Within a year they married, and Mary Jackson moved into Frank's square-hewn log house, seventy miles north of Battle River Prairie. They fetched Frank's two older sons from their mother's parents in Ferintosh; the baby was raised by his grandparents.

Giving up her job didn't mean giving up her practice; it just meant that she didn't get a salary or supplies. As well as caring for Keg River's four hundred residents, most of whom

Community was the key to success in the North, whether homesteading or healing. (Left), a twenty-hour 135-kilometre trip to the hospital at Peace River in May 1930 needed more than horsepower. (Above), Frank and Mary Jackson worked together for over 40 years. People said they served Keg River and the surrounding area so unstintingly that no amount of money could have compensated them. Not that the government tried.

were Métis, she taught the two boys by correspondence. In turn they taught her how to cook, milk a cow and perform all the other tasks of a northern housewife.

For the birth of her first child, Anne, she went to stay with her parents in England. When she found that her second was in breech position, she planned to go to hospital in Grande Prairie. But the baby arrived six weeks early, on a -72°F night in February 1935, and Frank delivered John Robert himself.

Frank and Mary Jackson spent the rest of their lives at Keg River, raising their children and healing their neighbours. In 1937 they set up a hospital, which they ran until 1950, when Frank gave up his trading post and took up farming, so successfully that he and Mary won the Alberta Master Farm Family Award in 1953. By this time both their children and Frank's elder sons were married and home-

steading, and his youngest son was an oilfield driller.

When Frank developed heart problems in 1974, at the age of 82, Mary retired to spend more time with him. She was 69, and had been practising medicine for 45 years. Frank died five years later, and she stayed on in their farmhouse.

Over the years many honours recognized Mary Percy Jackson's skill and dedication, among them the Order of Canada, the Alberta Order of Excellence, and an honorary LL.D. from the University of Alberta. She was especially moved when "The Voice of Native Women" named her Woman of the Year. In 1988, with the help of Cornelia Lehn, she published her memoirs, *The Homemade Brass Plate* (Cedar-Cott Enterprise, Sardis B.C.).

In 1996, Dr. Jackson moved from Keg River to Manning after falling and breaking her arms. In January 1998 she was still keeping abreast of the field of medicine and serving as a mentor to Alberta medical students.

—*J.T.*

ADr. Sutherland, then the only doctor in Peace River, had homesteaded there with two brothers. After graduating in medicine and serving in the Great War, he practised in Peace River from 1919 to 1963, and served sixteen years as mayor.

The people of the Peace played the same way they worked: they made do, improvised, and invited their neighbours to join them. [A] No diving board? No problem — for Ralph Hutchinson, anyway, as he prepares to dive off his horse into the 1930s' swimming hole in the Heart River, known to locals as "Bare-Ass Bend." [B] The Sokoloski family orchestra was a mainstay at get-togethers in the Fort Vermilion area. [C] The presence of a fiddler meant an impromptu dance at this picnic near Northmark, 18 miles southwest of Spirit River. [D] Robert Mehlum and R. Dale DeBolt operated a "ferry" in the DeBolt area. [E] A curling rink was a natural addition to Peace River. [F] The hills made skiing popular as well. [G] These Northmark men prepare to celebrate their first Christmas in their new home.

onslaught of drought, debt and despair (Vol.5, Sect.1, ch.1). Between 1931 and 1936, 5,000 settlers moved to Peace River country. The families who trekked there in search of a second chance had nothing more to lose. By 1933 only bush land was left, and in some new districts 95 per cent of the settlers were on relief, which had to be repaid by working on roads and railways, trapping or freighting. But here, like the first Peace settlers, they seldom went hungry because they could live off the land. Even in the worst years, there was enough game and produce to support a barter system.

"We had it pretty good up here in the Depression," says Edwin Ward, who was born in La Crete in the late Twenties. "My mother made up to 800 pounds of butter a month, traded for clothes and dry goods in the stores." Farther south in DeBolt, where dairy products were too abundant to have market value, "wooden money" (lumber) was the standard medium of exchange, and butter was used as axle grease. In 1936, in the depth of the drought, Peace River's $9.4-million crop earned real money, and residents spent more on groceries and dry goods than in any year since 1929. By January 1937, Grande Prairie was free of debt for the first time since its incorporation in 1919; an $11,000 bank surplus allowed the town to cut taxes.

Though these were encouraging signs, the Peace country never became the great granary touted by politicians. It grew the province's best wheat and its long summer daylight accelerated the growing season. But this didn't guarantee big crops: spring came late, frost came early, and heavy rain fell almost every September before the fields were dry enough to harvest. In 1933, 1935 and 1937, snow fell in summer. The introduction of early varieties of wheat boosted production in fertile grasslands such as Grande Prairie, but even those areas weren't profitable when the price of wheat bottomed out. In 1932, when the Peace shipped a record crop of more than 18 million bushels, top grade No.1 Northern hit a low of 36 cents a bushel.[12] Farmers paid 69 cents a

bushel to produce it; from 1930 to 1935, they didn't recover their investment. In 1934, when they expected a bumper crop of 19 million bushels, they couldn't raise the $30 cash necessary to buy binder twine. They didn't need it; autumn rain and early frost killed the harvest.

So the Depression forced the promising Peace to give up its dreams of immense wheat fields and ranches, and its inhabitants had to find new ways to make a living. The climate, too capricious for single crops, invited diversified farming. In 1927 J.B. Early planted half an acre of vegetables near Peace River; six years later his 18-acre garden yielded ten tons of tomatoes, and four

When sound equipment came to Grande Prairie in 1930, the Capitol Theatre was jammed with fans awaiting their first talkie. A week later the movie house burned down. Arson was suspected, and outraged citizens called for the lash.

tons each of cantaloupes and watermelons. Frances Mann, a young widow, had driven her four children from Moose Jaw to Peace River in a 1929 Essex after her husband's slow, painful death from gas poisoning in the Great War. She settled on a small farm and specialized in market gardening. Though prices were rock bottom — 25 cents a dozen for corn, 1½ cents a pound for cucumbers, $8.85 for two nearly grown lambs — her family thrived.[13]

Others switched from wheat to oats, with its consistently higher yields, or hay grown from timothy and other grasses enriched with legumes such as alfalfa and clover. As Robert Irwin explains, this mixture made land more fertile because the legumes restored nutrients, the grasses added fibre, and together they controlled both weeds and soil erosion. Homesteading in DeBolt in

[12]Marquis wheat, which ripened a week earlier and yielded more than Red Fife, was commonly grown in the Peace River district by 1911. After 1926, Garnet became the dominant variety because it matured several days earlier, even though it produced inferior flour. By 1940, Garnet had been overtaken by Red Bobs 222.

[13]After serving in the RCAF in the Second World War, Frances Mann's sons, John and James, ran a grocery business. John joined the fire department, retiring as chief, and James served 16 years on town council, four as mayor.

1932, Charlie Moore ordered Victory seed oats from Robert Cochrane of Clairmont, North America's foremost grower of timothy seed. To pay for them, he cashed in his life insurance policy. When the company withheld payment for sixty days, he cancelled the order. Cochrane wrote back, "Young man, you come and get your seed oats and pay later." Breaking land with a home made plough, seeding by hand, cutting with a neighbour's binder, Moore launched his seed-growing business. Encouraged by Cochrane, he specialized in Alsike clover. A new industry was born when the Peace River climate proved ideal for growing high quality forage seed, which could be shipped cheaply to profitable markets in eastern Canada.

Mike Raychyba found a new vocation by building a bigger *Russian Navy* with a cabin and kitchen, an upstart rival to the Hudson's Bay scow *Weenusk*. For eight summers he carried freight and passengers between Peace River and Fort Vermilion. In 1937, when nothing grew on his Prelate farm but Russian thistle, he brought his family to Peace River. By then, two other vessels manned by Nick Batt and Jack O'Sullivan were plying the same route, pushing one or two barges loaded with grain or livestock. Passengers who signalled with a white flag were picked up by a dinghy with an outboard motor and taken aboard the moving boats.

Alex Campbell, who brought his family to Peace River country on the *Russian Navy,* returned to his former work as a mechanic when he moved back to Fort Vermilion. Owning one of three cars in town, he ran a taxi and opened a garage where he repaired radios and farm machinery. For the local doctor he devised a snowmobile from a Ford Model A chassis (see photo on page 18); it cut Dr. H.A. Hamman's visits to remote regions from a week to two days.[14] With a gas engine he generated the first electricity in Fort Vermilion, which powered the hospital, doctor's house, hotel and stores.

The same spirit of enterprise led each settlement to build the institutions everyone needed, churches, schools and hospitals, that drew settlers together, whatever their circumstances or country of origin.[15] Ed Hughes wrote, "Looking back, I think of the people who came to DeBolt[16] with their many nationalities, religions, backgrounds and skills, blending together despite a terrible depression and creating an excellent community out of nothing."

Like most small villages Homestead, 30 miles northwest of Grande Prairie, opened its own school in 1931. Neighbours cut, hauled and hewed logs and hand-made everything from the schoolhouse to the desks. Another school built the same year became the community centre for

(Above) Charlie Moore, shown here with his two sons, helped start a new industry with borrowed machinery, but told the company he couldn't buy seed. The company gambled on him and won. (Below) Threshers being unloaded at Fort Vermilion, probably in 1934. Heavy machinery came in by river. (Opposite page) A threshing crew at work near Spirit River in 1930. For many the risks paid off.

Arras, west of Dawson Creek. "All gatherings were held there," wrote Ida Scharf Hopkins in *To the Peace River Country and On* (Richmond, B.C., c1973). "Our Women's Institute met once a month and planned dances, sports days and picnics. We encouraged each other. Quilts were made and raffled off to raise money with which we bought a carding machine to card the wool for home made quilts or spinning, a small loom to make mats, and equipment for the schools. The most important part was getting out to visit other women."

Almost every Friday night in Nampa, school desks were moved out to make room for a dance. Anna Nord wrote, "Gas lamps were lit and hung from the ceiling, a boiler of water was put on the stove for coffee, babies were put to sleep behind the piano and ladies would bring cake and sandwiches to serve at midnight. Men would pay 25 cents for a bit of floor wax and a token offering for the musicians. Horses would be tied at the hitching rail from eight o'clock at night to three o'clock in the morning."

A few larger towns enjoyed more sophisticated entertainment; people from surrounding districts flocked to the cinemas. When sound equipment came to Grande Prairie in 1930, the Capitol Theatre was jammed with fans awaiting their first talkie. A week later the movie house burned down. Arson was suspected, and outraged citizens called for the lash; the culprit, if he existed, was never found. The Boyd Theatre in Peace River began showing talkies the same year, and in 1932 it was refurbished with a flashing electric marquee and a grandiose lobby with sofas, potted palms, and a fireplace. For patrons with hearing problems, the front row of the balcony was fitted with earphones; families with babies were seated in a special glass-fronted "crying room".

Big or small, every community in the Peace celebrated Dominion Day. Lila Miller of Royce remembered, "Our first picnic was held July 1st, 1930, at Carter's ranch. Settlers came for miles around, walking, on horseback, riding in wagons. We had a wonderful time. There were ball games but best of all was the visiting with everyone. The ladies brought a bountiful lunch. We had a big supper and enough left for the dance at night. The picnic became a yearly event."

The need for companionship overrode hardships. In 1931 Marion and Margaret Gubrud and their neighbours, John and Evelyn Hillman, drove three miles to a party after supper: "As we had two small children, our Lou and the Hillmans' Florence, we put the sad-irons in the oven to warm our feet in the sleigh, and took all our blankets and quilts. When we got to the Holmquists, we found out it was 62°F below. There were twenty men and five women at the party. The women played out dancing and went to bed with the children. The men spent the night playing cards and sleeping around the heater. We woke up to the smell of meat frying, and Bob Holmquist toasted eight loaves of bread to feed us all."

The paradox of the Peace was born in the Thirties. Its residents were at once fiercely independent and inextricably united. "A man may become part of a city and not be unduly noticed, but when he plants himself in the middle of a half-mile square of land he can't help but become an individual," writes Ida Hopkins. "His qualities or lack of qualities are exposed to the world to see.

There were no accurate maps. There were no weather stations. And it was a map that Wop May drew on the back of an envelope that [local bush pilot] Bissell used when he flew me and my infant daughter to Keg River. This was one of the first times that I nearly became unstuck. We were flying down to Keg River — this was in 1932 — and a storm came in from the north... I remember vividly how he opened the side window of the plane and tried to rub the ice off the front, which was, of course, what we did in cars in those days, but it didn't do any good...
— Dr. Mary Percy Jackson

[14]Alex Campbell's daughter Jean remembers, "One night, waiting for Dad to bring the doctor home from a long trip, we heard a roar and saw red lights. 'Daddy's home!' Mother said, 'No, it's a chimney fire!' So we took buckets of water up to the attic and put it out."

[15]In 1931 there were 23 religious denominations in the Peace River country; with fewer than 1,500 residents, Grande Prairie alone had six resident ministers and two congregations served by circuit preachers.

[16]DeBolt was named for H.E. DeBolt, an early postmaster in the Peace and later (1940-1950) Social Credit MLA for Spirit River.

His ability to stand on his own two feet and yet co-operate with his neighbours could make the difference between success or failure."

Thus was bred the spirit that led the Peace country to pursue two related demands: recognition as a distinct region, and an outlet to the Pacific. The secessionist movement sparked by newspaper publisher Charles Frederick in 1927 (Vol.5, Sect.2, ch.2) was briefly reignited in 1936 when the Peace River Autonomy League pressed for a return to territorial status. Alberta was giving the region a raw deal, Frederick claimed, by exploiting its natural resources to float bonds, and giving it nothing in return but a share of the huge provincial debt. He called for an all-weather highway connection with southern Alberta, and a railway to the coast with reasonable freight charges. Neither threat nor appeal bore fruit.

In April 1938 Dr. F.A. Wyatt, professor of soils at the University of Alberta, told the Royal Commission on Dominion-Provincial Relations that the northern parklands could support 250,000 new settlers within the next 25 years. Three weeks later the Peace River Chamber of Commerce revived the idea of secession — this time including northern B.C. and the Mackenzie River basin right to the Arctic Ocean, but not Alaska. Universally damned by federal and provincial politicians, the proposal died again.

What the Peace chiefly wanted — had wanted for 25 years, and would go on wanting for many more — was the coast outlet, to export grain and import necessities without going through Edmonton. Canadian National president Sir Henry Thornton had reneged on his 1925 promise to build a railway to the coast when Peace River grain production doubled to 10,000 bushels. In 1930 the Canadian Pacific had surveyed four Rocky Mountain passes — the Monkman, Pine, Peace and Wapiti — but Ottawa and the railways wouldn't follow through with the cash. By now, with 8,000 cars in the Peace region, residents were willing to settle for a highway. Grande Prairie wanted a southern route. Alexander Monkman, a pioneer fur trader, rancher and prospector, had discovered an old Indian trail, only 132 miles long, that cut through the Rockies from Rio Grande, south of Beaverlodge, to Hansard, B.C., where a gravel road led to Prince George. With a group of farmers and businessmen, he formed the Monkman Pass Highway Association. In the summer of 1937, a volunteer crew of twenty young men began building the road. The work party, reinforced by new shifts, included three women cooks, one of them Monkman's 31-year-old daughter, Christina. Local residents donated food and funds for supplies. Grande Prairie had just opened the most northerly radio station in the British Empire, CFGP, which played five hours of music for a Radio Dance. That night, fifty dances held in halls throughout the Peace raised a total of $1079.80. With up to ninety men working at any one time, twenty miles of road and bridges were built in 1937, and sixty more in 1938. The Edmonton Chamber of Commerce promised funding if the MPHA ran a car through the pass. On September 3 a 1927 Model T Ford set out with a brave banner: PATHFINDER CAR, MONKMAN PASS HIGHWAY 1938. PEACE RIVER OUTLET TO THE PACIFIC. PRINCE GEORGE OR BUST! Two months later it was stopped by winter weather. In 1939 lack of cash slowed the project and the outbreak of the Second World War killed it. The Model T didn't make it through the pass until June 1967.

Meanwhile, residents north of the river championed a rival route through the Peace Pass. By 1940 volunteers had cleared a trail from Hines Creek to Rose Prairie, north of Fort St. John, where they too bogged down. But the Peace Pass and Monkman Pass ventures were widely respected as a symbol of self-reliance: without a cent of government money, the people of the Peace had worked together to challenge their perennial isolation.

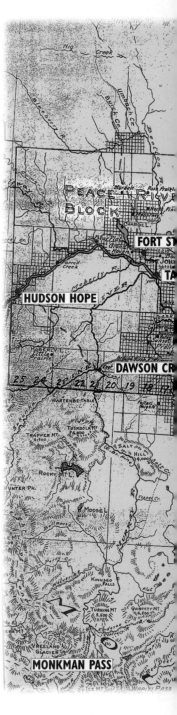

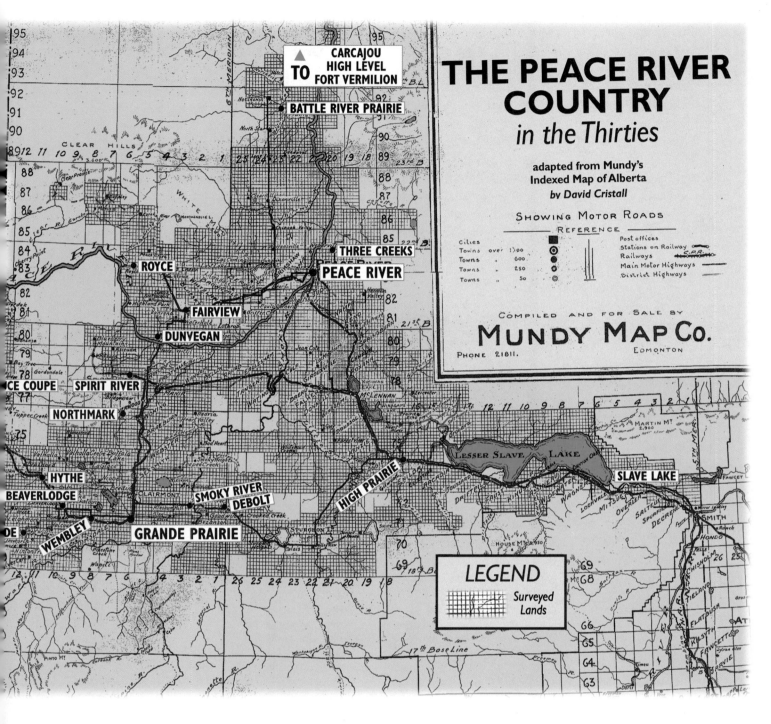

THE PEACE RIVER COUNTRY
in the Thirties

adapted from Mundy's
Indexed Map of Alberta
by David Cristall

SHOWING MOTOR ROADS
REFERENCE

Cities		
Towns over 1,000		Post offices
Towns " 600		Stations on Railway
Towns " 250		Railways
Towns " 50		Main Motor Highways
		District Highways

COMPILED AND FOR SALE BY

MUNDY MAP CO.

PHONE 21811.   EDMONTON

LEGEND
Surveyed Lands

TO CARCAJOU HIGH LEVEL FORT VERMILION

BATTLE RIVER PRAIRIE

THREE CREEKS

PEACE RIVER

ROYCE

FAIRVIEW

DUNVEGAN

SPIRIT RIVER

NORTHMARK

CE COUPE

HYTHE

BEAVERLODGE

WEMBLEY

GRANDE PRAIRIE

SMOKY RIVER DEBOLT

HIGH PRAIRIE

SLAVE LAKE

By the end of the decade, technology and local initiative began to open up the Peace. From 1937, Grande Prairie and Peace River had regular airport service and by the following year, Peace River Airways began flying to Fort Vermilion, Hay River and Yellowknife. In 1939, the regional telephone system was linked with Edmonton, giving residents their first chance to call "outside." That year, work began on a highway from Grimshaw to Hay River, boosting Peace River's hope of becoming the gateway to the mining fields of Yellowknife — a hope that would be realized in 1947, when the winter tractor road from the Meikle River to Great Slave Lake, hacked out as a make-work project for the unemployed during the Depression, became the Mackenzie Highway.

Even at the century's end the people of the Peace shared a lingering pride in belonging to a remote, independent community. As Fran Moore, curator of the DeBolt Museum and head of the 27 museums that made up "The Spirit of the Peace" at the end of the century, observed, "Anyone who arrived before 1970 has a sense of Peace River country as a special region."

The lavish overland junket of a French eccentric — Was he a dilettante, a spy, or just plain nuts?

TRUE, MONSIEUR BEDAUX BROUGHT HIS WIFE, MISTRESS, A SPANISH MAID AND A FLEET OF HALF-TRACKS, BUT NOT ALL THAT MUCH CHAMPAGNE

What the Peace River country lacked in the Thirties was ready cash and a route to the Pacific. In 1934 Charles Eugene Bedaux handed out plenty of the first and proposed to explore the second by travelling 1,200 miles overland from Edmonton to Telegraph Creek, B.C. The press seized on his plan; whether or not it solved regional problems, it made good copy. In May the *Edmonton Journal* reported that "the French multi-millionaire sportsman's party, which includes three women and several experts of international reputation, will comprise one of the best-equipped and certainly the most unorthodox expeditions ever to penetrate northern Canada."

The expedition was legendary, in that it spawned many conflicting accounts. Was Bedaux a dilettante embarking on a "champagne safari" with his American wife, Fern, his Italian-Swiss mistress, Bilonha Chiesa, their Spanish maid, Josefina Daly, and vast quantities of champagne, caviar, truffles and pâté de foie gras? Was he a Nazi sympathizer, spying out the route that would later become the Alaska Highway? Was he *crazy*?

The answer is complicated, as Jim Christy discovered while researching his book, *The Price of Power* (Toronto, Doubleday Canada, 1984). Bedaux, a short, forceful man often described as Napoleonic, had made a fortune by devising a time-and-

motion-study system which he sold to 600 major industries in eighteen countries. Though his ideas were later reviled by labour as a speed-up method of exploiting workers, clients such as Goodyear, DuPont and General Electric used them to streamline production.

Obsessed with efficiency, confident of his own skills, Bedaux set out from Edmonton clearly expecting to succeed. While hunting big game in northern B.C. in 1926, 1932 and 1933, he was struck by the need for a route to the coast. Now he assembled a team of experts who knew the unmapped country. Geologist Jack Bocock, who had organized his trip in 1932, hired two experienced surveyors, Ernest Lamarque and Frank Swannell. Bedaux's twenty tons of supplies included high-tech gear such as fireproof tents, folding tables and chairs, and bush toilets. He packed liquor, but probably only one case of champagne, which was shared by twenty-two people after a hard day on the trail.

Like most latter-day explorers, Bedaux hedged his bet by using clients to line up sponsors and publicity. News dispatches were released by his New York press agent, Austin Carson. Citroën provided a mechanic and five half-track tractors to be tested in rough terrain. Eastman Kodak rounded up an Academy Award-winning Hollywood cameraman, Floyd Crosby, to film the expedition.

Bedaux ensured his popularity in the Peace by spending more money than most residents had seen in a lifetime. He paid premium prices for every-

Charles Bedaux was more than willing to talk to reporters in Edmonton on July 6, 1934, as he tried to make his expedition the media event of the summer, and succeeded.

Accompanying Bedaux on his expedition were his beautiful wife, Fern, and his equally lovely mistress, Bilonha Chiesa. Despite such exotic erotics, veteran northerners doubtless regarded the whole enterpise as absurd.

then still in Fort St. John: "Do not think it possible for main party to reach here till end of August at earliest."

This was optimistic. It rained almost every day. Floundering in muskeg, the tractors got stuck and had to be dragged out with block and tackle. Once it took four hours to get them across a quarter-mile swamp. Their tracks and mechanical parts needed continual repairs. Often they moved only one or two miles a day. By August 1, when they reached Cameron River, only 58 miles out of Fort St. John, Bedaux decided they made better film footage than transportation. His "documentary" was fast turning into melodrama. Three nights later he had Crosby stage and shoot a fire in camp. "I dash across in frantic haste to save my tent — this is the cue for our buckaroo cowboys to drive the pack train in front of the camera," geographer Swannell wrote in his diary. "The others dash out of the tents with dunnage and Josefina finally emerges shrieking."

thing from packhorses to $7,000 for his wife's mink coat. He hired 53 cowboys at $4 a day — twice the going rate — chosen from 3,200 applicants. Edmonton responded by staging a champagne breakfast, a parade and a speech by Lieutenant-Governor William Walsh — as Bedaux set out on July 6. Villages along the route welcomed the party with banners and cheering crowds; at Grande Prairie it passed under a specially built arch.

The spectacular climax was filmed when the expedition reached the Halfway River where it surged against a 120-foot bank of sheer rock. Bedaux had his crew undercut the cliff so that it would collapse under the weight of two Citroëns. As the drivers jumped free, the big tractors plunged into the river, spilling their loads of empty boxes. Two days later another tractor was sent downstream on

Fanfare couldn't speed the big Citroëns crawling along trails turned to gumbo by heavy rain. They took ten days to reach Fort St. John, where Bedaux spent almost a week mending the tractors and waiting for better weather. When they left on July 22, Bedaux launched his backup plan. Even if they didn't make it, their endeavour would be recorded on film. The party spent 1½ hours posing for Crosby's camera; the pack train was unpacked and repacked; dozens of residents were paid $10 each to wave goodbye. Now the expedition entered little-known terrain. Since April 30, advance parties under Ernest Lamarque had been finding and clearing trails for the Citroëns. A month later, when the planned route through Prophet River proved impractical, they crossed the Muskwa River. There a trapper told them of a pass where that river met the Kwadacha. From there a rough trail led Lamarque to Whitewater Post (later Ware, B.C.), where he sent a message to Bedaux,

(Top) The Bedaux bravado was in evidence as he paraded his Citroëns at Exhibition Park before celebrity-struck Edmontonians. (Middle) With military precision, the group headed into the north, confident of coming out with the documentary of the century. (Bottom) It wasn't long before reality set in, and the wheels of the trucks sank into the gumbo of the Peace.

(Left) Bedaux at the reception held for him at Government House, shaking hands with Lieutenant-Governor William L. Walsh. No one seemed to be immune from his charm. (Right) Bedaux plainly enjoyed photographing his wife and his mistress together, as titillated Edmnontonians noted. Were they truly close to each other, people asked, or was this just another part of the performance that was Charles Bedaux's life?

a raft toward a cliff loaded with dynamite, which was intended to crash down on the car. The stunt failed: the dynamite fizzled and the raft swung clear to drift gently past. The other two Citroëns were abandoned.

Bedaux parlayed these fake events into headline news. "Nine Escape Death Narrowly When Three Tractors Are Lost," the Calgary *Albertan* reported under a New York dateline. The *Edmonton Journal* interviewed William Thomlinson, one of Bedaux's pack-riders, in Edmonton's Misericordia Hospital; he spoke vividly of the disasters, but admitted that he had simply suffered a torn tendon when his horse bucked him off. When Lamarque's party met a youngster whose partner had just drowned crossing the Kwadacha, Bedaux's agent reported the death as the expedition's first fatality.

The real victims were the horses. Before scrapping the Citroëns, Bedaux had brought in 58 more. Plodding through mud, in country that provided little forage, they were soon weary, starving and infected with hoof rot. Some died; some had to be shot. On September 4, two days after fording the Muskwa, they at last found a rich meadow beside a clear lake ringed by magnificent snow-capped mountains. Here the party camped for four days, while the horses grazed and rested. Mapping the terrain, Swannell named its features. "Fern Lake" was surrounded by peaks called after expedition members, the highest being "Mount Bedaux".

At Whitewater, Bedaux expected a message from Lamarque, telling him what route to follow. Far ahead at Telegraph Creek, Lamarque had

Josefina Daly, Mrs. Bedaux's maid, was given her own role in the movie "documenting" the trek.

indeed sent word by wireless: he had found a good route through Sifton Pass to Dease Lake. But a clerk in Vancouver failed to relay the message, and it never got to Bedaux. When the expedition reached Sifton Pass heavy snow was falling, food was running short, and the men and surviving horses were exhausted. Bedaux decided to give up. His party went down the Finlay and Peace rivers to Taylor, B.C., in five freighter canoes with outboard motors, then hired cars and trucks to Pouce Coupé. There Bedaux told reporters that he recommended a highway along the route discovered by Lamarque: "I believe Canada and the United States want an international road through there and I wanted to be the first to try it."

By the time the expedition passed through Beaverlodge on July 12, 1934, public enthusiasm had obviously waned. A far cry from the adulation in Edmonton, the faces of these spectators express incredulity — perhaps because they knew the Peace country better than southern Albertans did.

Bedaux's aims were, and still are, mystifying. When he invited the Duke of Windsor to marry Wallis Simpson at his château at Cande in 1937, was he luring the Duke into a German tour that endorsed Hitler's dictatorship? Or did he, as Jim Christy suggests, work with British agents, and encourage his European companies to protect Jews and sabotage the Nazis after France was occupied in 1940? Was he playing both sides, by trying to sell a trans-Sahara pipeline first to the Germans, then to the Americans?

Whatever his game, Bedaux lost. In September 1942 he and his wife were arrested by the Gestapo in Paris. After two weeks in a concentration camp, he was sent to Algiers to build the pipeline, carrying water one way and fuel the other. When the Allies occupied North Africa, he tried to persuade the U.S. to adopt his plan. An American agent raised doubts about Bedaux's allegiance: he was charged with collaborating with the Nazis and imprisoned in Miami, where he died of an overdose of sleeping pills on February 18, 1944.

Vilified, perhaps maligned, by a succession of Canadian journalists, Bedaux crossed Peace River history like a stray comet. This was perhaps the most straightforward of his many endeavours: he tried, and failed, to establish the long-awaited route to the coast.

Perhaps it was the fact that so many respected professionals were persuaded to accompany Bedaux that convinced some there must be covert motives behind Bedaux's journey. It seemed unbelievable that geographer Frank Swannell (left), geologist Jock Bocock (centre) and photographer Floyd D. Crosby (right) could be convinced for any amount of money to participate in a vanity expedition.

Section Four

FURY ON THE PRAIRIES

The fall of the UFA and the Social Credit explosion

Between 1930 and 1935, the swelling agony of Prairie farmers and the unemployed led to the gradual erosion of support for John Brownlee's UFA government. But this disillusionment turned into fury after court actions saw sex scandals surround the premier and one of his senior cabinet ministers. It also fanned the Social Credit movement, which spread like a fire on the Prairie, resulting in what is arguably the greatest election upset in Canadian history on August 22, 1935. Here in a typical 1935 election rally a speaker, too far from the camera to identify, harangues a crowd at Smoky Lake.

Premier John Edward Brownlee looks nonchalant in this April 1930 photo, taken at Mayfair Golf Course. Brownlee had good reason for high spirits. He had rounded out his first term of office with the return of Alberta's natural resources to provincial jurisdiction, and looked forward to being elected to a second term. However, within months the fabric of his administration would start to unravel.

CHAPTER ONE

Saving the Pools sends Alberta into a debt spiral

BENNETT SALVAGES THE ALBERTA TREASURY, BUT CLOSES THE POOLS' WORLD MARKETING FACILITIES, RUINING WOOD'S GREAT VISION

by GEORGE OAKE

As the man who had won control of natural resources for Alberta, and sold the white-elephant northern railways to the Canadian National and Canadian Pacific railways for $25 million, Premier John Brownlee confidently faced the 1930s. With a powerful mandate from the people, and a still-buoyant economy, he made light of ominous portents. The stock market crash of October 1929 then seemed an eastern calamity, scarcely noticed by most Albertans. They were more concerned about rising unemployment and falling prices for grain, the engine of the Alberta economy.

In the face of such danger signals — relief payments were costing the provincial treasury nearly $3,000 a day, and the price of a bushel of No.1 Northern wheat had dropped from $1.78 in July of 1929 to $1.20 by the end of January 1930 — Brownlee remained bullish. He blamed the jobless figures on recent immigrants, and assured nervous farmers in Calgary that wheat prices would soar again. These temporary setbacks were not insurmountable, he declared. But they were, as he would learn to his chagrin over the ensuing and increasingly painful years.

Like the premier and other federal and provincial leaders, newspapers paid scant attention to declining grain prices. No.1 Northern's 58-cent slide over six months was relegated to the business pages. "Fractional Fall in Wheat Values," said a one-column headline on page 21 of the *Calgary Herald* on January 3, 1930.

Grain officials confessed bewilderment. George W. Green, manager of the Ellison Milling and Elevator Company, called the decline "the most baffling question I have faced in 27 years in the grain business in Western Canada." On February 27, 1930, he told the *Lethbridge Herald*, "Everyone has been fooled — the pool and the grain trade. We have the wheat, but no one is buying it..."

That was the central dilemma for the Alberta Wheat Pool, the province-wide grain-handling co-operative that was proudly seen as at last giving farmers control over their marketing (Vol.5, Sect.2, ch.2). When the Pool opened its doors October 29, 1923, on the second floor of Calgary's Lougheed Building, it had signed more than 25,000 farmers. representing 2.4 million wheat acres, to five-year contracts. For several years the Pool thrived, thanks to a series of good crops, and a $15-million line of credit wrested from the banks. It could also count on solid government support. The government itself, after all, was the creation of the United Farmers of Alberta, the UFA, whose president Henry Wise Wood was also president of the Alberta Wheat Pool.

The Pool needed this line of credit to make an initial payment to its farmer members when they delivered their wheat to a local grain elevator. After a substantial volume of wheat had been sold by Canadian Co-operative Wheat Producers Ltd., the federally incorporated central selling agency that represented the three prairie pools, another interim payment was made, followed by a final payment at the end of the crop year.

Throughout the Roaring Twenties export markets boomed and Canadian wheat was the benchmark of quality around the world. Even Canada's banks, no friends to western farmers in the past, were happy, although they had insisted on a hedge before extending their multi-million dollar credit line. Their agreements with the Pool stipulated that initial payments to farmers must be 15 per cent less per bushel than the price wheat sold for on the open market. Notoriously tight-fisted bankers thought this margin would protect them if grain prices dropped. Equally confident,

---

'Everybody has been fooled — the Pool and the grain trade generally,' said the manager of a milling and elevator company. 'We have the wheat, but no one is buying it.'

---

the Alberta Wheat Pool guaranteed farmers a 1930 initial payment of $1 a bushel.

Short-sighted Pool officials couldn't grasp the scope of the precipitous slide in world wheat prices. They decided to hang on to their wheat until they could get a decent price for it. They withheld from market more than 48 million bushels of the low-quality 1928 crop. This strategy had no effect on the falling international market. Nonetheless, the three prairie pools kept back more than 44 million bushels of the 1929 crop.[1]

Pool directors were convinced that prices would eventually improve and Canadian farmers would reap a fair price or even a windfall on various foreign markets. But prices kept falling and the tactic of withholding wheat caused resentment among some of Canada's best customers in Europe. On February 8, 1930, *The People*, a British weekly, ran a front-page article claiming the Canadian wheat pool had stored its grain "to squeeze money out of our pockets," and declared the economic crisis in Canada was caused by the "most gigantic gamble in wheat ever known." In Canada, such inflammatory stories were blamed on what the *Winnipeg Free Press* called the "Millers' Trust," British grain brokers who resented dealing with colonial co-operatives that smacked of socialism or worse. But withholding wheat proved a disaster, and the Pool abandoned its foolhardy policy in 1930. The last grain of the 1929 crop was not sold until June 1931.

In 1930 the Pools tried another device to control wheat prices — compulsory pooling. For the previous five years, almost half the wheat crop had been sold on the open market, rather than through the Pools' central selling agency. Advocates of compulsory pooling argued that a monopoly would have more market clout to command fair prices. Alberta and Manitoba Pool members were lukewarm to the plan, but the militant Saskatchewan group, grandiloquently known as the United Farmers of Canada, were determined. With a mandate from 71 per cent of members, Saskatchewan Pool executives asked the provincial Liberal government to enact laws ensuring mandatory wheat pooling.

---

[1] The Canadian Wheat Pool was not alone in withholding wheat from international markets as a means of stabilizing prices. The total Canadian wheat carry-over from 1928 was 131 million bushels; and the 1929 carry-over was 140 million bushels.

In 1931 Robert Gardiner became president of the United Farmers of Alberta and a thorn in Brownlee's side. Under Gardiner's leadership the UFA moved to the left and became increasingly impatient with the premier's conservative proclivities.

Provincial Archives of Alberta, A 13980

When the government stalled through the fall session, Alexander McPhail, general manager of the Canadian wheat pool, threw his weight behind an idea he had initially opposed. Prodded by such endorsements, in March 1931 the Saskatchewan government reluctantly enacted the Referendum and Grain Marketing Bills, which required all Saskatchewan farmers to deliver their wheat to Pool facilities. Less than a month later the contentious laws were thrown out by the Saskatchewan Court of Appeal.

Meanwhile the Pools were finding it even harder to sell wheat abroad, as markets dried up and new sellers appeared. In 1930 the outbreak of a civil war cut China's demand for wheat. That year, Argentina began dumping wheat on the international market, and the Russians became net wheat exporters for the first time in sixteen years, selling more than 112 million bushels to Europe while their own people starved at home. European countries such as Germany, France and Italy responded by raising the duty on imported wheat to protect their own farmers. Spain kept its domestic price up by forbidding wheat imports.

Growing ever more desperate, the Pools' central selling agency tried to influence prices by buying more than $2-million worth of wheat futures on the international market, a speculative gamble with much the same odds as rolling the dice in a crap game. This fruitless ploy was abandoned in the grim winter of 1930. By mid-January prices were falling like snow, and bankers saw the 15 per cent margin that had once seemed enough to guarantee their loans evaporating as the Great Depression took hold. If the Pool paid out more in the initial payment than it could earn on

The wheat pool's central selling agency tried to influence prices by buying more than $2-million worth of wheat futures on the international market, a speculative gamble with much the same odds as rolling the dice in a crap game.

the international market, every bushel sold at a loss would edge the provincial Pools closer to defaulting on their loans. The banks warned the central selling agency that once their margin was gone they would force the agency to repay their equity by selling all the wheat then in stock. Given the large carry-overs of wheat from the 1928 and 1929 crops, such massive dumping on a soft market would have collapsed world prices and ensured the death of the pools.

Harried by the banks, losing their toehold in the international market. Officials of the pools turned to their provincial governments for salvation. In Alberta the appeal was a foregone conclusion. The UFA government could not turn down a call from the UFA organization that had put it in power.

Agriculture was the province's lifeblood. The total value of Alberta's 1929 agricultural production was more than $240 million. That year more than 16.3 million acres had been under cultivation, producing 88,181,000 bushels of spring wheat in addition to many other crops. Virtually every Alberta family had a stake in the price of wheat.

Brownlee and his counterparts, Saskatchewan Premier James Thomas Milton Anderson and Manitoba Premier John Bracken, knew that if the Pools went under, the whole Prairie economy might collapse. If they guaranteed the loans the banks had made to the Pools, how could they pay off the loans? If the Pools defaulted on the loans, the prairie provinces could be bankrupt. In late January the three Prairie premiers met in Regina with Wheat Pool officials, then in Winnipeg with the jittery bankers. "Prairie Provinces Guarantee Further Bank Loans to Pools," read the headlines in the February 5 *Edmonton Journal*. The subhead added, "Wheat Market Dangerously Close to Price Covered By Initial Loan; Further 15 per cent Security Assured."

When the government galloped to their rescue, the Wheat Pools breathed a sigh of relief. No one — pools, politicians or press — was yet willing to face reality. Even a small increase in prices turned newspapers into Pollyannas. "Foreigners After Our Wheat," screamed the banner headline of the *Lethbridge Herald* on March 21, 1930. The fine print told another story: rumours of Argentine grain export shortfalls had triggered a small price rally, which died by noon.

Such yearning for good news reflected newspaper readers' concern. As prices continued their inexorable decline, authorities tried to counter growing public pessimism. On February 6 the *Edmonton Journal* ran a report of a Winnipeg speech by federal Finance Minister Charles Dunning under the headline, "Grain Situation Is Not Alarming Dunning Insists." But the minister's message, "A way out can be found with cool and careful handling," offered no specific solutions.

Brownlee used almost every podium to refute the fears spreading like wheat rust. Gearing up for a spring election, on March 2 he told Edmonton's St. David's Society that there was no sound basis for "the prevalent pessimistic outlook." His exhortation had little effect on the price of grain. Ten days later, for the first time since 1923, No.1 Northern wheat fell below $1 a bushel, a figure that nudged the cost of production.[2]

Such portents didn't dissuade the premier from calling an election on April 24. Reminding Albertans of the UFA's achievements, he capitalized on the fact that almost every one of the "Brownlee government's" initiatives bore his personal stamp. This so impressed the Peace River UFA federal constituency association that, at the annual convention, they suggested raising his salary. He counted on his popularity to override the effect of plunging wheat prices. Even on June 14, five days before the election, when July wheat futures dropped below the critical $1-a-bushel mark and the Canadian Press reported, "Bedlam racked the wheat pit with holders unloading recklessly," Brownlee expected to win a second term.

On June 19 voters confirmed his victory. The UFA won forty seats, a drop of three from dissolution but still a substantial majority. The Liberals won only nine, the Conservatives a mere six. Labour and Independents split eight seats for a total of 63. With a solid mandate, a $582,000 budgetary surplus for 1929-1930, and a record of resolving federal-provincial problems, Brownlee was envied by other premiers with shakier political foundations. As the cracks in Alberta's bedrock widened, he assured the provincial Wheat Pool that agricultural prices were bottoming out and an upward swing was soon expected. His predictions were wrong. From a low of 96.5 cents a bushel two days after the election, July wheat futures dropped to 85 cents by the end of June. And 1930 promised a bountiful crop just as export markets were vanishing.

While crops swelled and prices dropped, the hard-pressed wheat pool found the bankers snapping at its heels. At the end of July, bank head offices in Toronto and Montreal suddenly reneged on their previous agreements and refused to advance any new funds unless the co-operatives provided market receipts for stored grain. This ultimatum spelled the end of the Pools. Without the provincially guaranteed bank loans, they couldn't pay their members and would be forced to buy and sell on a falling market.

Again Brownlee managed to bail them out. On the way to an Ontario holiday with his family, he was in Winnipeg on July 30, the day the bankers presented their demands. That afternoon he persuaded the banks to advance an extra $2 million to the pools, allowing the Western premiers time to bargain with the bankers. Wheat pool boss McPhail was less sanguine. "Most of the general managers showed a surprising ignorance of the matters under discussion and a great deal of stupidity in their ability to understand explanations," he wrote in his diary on August 5. "God help the country if these are the kind of men who carry such large responsibilities."

By the second week of August, the three western premiers ground out a new deal between the pools and the banks, by signing perilous new documents that protected the bankers from all financial risk. This stopgap agreement covered only the 1929 crop. What about the 1930 bumper crop now being harvested? The Pools set an initial price of 60 cents a bushel on No.1 Northern, which then seemed an ample margin.

From *The U.F.A.*, November 15, 1930

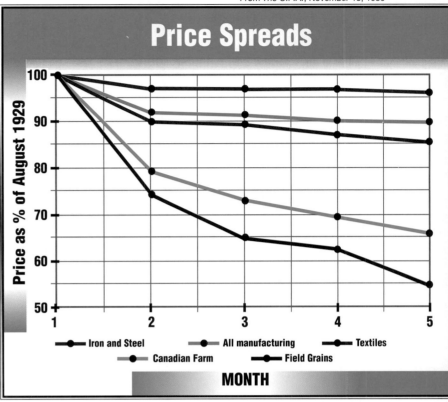

By 1930 the Wall Street crash had echoed through all sectors of the Canadian economy. But the farmers were paying the greatest price by far.

[2]In February, 1930 the price of No.1 Northern wheat fell to a low of $1.07 per bushel and continued its decline in March before stabilizing temporarily at about $1, a figure which translated into an Alberta farm gate price of roughly 70 cents, or the approximate cost of production. Thus any further decline would result in a net loss for farmers.

*The three Prairie premiers —
Manitoba's John Bracken (left),
Saskatchewan's J.T.M. Anderson
(centre), and John Brownlee —
united in 1930 in a desperate
effort to save the Pools. But their
success in Ottawa came too late.*

[3]"The decline in the net
income of farmers had been drastic
between 1927 and 1929," writes
E.J. Hanson in his thesis, *A Financial
History of Alberta: 1905-1950.* "Such
income fell further from $62 mil-
lion in 1929 to $6 million in 1933. In
1934 and 1935 agricultural income
rose to exceed $30 million in each
year. Thus, for the six successive
years, 1930-35, the net income
per farmer was less than $400
annually."

[4]A.J. McPhail died suddenly in
Regina on October 21, 1931, at the
age of 47, of complications following surgery for appendicitis, which
he had undergone two weeks prior
to his death.

Meanwhile the Prairie premiers made a vain appeal
to Richard Bedford Bennett, the newly elected Conservative prime minister from Calgary, who refused to put a
70-cent floor price on wheat. When the price of top
grade wheat slipped from 92 cents in August to 78 cents
in October, dumbfounded Pool officials reduced their initial payment on the 1930 crop to 55 cents a bushel.

Desperately seeking solutions, Brownlee suggested
that the Pools issue long-term public bonds, to be repaid
so gradually that Pool members wouldn't face heavy
deductions. The banks dismissed the idea of what they
considered junk bonds. Next Brownlee proposed two
drastic ways of reducing the Pool's liability: withholding
funds reserved for the final payment on the 1928 crop,
and debiting the accounts of members who had been
overpaid in 1929. Since Alberta's loan guarantees were
propping them up, Pool officials reluctantly agreed.
Broke and bewildered, the farmers had no fight left in
them.[3]

On November 11, when Canadian over-production
and higher European tariff barriers had pushed wheat
prices down to 64 cents a bushel, Brownlee again asked
the federal government's help. "Cannot too strongly urge some action necessary
prevent great revulsion of public opinion," he telegraphed Bennett. "Meeting already called farmers' organizations three provinces. We cannot too strongly urge upon Dominion Government
necessity some action to prevent entire collapse agricultural industry." Ironically the prime minister, who had allied himself with eastern manufacturers by protecting them from international
competition, simply wired back that he was "deeply concerned about the whole matter."

That night the prairie premiers met Pool and bank officials in Bracken's office. The bankers
finally accepted an agreement that would prevent the financial collapse of the Pools. They agreed
to defer their loans if the premiers would again guarantee them against future loss. McPhail had to
sign a document agreeing to appoint a general manager for the Pool approved by the banks. The
banks' head offices in Montreal and Toronto refused to honour the agreement and the three west-

---

**When the premiers bargained with the bankers, Wheat Pool general
manager Alexander McPhail wrote, 'Most showed a surprising
ignorance of the matters under discussion and a great deal of
stupidity in their ability to understand explanations. God help the
country.'**

---

ern premiers again rushed east for an emergency meeting with bank executives who said they
would foreclose on their loans unless the federal government put its financial clout behind the
bankrupt Pools. Travelling with them, McPhail wrote, "Banks seem to feel if Bennett does not do
anything to insure them against loss they will close out the pool and take over the wheat... The
vultures are gathering."

When the premiers reached Ottawa, acting prime minister Sir George Perley stonewalled
Brownlee's suggestions of a floor price for grain, financial backing and a stabilization board to buy
wheat when it fell below accepted levels. A direct appeal to Bennett, then attending an Imperial
Conference in London, produced an ambiguous reply that Ottawa *might* lend the provinces money
to protect the banks.

Now the contest was down to the wire. The banks set November 20 as the day they would
foreclose on the pools, western agriculture's greatest marketing achievement. Spurred by this
imminent political and economic catastrophe, Bennett at last assured the Canadian Bankers'
Association that the federal treasury would guarantee Pool loans. Even staunchly Conservative

newspapers favoured the deal. The government hadn't gone into the wheat business, explained the *Ottawa Journal*: "A step taken in an emergency to tide over a crisis has nothing to do with a permanent policy; and if what the government has done can check the downward march of the wheat market it will benefit the whole country."

Bennett's move came too late. The wheat price skidded to 56 cents a bushel in later December, four cents less than the original 60-cent initial payment and 14 cents below the cost of producing a bushel of top grade wheat. Though Brownlee professed optimism — the *Edmonton Journal*'s December 27 headline was "Depression Has Hit Bottom, Curve Upward From Now On, Premier Brownlee Decrees" — he might as well have decreed that the North Saskatchewan run upstream.

The only people in a position to issue decrees were the bankers, who insisted that the wheat pool make good on its commitment to appoint a general manager they approved, notably John McFarland, general manager of the Alberta Pacific Grain Company and a close friend of Bennett. Appointed on December 10, he closed the Pool's overseas offices, ending its marketing capability. McPhail, who vainly fought the move, wrote that McFarland "has no understanding of the farmers' viewpoint or any idea other than to perpetuate old methods of doing business."

Replacing McPhail[4] and the Canadian wheat pool's board, McFarland became a one-man export agency, selling pool wheat through the Winnipeg Grain Exchange, the very agency the pools had tried to circumvent by direct marketing from their overseas offices.[5] McFarland's appointment and his subsequent actions killed the barely realized dream of a farmer-owned grain marketing co-operative. Without the central selling agency, the Canadian pool reverted to its original status, a farmer-owned elevator system in each prairie province.

What UFA president Henry Wise Wood had extolled as the "ultimate achievement" of the farmer co-operative had been wiped out in less than a year. If the architect of the Pool's greatest achievement was devastated by seeing his life's work destroyed, he would say only that the big mistake had been fixing a $1 initial payment per bushel in 1929. Still a champion of co-operative marketing, he remained Alberta Wheat Pool president until 1937, just four years before he died. In 1931 he refused to run for another term as president of the UFA. He watched from the sidelines as the organization he had cautiously nurtured for fifteen years dissolved into factions of socialists and Social Crediters, slowly becoming irrelevant in an age of more militant populism.

In a very real sense 1930 represented a loss of innocence for the UFA as an organization and a government. The dream of a vast farmer marketing co-operative had vanished overnight, along with the voter goodwill that had granted the UFA a third term in office. Though the 1930 wheat crop was one-third larger than the previous year's, the drop in farm-gate prices from $1.02 to 45 cents a bushel meant that farm income was down by more than 50 per cent. On June 1, 1931, 27,846 people — 24 per cent of all Alberta wage earners — were unemployed. By the end of the year more than 40,000 Albertans were on government relief and the costs were staggering.

A flurry of legislation was enacted to deal with various aspects of the problem. A special act was passed to authorize temporary seed grain advances, financed by loans from Ottawa. Cabinet was authorized to raise funds by way of loans payable within five years — a mistake, as time would show.

Farmers who could not meet their debts in 1929 had a year's grace under the 1923 Debt Adjustment Act (Vol.5, Sect.1, ch.1) but foreclosures multiplied in 1930. Government efforts to go to bat for individual farmers with creditors proved futile. The UFA 1931 convention in Calgary passed a resolution calling for the cost of necessary government services to be confiscated from the profits and reserves of commercial institutions (read "banks"), but the government resisted such radical solutions in favour of a mild compromise. The 1923 act was repealed and replaced with the Debt Adjustment Act of 1931, which enabled municipal councils to pass a bylaw providing for the consolidation and payment in instalments of tax arrears. It also set up a review board with all the powers of a commission under the Public Inquiries Act to attempt amicable settlement of debts. Another act established the Alberta Rural Credit Corporation in order to co-ordinate and consolidate the financial affairs of the province's co-operative credit societies, many of which were in

Henry Wise Wood could do nothing but watch as the organization he had built and guided for more than a decade crumbled. After refusing to run for the presidency of the UFA in 1931, the year this photo was taken, Wood outwardly maintained his faith in the co-operative movement, but his eyes told something of the pain he must have felt.

[5]In June 1931, Prime Minister R.B. Bennett agreed to McFarland's request for a federal guarantee to back the Pool's price stabilization operations (the risky purchase of wheat futures on the international markets), according to William Kirby Rolph in his biography, *Henry Wise Wood of Alberta* (University of Toronto Press, 1950). "Despite the fears in many quarters that the guarantee would cost the federal government millions of dollars, McFarland eventually achieved a profit of over $9.6 million," writes Rolph.

default on government loans.

Such legislative Band-Aids, which reflected Brownlee's prudence, showed that the UFA government still didn't grasp the depth of the economic wounds bleeding Albertans dry. But they did see that the treasury was nearly empty, and Brownlee insisted on some tough cost-cutting measures. Government agricultural schools at Claresholm and Raymond were closed "temporarily." Almost 1,000 Alberta civil servants lost their jobs as the payroll dropped from 2,566 in January 1930 to 1,600 in December 1931, and many of the survivors suffered wage cutbacks of between 4 and 10 per cent.

When the last remnants of the 1929 crop were sold in June 1931, the net overpayment totalled a whopping $22 million, of which Alberta's share was more than $5.5 million.[6] Bennett had pacified the bankers by guaranteeing the 1930 crop, but he didn't intend to offer similar support in 1931. Brownlee was instrumental in forging an agreement — no mean feat considering the participants included three provinces, three pools and seven banks — that was as creative as it was complex.

The three provincial governments issued 4.5 per cent bonds (at 2 per cent discount) to the banks to cover their share of the liability. The provincial Pools in turn issued 5 per cent twenty-year amortization bonds to their respective governments in corresponding amounts. The banks were secured by the elevator assets of the Pools, which in Alberta and Saskatchewan were worth more than their

MENACED!

The wolves, in the forms of bankers, politicians and market conditions, were circling by August 15, 1931, and the UFA knew it. However big and powerful the farmers' organization had once been, it knew it wasn't invincible.

pledge of security to the governments. Even when the Manitoba Pool declared bankruptcy in November 1932, the deal Brownlee had cobbled together remained intact. Manitoba's government agreed to absorb $1.4 million of its Pool's liability to the banks and to accept security for the balance in the stock of the reorganized Manitoba Pool Elevator Company.

Instead of supporting Brownlee's initiative, Bennett undermined it. For years western farmers had been complaining bitterly that futures trading by the Winnipeg Grain Exchange was a major cause of the wheat price collapse. In a cynical sop to the farmers and Pools, Bennett appointed the British economist Sir Josiah Stamp to head a royal commission "to determine whether or not the sale of grain futures is injurious." The imported commissioner added little to previous inquiries, and concluded that "futures trading, even with its disadvantages... is of distinct benefit to the producer in the price which he receives." Naturally enough, the farmers felt betrayed.

In 1931 wheat prices stabilized at last. As early as January 3, the *Edmonton Journal* reported May wheat futures were up to 58 cents a bushel. When the price reached 70 cents in November the paper headlined the "Soaring Price for Grain." But Brownlee's promise of better times already

[6]Throughout the twenty years after the termination of contract pooling in 1931, the three provincial elevator systems prospered, expanded, and, to a certain extent, diversified their activities. Each one liquidated in full its financial obligation for the 1929 over-payment to its respective provincial government. The Alberta Pool made its final payment on June 1, 1947, the Saskatchewan Pool in September 1949, and the Manitoba organization a month later. By the end of the 1950-51 crop year, the three pool elevator systems had declared patronage dividends to a total of approximately $50 million. — Vernon C. Fowke, *The National Policy and the Wheat Economy* (University of Toronto Press, 1957).

The *Edmonton Journal* headline on December 27, 1930, read, 'Depression Has Hit Bottom, Curve Upward From Now On, Premier Brownlee Decrees.' He might as well have decreed that the North Saskatchewan run upstream.

---

had a hollow ring. That year a mini-drought in parts of southern Alberta had a widespread psychological effect. Bankers became even more reluctant to grant farm loans, and when they refused to advance funds to buy binder twine, the rough string needed to bind wheat sheaves for threshing, farmers were outraged.

Brownlee recognized that bank strategy was aimed at forcing the provincial government to guarantee binder twine loans. Though he joined his fellow prairie premiers in backing the loans, he insisted the guarantee be kept secret to thwart speculators. Farmers who had been refused loans were quietly told to reapply, and bank executives ordered their rural branches to approve the loans since the government would back the farmers' notes. By 1932, $23,960 in binder twine loans were outstanding. That year 8,575 farmers received these loans and the government posted a guarantee for more than $350,000 with the banks. At year end, $112,348 was still outstanding.

The government whittled down bad binder twine loans to $90,000 in early 1933, but clearly Brownlee's treasury couldn't afford the spiralling costs. The UFA government got off the hook by enacting the Binder Twine Securities Act, which allowed farmers to buy 3.5 pounds of twine per acre of wheat on credit, using part of their forthcoming crop as collateral by giving the seller a crop mortgage note.

Meanwhile Brownlee faced a more serious problem. Low wheat prices and the southern mini-drought combined to force a growing number of farmers to default on taxes. This meant that many school districts ran out of operating funds and had turned to the provincial government.

During a conference in the spring of 1931, Bennett had told Brownlee that Ottawa would pick up part of the tab to keep schools operating, but the wily premier asked the prime minister not to reveal his generous offer. In a letter to MP Henry Spencer, Brownlee explained that "any general statement would mean the municipalities would throw up their hands and the banks would insist on government guarantees." To his dismay, this was already happening in Manitoba and Saskatchewan. So far Alberta, by encouraging deals between banks and municipalities, had kept schools running without provincial guarantees. Even if the province had to provide loans for the next school year, Alberta would be one step ahead of the other prairie provinces.

More than 600 of the 3,427 teachers employed by Alberta's rural school districts in 1932 were earning less than the minimum annual salary of $840. Some were working for as little as $500 a year, but that was still $100 more than the average farm family income in 1933.

Teachers' salaries, binder twine loans and above all massive relief costs soon drained the provincial treasury. The New York money markets, usually the best source of loans to provinces, began turning down applications from struggling Canadian governments. Only Brownlee's appeal to Bennett for interim credit from the federal government kept Alberta from defaulting on a bond interest payment due in U.S. dollars in New York on October 1, 1931. In exchange for its support, Ottawa insisted on provincial cutbacks.

In January 1932, Alberta again turned to the federal government, when the province came within hours of defaulting on a $3-million bond maturity. The Bank of Manhattan agreed to

---

If Henry Wise Wood was devastated by seeing his life's work destroyed, he would say only that the big mistake had been fixing a $1 initial payment per bushel to Wheat Pool members in 1929.

---

renew a third of the issue for 90 days at 6 per cent only after Bennett promised that no further renewal would be requested. Finally the entire renewal of the bond issue was accomplished by a loan from the federal government. Alberta had to cover other liabilities by floating a new sinking fund debenture series for $15 million, paying 6 per cent interest, then a record high, and discounted to 95.25 per $100 — the most expensive financing the province had yet undertaken.

Brownlee was increasingly frustrated by the impossibility of reconciling spiralling relief costs and shrinking revenues. Farmers wanted money for seed grain and binder twine. City people wanted freight subsidies on coal and more generous unemployment relief. And now the school districts had joined the chorus for emergency funds. A competing demand for reduced taxation was clearly an impossible dream as the treasury bottomed out. The premier testily warned Albertans that the government couldn't pay out unless the people paid in: "If present conditions have to be faced for another year or more, the government will be obliged to put into effect drastic economies or to substantially increase taxation, or both."

In the fiscal year ending March 31, 1931, the government racked up a deficit of more than $2.4 million, the first provincial red ink in seven years. Over the next year the deficit reached more than $5 million. Brownlee, who viewed debt like a disease, imposed even more stringent economies. A new provincial income tax lowered exemptions to $750 for single persons and $1,500 for married men, raising an extra $1.3 million. By now Alberta's farmers were so broke that, even with the lower exemptions, few had any taxable income.

Corporate taxes were increased only 4 per cent even though Brownlee noted that Calgary Power paid just $1,000 provincial tax on income of almost $500,000 in 1931, and Canadian Utilities paid a total of $25 in taxes. Disbanding the Alberta Provincial Police and replacing it with

Whatever his problems, Brownlee could still draw crowds. And the people of the Peace area had not forgotten that he had been the first premier to visit that part of the province (see Vol.5 p.87). This photo was taken in 1929 at the community hall in DeBolt during that tour.

the RCMP in 1932 reduced the price of policing to fixed annual costs shared with Ottawa. The Debt Adjustment Act was modified again to include retail merchants, to whom Alberta farmers now owed $40 million.

Beleaguered by the economy, Brownlee was fast falling out of favour with his own organization. Since Henry Wise Wood had retired, the UFA had lost its Christian overtones and had become increasingly radical under its new president, Robert Gardiner. Membership, down from 31,000 in 1921 to 10,351 in 1931, hit an all-time low of 4,098 in 1932. Some members were soon deserting to the new Social Credit movement or the Co-operative Commonwealth Federation (CCF), the socialist forerunner of the New Democratic Party. Many others simply couldn't afford to pay dues.

The new UFA executive had little sympathy with Brownlee's fiscal retrenchment. In his presidential address at the annual UFA convention in Edmonton on January 22, 1932, Gardiner made a thinly veiled attack on the premier. "To reduce the power of the people to purchase the goods they need, when these goods can be produced in abundance, is not economy," he thundered. "Yet the further reduction of the community's income is the only remedy prescribed by those who are concerned to retain the present economic system intact."

On June 1, 1931, 24 per cent of all Alberta wage earners were unemployed. By the end of that year more than 40,000 Albertans were on government relief. The costs were staggering.

The UFA convention, which two years earlier considered giving the premier a raise, was now passing resolutions that could only make his task harder. The perennial demand for a complete debt moratorium had even more supporters this time. One proposal urged Ottawa to provide a subsidy of $1 an acre for all seeded land. Others called for a nationalized monetary system and inflated currency, and public ownership of all land, radio broadcasting and power development. Although the 1931 call for secession from "the Dominion of Canada" was not repeated, the farmers were clearly fed up with government.

Brownlee lost still more public sympathy when he ordered the RCMP to disperse a hunger march on the legislature in November 1932 (Sect.1, ch.1). Meanwhile Gardiner, who was leader of the Progressives in the House of Commons as well as president of the provincial UFA, was urging the confiscation of wealth from wealthy Canadians. If he were minister of Finance for a day, he told the House, he would allow rich men $20,000 or $25,000 a year, and tax away 99 per cent of their income above that figure.

The premier tried to curb the more extreme proposals of his former allies by assuring the public that conservative measures would work better than reckless reforms, but his efforts were undermined by economic forces beyond his control. The international price of grain started to slide again. By late October 1932, wheat dropped to a new low of 45 cents a bushel. Nobody could figure out what was wrong. Gardiner attributed the decline to "hoarding of money in banks."

Glenbow Archives, NA-3657-6

Others blamed the civil war in China or that mysterious scapegoat, sunspots.

Initial payment for the 1931-32 crop had been set at 40 cents a bushel, including a 5-cent bonus on the 1931 crop paid by Ottawa. Surely the international price of wheat wouldn't fall below that meagre level. But it did. By December 16, 1932, it hit 38 cents. Wheat, the mainspring of western agriculture, was almost worthless on world markets.

Albertans were becoming desperate and calls mounted for a government-legislated moratorium on debt, which Brownlee opposed. As a lawyer he knew that such a law would not only conflict with the federal Bankruptcy Act, but would make the province a pariah among creditors, unable to borrow money for public services and relief. It would force farmers to make cash transactions, which they couldn't afford, while safeguarding borrowers who didn't need its protection.

Besieged with letters and petitions pleading for debt relief through the grim winter of 1933, Brownlee was pressed into legislation that came within a whisker of a moratorium. The 1933 Debt Adjustment Act, which amended and consolidated the previous act, required a creditor seeking foreclosure on a debt to apply to one of a number of three-member government-appointed boards set up throughout the province. Conferring with debtor and creditor, the board tried to work out an amicable arrange-

There weren't many people who had a guaranteed income in the 1930s, but William Powley, shown here with his family near Smoky Lake in 1936, was one of them. As a binder twine salesman for McCormick-Deering, he was selling a product for which payment had first been provided surreptitiously by government, then later guaranteed by legislation.

The final blow to the tottering UFA government would come not from the grain markets, not from the banks, not from Ottawa, not even from the dead-broke farmers and the unemployed, but from a 22-year-old junior stenographer in Brownlee's own government.

ment for repayment. Only if this failed could the creditor sue, with written permission from the board. The act was also broadened to cover individual homeowners as well as farmers and retail merchants. Though not a perfect solution, the new law was generally admired and imitated. Manitoba, Saskatchewan and Ontario adopted similar legislation, and envoys from Franklin D. Roosevelt interviewed Brownlee about the act, which the American presidential candidate considered one of the premier's best accomplishments.

Brownlee's financial expertise was recognized when he was the sole westerner appointed to a Royal Commission on Banking and Currency in the summer of 1933. The only commissioner to recommend a publicly owned central bank, he was congratulated by his tepid ally, Robert Gardiner.

But Brownlee had used up most of his political capital and economic credit. The UFA government appeared isolated and alienated from the increasingly radicalized UFA organization. By 1934, 5,943 urban families — a total of 24,032 people — were on relief. Yet the premier wouldn't respond to ever more desperate appeals for substantial increases in food, clothing and rental allowances. He was obsessed with the provincial debt, which the previous year's deficit had increased by $2 million. With $425,000 paid out each month, relief was costing Alberta more than $5 million per year. By now the province's debt to Ottawa, mainly for relief, amounted to $8 million.

Now another long-simmering problem boiled over. Alberta's provincially owned telephone system was carrying $10.5 million in capital loans. In 1933, more than 6,000 Calgary phones, and 142 rural lines, had been temporarily or permanently disconnected for non-payment of charges. A consultant recommended wiping out the $10.5 million debt with the stroke of a pen, and spending another $5 million to recondition rural lines. It was enough to make a grown man cry — and many probably did. But the government did nothing.

Could the tottering UFA government fare worse? It could indeed. But the final blow was to come, not from the grain markets, not from the banks, not from Ottawa, not even from the dead-broke farmers and the unemployed, but from a 22-year-old junior stenographer in Brownlee's own administration.

The crop that promised prosperity
BUT IN TWO YEARS THE SUGAR-BEET FARMERS FARED AS BADLY AS THE GRAIN MEN

The *Lethbridge Herald* headline in the gloomy fall of 1930 seemed to suggest a shining new option for Alberta's suffering farmers: "Huge Sum Will Go Out to Growers." What they were growing were sugar beets, the succulent root crop local Mormon settlers had been cultivating since the late 19th century. Dependent on irrigation, the industry took off when a 115-mile canal was built from Kimball to Lethbridge. By 1930 the district grew more than 14,000 acres of beets and produced a 131,000-ton crop worth $858,000. Soon farmers throughout the province, dismayed by the falling wheat market, were planting beets. But within two seasons beet growers were in the same sad state as grain farmers.

The southern Alberta sugar-beet industry was centred at the "Sugar City" of Raymond, named for the eldest son of Jesse Knight, a Utah magnate who bought a 30,000-acre block and set up a sugar processing plant there in 1903. Rebuilt in 1925 by the Mormon-controlled Utah-Idaho Sugar Company, the factory was sold five years later to Canadian Sugar Factories Ltd., owned by Vancouver tycoon Ernest T. Rogers. Rogers planned to shut down the Alberta plant, the only obstacle to his Western Canada cane-sugar monopoly, but he was outmanoeuvred by Utah-Idaho, which refused to leave local Mormons without a market for their beets. As a condition of sale, the company stipulated that the Raymond factory had to operate through the next decade.

Trapped in an unwanted venture, Rogers set out to make a profit — 20 per cent the first year — by running the factory around the clock, processing the 1931 harvest of 105,000 tons to produce 2,000 pounds of sugar every 24 hours, and cutting his price to the Mormon farmers, who had no other market. At $5.50 a ton, they were getting less than their production costs. In 1932 the Raymond town council, faced with mounting tax arrears, decided to issue scrip for up to 40 per cent of its payroll and local bills. All but $200 of the worthless paper came back to the town treasury as tax payments.

By then, sugar-beet farmers throughout southern Alberta were appealing to Edmonton and Ottawa for funds. The federal government responded by setting up a committee to consider ways of salvaging the industry. Chaired by Lethbridge Conservative MP Dr. John S. Stewart, it recommended supporting measures, but its report was disregarded. Even former Alberta premier Charles Stewart, now a Liberal MP, opposed increased tariffs or bonuses for a crop that supplied less than 10 per cent of the domestic market. Most sugar consumed in Canada came from cane imported by Rogers and other powerful companies, which strongly opposed any concessions to the sugar-beet industry. Bennett's 1933 budget put a 2-cent-a-pound excise tax on raw and refined sugar, regardless of its origin; though the cabinet later reduced this to one cent a hundredweight for sugar grown and processed in Canada, the growers saw the tax as proof that Ottawa was in thrall to the Montreal importers.

But the provincial UFA government supported expansion

Salvation in sugar beets — pictures like this one told the story of wealth that the rest of the agricultural sector could only dream of in the 1930s. What was hidden from view were discontented growers, and workers who wanted a share of those riches.

of the industry, and its subsidies enabled Canadian Sugar Industries to build bigger bins. In 1934 an over 170,000-ton crop yielded a record 50 million pounds of sugar, and the growers collected close to $1 million. When a Utah sugar company tried to make a deal with the government to build a refinery in southern Alberta, Rogers-owned Canadian Sugar forestalled a potential competitor by setting up a second plant of its own, a $1-million refinery near Picture Butte built in 1935 with the help of tax concessions from the province.

While the farmers looked forward to modest gains, their workers were fed up with their poorly paid, back-breaking labour. Mainly Hungarian immigrants, they signed an annual contract with individual growers who paid them an agreed price for each acre worked. In the late 1920s, their average earnings represented 38.6 per cent of the farmers' return; in the early 1930s they got only 28.3 per cent, even though the tonnage of beets per acre had increased. In 1935 the Growers' Association dropped their rate from $22 an acre to $17, plus bonuses for high tonnage and clean fields. That April, radical

organizers encouraged the workers to strike for better contracts.

The provincial government traced the agitation to the Communist-affiliated Farmers' Unity League. Joe Sutton, assistant colonization manager for the Lethbridge Northern Irrigation District, urged F.S. Grisdale, the minister in charge of irrigation (vital to the industry), to squelch the strike by arresting ringleaders and withholding workers' relief payments. Sutton didn't grasp the fact that beet workers were being asked to take a $5-an-acre cut in their wages at the depth of the Depression.

Backing the growers, the provincial government managed to keep the strike out of the papers. But a union declaration charged that a "Fascist mob" assisted by two RCMP members tried to evict the beet workers and their families by breaking into their shacks and tossing out all their belongings. Some growers, like W.H. Childress of Iron Springs, sympathized with the workers. On May 5 Childress complained to the Beet Growers' Association that he had been threatened by a committee of vigilantes, who claimed to have letters warning that "Reds" like him planned to burn buildings and rape local women. If such letters existed, Childress wrote, they should be turned over to the police. The association expelled him, the Rogers interests refused to sign a contract with him, and he was forced out of the industry. By mid-May the strike was broken and most workers were back hoeing beets.

Next year the growers demanded a new deal from the two Rogers refineries. Instead of a negotiated price per ton of beets, they wanted a 50 per cent share of sugar sales. Rogers agreed because they feared an alliance between the farmers and their workers, now enrolled into the Communist-inspired Beet Workers Industrial Union. Given this assurance, the growers broke off negotiations with their workers, who responded by striking again. The farmers threw them out of their shacks, and replaced them with unemployed men from Calgary and Edmonton. On May 27 they gave the strikers 24 hours to renounce all Communist ties, and get back to work. Next day most workers returned to the fields, accepting the growers' price of $20 an acre.

Despite the year's turmoil, a bumper crop set a record: Albertan sugar-beet production earned $2,350,000. By 1939, with no help from the federal government, the industry paid farmers $1,267,000. As the president of the Alberta Sugar Beet Growers' Association later acknowledged, the only people who didn't profit were the immigrant workers.

—*G.O.*

CHAPTER TWO

The triumph and fall of the first Albertan to make prime minister

CALGARY'S R.B. BENNETT BEGAN AS A STRICT RIGHT-WING TORY CAPITALIST BUT AFTER YEARS OF TRIAL AND FAILURE LAUNCHED CANADA'S WELFARE STATE

by GEORGE OAKE

Richard Bedford Bennett had perhaps the worst luck with timing of any Canadian prime minister. He achieved power at the onset of the Great Depression. If he had rapidly attacked its problems and had made some headway against them, he would no doubt have come to be revered as an outstanding leader, rather than reviled as the man who drove starving Westerners from their farms and ran roughshod over civil rights by beating up jobless strikers in Regina. Finally his spectacular conversion from right-wing free-marketer to left-wing interventionist came too late in his term to stave off an electoral catastrophe, yet soon enough to set in motion Canada's transformation into a welfare state.

When the 60-year-old millionaire from Calgary was sworn in on August 7, 1930, Canada's economy was crumbling.[1] The stock market had collapsed in October 1929, wheat prices were falling, foreign markets were shrinking, unemployment was soaring, and bankruptcy rates were exploding. But Bennett was riding high. Having won the job he sought all his life, he wasn't going to let a recession stand in his way. Throughout his election campaign he had exuded optimism and addressed the issues, unlike the incumbent Liberals who tried to ignore economic problems for which they were inevitably blamed. His major campaign speech repeatedly promised his party would "find work for all who are willing to work," an economic feat that would be accomplished by invoking the old Tory cure-all of high tariffs.[2]

When the votes were counted in the early morning hours of July 29, 1930, Bennett had done what his predecessor and friend, Arthur Meighen, could never do — convincingly thrash the wily Mackenzie King and his Liberal machine. He had increased Conservative seats from 91 in 1926 to a solid majority of 137 in 1930, slashing the Liberals from 128 to 91. Significantly, the Progressives and other minority parties won only seventeen seats, the lowest total since 1917. And Bennett's mandate was truly national: the Conservatives won 25 seats in Quebec, twenty more than they held in 1926. The party also made gains in Ontario, Prince Edward Island, Manitoba, Saskatchewan and Alberta, which went from one to three Tory seats. "Thousands Welcome Calgary's Own Prime Minister" proclaimed the *Herald* when Bennett came home to a civic reception in August. Voters expected miracles from a leader who promised to boost Canada's economy in a new era that would create jobs and revive the prosperity of the 1920s.

Bennett attacked the task with zeal, retaining the key portfolios of finance and external affairs. This inability to delegate responsibility soon alienated colleagues who found him distant and unforgiving. *Ottawa Journal* editor Grattan O'Leary found he was "not a consensus man." He was "not above asking the opinions of others, he was only above accepting them." Even Lord Beaverbrook, a lifelong confidant, acknowledged that Bennett "regarded his cabinet colleagues as subordinates." He described his friend as rigid and arrogant, an attitude inculcated in childhood by a Methodist mother who expected her eldest son to be a paragon (Vol.2, Sect.1, ch.2). Bennett brought her stern principles to the prime minister's office. There he immediately called a special session of Parliament to pass three major acts, none designed to help Western farmers, even though he had lived and worked in Calgary for more than thirty years.

The Unemployment Relief Act allocated $4 million for direct relief, and $16 million for federal

[1] Bennett's luck in politics was in inverse proportion to his luck in business. As solicitor for the Canadian Pacific Railway, he acquired large tracts of CPR land, which he sold at handsome profits to American settlers. With $100,000 borrowed from Max Aitken, later Lord Beaverbrook, he helped found what became the Canada Cement Company (later Lafarge Canada). The two friends also backed Calgary Power, of which Bennett was president for ten years, and the Alberta Pacific Grain Company, which eventually netted Bennett $1,350,000.

Bennett also profited from a small investment in the first oil well discovered in Turner Valley, which grew into Royalite Oil, a subsidiary of Imperial Oil. E. B. Eddy's widow left him a third of her estate: when her brother died, Bennett inherited his share, which gave him a controlling interest in the wood processing giant. Six months before the stock-market crash in October of 1929 Bennett sold most of his equities and advised his friends to do the same.

[2] For the first time in a Canadian election the cult of personality may have been a significant factor because of a new technological device — radio. King was an unemotional speaker who spoke in a monotone while Bennett was an accomplished orator, ebullient and emotional. By 1930 there were 450,000 radios in Canada, which meant that Bennett's keynote speech could be heard by two million people.

public works such as wharves and bridges. Although Bennett admitted that the number of unemployed Canadians, then at least 117,000, would probably increase in winter, he portrayed the act as "work, not charity." The other two measures made good on his promise to protect Canadian manufacturers. One imposed higher tariffs on 130 imported items. A few months later he raised tariffs on an additional 400 items, including fresh vegetables, which made food more expensive for most Canadian families during the long winter months.[3] The second, an amendment to the Canada Customs Act, increased the maximum anti-dumping duties to 50 per cent from 15 per cent.

After adjourning the House of Commons on September 22, Bennett ignored rising economic problems in Canada while he attended the 1930 Imperial Conference in London. Anglophile, imperialist, head of the senior British dominion, Bennett didn't understand that the meeting was irrelevant to Canadian concerns. He saw it as an opportunity to argue for lower tariffs on goods traded within the British Empire. His notion of imperial preference wasn't welcomed by Ramsay MacDonald's Labour government. Britain wouldn't satisfy former colonials by sacrificing its ability to buy cheaper foreign wheat. The British press looked askance at an upstart Canadian who tried to talk business at a conference staged only to affirm the bonds of empire.

In Canada Bennett's failure to influence opinion was interpreted as weakness. His further absence, on holiday in Ireland, annoyed the three Prairie premiers who had gone to Ottawa begging for a guaranteed minimum price for wheat, only to be told that nothing could be decided until Bennett came home.

Richard Bedford Bennett became prime minister of Canada in the summer of 1930, at a time when many believed that the worldwide Depression would soon pass. Bennett was one of them, and the election promises that he could not possibly have kept would haunt him throughout his term in public office and beyond.

When he returned, his first public speech suggested he was unaware that the Depression was now world wide. Instead, he told 10,000 people in Regina on December 30, 1930, Canada's economic problems were entirely the fault of the Liberals and their "accumulation of many years of mistakes for which I am not responsible." He promised that the new Tory government would clean up the mess, and reminded his listeners that the $20 million pledged by Ottawa, plus $40 million in railway projects, amounted to $60 million spent on relief work. Two days later, in his annual New Year's address in Calgary, he declared that hard times were over: "We have all suffered, but we have all survived the greatest Depression of which this old world has record."

He was outrageously wrong. The Depression was intensifying all over the country, especially

Not just a Westerner, but a Calgarian, R.B. Bennett received a tumultuous welcome on his first trip home as prime minister. Here he is greeted at the train station by (L-R) Charles Jackson, Anglican Bishop Cyprian Pinkham and Mary Pinkham.

in Alberta. The province's relief rate had doubled since 1929: by January 31, 1931, 2,717 heads of families and 8,489 single men were on direct relief.

While Bennett insisted that the country was shaking off the economic blues and marching steadfastly into a brilliant future, there were signs that the government was worried. The first of a number of anti-immigration laws under Bennett's administration was a cabinet order passed on February 16, 1931, banning assisted immigration for two years on the grounds that Canada already had enough farmhands, unskilled labourers and household workers to supply its needs until 1933.

Though communist attempts to exploit and organize the unemployed met only marginal success in a few spots across the country, they terrified the conservative establishment. In the summer of 1931 an Ontario court ruled that the Communist Party of Canada was illegal, and sent five of its leaders to jail. King's Liberal government had repeatedly tried to repeal the odious Section 98 of the Criminal Code which allowed the imprisonment of politicians espousing sedition, but the Conservative Senate majority always vetoed the bill. With Bennett in power, repeal was out of the question. Bennett loathed and feared Communism, and at this point he so distrusted socialism that he and his colleagues referred to leftists as "Reds" and "Bolsheviks."

If the government had qualms about unemployment, they weren't revealed when Parliament reconvened in March 1931; the word wasn't even mentioned in the throne speech. A month later Bennett, announcing that he would never peg wheat prices, told the House, "The cry of Western insolvency is hurtful and unjust and greatly overdrawn." When Alberta Progressive MPs pressed for banking reform, he dismissed them by responding, "The banking system of Canada is adequate to the needs of the country and no reason exists for a change." Neither of these statements, which made front-page headlines in Western newspapers, endeared Bennett to hard-pressed farmers. Bennett's reluctance to acknowledge urban poverty was equally alienating. Approached by a delegation from the communist-inspired Workers' Unity League who wanted free state unemployment insurance, he bluntly replied, "We will not put a premium on idleness, and we will not put our people on the dole."

Through the spring of 1931, Bennett put his principles into practice by working from early morning until past midnight. He began each day reading files and dictating letters, spent afternoons in the House proposing measures and defending them against opposition challenges, and

[3]Bennett slapped tariffs on almost everything imported by Canadians. The mystifying duties on a pound of imported fresh vegetables included: asparagus, 15¢; lettuce, 5¢; green onions and shallots, 5¢; onion sets, 15¢; potatoes, 6¢; and spinach, 5¢.

then returned to his office. But his efforts did little to counter the Depression. When the price of wheat fell below 50 cents he evaded the issue by establishing a royal commission.

Bennett's first budget, brought down on June 1, 1931, reflected his laissez-faire capitalism. To meet a $75-million shortfall he increased the federal sales tax to 4 per cent from 1 per cent and lowered personal income tax deductions, while reducing the tax rate on higher incomes and eliminating tax on dividends from Canadian stocks. Though corporate tax was raised to ten per cent from 8 per cent, the overall effect on those with modest incomes was so harsh that the measures were resented throughout the country. All but the most pro-Tory papers endorsed the left-wing *Canadian Forum*'s assessment of a budget made up of "presents to the wealthy and greater burdens on the poor."

The Relief Act of 1930, which even Bennett had called a "palliative" measure, was not working. In a country of 10.5 million people, 437,000 were unemployed by the second quarter of 1931, and the figure didn't include agricultural workers. The $4 million spent on direct relief was too little to have impact, and critics claimed that most of the $16 million earmarked for public works under the Relief Act had been used by the provinces for political projects.

The government responded by passing another "temporary" measure, the Unemployment and Farm Relief Act of 1931. It promised relief funding until March 1, 1932 — but Bennett refused to reveal the amount. Ottawa would pay half the cost of public works, the rest being divided equally between province and municipality. Because Bennett considered that direct relief sapped the moral fibre of recipients, the Dominion government would pay only a third of such costs, and took other steps to hold them down. To keep unemployed single men off relief (and away from agitators), they would be moved from the cities to rural construction camps and given room, board and 20 cents a day. Those who refused to go could be imprisoned by the RCMP.

Bennett belatedly acknowledged the plight of the West on July 2, when he told the House that the Alberta and Saskatchewan drought was "the greatest national calamity that has ever overtaken the country." But the half-measures he took indicated that he had decided to wait out the Depression. When he introduced freight rate amendments that allowed Ottawa to absorb a 5-cent transportation subsidy for each bushel of wheat exported in the 1931 crop year, the UFA dismissed

[4]If this was Bennett's first tentative step into the realm of social legislation, it was merely an aid to Depression-ridden provincial treasuries. The original bill, enacted by Mackenzie King's Liberals in 1927, was mean-spirited and parsimonious, as John Herd and Allen Seager explain in the following passage from their book *Canada 1922-1939: Decades of Discord* (Toronto, McClelland and Stewart, 1985): "The pension scheme introduced [in 1927] was scarcely the harbinger of the welfare state. It provided British subjects over the age of 70, and with 20 years residence in Canada, with $20 a month, if they could demonstrate in a means test that their annual income from all sources was less than $125. On the pensioner's death, the pension was to be repaid by the sale of any property remaining in the estate — with five per cent compound interest added... Many elderly Canadians were left without pensions until the mid-thirties when the Maritime provinces and Quebec at last signed agreements with Ottawa."

[5]The Banff-Jasper Highway construction was begun as a federal relief project in 1931 and was completed in 1939.

'Bennett was not a consensus man,' said *Ottawa Journal* editor Grattan O'Leary. 'He was not above asking the opinions of others, he was only above accepting them.'

them as a sop to wealthy farmers, useless to those whose crops were hailed or dried out. In July the federal government announced it would buy two million bushels of wheat to be ground into 450,000 barrels of flour and sold at bargain prices to poor families in drought-stricken areas of Western Canada. It also introduced a bill that raised Ottawa's contribution to the cost of old-age pensions to 75 per cent from 50 per cent.[4] On a Western tour in August 1931, Bennett promised "work for all who desire it" and proclaimed that, "Change must come in the minds of men, not in their pockets or bank balances." Such platitudes rang hollow in the ears of dispirited Westerners racked by unemployment, drought, grasshoppers and poverty. More men were put to work on highway construction in Alberta, including 300 men picked to build the Banff-Jasper Highway.[5] Back in Ottawa on September 5, Bennett decreed a "fair wage rate" and an eight-hour day for workers on relief projects. Despite these minimal measures, the Unemployment and Farm Relief Act was a bust. On September 15, Ottawa announced it would close down 700 miles of northern telegraph lines, shutting twelve offices between Edmonton and Pouce Coupé, and putting 28 linemen and operators out of work.

Through the autumn the 61-year-old prime minister involved himself in the preparation of every major bill for the upcoming 1932 session. By the end of October he was exhausted. When his doctors said he needed a rest he headed for his second home — England — where he spent weeks consulting government officials about the next Imperial Conference, which, much to his delight, was scheduled for the summer of 1932 in Ottawa.

Meanwhile hard times got harder. By March 1932 the national unemployment figure was up

Bennett is my shepherd— I am in want. He maketh me lie down on park benches, he leadeth me beside great need, he restoreth my doubt in the Conservative Party, he leadeth me in the path of destruction for the party's sake. Yea though I walk through the valley of starvation I do fear evil for he is against me. He prepareth a reduction in my salary, in the presence of mine enemies, he anointed my income with taxes, my expenses runneth over my income. Surely unemployment and poverty will follow me all the days of the Conservative administration. And I will dwell in a rented house forever.
—*Medicine Hat News*, May 21, 1931.

[6]General Andrew McNaughton kept charts recording the disturbances in relief camps judged significant enough to be reported to National Defence Headquarters. There were 57 such disturbances between June 27, 1933, and March 31, 1934; at least 21 of the inmates involved received prison sentences. Up to December 31, 1933, a total of 3,379 men were expelled from the camps for disciplinary reasons or left in protest. Not a single month passed from the time the camps were established when there were not disturbances of sufficient magnitude to report to National Defence Headquarters. — Lorne A. Brown, *The Bennett Government, Political Stability and the Politics of the Unemployment Relief Camps, 1930-1935* (Queen's University PhD. thesis, 1979).

to 571,000. Parliament was recalled a month early, in February, to extend the lame Relief Act to the end of May — a short-sighted stopgap — and to allow the new Finance minister, E.N. Rhodes, to present his first budget. At a time when Canadians sorely needed tax relief, the budget was even tougher than that of the previous year. A special excise duty was piled upon already high tariffs, and personal income tax exemptions were drastically reduced in order to increase the number of taxpayers. While the sales tax, which hit the poor hardest, went from 4 per cent to 6 per cent, corporate taxes were minimally raised from 10 per cent to 11 per cent. All civil servants — except judges, RCMP officers and members of the armed forces, the people who would enforce Bennett's "peace, order and good government" — faced 10 per cent salary cuts, later modified to 5 per cent for those earning less than $1,200 a year.

In an abrupt reversal of policy, Bennett also decided to cut back public works and rely on direct relief provided by all levels of government. As Alberta premier John Brownlee pointed out when the prime minister announced his intentions in April, the cost of direct relief would be less than half that of the work projects, which the provinces could no longer afford.

Since the Unemployment and Farm Relief Act would run out in May, the government passed a third Relief Act. It required the Dominion, the provinces and the municipalities to share direct relief costs equally. Ottawa would lend the provinces enough money to cover the share of the many municipal governments already bankrupt. Single men who didn't qualify for local relief would be sent to western farms as labourers. Urban families on relief would receive $600 over three years to establish themselves on the land.

The first relief act had been inadequate, the second a failure, and the third was a disaster that did nothing to mitigate the Depression. Immigration and Colonization Minister W.A. Gordon boasted that 200,000 of the urban jobless would eventually be resettled on farms across Canada. Fewer than 7,000 families moved, and many of these simply transferred from urban to rural relief

---

In his New Year's Day address in 1931, Bennett told a Calgary audience that the hard times were over: 'We have all suffered, but we have all survived the greatest Depression of which this old world has record.' He was outrageously wrong.

---

rolls. Bennett's decision to put the relief camps under army jurisdiction was equally ill-judged. The very things he dreaded, unrest and strikes, were bred by military discipline, poor food and inadequate winter clothing.[6]

In July 1932 Bennett laid aside domestic crises to play host to the Imperial Conference in Ottawa. Since Great Britain's new prime minister, Stanley Baldwin, was a fellow Conservative, Bennett felt sure he could push through his pet project, a tariff-free economic union of the British Empire. His hopes were dashed when Britain's request for tariff concessions that would enable its textile manufacturers to crack the Canadian market was resisted by Montreal textile barons determined to retain their monopoly. They persuaded their local MP, Secretary of State Charles H. Cahan, to threaten resignation. Thus Bennett's dream was trashed by his own party's supporters. Britain retaliated by buying Russian timber.

The $300,000 cost of the fruitless international gala was bitterly resented by impoverished Canadians. Under the prime minister who had promised to conquer world markets, the gross domestic product had shrunk from $5.7 billion in 1930 to $3.5 billion in 1933. He had guaranteed jobs, but in September of 1932 one in four workers was unemployed. He had vowed citizens would never have to go on the dole, but more than 250,000 Canadian families were on direct relief by Christmas.

Yet Bennett was still determined to take a hard line. For more than two years unemployed men had been allowed to travel free in empty freight cars on both major railways. At a meeting in Calgary's Palliser Hotel in September, the four western premiers asked Bennett to increase Ottawa's share of direct relief to 50 per cent, because city relief programs were swamped by an influx of transients. Bennett immediately announced that free train travel for single unemployed men would cease as of September 30, 1932 — and the police would enforce it. Destitute men were advised to return home before the ban took effect to avoid maximum sentences under the Railway Act.

Intended to lighten the burden on municipal relief by getting single men out of town, the ruling had the opposite effect. Transients working on the southern Alberta harvest headed for the cities in the last week of September. In October the ban caused a 33 per cent increase in Alberta's jail population, as police arrested men hitching rides that were now illegal.

In the spring of 1933, with unemployment up to 708,000, its highest point in the decade, Bennett brought down a budget that continued his stingy relief policy. A total of $25 million would be provided for direct relief among the 1,357,562 men, women and children now officially on the dole. Again, personal and corporate taxes were increased, by $70 million. The government's estimate of a $2-million surplus for 1933-34 was misleading, since they had failed to account for the Canadian National Railways deficit and for the money already spent on relief. Pointing out that the public debt had risen by $156,133,000 over the past fiscal year, on March 22 the *Calgary Herald* said, "The federal budget reveals that the government has no original ideas on how to deal with a situation created by declining trade and diminishing public revenue."

The West's initial respect for Bennett, long since soured to loathing, now turned to wry ridicule. Horse-drawn cars became "Bennett buggies," abandoned farms were "Bennett barnyards," shanty towns were called "Bennett boroughs," and boiled grain was sarcastically known as "Bennett coffee." His portly figure, in top hat, morning coat, waistcoat and striped trousers, was a natural target for caricaturists who could lampoon him as a capitalist simply by drawing him as he looked. A rich bachelor, he had nothing in common with ordinary Albertans. In Calgary, he had lived in a suite in the Palliser Hotel; in Ottawa, he occupied a lavishly remodelled suite in the Chateau Laurier. Though he maintained his lifelong abhorrence of alcohol and tobacco, he ate heavy meals with plenty of sweets.

Yet Bennett, like Mackenzie King, was far more complex than his public image. Both men were intensely private; both lacked cronies who might have revealed other aspects of their nature. King, a canny politician, confided uncanny notions only to his diaries; Bennett, whose political instincts were minimal, hid his redeeming qualities. Thousands of Canadians pleaded for his help in the early 1930s; few people knew that he often answered these letters himself, not with platitudes, but with sound advice and $5 or $10 from his own pocket.

Gradually, in 1933 and 1934, Bennett recognized that his high-handed measures hadn't countered the unprecedented crisis of the Depression. When all his initiatives failed he began, belatedly and spasmodically, to embark on radical measures.

Despite his inadequate response to unemployment, Bennett had shown some awareness of national concerns in 1932 when, in response to the Privy Council's ruling that Ottawa had jurisdiction over radio broadcasting, he set up an inquiry that led to the creation of the state-owned Canadian Broadcasting Corporation (see sidebar). At the first federal-provincial conference in January of 1933 he appalled fellow Tories by backing a contributory unemployment insurance scheme. His 1933 budget further astonished his cabinet by recommending a royal commission on banking, which endorsed the creation of a central Bank of Canada.

Canada's chartered banks strenuously resisted this idea. As well as giving up issuing their own currency, they would have to transfer their gold reserves to the central bank at par value, forfeiting the profits they made while gold rose from $20.65 to $35.40 an ounce. Nevertheless, the Bank of Canada was established by Parliament on June 28, 1934,

"We will blast our way into the markets of the world." Bennett worked hard to fulfil this campaign promise, hosting the Imperial Conference in 1932 and meeting with American president Franklin Delano Roosevelt (below) in 1933 to discuss trade, all to no avail.

National Archives of Canada, c198

when the unanimous vote of 97 Conservatives defeated the unanimous vote of 50 Liberals.

Meanwhile Bennett's brother-in-law, William Herridge, encouraged the prime minister's new-born radicalism. Before marrying Mildred Bennett, Herridge had been Bennett's lawyer and speech writer. Now, as Canada's first minister to the United States, he admired President Franklin Delano Roosevelt's New Deal, a massive public works program designed to fight the Depression. But Bennett wasn't yet ready to try extreme measures. After his first meeting with the American president on April 27, 1933, when the two leaders discussed a trade treaty, he retained his policy of high tariffs. Since imports mightily exceeded exports, he felt that he had to provide employment and lower the national deficit by protecting the domestic market.

Although 1933 marked the turning point in the Great Depression, as unemployment rates at

He loved women, but would never marry one
Sad, lonely Bennett mourned the loss of his beloved little sister

Beneath R.B. Bennett's camouflage of striped pants and morning coat lurked an emotional personality few Canadians ever glimpsed. Like Mackenzie King, another life-long bachelor with a doting and ambitious mother, he loved women but never committed himself to marriage. "He liked the society of ladies, and at dinners he always preferred mixed company," said his friend Lord Beaverbrook.

Yet Bennett was only 34 when he wrote to Beaverbrook, lamenting that it was too late for him to marry. "I guess I have made a mistake but it cannot be reme-died. May I say, though, that I think a woman, to be a wife in the best and true sense of the term must, while being domestic in her tastes, have much larger sympathies and mental qualities as to be able to enter into the ambition and hopes of her husband, whatever they may be."

Speculation about Bennett's private life must rely mainly on conjecture. He destroyed all his correspondence with his mother, Henrietta Stiles Bennett,▲ and with the women he courted. After his death, many of his personal letters and papers were burned by Alice Millar, his confidential secretary.

His first romance, at 18, foreshadowed the paradoxical nature of his relationship with women. Appointed principal of the school at Douglastown, N.B., in 1888, he took out Alma Russell, daughter of the local postmaster. Though the friendship appeared to cool when he entered Dalhousie University to study law in 1891, the following year he drove her to the station when

University of New Brunswick Archives

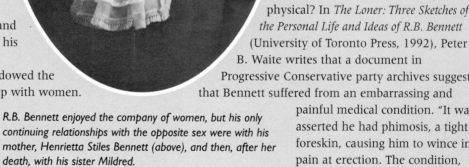

R.B. Bennett enjoyed the company of women, but his only continuing relationships with the opposite sex were with his mother, Henrietta Stiles Bennett (above), and then, after her death, with his sister Mildred.

she left to join her family in Victoria, and corresponded with her until the year before he died.

When Bennett moved to Calgary to join Senator James Lougheed's law firm, he led an active social life centred on the Methodist church, but remained staid, studious, and apparently unattached. After he was elected MP for Calgary West in 1911, a series of Ottawa women were linked with his name. One was Edith Cochrane, whose father, powerful Ontario Tory Frank Cochrane, discouraged Bennett's courtship. Another was Jennie Eddy, widow of Ezra Butler Eddy, who had expanded his small match company into a wood and paper industry worth more than $4 million when he died in 1906. She often asked Bennett's legal advice about her husband's estate, and when she died she left him a con-trolling interest in the Eddy Match Company, making him one of the richest men in Canada.

Bennett was 47 in 1917. He was wealthy, successful and in the prime of life, but women seemed to slip by him. Was the reason psychological, or physical? In *The Loner: Three Sketches of the Personal Life and Ideas of R.B. Bennett* (University of Toronto Press, 1992), Peter B. Waite writes that a document in Progressive Conservative party archives suggests that Bennett suffered from an embarrassing and painful medical condition. "It was asserted he had phimosis, a tight foreskin, causing him to wince in pain at erection. The condition, not uncommon, is easily reme-died by surgery now, but in Dick Bennett's adolescence and early manhood it was not," Waite writes. "He was tall,

last began falling, Bennett was so discouraged by the ineffectiveness of his policies that he considered retirement. Across the country, Tory support was crumbling. Voters in British Columbia and Nova Scotia rejected incumbent Conservative governments, and in federal by-elections in Saskatchewan, Quebec and New Brunswick, the Tories finished a dismal third. Perversely, in March 1934 Bennett responded by enacting legislation that reinstituted the conferring of non-heritable titles, a practice restricted in 1919 as repugnant to egalitarian Canadians.

If such reactionary measures pacified his conservative colleagues, they incited more progressive cabinet members to push for change. Harry Stevens, Bennett's minister of Trade and Commerce, was a small businessman from Vancouver who harboured a deep resentment for the big corporations that backed the Conservative party. At a shoe retailers' convention in Toronto, he

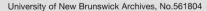

In the absence of a wife, Bennett's then unmarried sister, Mildred, assisted him at public functions and acted privately as his confidante. Mildred, who was devoted to her brother, seems to have relished the task, and relinquished it only upon her marriage. (Above) R.B. Bennett was sworn in as prime minister on August 7, 1930, with his supportive younger sister at his side. She was able to step into this very public role with apparent ease, having served her brother in this capacity earlier (upper right). In 1928, for example, she acted as hostess for Viscount and Lady Willingdon when the governor-general and his wife visited the Calgary Stampede (right).

handsome and well turned out. But while his approach was frequently bold, he was fundamentally shy; his condition would only have made that shyness worse."

Another factor that may have inhibited Bennett's romantic instincts was his devotion to his sister Mildred, 19 years his junior.[B] He paid all her expenses at Mount Allison University, and after their mother died in 1914 Mildred seemed to take her place in his affection. Living with her

accused major department stores of using mass buying power to blackmail manufacturers into low prices that forced smaller merchants to cut wages and run sweatshops. Hailed as the champion of the independent businessman, Stevens invited the wrath of department stores such as Eaton's, major Conservative contributors who promptly complained to the prime minister. He offered to resign, but Bennett refused to create a martyr of a man whose speech attracted more than 100 favourable letters a day. Instead, he gave Stevens the chairmanship of an eleven-man parliamentary special committee to "investigate the causes of the large price spreads between producers' costs and retail prices."

In more than sixty public meetings, the Price Spreads Commission revealed widespread exploitation, especially in Quebec, where some workers were paid only $1.50 for a 75-hour

Hazel Colville may have been the love of R.B. Bennett's life. Some speculated that the feelings that she stirred in the aging prime minister had something to do with her resemblance to his sister Mildred. Whatever sparked the attraction, she soon grew weary of him.

sister, Evelyn, and her husband in Vancouver, she often visited Bennett in Calgary, and in 1929 she moved into his suite at the Palliser Hotel. There she became his political and personal chatelaine, a role she continued to play after they moved to the Chateau Laurier in Ottawa. Although no one suggested any impropriety in their relationship, they were emotionally closer than many married couples. Bennett's biographer Ernest Watkins recounts a remark that suggests his dependence on her. To Alice Millar she said, "Don't ever walk out on Dick. We're the bumpers on his car. We can save him a lot of damage."

Yet, while Mildred always said she would be married on the same day her brother wed and not before, she broke her vow and married William Herridge on April 14, 1931. When she moved out of the Chateau Laurier suite, she wrote an impassioned note of farewell: "Dick, my dear dear brother, I cannot leave this address without a little note to you — if I could only say all that's in my heart but I can't — and I know that you realize that in the midst of my most sacred and divine love you have never for a moment been

and finest brother a sister ever had — Ever and forever, Your devoted sister, Mildred."**C**

Bennett missed his sister terribly, but barely a year later, at 62, he fell in love. Hazel Beatrice Kemp Colville was attractive, intelligent, wealthy, elegant and probably the most sophisticated woman Bennett had ever met. She was the daughter of Sir Edward Kemp, a Methodist millionaire manufacturer and keeper of the Conservative flame in Toronto. Bennett had known the family for years; he and Kemp had served briefly together in Prime Minister Arthur Meighen's 1920-1921 cabinet. Now Hazel was 44 and twice widowed. Her first husband, Francis Stephens, died in the 1918 influenza epidemic after serving in France during the Great War, leaving her with a daughter born in 1912. Her second was another veteran, Arthur Colville, a lawyer in Toronto and then Montreal, who died of throat cancer in 1931. Both left sizable estates and Hazel used some of her inheritance to buy and restore the manor house of Pierre le Gardeur de Repentigny at Mascouche, northeast of Montreal.

'Ever your grateful & devoted old man,' wrote Bennett to Hazel Colville. 'Oh my dear how I miss you. I really am just a poor weak emotional man, hungry for a sight of you.'

---

out of my mind — In fact, I sometimes wonder if I am not going to be very lonely for you. I've not changed and never will. I sometimes think that loving Bill as I do — I've loved and valued you even more — I can't write more my darling Dick, but always my adoration and devotion to the grandest

In January 1930 she had written to Bennett, then minister of Justice, about immigration policy. When her husband died, their correspondence became more personal. After playing host to the Imperial Conference in the summer of 1932, the prime minister spent four days at Mascouche. He

week.[7] Stevens's inquiry was the most popular initiative undertaken by the Bennett government, but he went too far on June 25, 1934. Addressing the Conservative Study Group, an informal luncheon group of party faithful, he launched a blistering attack on individual corporate leaders and Canada's economic structure and had 3,000 copies of his speech privately distributed. The country's foremost Liberal papers, the *Toronto Star* and the *Winnipeg Free Press*, published the text, provoking a libel threat from the president of the Robert Simpson Company which, though never carried out, widened the breach between Bennett and Stevens. In October, when Secretary of State Cahan (nicknamed Dino for dinosaur) ripped into Stevens, the Vancouver MP again tendered his resignation from the cabinet, and this time Bennett accepted it.

But he was clearly impressed by the public acclaim for Stevens's crusade, and some historians

hurried back to Ottawa for a civic reception, at which he suggested that he might leave politics. On August 27, he wrote Hazel, "Beloved, all day yesterday, a day of great contrasts and amazing experiences, you were with me. The city address was quite too trying at 11. Somehow it shook the very foundations of my being and I'm afraid it was not because of the reasons assigned by the *Mail and Empire* today, but because just before I replied that dear face was so clear and near beside me, just over the right shoulder but with tears in her eyes: it was quite too real for words..." Ending with, "Ever your grateful and devoted old man," he added a tender postscript, "I am going to mail this without waiting — Oh my dear how I miss you. I really am just a poor weak emotional man, hungry for a sight of you."[D]

By mid-September he was spending most weekends with Hazel Colville. He kept his trysts hidden by taking his official car to a halfway point, often Hawkesbury, where Mrs. Colville's car picked him up. On weekdays, while he ran the government of Canada, letters flew between Ottawa and Mascouche. In October, his courtship began to run aground. A letter from Hazel, which he referred to as a "moving communication," clearly expressed doubts about their relationship. After visiting her on the weekend of October 29, he wrote a letter warning her against "introspection" and promising that they would find peace together. Next day he wrote again, speaking of their relationship in the past tense.

"It has meant so much to me to be able to go down to your place on the weekend: What delightful anticipation and of joyous realization — care has dropped from me as a mantle discarded... I shall ever hold that deep and indescribable devotion for you that so strangely has come upon me at this late hour of life: And it has all been good for me: Sweetened my views of life and people and made me a much happier person even tho' I do find it irksome to be so held in leash by the party I lead — It is not only unfair but I cannot permit it to continue much longer... This is in the nature of a 'peace offering.' I am so happy when I am at the manor house and with you."

By then American and Canadian newspapers had reported rumours of impending marriage, which Bennett tried vainly to squelch. When he went to England in December 1932, reporters asked if he was about to marry a mysterious widow and move to Britain. Under the headline "Premier Bennett Refuses to Discuss Private Affairs," the *Edmonton Journal* quoted him, "Although I am a public man I am entitled to the amenities of polite society, and I decline to discuss my personal affairs."

But Hazel Colville's affection was fading. In March 1933 she left for a two-month visit to Europe and her correspondence with Bennett dwindled. Her last letter, written on September 21, 1933, consisted of two words: "No! Dick." Bennett made one last attempt to win her hand. Early in 1934 he visited her Montreal house. It was their last meeting, from which he stalked out so angrily that he forgot his blackthorn stick. The love of his life had emphatically jilted him, just as the Canadian electorate did as soon as it got the chance in 1935.

— *G.O.*

[A] "[My mother] was the mainspring of my life. It was my ambition and joy to please her; to have her see that the care and effort she bestowed on me were not in vain. She had the finest mind I have known. All that I am or may be I owe to her. She was a teacher, guide, adviser, companion, counsellor, friend and above all an impartial and candid critic." — R.B. Bennett (from the Alma Russell Papers, Saint John Museum).

[B] Despite an unhappy marriage, Bennett's parents had six children: Richard Bedford, born 1870; Henry, 1872, who died four years later; Evelyn, 1874; Ronald, 1896; George, 1891; and Mildred, 1889. Richard was financially generous but cold-hearted to members of his family who didn't measure up to his high standards. When George became an alcoholic after returning from the Great War, Bennett banished him to Fort McMurray, on an allowance of $125 a month, assigned Edmonton lawyer Ray Milner to pay his debts after his urban binges, and paid for his daughter's secretarial course through intermediaries.

[C] When Mildred Herridge died of a long illness in a New York hospital on May 11, 1938, at the age of 49, Bennett was so distraught that he shut himself in her old room at the Chateau Laurier, alternately pacing back and forth and reading the Book of Ruth.

[D] All R.B. Bennett's letters to Hazel Colville quoted here are from Peter Busby Waite's *The Loner: Three Sketches of the Personal Life and Ideas of R.B. Bennett, 1870-1947*. Readers may wonder how this sequence of letters survived when so much of Bennett's private correspondence was destroyed. Waite explains: "Hazel Colville worried about those love letters from R.B.. On November 24, 1932, she took all her letters from him, sealed them, and handed them to the Royal Trust, Montreal. On the wrapping was written: 'Not to be opened by anyone. Can be given to my daughter in 1950 if not destroyed by me before that date.' They never were destroyed."

[7]The opening hearings revealed that since 1927 Canada Packers had made profits averaging $900,000 a year, while paying farmers as little as 1.5¢ a pound for beef that retailed for 19¢. In 1933 the T. Eaton Company had paid its forty directors an average of $35,000 each, while paying its 25,736 other employees salaries averaging $970. In short, the larger the firm, the greater its profits and the lower its wages. — Richard Wilbur, *The Bennett Administration 1930-1935* (The Canadian Historical Association, Historical Booklet No. 24).

[8]In the late 1920s British Columbia passed legislation giving the dairy and produce industries the right to form cartels. If 75 per cent of the growers or dairy farmers in an area voted to establish a marketing practice, such as a fixed price or a production quota, the decision was legally binding on all producers. In the early 1930s this legislation was ruled unconstitutional. It invaded the federal jurisdiction over interprovincial and international trade; and deducting the cost of operating the marketing board from the sale price of the commodity constituted an indirect tax, which meant that federal authority was required. — Alvin Finkel, *Business and Social Reform in the Thirties* (James Lorimer and Company, 1979).

[9]The New Deal was essentially a continuation of the U.S. Progressive Movement, although on a broader scale and with more intellectual sophistication. Like Progressivism it had no coherent program or philosophy, but was based on the pragmatic belief that wherever there was a maladjustment in the economic system the government should intervene in order to remedy it... The farmers were enabled to restrict agricultural production and thereby to raise farm prices while wage earners acquired a legal right to form trade unions and bargain collectively, by which means they could raise their wages and reduce their hours of labour. Social security legislation, moreover, provided wage earners with unemployment and old age insurance. — Henry Bamford Parkes, *The American Experience* (N.Y., Vintage Books, 1959).

consider it one of the factors in his conversion to radicalism. By now, after losing two more provincial elections and four by-elections, the Tories were besieged and deeply divided between reactionaries like Cahan and progressives like Railways and Canals Minister Robert J. Manion, who urged more government spending on public works. Bennett, exhausted by overwork and suffering from marginal diabetes and irregular heartbeat, seemed readier to address peoples' hardships, especially in Western Canada.

For example, on March 15, 1934, while the Price Spreads Commission was grilling corporate barons, Bennett's Agriculture minister Robert Weir introduced the controversial Natural Products Marketing Bill, which set up federal marketing boards for most of Canada's agricultural products, from wheat to meat, as well as natural resources such as lumber.[8] Many Western farmers applauded the bill because it guaranteed better prices. After weeks of bitter debate the bill passed with support from socialists and even one Liberal, former Agriculture minister W.R. Motherwell. Bennett, the consummate Conservative capitalist, had just said "aye" to the most intrusive bill in Canadian history. What was happening?

During the same session the government passed the Farmers' Creditors' Arrangements Act, based on a similar Alberta law designed by Premier Brownlee to forestall farm foreclosures and bankruptcy. Like the provincial act, it appointed a government board to mediate between debtors and creditors. If negotiations broke down, the board could order compulsory arbitration, and if necessary write down the debt and reschedule repayment. This act, compromising the law of contracts, was another apparent reversal of philosophy by a formerly deep-blue Conservative regime.

In April 1931 the prime minister announced that he would never peg wheat prices. In the House of Commons he declared, 'The cry of Western insolvency is hurtful and unjust and clearly overdrawn.'

Welcomed by farmers, these new policies were scarcely noticed by destitute city residents and unemployed men in the bush camps. What they wanted was sweeping reform like Roosevelt's New Deal. Tuning their radios to the president's Sunday evening "fireside chats,"[9] Canadians wanted their own new deal. Bennett tried to ride Roosevelt's coattails by presenting the 1934 farm bills as the harbinger of a new thrust, but meanwhile he was cutting back provincial subsidies for relief and public works. The funding that filtered down to Edmonton, Calgary and Lethbridge was only a third of the amount each city had requested.

With the deadline for an election only a year hence, Bennett's advisors pressed him to adopt more generous policies. Most influential of these was his brother-in-law in Washington. Throughout 1934 Herridge continually urged Bennett to abandon old-fashioned Toryism and recognize, as Roosevelt had, that government intervention was the way of the future. His advice was seconded by Bennett's executive assistant, Rod Finlayson. Herridge and Finlayson, who had both been Liberals before they became involved with Bennett, often worked in tandem to persuade the prime minister to follow a course of action. Now they effected a transformation.

In early January 1935, Bennett astounded the nation with a series of prime-time radio broadcasts that turned Tory principles on their ear. He paid the costs out of his own pocket, and didn't consult his ministers, who had no idea of what to expect. Carried on 38 stations across the nine provinces, the five thirty-minute addresses were crafted by Herridge and Finlayson. In the first, on January 2, the prime minister declared, "Reform means government control and regulation. It means the end of laissez-faire." Two nights later the second broadcast promised uniform wages, an eight-hour day, a maximum work week, new acts reforming unemployment insurance, health insurance and old-age pensions, and higher taxes for the rich. Farm debt would be scaled down and a new law would provide protection from monopolistic purchasers and "economic parasites." The third speech, on January 7, proclaimed that "the corporate strength of the state should be used to assist farmers to secure their operating capital at low interest rates." The last two broadcasts reviewed earlier legislation and launched a pre-election attack on the Liberals. By this time Bennett's audience was an estimated eight million of Canada's 10.5 million residents.

Reaction was swift and predictable. The Conservative establishment was horrified. Bennett

Hail the conqueror

R.B. Bennett, the quintissential Calgarian before his election as prime minister, contributed to the life of his adopted home in many arenas. [A] Bennett (left) confers with Pat Burns at the 1928 Calgary Stampede. He is shown in [B] visiting the Calgary Junior Red Cross hospital's school for longterm patients. In [D] he is posing with a child identified only as Dianne, along with Matron F.E.C. Reid and J.A. MacLeod, president of the Alberta Red Cross. [C] This medal for general academic proficiency was awarded by Bennett's educational foundation to Carmen Barkley, a Grade 9 student in the Brushy Ridge School District.

Glenbow Archives, McDermid Collection, NB-16-175

Glenbow Archives, NA-3087-7

Glenbow Archives, NA-3218-5

Glenbow Archives, NA-3087-6

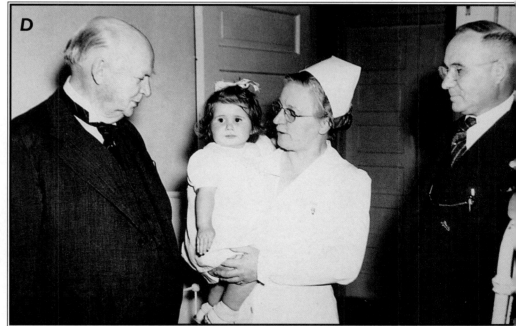

For five years Bennett was under attack by the cartoonist Arch Dale

Arch Dale, of the Winnipeg Free Press was already a veteran of many political wars when R.B. Bennett took office as prime minister in 1930. Dale kept up the assault until Bennett was finally driven out. In [A] Dale spoofs Bennett's pledge that Canadians would "blast our way into the markets of the world." (We didn't.) In [B] and [H] he heaps scorn on Bennett's plan to restore British titles for Canadian citizens. In [C] and [D] he chides Bennett's quest for reciprocity with the U.S., something Bennett had hitherto opposed. In [E], [F] and [G] he targets Bennett's habit of reducing his cabinet ministers to lackeys. Bennett left office in October 1935, two months after Alberta's William Aberhart assumed the premiership, just in time to become Dale's next victim.

hastily assured Tories that he wasn't introducing socialism, let alone Communism; he was simply proposing legislation that would "ensure the more successful operation of the capitalist system." But Herridge recognized that ordinary Canadians wanted action, not promises.

When he and Finlayson met with Bennett to discuss their usual task of drafting the throne speech, Herridge overrode the prime minister's qualms and produced an address that echoed the broadcasts. After it was delivered on January 17, the government tabled new laws. They laid the foundation for the modern welfare state that would dominate Canadian public policy for the next fifty years. The Conservatives expected Mackenzie King to oppose the reforms, allowing them to

How the squabbles over radio produced the CBC
The broadcast czar was called a polecat and Judas, but not for long

Among the woes that burdened R.B. Bennett when he became prime minister at the outset of the Depression was a conflict almost unrelated to drought, unemployment and poverty. It focused on whether the new medium of radio broadcasting should be under public or private control. Two lobbying groups had already squared off against each other.

On the private side was the Association of Canadian Broadcasters, a loose coalition of private, commercial broadcasters headed by Ernie Bushnell, manager of a Toronto radio station and the inventor of singing commercials.▲ On the public side was the Canadian Radio League, headed by Graham Spry, Rhodes scholar and national secretary of the Association of Canadian Clubs. Among its more than 600,000 influential members were university presidents, provincial education officials, women's groups, farm organizations, and fifty newspapers whose advertising revenue was threatened by competition from private radio. The two camps represented the classic Canadian fight: unfettered free enterprise versus complete government control.

Federal control over broadcasting had existed as long as Alberta. Since 1905, a series of acts had regulated and licensed telegraph and radio transmission. But privately owned stations proliferated, even though advertising was banned until 1925. By 1929 Canada had more than 75 English and French stations, most of them operated by newspapers, radio manufacturers and ham radio clubs; the University of Alberta's station was CKUA. The CNR ran a fifteen-station network, connecting its own outlets in Vancouver, Ottawa and Moncton with leased private stations. The railway was experimenting with broadcasts to moving trains, and many parlour cars had uniformed operators and headsets for passengers.

Nearly 300,000 Canadians owned radios, for which they paid a $1 government licensing fee. Except on Saturday

National Archives of Canada PA 117913

CBC champion Graham Spry.

nights, when listening to the hockey games became a national pastime, four out of five tuned in to American programs. With the bright exception of the CNR network, most Canadian stations found it cheaper to use recorded U.S. music, comedy and drama. Listeners also got programs directly from the U.S. where burgeoning advertising revenue financed powerful 50,000-watt transmitters that blocked Canadian stations operating on 1,000 watts or less. Though diplomatic negotiations with the United States and Mexico eventually solved this problem, domestic radio was plagued by the familiar demons of nationalism, religious bigotry and even that substance government controlled even more tightly than radio — alcohol.

In 1928, Liberals were concerned because several stations owned by Bible societies were airing anti-Catholic messages. In Saskatchewan, one even rented time to the Ku Klux Klan. The government forced the fundamentalist stations off the air by re-allocating some broadcast frequencies. When one was assigned to distillers Gooderham & Worts Ltd. to create CKWG in Toronto, King was accused of favouring booze over the Bible.

Nationalism surfaced in 1929, when Toronto stations began affiliating with U.S. networks. CFRB joined the Columbia Broadcasting System (CBS), and CKWG signed up with the National Broadcasting Company (NBC). The government iced the issue by appointing Canada's first royal commission on broadcasting, chaired by Sir John Aird, president of the Canadian Bank of Commerce. The other members were Augustin Frigon, director general of technical education in Quebec, and *Ottawa Citizen* editor Charles Bowman, a rare journalistic supporter of Social Credit ideas. After hearings in 25 Canadian centres and fact-finding trips to the U.S., Britain and several European countries, the Aird Commission tabled its report.

castigate the Liberals as reactionaries in the upcoming election. King outwitted them. Instead of moving a no-confidence motion, he accepted Bennett's ideas in principle but insisted on debating each new law on the floor of the House.

But the legislation was not yet drafted. Taken by surprise, the Conservatives had to scramble to frame each bill, but managed to introduce and pass fourteen major bills in the spring session. Most important was a federal unemployment insurance scheme whose principles lasted more than sixty years. Other acts overhauled Canadian labour laws, providing for weekly holidays, minimum wage machinery and limitations on weekly hours of work, based on the International Labour

The major recommendations: the creation of seven 50,000-watt radio transmitters nationwide; federal control of all broadcasting with no commercials of any kind; tripling annual radio licence fees to $3; prohibition of controversial statements and attacks by one religion on another and restrictions on political broadcasting. To the satisfaction of the government, who saw publishers as powerful allies or enemies, most newspapers endorsed the Aird Report.

But it gathered dust as the 1930 election approached and the Depression sank its teeth into the economy. R.B. Bennett's Conservatives had enough on their plate without refereeing between the vocal zealots of public and private radio. Moreover, the provinces had entered the fray. Quebec Premier Louis Alexandre Taschereau led the charge, demanding provincial control of broadcasting without federal interference.

With the legal obstacles out of the way — provincial rights were a delicate matter even in the 1930s — Bennett established a parliamentary committee in March 1932 to consider the Aird Report. Delivered in May, the committee's report was a typically Canadian compromise that supported public ownership and control of a national broadcasting system, but allowed room for private stations in the broadcasting mix. The MPs recommended a government-appointed three-man commission with complete authority over programming and technical performance and the ability to recommend on licensing. The national network would be a hybrid, staffed by civil servants but financially self-sustaining, through licensing fees and limited advertising.

Most of the committee's recommendations were adopted in the Canadian Radio Broadcasting Act passed on May 26, 1932. Prompted by the influential supporters of the Radio League, and his own anglophile admiration of the BBC model, Bennett took the nationalist route as far as he could, given that his government couldn't afford to subsidize a Canadian network to compete with U.S. stations. When the Canadian Radio Broadcasting Commission (CRBC) went on

National Archives of Canada, 125792

Free enterpriser Ernie Bushnell.

the air in 1933, offering about 48 hours a week in English and French, it was thwarted by lack of money and independence. A Rube Goldberg machine, it borrowed its equipment from the CNR, owned or leased some stations, and booked time on other private stations. Every commercial had to be vetted by one of the three commissioners.

It had other problems. It routinely ran broadcasts in Canada by "Judge Rutherford," chief prophet of the Jehovah's Witnsses, whose verbal assaults on all Christian clergy took raw invective into the realm of the esoteric. Joseph Franklin Rutherford, known as Judge to his following, launched a vitriolic attack on the commission in Witness publications. He called the chairman, among other things, "a liar, a thief, a Judas and polecat and therefore fit to associate only with clergy."

Ironically, it was political, not religious, broadcasting that killed the CRBC. In the thick of the 1935 federal election campaign, it allowed a thinly veiled anti-Liberal drama entitled *Uncle Sage* to air coast to coast. Sponsored by the Conservative party's advertising agency, the program was axed when King regained power. He immediately ordered that the CRBC be investigated by a Liberal-dominated committee, which recommended replacing it with a crown corporation. On November 2, 1936, a new broadcasting act created the Canadian Broadcasting Corporation.

In the end, the creation of the CBC was quintessentially Canadian. The Conservative prime minister who laid the foundations of one of our most nationalist organizations was a devoted anglophile; the Liberal prime minister who actually created modern state-controlled broadcasting was a devoted free enterpriser opposed to socialism of any kind.

—*G.O.*

AErnest L. Bushnell was manager of CFRB and CKCN in Toronto between 1929 and 1933. He later started the first agency geared to radio advertising. After joining the CBC at 45 and retiring thirteen years later as a vice-president, he created his own private broadcasting empire, Bushnell Communications Ltd.

Canada's old money...

Currency courtesy of West Edmonton Coin and Stamp Corporation. Photography by Philippa Byfield.

...and the new

Currency courtesy of West Edmonton Coin and Stamp Corporation. Photography by Philippa Byfield.

With the passage by the Bennett government of the Bank of Canada Act, the old system of bank-note currency (shown on the opposite page) came to an end in 1935, to be replaced by the new Bank of Canada currency (this page). Where the old tender was issued by the chartered banks and might feature portraits of royalty or distinguished Canadians, the new hewed strictly to the monarchy. Thus the five-dollar bill featured Edward VIII, who as Prince of Wales was familiar to Albertans because of his ranch west of High River (Vol.5, p.193). He would reign briefly in 1935 and 1936, then abdicate in favour of his brother. The latter would become George VI. Their sister, the Princess Mary, appears on the ten-dollar bill. The child on the twenty-dollar bill is George VI's daughter Princess Elizabeth, who as Elizabeth II would reign for nearly half the century very much in the tradition of her parents, grandparents and great grandmother, Queen Victoria. Problems would arise in the generation that followed Elizabeth II, whose children would plunge the monarchy into wide disfavour through divorce and scandal. Along with the bank-issued currency, something else disappeared in 1935, notably Canada's four-dollar bill (opposite page).

Conference of 1919. The Farmers' Creditors' Arrangements Act and the Natural Products Marketing Act were updated. An amendment to the Criminal Code made it an offence to cut prices in order to eliminate competitors. The Price Spreads Commission's recommendations were implemented in the Dominion Trades Industry Act, which proposed sweeping new powers to regulate industry. Westerners benefited from the establishment of a new Canada Wheat Board, a marketing agency, and the Prairie Farm Rehabilitation Act, designed to teach dryland farming techniques in the dustbowl. A Dominion Housing Bill was proposed to create cheaper and better housing. New relief and public works construction bills were introduced and a bill setting up the Economic Council of Canada was tabled.

Money was finally going to flow in rivers from federal coffers into the parched provinces. It was a massive social engineering blueprint, magnificent on paper, but a mess when the government attempted to implement it. Only parts of the vaunted New Deal legislation dribbled into the Commons, and what did make it through was for many people too little too late, which prompted Mackenzie King's partisan dismissal of the reforms as a "deathbed repentance."

Meanwhile, the man who ordinarily oversaw all government bills with a critical eye and a meddlesome hand was out of action. In February, a secret meeting between Bennett and Harry Stevens, engineered by Robert Manion, hadn't achieved a reconciliation. A few days later Bennett took to his bed in the Chateau Laurier with a bad cold that turned into a mild heart attack. In his absence King had a field day in the House, provoking Stevens into explaining why he left cabinet, and prodding for soft spots in a government rapidly falling apart. When Bennett recovered on April 16, he fled to England to attend George V's Silver Jubilee celebrations, delaying his return to the House of Commons until May 20.

Meanwhile Stevens had renewed his attacks on big business, threatening to name the "twelve men who controlled 50 per cent of the nation's wealth." When the minister of Justice admitted that parts of the bill implementing the Price Spread Commission's recommendations went beyond the jurisdiction of the constitution, Stevens told reporters, "I have no patience with this government's attitude of waiting for legal opinions."

Taking his cue from the maverick Tory backbencher, Mackenzie King simply waited for the British Privy Council to rule on the constitutionality of the government bills.[10] The U.S. Supreme Court's recent declaration that Roosevelt's National Recovery Act was unconstitutional cast more doubt on Bennett's new thrust.

Worn down by five years of fighting the Depression the 65-year-old prime minister wanted nothing more than retirement, but felt he had to check Stevens by leading his party into the long-awaited election. After Parliament was prorogued on July 6, Stevens announced the formation of

Bennett belatedly acknowledged the plight of the West on July 2, 1931, when he told the House that the Alberta and Saskatchewan drought was 'the greatest national calamity that has ever overtaken the country.'

his Reconstruction Party to re-establish government for the benefit of the majority.

The smell of Tory blood attracted a swarm of electoral aspirants. Besides the Liberals and Conservatives, Stevens fielded 174 Reconstructionists. J.S. Woodsworth's Co-operative Commonwealth Federation (CCF) ran 118 candidates. The field included 45 federal Social Crediters, buoyed by their victory in Alberta, and 81 other assorted candidates, each with a different proposal for solving the nation's problems.

The Liberals took a look at this motley array and ran on a slogan: "King or chaos." They didn't bother to trump Bennett's New Deal; who needed an election platform when you could point to Bennett's record?

What else might go wrong as the government stumbled along the campaign trail? It could shoot itself in the foot — and it did ten days after the writ dropped.

Inmates of government labour camps had begun an "On to Ottawa" march to protest against camp conditions and the government's failure to soften the Depression. Riding freight cars across

Prime Minister Bennett tried to use the popularity of Harry Stevens (below) to his advantage, but his plan backfired. Rather than boost his government's image, Stevens' personal popularity served to divide the beleaguered cabinet and, some historians believe, forced Bennett to align with Robert Manion, minister of Railways and Canals, and the other more radical members of his party (left).

the Prairies, the "marchers" gained momentum and reinforcements as they moved east. Communist agitators were among the unemployed trekkers, but certainly didn't speak for the majority.

Fearing insurrection, the Bennett government ordered the march stopped in Regina on July 1, Dominion Day. When the dust cleared one policeman was dead, hundreds of people injured and scores of protesters arrested. The government could not have picked a more inappropriate day to crack down; its response reinforced the idea that Ottawa cared little for the jobless victims of the continuing Depression.

Throughout the campaign Bennett was a lonely figure, the only remaining Conservative leader in Canada. One of his cabinet had died and eight others did not run. Everyone expected the Liberals to win on October 23, and so they did, resoundingly. King's Grits won 171 of the 245 seats in the House of Commons, reducing the Tories to 39 seats, their lowest tally since Confederation. The CCF won seven; Social Credit won fifteen in Alberta and two in Saskatchewan. Eleven independents including one Reconstructionist, Harry Stevens, made up the new Parliament.

In terms of the popular vote, Bennett's defeat was less catastrophic. The Conservatives won thirty per cent and the Liberals' share actually dropped to only forty per cent. As Professor Blair Neatby remarked, if the choice was between King and chaos a majority of voters chose chaos. What really beat Bennett was the same thing that brought him to power — the Depression, which by now had embittered him towards friends and foes alike. Despite the overwhelming Liberal victory, he blamed Stevens for his defeat, even though the Reconstructionists effectively split the vote in only 48 ridings. He resented his Conservative colleagues for relying on his deep pockets to provide funding. Above all, he suffered the indignity of seeing a man he considered unprincipled govern the country. He had to watch King gloat when the British Privy Council declared most of the Conservative New Deal legislation unconstitutional under the British North America Act.[11]

In 1938 he was devastated by the death of Mildred, the much younger sister who had taken his mother's place in his heart. When he resigned later that year, his farewell speech in the House was as chilly as an Ottawa winter. He told his colleagues, "I shall never forget your kindness at times, or your cruelty at others."

The following January he moved to England, always his favourite refuge, and bought a sixty-acre property from his old friend Lord Beaverbrook, next door to Beaverbrook's estate, Cherkly, at Mickleham in Surrey, twenty miles south of London. He spent more than $100,000 refurbishing Juniper Hill, which became his first and last real home. But he made few friends among the Tory establishment. His hopes of a knighthood were thwarted by Prime Minister Neville Chamberlain, who had not been impressed by his conducting of the 1932 Imperial Conference. When war came in September of 1939, there were no important jobs for the former prime minister. Bennett, always a man of action and purpose, must have envied Beaverbrook's appointments to the epicentre of wartime production.

After Winston Churchill replaced Chamberlain as prime minister Bennett was awarded a peerage, thanks to Beaverbrook's lobbying. On June 15, 1941, Bennett became Viscount Bennett of Mickleham, Calgary and Hopewell. He relished the honour, but his spirit was shattered in August

Historian A.R.M. Lower (left) was blunt in his assessment of R.B. Bennett, dismissing him as a "man whose love of dominance reduced his ministers to nonentities and vitiated his career." James H. Gray, on the other hand, considered him a maverick progressive, who eventually tried to come to grips with the Depression, especially in western Canada. The final word may not have been spoken.

Immigration and Colonization Minister W.A. Gordon boasted that 200,000 of the urban jobless would eventually be resettled on farms across Canada. Fewer than 7,000 families moved, and many of these simply transferred from urban to rural relief rolls.

1944, when two of his nephews were killed in action within nine days. On the evening of June 26, 1947, he was taking a hot bath when he died of heart failure, a week before his 77th birthday.

To the century's end Bennett would remain a villain in Canadian eyes. In his seminal history, *Colony to Nation* (Toronto, Longmans, Green, 1946), Arthur R.M. Lower delivered a scathing judgment: "Here was a man with great force of character, with rugged sincerity, with the concern for his fellows characteristic of his Methodist traditions and with the deep irrational prejudices of a Loyalist background, yet a man whose love of dominance reduced his ministers to nonentities and vitiated his career." Lower believed that Bennett so distrusted democracy that he exercised inordinate executive power over tariffs and encouraged the RCMP to encroach on civil liberties.

Yet other historians, such as James H. Gray, see Bennett as a maverick progressive who eventually tried to break the Depression while the Liberal Opposition suggested nothing to combat the desperate situation of Westerners. "The Bennett New Deal ought to have carried the West for the Conservatives," he argues in his memoir, *Troublemaker* (Toronto, Macmillan, 1978), citing the renewal of the Wheat Board, the establishment of farmer-operated marketing boards to

11 "[The Privy Council's] performance in those cases is surely a monument to judicial rigidity and to a complacence which admits of no respectable explanation unless it be that the blinders fashioned by Viscount Haldane's opinions permitted no deviation from the course on which he set Canadian constitutional interpretation."
— Bora Laskin, late chief justice of the Supreme Court of Canada, quoted in *The Bennett New Deal: Fraud or Portent*, by J.R.H. Wilbur (Toronto, Copp Clark, c1968).

FURY ON THE PRAIRIES

enable producers to combat chain-store pricing policies, and the Farmers' Creditors' Arrangement Act as legislative landmarks.

Does Bennett deserve the credit for the Canadian New Deal? He had always been a laissez-faire capitalist, solidly against government intervention in the marketplace. In 1934, when the first glimmers of his conversion from the economics of Adam Smith to those of John Maynard Keynes surfaced, Bennett was weakened by overeating and underexercising; Canadians were suffering from the opposite problems. His speeches, written by Herridge and Finlayson, were a desperate attempt to win re-election after nearly five misguided years.

R.B. Bennett was an obstinate, contradictory man, who won power too late to stop the Depression and waited too long to combat it. "For this star-crossed millionaire Tory from Calgary, the times were hopelessly out of joint," James Gray writes. Ironically, he adds, this arch-conservative "was the real father of the Canadian welfare state, who set the country on a course from which it could never retreat. And he did it, not with his New Deal package, but with the fiscal and legislative precedents he set during his half decade in power."

Emboldened, perhaps, by the fact that FDR's National Recovery Act had been declared unconstitutional, Mackenzie King opposed Bennett's similar legislation, which had been upheld by the Canadian courts. King, however, took it to the British Privy Council and with few exceptions, they were similarly invalidated.

Country Guide, July 1936

Though both the Tories and the Liberals shuddered, the Wheat Board was born out of sheer desperation

AS THE UNSOLD GRAIN GREW INTO MOUNTAINOUS PROPORTIONS, AND BENNETT'S TRADE DEAL FELL THROUGH, IT WAS THE ONLY OPTION LEFT

The Canadian Wheat Board of 1935 was created by a Conservative government opposed to state regulation, and nurtured by a Liberal government equally wary of intervention. But it was greeted as a godsend by Western wheat farmers, who had been lobbying for one since 1920, when a wartime wheat marketing agency had been scrapped under pressure from businessmen, who resented its fixed prices (Vol.5, Sect.1, ch.2).

Thereafter, Canadian governments had vetoed the idea of a marketing board because it would interfere with laissez-faire capitalism. As an ultra-capitalist and former grain merchant, R.B. Bennett had opposed it for years, ignoring three successive resolutions of the United Farmers of Alberta calling for the establishment of such a board.

However, in 1930 things changed radically. In return for guaranteeing the debts of the prairie wheat pools' central marketing agency, Bennett insisted that a federal appointee take the agency over. He installed his friend John McFarland as its general manager, in charge of disposing of the huge stock the Pools had stored in hopes of better prices.

But prices kept falling, and this forced McFarland into a ludicrous situation. In August 1933 he convinced the Winnipeg Grain Exchange to support a floor price of more than 70 cents a bushel for October futures. Speculators wouldn't pay that. So he had to buy almost 20 million bushels on the international market to maintain the price on the wheat Canadian farmers had already contracted to deliver. In other words, he was buying large quantities of foreign grain while sitting on a huge pile of unsaleable

R.B. Bennett may have thought he was doing his friend a favour when he appointed John I. McFarland head of the wheat pools' marketing agency. What he was, in fact, accomplishing was giving his colleague a headache that only a greater agony — the Second World War — could cure.

domestic wheat that by 1935 amounted to 235 million bushels.

Also in August 1933 Bennett signed an agreement by which the four main wheat exporting countries — Canada, the United States, Australia and Argentina — set lower export quotas. As the pressure mounted to put the marketing of all Canadian grain in the hands of one government-appointed board, he still balked. "I have committed the Dominion of Canada, particularly the wheat growing provinces, the grain trade, the wheat pools, the wheat farmers, to an international obligation," he told a federal-provincial conference in 1934. "I will not agree to a national wheat board to administer the delivery of Canada's quota and organize the surplus, if any, because this would endanger the capital investments of the grain trade."

His stand enraged farmers and events seem to vindicate them. Bennett's international agreement soon fell apart because Argentina broke faith, while drought and rust prevented Canada from meeting its quota of 200 million bushels anyway. Then politics intervened. McFarland warned the prime minister that the Liberals were about to unveil a policy for the creation of a national wheat board in early 1935, an election year. Bennett and some traders began to recognize the need for some kind of government involvement in wheat marketing. Even bankers liked the idea of stable prices to underpin their loans. Moreover the wheat board proposal accorded well with Bennett's New Deal, his strategy to get his Depression-racked government re-elected (see main chapter).

On June 10, 1935, he acted, introducing legislation that created a three-man grain board charged with "the orderly

McFarland was forced to continue the Pools' policy of withholding wheat from the market in the hope of forcing the price up, which meant buying foreign wheat for domestic need. This situation seemed ludicrous to Arch Dale at the Winnipeg Free Press, as it did to many in the Prairies.

marketing of wheat in interprovincial and export trade." The board's extraordinary mandate gave it a monopoly on buying and selling wheat from all sources within Canada, licensing and regulating all grain elevators and even setting up its own elevators with cabinet approval. Oats, barley, rye and flax produced in the four western provinces could also be bought, sold and stored by the board. Wheat contracts between the three western pools, their farmer-members and their customers, previously guaranteed by Ottawa under various relief acts, would now be under the aegis of the all-powerful board.

When the bill hit the floor of the Commons the grain industry and business interests hit the roof. Boards of trade across the land joined the grain traders to fight the compulsory features of the bill. Government or not, they said, it would soon work all the evils of monopoly. Mackenzie King's Liberals supported the business lobby in its stance, as did some members of Bennett's Tory caucus who whispered that it was a "step in the direction of state socialism."

As the anti-board lobby geared up for an all-out assault, farm newspapers issued a call for the bill's defence. "If the

farmers of Western Canada want a Grain Board to market their wheat and coarse grains, getting the best prices obtainable on the world's markets," declared the *Western Producer* on June 21, 1935, "they should say so in the most definite and positive terms AT ONCE." It warned that the Winnipeg Grain Exchange and the grain trade were planning to "wreck the bill if they can."

And they did. Rather than earning the votes of Western farmers by standing up to vociferous opposition, Bennett backed down. He set up a special committee "to hear the industry's point of view," then passed a compromise bill in August that bore little resemblance to the original. The only grain left under the board's jurisdiction was wheat.[C] Gone were the board's monopoly powers, although it retained control of all elevator licences and could set a minimum price per bushel on wheat bought from producers. McFarland, who saw the Wheat Board as a necessary evil, was named its chairman.

A weakened Wheat Board was back in business, but for how long? When the Liberals swept Bennett's Tories from

The U.F.A., May 2, 1932

secretary of the Winnipeg Grain Exchange. The board set a minimum price of 87.6 cents a bushel for the 1936 crop year, below market value since prices were now rising. Government ministers suggested that farmers who wouldn't accept it could sell their wheat privately.

In 1936 the Liberals set up a royal commission, the third such inquiry in twelve years, to study alternative methods of marketing grain. The commission was headed by W.F.A. Turgeon, a former Saskatchewan Liberal cabinet minister. When his report was tabled in 1938, it supported the government's policy of scrapping the board and returning to free enterprise. But the government couldn't act on its recommendations because international wheat prices were once again falling, and the protectionist policies of many importing countries were strangling demand. Ottawa set the minimum price at 80 cents a bushel to ensure the repayment of bankers' loans and the purchasing power of farmers.

power in September 1935, scrapping the board was near the top of their agenda. Three months later McFarland was replaced by James Murray, vice-president and general manager of the Alberta Pacific Grain Company and a former

Next year, when the government lowered the minimum price to 60 cents in the hope of forcing producers to return to the free market, Western interests tried to shore up the Wheat Board by forming the Committee on Markets

Winnipeg Free Press, January 19, 1935

Winnipeg Free Press, January 17, 1935

As the depression progressed, disenchantment with the system grew into cynicism. (Top) This 1932 U.F.A. cartoon expresses the alienation felt by western farmers. (Above) In 1935 Arch Dale observed that politics created some strange bedfellows, i.e., that Bennett's New Deal seemed uncomfortably close to Woodsworth's CCF platform. (Right) Mackenzie King's smile would prove to be prophetic.

In 1935 the Winnipeg Grain Exchange, vowed unalterable enemy of Bennett's wheat board bill, is shown here in full fury.

and Agricultural Readjustment, an umbrella group that included representatives from Prairie governments, farm

the ashes of the Depression and dodged plans by both Liberal and Conservative governments to shoot it down. But

---

Crerar warned King that if Ottawa folded the board Westerners had fought so long and hard to revive, both prairie farmers and businessmen might reject the Liberals, jeopardizing eight to ten seats in Manitoba alone.

---

organizations and boards of trade from Edmonton, Calgary, Saskatoon and Regina. Its delegates put their case to cabinet in April 1939.

By now King's government, like Bennett's before it, was rethinking its opposition to government intervention in the grain trade. It was moved by the argument that other wheat-producing nations exercised control over markets, and even more strongly by political reality. Mines and Natural Resources Minister Thomas Crerar warned King that if Ottawa folded the board Westerners had fought so long and hard to revive, both prairie farmers and business-men might reject the Liberals in the upcoming 1940 election, jeopardizing eight to ten seats in Manitoba alone. Later that year the government raised its wheat price guarantee to 80¢ a bushel, evidence that the Wheat Board would survive.

Then came the Second World War. If the Wheat Board was not in place and it would have been invented to ensure wartime supply. Like a phoenix, the board had risen from

the debate on it was far from over, and its benefit to western farmers far from conclusive.

— *G.O.*

[A]Bennett was one of the most prominent businessmen in the private grain trade before he became prime minister. He had acted as agent for his old friend Max Aitken, later Lord Beaverbrook, in the merger that created the Alberta Pacific Grain Company, which owned and operated more than 300 grain elevators across the West by the mid-1920s. Bennett was a director of the company and made large profits from its operations until he sold his interest in 1924.

[B]McFarland, who was manager of the Alberta Pacific Grain Company, owned 45 of the 113 elevators in the original merger that created the company and held a controlling interest in the firm until 1926.

[C]From 1935 to 1943 the Wheat Board operated as a voluntary marketing agency, buying wheat from farmers at a fixed initial price. In September of 1943, when food production was part of the war effort, the Wheat Board was given the exclusive wheat marketing powers that it would retain until the century's last decade. The powers of the board were extended again in 1949, amidst great controversy, to cover the marketing of oats and barley.

CHAPTER THREE

She destroyed a government and ended a premier's career

VIVIAN MACMILLAN'S CLAIM THAT BROWNLEE MADE HER HIS SEXUAL PET CREATES ALBERTA'S MOST FAMOUS LAWSUIT AND DOOMS FOREVER THE UFA

by JANICE TYRWHITT

That the United Farmers government of Alberta should be terminated by the Depression was altogether probable because every provincial government in Canada but one would be defeated between 1930 and 1935. That it should be ruined by debt and pulverized by radical politics was also foreseeable for that was the temper of the times. But that it should be brought to permanent political ruin at the hands of a 22-year-old government stenographer and watch its revered leader destroyed as a politician, that was not foreseeable nor even imaginable. Yet such was the fate of the UFA and such was the devastation wrought by Vivian MacMillan, the church organist from Edson and one of the the most famous women in the 20th-century history of Alberta.

The suit she brought against Premier John Brownlee for "seduction" resulted in Alberta's most celebrated court case which made the front page of just about every paper in the country. It also touched off a scandal that overshadowed even the sensational divorce of Brownlee's minister of public works, Oran L. McPherson (see sidebar). What emerged was a yarn so tangled that some of its loose ends have never been tied down. Was this young woman the victim of a powerful and unprincipled man who first beguiled, then forced her into an adulterous relationship? The lurid story she told was so circumstantial in its details, and so bizarre, that many believed she couldn't have invented it. Brownlee's supporters were convinced that it *was* invented — not by Vivian but by her boyfriend, John Caldwell, whom they suspected of being backed by Brownlee's Liberal opponents. For the rest of her life, Vivian would maintain that her account was true; for the rest of his, Brownlee would deny it.

Vivian MacMillan was first introduced to Brownlee when she was sixteen, at a banquet for the visiting premier and Lieutenant-Governor W.G. Egbert held in her hometown of Edson in the summer of 1928. Her father, Allan, was assistant foreman in the local CNR shops; he and his wife, Letha Maude, were Baptists who regularly attended church with Vivian and her elder brother, Harry. Next year Vivian served as a Sunday school teacher and organist.

In July 1930, MLA Chris Pattinson invited Brownlee to make his second official visit to Edson. MacMillan was now mayor of the town, and with his wife and daughter he drove the premier to a picnic at Shining Bank on the McLeod River, an hour's drive from Edson. When he mentioned that Vivian had finished high school, Brownlee suggested she take a business course in Edmonton.

With her parents' approval, Vivian went to Edmonton on August 31, 1930, accompanied by her mother, who stayed three days. Vivian took lodgings at the YWCA and enrolled in a secretarial course at Alberta College. Soon she began visiting the premier's house in the Garneau district on the city's south side[1]. The Brownlees' sons, Jack and Alan, were then sixteen and fourteen. In 1919 the birth of a stillborn daughter, followed by a tubercular infection, affected Florence Brownlee's health for several years (Vol.5, Sect.2, ch.3). During the trial, she and her husband testified that since 1928, when doctors at the Mayo Clinic pronounced her physically sound, she had lived a normal life.

By her own account, Vivian was seduced by the premier in October 1930, and had frequent sexual intercourse with him until the spring of 1933. This was the accusation that confronted

[1] The site of Brownlee's house at 11151 88th Avenue has now been absorbed by the Timms Centre for the Arts.

Vivian MacMillan won her seduction case against Premier Brownlee and helped bring down a government, only to find herself labelled "The Girl In The Red Velvet Studebaker."

Brownlee when, on August 3, 1933, the law firm of Maclean, Short & Kane wrote, "We have been instructed to commence action against you for damages for seduction of Miss Vivian MacMillan."

What prompted Vivian and her father, as joint plaintiffs, to launch the civil suit? In September 1932, she had met and fallen in love with John Caldwell, an Edmonton United Church minister's son who was then a third-year medical student at the University of Alberta. When she came back to Edmonton after spending Christmas with her parents, both Caldwell and the Brownlees met her at the station. According to Vivian, rather than shaking Caldwell's hand, Brownlee turned and walked away.

In January Caldwell asked Vivian to marry him. Refusing, she confessed her relationship with Brownlee. Caldwell was shocked into withdrawing his proposal, but promised to help her escape from what she described as the premier's inexorable demands. On May 23 he consulted Neil Douglas Maclean, KC, who had represented Cora McPherson in her suit against her husband.[2] A dedicated Liberal, Maclean was known for his thorough grasp of law and fierce loyalty to his clients, especially women trapped in repressive relationships. He agreed to act for Vivian MacMillan. On July 5, his attempts to gather evidence against Brownlee included a car chase through Edmonton streets.

Maclean's letter reached the premier at his rented cottage at Sylvan Lake just as he was about to leave for a three-month stint on the Royal Commission on Banking and Currency in Ottawa.[3] Brownlee promptly hired a formidable legal team headed by two Calgary KCs, Arthur Leroy Smith and Marshall Menzies Porter. Smith was nationally respected as a criminal trial lawyer; during a courtroom skirmish, no one could better articulate and apply the rules of evidence, practice and procedure. Porter, an equally skilled litigator, was the premier's close friend and advisor to the Alberta government.

At 11 a.m. on September 22, Maclean entered the MacMillans' statement of claim, which set out in lurid detail Vivian's account of her relationship with Brownlee. "Solely by reason of the Defendant's actions to her," it alleged, "the said Vivian MacMillan became physically and mentally ill and suffered a nervous breakdown and was ill during the months of June, July, August and September 1932 and was forced to leave her position and return to her Father's home. When the said Vivian MacMillan returned to Edmonton in October 1932, the Defendant, in spite of her illness,

---

Vivian MacMillan swore that the premier told her it was her duty to save his wife's life by giving in to his demands. 'He said that if she ever became pregnant it would kill her. That was one way I could show my gratitude to her and to himself.'

---

insisted upon her resuming relations with him." Maclean leaked a copy of the statement to the Liberal *Edmonton Bulletin*, which splattered the whole text over the front page of its noon edition.

Suspecting that the suit had been instigated by his Liberal opponents, the premier called his attorney-general, John Lymburn, and told him that the allegation was not only a lie but an attempt at extortion, a criminal act that allowed the affair to be investigated at government expense.

Lymburn immediately assigned UFA troubleshooter Harry Brace, a former APP officer who was now provincial superintendent of insurance, to delve into the lives of Maclean, Vivian MacMillan and John Caldwell. Brace then hired three local private detectives.[4] To arm himself against the examination for discovery, Brownlee was deliberately kept in the dark about Brace and his operatives.

In the fall of 1933, the three detectives told Brace that they had interviewed Vivian's friends in Edson, staff at the legislature, and even Brownlee's maids. Their information was incorporated into Brace's handwritten reports. According to those notes, Bob Dudley pretended to be a loan shark. Meeting him in a room at the Corona Hotel, Caldwell said he had engineered the lawsuit, and could repay a loan because he expected to make a lot of money out of the case by December. Dudley asked Caldwell to come back at 11 p.m. Before Caldwell returned, Dudley hired Harold Allen, an RCMP special constable, to hide in the room. Allen made shorthand notes of the ensuing discussion. Dudley said that Caldwell admitted that he and twelve others had been asked to gather evidence against the premier. When the Liberals were elected, he expected to be rewarded.

[2] Maclean had a longstanding grudge against Brownlee. They first fell out in the Twenties, when Maclean was charged with drinking and driving. After putting his Packard into a highway ditch near Millet, he tried to drive off while being hauled out, causing injury and damage. Since his practice required him to drive, he was appalled at the prospect of losing his licence. The case was referred to Brownlee, then attorney-general, who refused to reduce or dismiss it.

[3] There he was effective, as James Gray notes in his book *Talk to My Lawyer*. When the Macmillan Commission recommended the establishment of the Bank of Canada, Brownlee drafted the bank's corporate structure.

[4] Later in court, Maclean asked Brownlee if one of the detectives was "the same gentleman that spent a while in Fort Saskatchewan [prison] a year or two ago?"

Edmonton Journal, 5 July, 1934.

Glenbow Archives, McDermid Collection, ND-3-5545

Premier John Brownlee won a triumphant second election victory in 1930 (R) but his sexual escapade pushed him first into court, then into disgrace and finally into resigning within four years. The drawing (left) was published by the Edmonton Journal the day he resigned.

Harry Brace also examined a statement by the wife of one of his detectives. Doris Audrey Schwantge claimed that Neil Maclean had tried to bribe her to seduce the premier so that Mrs. Brownlee could get a divorce. Unsupported by evidence, her allegation fell apart.

One of Brace's operatives tracked down Carol H. Snell, Vivian's high school Latin teacher and fellow Baptist, who had proposed to her in the spring of 1929. Then seventeen, she refused, but they remained friends. In 1933 he was working as a private tutor in Bear River, Nova Scotia. While hinting at extortion, Brace's account was scarcely reassuring:

Snell will testify that Vivian MacMillan told him in 1932 that she was having a sexual relationship with J.E. Brownlee but did not at that time suggest that it was in any way against her will or ever had been. At the same time she stated to him that she could put J.E. Brownlee any place she wanted because there was nothing that his political opponents

Florence Brownlee stuck by her husband through the whole sordid trial, flatly denying Vivian helped save her life by sleeping with her husband. This photo was taken the year of the trial.

would not give to get from her the information she had just given Snell.

Brace's attempts to discredit Maclean also included allegations that he had drafted false affidavits of documents, supplied the *Edmonton Bulletin* with sensational news, and offered a girl $100 to seduce Brownlee during the Edmonton Exhibition in 1933. All these allegations were intended to deter the MacMillans from suing by forcing Maclean to withdraw from the case. In this they failed. Nor were any of Brace's findings offered in court, when Brownlee's lawyers could have used them to show that the suit was a frame-up designed to defame the premier.

On November 13, 1933, Brownlee's lawyer filed two documents in Supreme Court. One was a statement of defence, which denied the allegations made in the MacMillans' statement of claim on the grounds that they were "false, frivolous, vexatious and scandalous." The second was a counterclaim that named John Caldwell and Vivian MacMillan as co-conspirators in a plan to extort money from the premier and defame his reputation. On November 18 Maclean filed his defence to counterclaim, which reiterated that the allegations against the premier were true and denied any conspiracy. At the same time Allan MacMillan denied that the lawsuit had any political motivation. "I am taking this action as any other father would take it," he declared, "to protect the young girls of this province."

In April 1934 Maclean presented to court a sworn statement that a stenographer in Harry Brace's department had gone to Vivian's boarding house, and told Vivian that she had been sent by a man with the authority and money to settle the action against Brownlee. Next morning Maclean telephoned Brace, who denied that his employee had any authority to make such an offer. "He told me that the 'big fellow' had given him a job to do and that in his position, he could not refuse to do it," Maclean testified.

In the examinations for discovery, held in May and June 1934, the plaintiffs and defendant were questioned under oath by their opponents' lawyers, to learn what evidence would be used against their clients. Maclean asked Brownlee about Harry Brace's investigation. The premier said that he had been told little beyond the fact that the government had spent about $1,400 (then about two years' salary for the average civil servant), which he had repaid from his own pocket.

When Brownlee's lawyers examined John Caldwell on May 25, they didn't ask him about his alleged conversation with Dudley at the Corona Hotel, or any questions related to the premier's accusation that he was furthering a conspiracy for gain. But he did explain why he and Neil Maclean had chased Brownlee through Edmonton the night of July 5. At the end of June Vivian had not yet broken off with the premier because she seemed to be afraid of him. On July 3 he watched Brownlee dropping Vivian near her lodgings, after midnight. When Vivian said she couldn't see him on July 5, he rented a car from Grey-Line Taxi, picked up Maclean, waited outside her boarding house, and saw her walking to 109th Street and 99th Avenue, where the premier picked her up about 10 p.m. Caldwell followed them as they zigzagged around downtown Edmonton, and eventually saw Vivian leaving the car near her home.

A younger Vivian with her parents Allan and Letha Maude. They first met Brownlee when, as a 16-year-old Girl Guide, Vivian helped serve at an Edson dinner in his honour.

Maclean chose trial by jury. He pressed for an early court date, and after Arthur Smith was granted some adjournments, the trial was set for June 18. But on June 3, Smith was badly injured in a car accident near Okotoks, and taken to a Calgary hospital with a broken collarbone. All the tendons in his right hand had been severed. Marshall Porter applied for an adjournment and, over Maclean's objections, the trial was postponed a week.

By ten o'clock on Monday morning, June 25, spectators jammed the halls of the Edmonton courthouse and overflowed onto 100th Street. Within the sombre supreme civil courtroom, with

Brownlee used threats and endearments to maintain their relationship, Vivian claimed. Over the next two years, she said she had intercourse with the premier in his car, his office and his own house.

its navy blue walls and dark oak furnishings, every one of the 75 seats in the public section was filled. Premier Brownlee, wearing a grey suit, sat with his wife and the defense counsel table.

Presiding over the trial was the Honourable William Carlos Ives, acting chief justice of the supreme court of Alberta. "Cowboy Billy Ives", as he was known (not always affectionately), made short work of the preliminaries. Arthur Smith, his bandaged right arm in a sling, was granted permission to appear without his barrister's robes. Six male jurors were quickly chosen: a

Stony Plain farmer and five businessmen (two from Edmonton, two from Wainwright and one from Athabasca). Maclean briefly addressed the jury, and portions of the premier's pre-trial discovery were read into the record.

At 11:45 the morning of June 25, Vivian MacMillan was called as a witness. Just past her 22nd birthday, she wore a white coat, brown checked dress, brown silk stockings and white shoes[5]. Questioned by Maclean, she described the premier's visit to Edson in July 1930. On the way to the picnic, Brownlee remarked, "You have a very beautiful daughter here, Mrs. MacMillan,

Charges of wife-swapping against Brownlee's works minister were merely a curtain-raiser

A JUDICIAL COVERUP FAILED TO CONCEAL ORAN MCPHERSON'S CLOSET DIVORCE

by J.F.J. PEREIRA

Before the seduction suit against Premier John Brownlee broke in the newspapers, the province had already been shocked, dismayed and titillated by an earlier sex scandal involving Brownlee's public works minister, Oran Leo McPherson, who was rumoured to be involved in wife-swapping. As it turned out, this wasn't quite true. In fact that was the problem.

Brownlee's high profile soon eclipsed the McPherson case, but the extra-marital adventures of "Tony" McPherson received their full share of public attention at the time. (Ironically, "Tony" was originally a pet name bestowed by his wife Cora during their courtship, but over the years it had become a nickname used by everyone.)

McPherson, who farmed in the Vulcan area, was well known throughout the province. He had been an active member of the United Farmers of Alberta since 1909, and was among those who led the UFA into direct political action in the general election of 1921. This brought the UFA to power in a stunning, totally unexpected defeat of the Liberal government (Vol.4, Sect.5, ch.3).

McPherson himself was elected, and his abilities were recognized by his selection as speaker of the Legislature, in which post he served until 1926.

By the winter of 1925-26, there were rumours of a cabinet post for McPherson. He was returned to the Legislature in the 1926 election and before the end of the year he became minister of public works. In 1928, the McPhersons moved to Edmonton.

The works portfolio included highways, jails and a number of other responsibilities later assigned to other ministries.

Edmonton Bulletin, 26 May, 1933

Cora McPherson gave into her husband's every outlandish request, until he left her to starve. Then she fought back, right up to the Privy Council in England.

Apart from the constant drumfire of criticism over highways which went with the job, Tony McPherson attracted little adverse notice. At the same time his personal popularity increased to the extent that in the election of 1930 he was returned by acclamation, and his political future seemed assured. However, by then the seeds of the scandal that would bring him down had already been sown.

In the spring of 1929 the McPhersons attended the "Armistice Ball" at the Edmonton Armouries where they met Leroy and Helen Mattern. Roy Mattern, a high-school science teacher, was also a major in the reserve army and aide-de-camp to the lieutenant-governor. His wartime marriage to Helen, however, had not been a happy one. Helen had already considered a Reno divorce and changed her mind. They now lived disconsolately together in Edmonton.

The couples began seeing more of one another. McPherson at least began seeing far too much of Helen Mattern who by 1930, was a frequent overnight guest at the McPherson home — sometimes, according to subsequent evidence, in the McPhersons' bed.

In the spring of 1930 the McPhersons, accompanied by Helen, made a holiday visit to Victoria. By the time they returned to Edmonton in mid-April, an agreement had been arrived at for the McPhersons to divorce so that Tony could marry Helen. It is not altogether clear whether Roy and Cora were also to marry, but Cora certainly acquiesced in the divorce scheme and at some point Roy Mattern was persuaded to become a party to it. In any event Helen moved

what are you going to do with her?" Dismissing her studies in music as "a useless occupation," he suggested that Vivian take a business course in Edmonton. When her mother protested that she was too young to leave home, he offered to act as her guardian in the city, and guaranteed her a job when she graduated. At the Memorial Hall that evening, he danced with her five times and told her that she would "grow up to be a very beautiful woman and he hoped she would see her way clear going to Edmonton."

The Saturday after she moved to the YWCA, Brownlee telephoned and said, "A little bird told

into the McPherson home, and a campaign was begun aimed at driving Cora out.

In the 1930s a divorce was no passing incident. The only legal ground for it was adultery. And in the Alberta of that day, the mere mention of such a thing was enough to demolish a political career. If McPherson were to survive as a politician, therefore, the divorce had to be kept quiet.

The first outsider made privy to this arrangement was J.L. Lymburn, the attorney-general. McPherson consulted him as to divorce procedures. The second was Lymburn's law partner, Mayne Reid, who agreed to act for McPherson as a favour to Lymburn.

In January 1931, Cora left McPherson and went to Saskatoon. During the following month, in order to provide McPherson with the evidence of adultery, Cora McPherson spent two nights in a Saskatoon hotel room with Roy Mattern. He had quit teaching and moved to Winnipeg as office manager with Canadian Airways Ltd., leaving Helen behind. But he travelled to Saskatoon and met Cora there by arrangement. Two private detectives, hired for the purpose, were witnesses to this occurrence and on March 17 McPherson's notice for divorce was served on Cora in Saskatoon. Though the circle of those "in the know" continued to expand, no word leaked out to the news media.

As a favour to "Tony," Mr. Justice Thomas Tweedie agreed to hear the McPhersons' divorce action under extraordinary circumstances. He arranged for it to be heard in the judges' library of the Edmonton courthouse during the noon hour of April 22, 1931, when the building would likely be deserted. There Tweedie, unrobed, sat in judgment just long enough to grant McPherson a divorce decree and award him custody of his children. Anyone passing the room would scarcely suspect a judicial proceeding was going on. And anyway, there was a brass plate on the door that read "private." In the room were five people: McPherson, Reid, Tweedie, a clerk and a court

Provincial Archives of Alberta, 90.98/SE

Oran McPherson's divorce might have escaped the media's notice. If he hadn't been stingy, his shenanigans might never have become front-page news.

reporter. Several weeks later Helen Mattern also received a divorce on the same evidence. The circle had been expanded again, but still no one talked.

Now however, events began to unfold with soap-opera dramatics. Cora followed Roy Mattern back to Winnipeg, apparently in the expectation that they would be married. When it became obvious that this was not going to happen, and that she was stranded in Winnipeg without funds, she reported her situation to her ex-husband and asked him for advice. He flew immediately to Winnipeg. Be more aggressive with Mattern, he said. Be less inhibited. Work on it. All to no avail. Mattern just wasn't interested. She was penniless and suffering, she said. Suffering, replied McPherson, was in the long run good for the soul.

Cora then wrote that she would challenge the divorce proceedings and return to McPherson. The latter, meanwhile, went ahead with marriage to Helen, and Cora went to stay with her sister in Great Falls, Montana. In July 1932, Tony and Helen were married — in secret — by a friend of McPherson's, a clergyman who, incidently, doubled as Alberta's movie censor. It later emerged that the cleric had renewed his licence to perform weddings only a day earlier, specifically so that he could perform this particular marriage.

At this point, however, McPherson grievously erred. He pushed the pitiable Cora one step too far. As part of the divorce agreement he had been making maintenance payments to Cora of $75 a month. Then as salary reductions hit the government and his $8,000 ministerial salary was cut to $7,000 he in turn cut back Cora to $40 a month. Then, after his marriage Helen, he stopped the payments entirely. This left Cora desperate. By October 8, she was back in Edmonton, where she consulted a lawyer from Mundare named Harry White, who just happened to be a dedicated Liberal, the party that McPherson's UFA had ousted from power eleven years before.

me you were here and I thought I would phone you up. I would like you to come over to my home on Sunday afternoon and meet Mrs. Brownlee and the boys." The next day, he and his wife picked her up at the YWCA and drove her home that evening. Vivian testified, "Mrs. Brownlee said she hoped I would feel free to come over any time, and I started going over two or three times a week... I became very fond of Mrs. Brownlee and I had a very deep respect for Mr. Brownlee."

Vivian testified that she was alone with Brownlee for the first time on Sunday, October 5,

It seems likely that it was White who first sensed an opportunity to embarrass the UFA government. In any event, he discussed the matter with another Liberal lawyer, George Van Allen, and he in turn conveyed a report of the situation to yet another Liberal, the prominent Edmonton barrister Neil D. Maclean. On October 15, 1932, Maclean filed a statement of claim asking the courts to set aside Cora McPherson's divorce on the ground that it had been obtained by fraud and collusion.

Waterways railway scandal that destroyed the Liberal Rutherford government (Vol.2, Sect.6, ch.2).

Mr. Justice Frank Ford threw the affidavit out, but that did not prevent its contents from becoming public. Before long it had surfaced in the constituency of Camrose, where a by-election campaign was under way. And from there it reached the Toronto scandal sheet *Hush*, which published it in three instalments. (McPherson initiated libel suits against everyone who might in any way be held responsible, but these had no effect.)

The trial of Cora McPherson's claim did not open until May 8, 1933 — almost seven months after it had been entered. By that time the shape of the whole story was general knowledge. Nevertheless, further tantalizing details came out in the fourteen days of relentless testimony. Sample 1: During the 1930 election campaign both Cora McPherson and Helen Mattern had accompanied McPherson on various trips — Cora tagging along to "protect McPherson's reputation." Sample 2: In their trip to Victoria, all three, Cora, Helen and McPherson, slept three in one bed with Helen in the middle.

Roy and Helen Mattern had a marriage on the rocks, but with an infatuated Tony McPherson ready to do anything required to make Helen his, their problems were solved.

The *Edmonton Bulletin* carried a complete transcript of the trial every day, sometimes running to more than eight full columns of the newspaper. From this the public learned how Cora was going through "change of life,"

Cora by this time was living on relief. She could not have retained the most down-and-out legal hack in the province. Yet she was represented by a team that included both Maclean and Van Allen. They must have been acting without fee or hope or promise of fee. They were plainly motivated, therefore, by politics. So, anyway, the UFA would contend for years to come. Whatever their motive, Cora's statement of claim brought to an abrupt end the secrecy.

The statement was accompanied by an affidavit spelling out the whole seamy background to the divorce. An objection to this document was entered by McPherson's lawyer, S.B. Woods, (ironically the same Sydney B. Woods who as deputy attorney-general had been involved in the

how she had denied sex to her husband, how she had fallen in love with Mattern, six years her junior, how her husband had fallen in love with Mattern's wife Helen, how the three — Cora, Helen and Tony — had travelled together and how Helen had "raged" when she felt herself denied full access to the family, how Cora had followed Mattern to Winnipeg only to find he in turn had fallen in love with a younger woman whom he soon married, and Cora was left alone in a single room, separated from her children, her home, her friends.

The "society women" (as the *Edmonton Bulletin* called them) who packed the courtroom wept so openly and loudly as Cora testified that the judge suggested they get out. They didn't. Tony wept too as he told how he had "frantically"

when he drove her home from afternoon tea with his family. Maclean's examination elicited the following exchange:

Q. Just what happened on this occasion?

A. When I got into the car Mr. Brownlee took my hand and told me that I was a very beautiful girl and that I would grow into a very beautiful woman. He asked me what I knew about life.

---

pleaded with Cora not to leave him and the children and how he had been devastated by her departure to live with Mattern This was a story that Cora's counsel, the sceptical Van Allen, acidly ripped to shreds in summation. Why, he demanded, had McPherson remained such a friend of Mattern, the man who had "stolen" his wife and wrecked his home? "Any decent man wanting to protect his wife from an adulterous invader would have thrown him out the window. Instead he kissed his wife and let her go out into the night with her adulterer." At one point, during relentless cross-examination, McPherson lost his composure altogether and was left muttering incomprehensibly in the witness box until a recess was called.

Long before the trial ended, McPherson's once-promising political career lay in ruins. He was 47. The end was postponed, however. Though by now an obvious liability to the government, he was not dropped from the cabinet. Hence further disclosures injured the Brownlee administration even more.

And further disclosures there were. Cora's counsel had somehow learned of the curious Tweedie-conducted lunch-hour divorce proceeding and launched another legal action

the Social Credit onslaught.

The reader of this record, sixty-five years later, may easily conclude that Helen Mattern was a predator with the strong wish to improve her lot by dropping a schoolteacher husband in favour of one who was not only a cabinet minister but owned a substantial farm, and perhaps that is so.

After Tony was out of the cabinet he and Helen moved to the farm, just outside Vulcan, where they remained for the next fourteen years. At some point during the 1940s they became speakers on the Christian Science lecture circuit in the United States. In the fall of 1948 they moved to Vancouver and a few months later to Victoria where McPherson died on May 23 at the age of 63.

Cora McPherson was still in the news on June 2, 1936, when she applied for support of $900 a year. (At that point she was still represented by George Van Allen.) Little was heard of her thereafter, however, until a local history of the Vulcan area was published in 1973. The book includes a reminiscence by Cora McPherson, then living in Alexandria, Virginia, of her years on the Vulcan farm. No mention is made of the scandal.

During the 1930 election campaign both Cora McPherson and Helen Mattern had accompanied McPherson on various trips — Cora tagging along to 'protect McPherson's reputation.' Then in their trip to Victoria, all three, Cora, Helen and McPherson, slept three in one bed with Helen in the middle, the public learned.

to dissolve the divorce. This was still before the courts when the suit against Brownlee began. That fact briefly saved McPherson's job. How could Brownlee jettison a minister for unseemly behaviour when he faced worse accusations himself? So McPherson stayed on as works minister for more than a year until Brownlee himself resigned and his successor, Gavin Reid, chose a cabinet that did not include him.

With the Brownlee case now making the front page of newspapers all over Canada, the McPherson affair continued under lesser headlines as it proceeded all the way to the judicial committee of the Privy Council in England, which ruled that the right to trial in open court had been violated in the divorce action. But the council did not grant Cora's request for a reversal of the divorce because McPherson had remarried.

Tony, meanwhile, was out of the cabinet as of July 13, 1934, but retained his seat in the Legislature and in fact stood for election again in 1935, when he went down under

Of Roy Mattern's fortunes after 1933 virtually nothing is known. His part in the divorce arrangement was over long before the trial of Cora McPherson's first claim had ended, and he seems to have been forgotten immediately in the sensational aftermath of that trial. He, like the McPhersons, had been a victim of his wife's machinations, but where Tony had been a willing if not eager victim and Cora a most reluctant one, Mattern seems to have been no more than an amiably complaisant accomplice.

One other victim of the affair was the judge Thomas Tweedie, who for years after was hassled about his lunch-hour divorce hearing in the library. James H. Gray in his anecdotal history of the Alberta legal profession, *Talk to My Lawyer*, recalls a typical incident. He was off to Edmonton to hold court, Tweedie one day told the acerbic Calgary trial lawyer McKinley Cameron. "You better be careful, Tom," replied Cameron, "and don't get to holding court in the shit house."

Neil Maclean, Vivian's lawyer, was so devoted to her cause and his Liberal politics, he worked on the case for eight years and never charged her a penny.

Q. What was your answer to that?

A. I said I did not know what he meant exactly, but that I probably knew what any young girl of eighteen did and he suggested that I come out with him, that he was lonely.

Q. And what did you say to that?

A. I thought that it was very strange but arranged to go out with him the following Monday night.

Q. Was there any meeting arranged by Mr. Brownlee?

A. Yes, he arranged to meet me in front of the YWCA at nine o'clock in the evening.

Q. Did you meet him there?

A. Yes.

Q. And what happened?

A. We went for a drive out on the Jasper Highway about six miles from the city. We turned down a side road going south and parked about two miles down that road off the main highway.

Q. Is there any way you can identify that road?

A. Yes, there is a large ditch on the road going south, like an irrigation ditch. It is on the left side of the road.

Q. Now, what occurred on that trip?

A. On that trip Premier Brownlee told he had been madly in love with me for some time, and that sure I could not have helped knowing. He told me that he was very, very lonely, and that he and Mrs. Brownlee had not been living together as man and wife for a good number of years, and he just could not go on any longer unless I would give in to him. He told me it would be a matter of saving Mrs. Brownlee's life. He said that if she ever became pregnant it would kill her.

Q. What was your answer to this proposal?

A. I told him I thought such a thing was a sin.

Q. What did he say to that?

A. He just laughed at that and he told me that if his daughter had lived, and had done the thing he was asking me to do, he would have been proud of her. He told me he could not go on as

---

'He told me I knew what would happen if I broke off with him,' Vivian testified. 'It would probably cost Mrs. Brownlee her life and I would be out of a job and he would certainly see that I did not get another position in the province of Alberta.'

---

premier of the Province of Alberta if I did not give in to him. And that his whole home life would be ruined unless I did as he asked, and that it would probably be the cause of Mrs. Brownlee's death. He told me that he and Mrs. Brownlee had not lived together for many years as man and wife. After the birth of the last child the doctor had told him that if she became pregnant again she would likely lose her life, and in addition to that there was a tubercular condition from which she was three or four years convalescing.

Q. What else did he say?

A. He asked me what I thought of Mrs. Brownlee. I told him that I thought a lot of her. He said that this was one way I could show my friendship and gratitude to her and to himself.

Q. And what was your reply to that?

A. I told him that if there was any other way of showing my gratitude I would be glad to do it, but he said that was the only way.

Q. Where did this conversation take place?

A. On the side road.

Q. Did you stay there parked long?

A. No, not long.

Q. Did anything further occur that evening?

A. Mr. Brownlee had his arms around me and was kissing me.

Q. Did he take you back to the YWCA?

A. Yes, he drove me back and left me out in front of the YWCA.

Q. Had you given him any definite answer about what he had been saying to you?

A. No, he just asked me to think about it.

Q. When was the next occasion when you went out with Mr. Brownlee?

A. The week following. Sunday night he again drove me home. He asked me on this occasion if I would like to learn to drive the car. I said I knew how to drive a car, as I drove the car at home in Edson. He said that his car was larger than the one that we had at Edson. And he said I would like to talk to you about the discussion of the other night. He asked me to meet him the following night.

Q. Did you meet him again?

A. Yes.

Q. Where did you go?

A. Out the same road as before.

Q. What car was Mr. Brownlee driving?

A. The large Studebaker.

Q. What was the licence number of that car?

A. 31884.

Q. What size of car is that?

A. An eight-cylinder car.

Q. Is it a big car?

A. Yes, a large car.

Q. Lots of room in it?

A. Yes.

Q. How are the seats? Are they wide?

A. Yes, quite wide.

Q. What time was it when he picked you up?

A. About ten o'clock.

Q. Had that all been arranged the previous day?

A. Yes.

Q. When he was driving you home?

A. Yes.

Q. Now, what happened on that occasion?

A. On the way out Mr. Brownlee repeated that he was madly in love with me and told me how much I would be doing for him and his family if I gave in to him; that he thought it was my duty to do it to show my gratitude to Mrs. Brownlee and himself for being so kind to me. When we got to the side of the road where we stopped, he suggested we sit in the back seat of the car. We got in the back seat. He again made love to me and told me how much he loved me and was kissing me. He said he thought it was my duty to give in to him to

His skill as a litigator and his close friendship with the premier made Calgarian Marshall Menzies Porter, KC, an obvious choice for the Brownlee defence team.

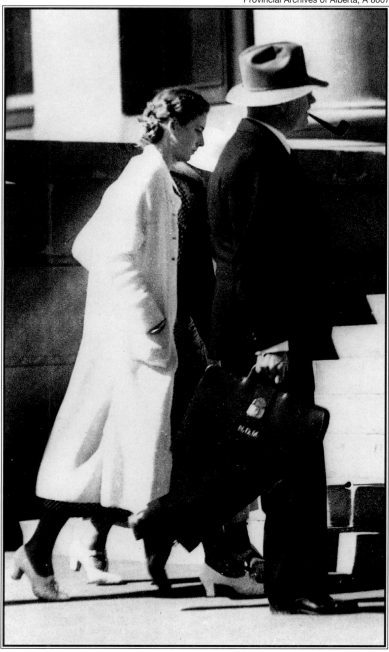

After two days and more than 1500 cross-examination questions, neither Vivian nor Maclean were surprised there were some discrepancies in her story.

6 The smaller car was a grey Studebaker that, Brownlee testified, was not bought until June 1932. He admitted that its front seat, like that of his Hupmobile, was "cut down" so that it could be laid flat lengthwise. Public indignation focussed not on these particulars but on the alleged use of any taxpayer-funded car for the purpose of seduction.

save his wife and family. He had his arms around me and while telling me this he forced me onto the seat of the car. I fought against him, but on this occasion he gained partial entrance. He flew into a rage because I resisted him, and he got into the front seat of the car.

Q. You say he gained partial entrance. I know it is very distasteful, but would you kindly tell me exactly what he did.

A. When he forced me down he had one arm around me. With one hand he raised my clothes and unfastened his own clothes and tried to have sexual intercourse with me.

Q. Did he succeed on that occasion?

A. No, not on that occasion.

Q. Then what did you do?

A. I fought against him, and because of my resistance he flew into a rage and got into the front seat and drove away. He drove to the Government Garage near the old Parliament Buildings to change the cars.

Q. What were your feelings at this time?

A. I was terrified.

Q. Just what do you mean when you say he drove down there to change cars?

A. He was driving the large car No. 31884, and for some reason changed to the small Studebaker 104.**6**

Q. What happened then?

A. Then he backed the smaller car out of the garage. When he came to get into the large car to drive in I got out and when he backed the smaller car out of the garage and drove up beside me, I opened the door to get in beside him, he told me to get in the back seat because I was not fit to ride with him. I said all right then, I would walk home. I elected to walk but Mr. Brownlee drove up and asked me to get in. On the way home he apologized, and said he must have lost his head to act that way, but that he was so disappointed that I was not going to do what he wanted.

Q. He did drive you to the Y that night?

A. Yes.

Q. When was the next occasion on which you went out with Premier Brownlee alone?

A. On Sunday night the last week in October.

Q. The first time that you went out was the first week in October. The second then a week after. And then on the last week in October. So then you were not out with him the third week, there must have been a week intervening when you were not out with him. Did you go over to the Brownlees?

A. No.

Q. Did you telephone?

A. No.

Q. Had you got into the habit of telephoning Mrs. Brownlee every day?

A. I just could not bear the thought of telephoning her pretending to be her friend when the fact that I was not going out with Mr. Brownlee might mean her death. Mrs. Brownlee telephoned and asked me to go over.

Q. Mrs. Brownlee telephoned you?

A. Yes. I did not go over.

Q. So there was a week intervening when you did not go over?

A. Yes. Mrs. Brownlee telephoned Sunday afternoon and asked if I would like to go for a drive and come back there for tea. I said yes. So Mr. Brownlee and Mrs. Brownlee called for me. In the evening when it was time to go home Mr. Brownlee drove me home himself. We did not go straight home. We went for a drive out into the country.

Q. Where did you go?

A. We went south on 9th Street to Whyte Avenue and then went as far east as the Post Office, then turned and went south again and drove out until we came to a graveyard.
There is a graveyard out there and a fox farm is next to it. Then we turned west for about half a mile.

Q. Was Mr. Brownlee again alone with you in the car?

A. Yes.

Q. What car was it?

A. The large Studebaker.

Q. Tell us what happened on that occasion?

A. Mr. Brownlee said he had something very important to talk to me about, and he hoped I would tell the truth about it, no matter how badly the evidence would be against me.

Q. And what was that?

A. He asked me if I had ever had intercourse with any other man. I told him no, I never had, and he said, "Viv, you must have had, because the first night there was no evidence to show that

Brownlee's statement of defence described Vivian's claims as 'false, frivolous, vexatious and scandalous.' For the rest of his life he would insist on they were false; for the rest of hers she would insist they were true.

there had never been another man." He said that I should prove there had never been another man. I said, well, if he could not take my word for it there was nothing I could do about it.

He then replied to me that he thought it was my duty to give in to him and save Mrs. Brownlee's life, his future and the honour of his family. I said I could not do anything like that, but I would gladly help Mrs. Brownlee in any other way. And he said that was the only way I could help.

He parked the car and asked me to get in the back seat, and said he would not touch me if I would get in the back seat, but I had only been in the back seat a few minutes when he said again, that if his daughter had lived he would be proud to have her do the thing he asked me to do. All this time he had his arms around me and was kissing me.

He again forced me down onto the back seat of the car. I fought against him but this time he was too determined to be moved by my tears or pleas. He again had one arm around me, holding me down on the seat of the car. He used his other hand to raise my clothes and undo his own. On that occasion we had complete sexual intercourse.[7] When he had been completely satisfied he sat on the back seat of the car and took me in his arms and said how wonderful I was, and that it was strange that he had to wait until he was an old man before he found the woman he really loved. He said how proud he was that I had been so unselfish as to do the thing he had asked me to do. He then asked me why I was trembling. I said I was afraid I might become pregnant, and he said not to worry about that because he knew about some pills and that if I took them at the end of each month before menstruating I need not be afraid.[8]

Q. And that was on a Sunday night. The last week in October?

A. Yes.

Q. And when did you see Mr. Brownlee again?

A. On Sunday night before letting me out at the "Y" he asked if he could see me on Wednesday night. Then on Monday evening he telephoned and said he had some wonderful news for me and asked if he could see me on Tuesday night. He asked me how I had been feeling and I said I had been ill. On Tuesday night he picked me up by the funeral home at ten o'clock.

When I got into the car he apologized for accusing me of having anything to do with any

[7] Brownlee was then 46, stood 6'4", and weighed more than 200 pounds. Vivian MacMillan was 5'7" and weighed about 150 pounds.

[8] These contraceptive pills were described by the *Edmonton Bulletin* as "apergols."

other man, because, he said, the condition of his clothes was such that he was afraid Mrs. Brownlee would notice something. He said he was so glad he was the first man, and again he went on to tell me how madly in love he was with me, and telling me what a wonderful thing I had done for his family, because I was saving Mrs. Brownlee's life.

Q. Where did you go this Tuesday night?

A. Out on the same road.

Q. Was that a well-travelled road?

A. I imagine it would be travelled by farmers, but there was very little traffic at that time.

Q. On this Tuesday night did you have connection with Premier Brownlee?

A. I did.

Q. From then on tell us what happened.

A. From then on during the time I stayed at the YWCA Mr. Brownlee telephoned me on an average of two or three times a week. We would go for a ride out on the same road generally. Sometimes, he would drive me out along the south road. During the winter of 1930 and the spring of 1931 he always picked me up on 100 Avenue and 103 Street.

Q. During that fall and winter of 1931 were you continuing going over to Brownlee's house?

A. Yes, twice a week, nearly every week.

Q. How did Mrs. Brownlee act toward you?

A. Mrs. Brownlee was very nice to me.

When Vivian finished her studies at Alberta College at the end of June 1931, leaving without a diploma because she had completed only six months of a ten-month course, Brownlee was out of town. But he had already introduced her to Fred Smailes, the civil service commissioner, who hired her as a junior stenographer in the attorney-general's department, on the same corridor as the premier's office. When she next saw Brownlee, he said, "I suppose you think you are clever going down and getting a position by yourself, but it was all arranged."

Now a working girl, Vivian left the YMCA and, over the next two years, lived in a series of Edmonton boarding houses. If her lodgings were on a well-lit street, Brownlee would pick her up at a less conspicuous corner. Vivian didn't enjoy sex: "It was a shock to my system and I was always worrying about becoming pregnant, even though I was taking pills."

Brownlee's defence counsel, Arthur Smith, put 1,584 questions to Vivian over two days in withering salvoes of rapid-fire cross-questioning that twice reduced her to tears. A cynical onlooker remarked, 'Each tear is worth $5,000.'

Gradually recognizing, she said, that the premier was taking advantage of her, Vivian vainly tried to break free. Brownlee used threats and endearments to maintain their relationship. Over the next two years, Vivian claimed, she had intercourse with Brownlee many times, in his car, his office and his own house. She stayed there for three days in September 1933 when his wife invited Vivian's mother to join her on a trip to Vancouver. Since her maid was away, Florence Brownlee asked Vivian to move in. One night Brownlee spent in Calgary; the other two, he slept with Vivian.

Vivian's most damning evidence was perhaps her recollection of several weeks spent at the

From the start of the trial the courtroom was packed, with the overflow of people crammed into the halls, the rotunda and out on the sidewalk.

premier's house in the spring of 1932. Florence Brownlee shared the south bedroom with Alan, who sometimes walked in his sleep. Brownlee and Jack, a tall, nervous sixteen-year-old who feared the dark and occasionally woke up screaming, had twin beds eighteen inches apart in the north bedroom overlooking the street. Beside it was a room that Vivian shared with the maid, Jean McCloy. During that time, Brownlee established a routine which he and Vivian followed almost every night that he wasn't away on business. He would walk down the hall to the bathroom, and run the water in the basin as a signal for her to join him. She followed him back to his room, keeping time with his footsteps so that only one person could be heard walking on the squeaky floor. She would enter the room behind Brownlee, who wore a big woolly dressing gown. Once, when Jack moved and muttered, Brownlee turned on the light, and his son slumbered on.

One day Vivian collapsed on the way to work. Mrs. Brownlee took her to the University Hospital, and three days later her mother took her home to Edson to rest from what Vivian described as a nervous breakdown: "I was getting very tired and those pills I was taking upset me and I kept getting a very severe pain in my left side. I had lost about thirty pounds."

When she met and soon fell in love with Johnny Caldwell in the fall of 1933, she determined to end her relationship with the premier but, she said, "He told me I knew what would happen if I broke off with him; that it would probably cost Mrs. Brownlee her life and I would be out of a position and he would certainly see that I did not get another position in the province of Alberta."

Not surprisingly, both John and Florence Brownlee sensed that Vivian's affection was cooling. In February, the premier blamed John Caldwell, and told her that a young man had nothing to offer, whereas he had everything to offer. Some weeks later his wife more astutely asked, "Are you sure Mr. Brownlee has not done anything to you?" No, said Vivian, but the lie strengthened her resolve. On a Sunday morning in May of 1933, she refused to let him take her to his office. Furious, he drove her to the First Baptist Church and told her she would not be welcome at tea that afternoon. But he soon resumed his attentions: "He was playing with me like a cat plays with a mouse."

Vivian's continued visits to the Brownlees exhausted John Caldwell's patience. "He asked me if I was ever going to stop going over there... I told him that I just couldn't, because Mr. Brownlee was too strong, and I asked him what I should do about it. He said he would consult a lawyer."

On May 24, the day after Caldwell's first meeting with Neil Maclean, she agreed to write a statement which was sworn before lawyer George L. Parney. Even though she resigned her job that day, she didn't end her relationship with the premier. On June 27 and July 3, they again had intercourse on country roads. When he picked her up two nights later, he suggested going to his house, since his wife and sons were away at Sylvan Lake. That evening they were trailed by Neil Maclean and John Caldwell. At that point, Vivian said, neither she nor Brownlee knew who was in the car following them. Unable to shake it, the premier dropped her off near her lodgings. In the middle of July, she told her parents about her relationship with the premier. MacMillan consulted Maclean and instructed him to sue.

On Tuesday morning Smith began his cross-examination, which he well knew would be crucial to the premier's countersuit as well as his trial. By ruling that some of Maclean's questions were inadmissible, Judge Ives had already made it clear that he had little sympathy for the plaintiff. But she was attractive and quick-thinking, and the jury might well believe her story. So Smith challenged her as a wanton perjurer and savaged every detail of her evidence.

The *Edmonton Bulletin*'s coverage was unashamedly partisan. That morning Albertans read court reporter J.S. Cowper's account of Monday's proceedings under bold red headlines, "Vivian Testifies to Harrowing Ordeal" and "Premier Brownlee is Pictured Love-torn for Girl Companion." Cowper described Vivian as "pallid of face but with eyes feverishly bright like a deer at bay before the hunter... Not even when her voice choked with sobs did she ask for any quarter. Forcing back tears, she gave answer to the questions designed to tear away all privacies of soul and body and expose her inner consciousness to the jury."

Barely able to write with his injured hand, Smith had to rely on his remarkably precise memory of what she had said the previous day. He confronted her on why she came to Edmonton, her claimed concern for Mrs. Brownlee and the family, how she got her job, her allegedly failed

---

Mrs. MacMillan described the premier's visit to her in Edson: 'Mr. Brownlee suggested did I realize that Vivian's name would be ruined forever it this came out. I said, 'Do you realize what it will do to your own name, Mr. Brownlee?'

---

health, her friends, her love life before 1930 and after, her interest in Caldwell and her expectation of reward from the case itself. Smith put 1,584 questions to her over two days in what even the cautious *Edmonton Journal* described as "withering salvoes of rapid-fire cross-questioning," that twice reduced her to tears. A cynical onlooker remarked, "Each tear is worth $5,000."

Hammering Vivian about her testimony in court and in the examination for discovery, Smith managed to establish some inconsistencies. Vivian said she hadn't considered going to the University of Alberta before meeting Brownlee. Smith produced letters proving that she had requested and received information about a course in music and English. He cast doubt on her assertion that Brownlee had offered to be her guardian:

Q. You say that Brownlee said that if you came down to Edmonton his home would be your home and he would act as your guardian?
A. Yes, sir.

The Brownlee residence at 11151 88th Avenue, where, according to her testimony, Vivian regularly had tea with Florence and sometimes sex with the premier.

Q. He used the word guardian?

A. Yes, sir.

Q. Are you quite sure of that?

A. Positive.

Q. And that they would look after you. I suppose that means Mr. and Mrs. Brownlee?

A. Yes.

Q. Did it strike you that there was something remarkably hasty about that?

A. I remarked about it being strange that Mr. Brownlee had taken such a great interest in me.

Q. You did discuss it with your parents and wondered why he had taken such an interest in you?

A. Yes.

Q. Did they think he had acted hastily?

A. No, sir.

Later Smith confronted Vivian with her father's testimony at the examination for discovery, in which MacMillan admitted that Brownlee had not actually used the word "guardian," but had implied it: "He said, 'We will look after her.'" Vivian maintained that Brownlee had offered to be her guardian.

Q. When a man you had only seen and been in conversation with a few moments in the presence of your parents says he is going to be your guardian, did that not strike you as a little startling?

A. No. It was not startling.

Q. Well then, striking, unusual?

A. It just made me wonder why he was taking so much interest in me.

Why, asked Smith, had she enrolled in a commercial course at Alberta College without consulting Brownlee?

Artwork by Lyle Grant

Vivian would follow Brownlee back to the bedroom he shared with his younger son, carefully keeping time with his footsteps so Mrs. Brownlee would only hear a single person walking on the squeaking floor.

Q. Neither you nor your father or mother communicated with Brownlee then from the time he was there until you came to Edmonton. You went to Alberta College and arranged about your own studies without consulting this guardian?

A. Yes.

Q. And you decided that you would not live in residence at Alberta College?

A. Yes.

Q. And your mother was with you when you made that decision?

A. Yes.

Q. And the reason was because the evening restrictions were too close. In other words, that you would not have sufficient freedom in the evening?

A. Yes.

Q. And you and your mother chose for you to live at the YWCA?

A. Yes.

Q. So the man and his wife who were to act as your guardian and look after you were not even consulted as to where you should stay?

A. When Mr. Brownlee was in Edson he had suggested that I stay at the YWCA.

Q. When did you think that up?

A. When you asked me about it.

Smith ridiculed Vivian's notion that Brownlee had ulterior motives when he suggested that she take a course in Edmonton.

Q. You still say that in that hour [during the drive to Sylvan Lake] he made up his mind to entice you from your home and seduce you. You don't believe that, do you?

A. After what happened when I came to Edmonton I believe he had that idea.

Q. When did you first get that idea?

A. When I first went out with Mr. Brownlee alone.

Q. It is a terrible thing to think that you, a young girl, would think that a man enticed you from your home with the purpose of seducing you.

A. I didn't understand you when you said that first.

Q. All right, go ahead, take your time.

A. It would be after I'd been going out with him for about a year.

Q. So that it would be some time in the fall of 1931 that you got the idea?

A. Yes.

Q. Where were you when you got the idea?

A. I didn't get it all at once. It was gradual.

Q. Can you give me any idea when this terrible thought occurred to you?

A. It would be in the first year that I was working in the Parliament Buildings.

Q. So that he had been having intercourse with you for a year and the thought hadn't occurred to you that he had brought you down from Edson for that purpose.

A. No.

Q. What happened to put it into your mind?

A. I would hear girls talking about men and I was working in the Attorney-General's department and there were always all sorts of files to read about men getting young girls into trouble and I started to have my suspicions that perhaps Mr. Brownlee wasn't in love with me.

When did Brownlee first call Vivian to invite her to tea?

Smith suggested that she had first visited the Brownlees on September 14, not September 7. He asked, "Did Mr. Brownlee telephone you on Saturday, the 6th?" Vivian answered, "I am quite sure it was the 6th. If it was not that Saturday then it would be the Saturday following."

Vivian broke down when Smith questioned her about Brownlee's early advances:

Q. So here you were, frequenting the Brownlee household for three years. He had promised to be your guardian and look after you and you never even mentioned this to Mrs. Brownlee. [Miss MacMillan burst into tears.] Why did you not?

A. Because Mrs. Brownlee was being very kind to me and I assumed that Mr. Brownlee had told her of the conversation.

Q. You told me about Sunday night and that he called for you on the Monday night, that would be the 6th, and that night he drove you to the country.

A. Yes, sir.

Q. And then you had some conversation in the car to the effect that Mr. Brownlee was a lonely man. [Witness again breaks down but quickly recovers.]

Q. Was his wife mentioned that night?

A. Yes, sir.

Vivian's lawyer, Neil Maclean, challenged defence counsel Smith's dismissal of backseat coupling as physically impossible: 'Ask any taxi driver, any policeman.'

Q. He told you that if he had sexual intercourse with his wife it would kill her?

A. He said that if she became pregnant it would kill her.

Q. In the examination for discovery you told me that it was sexual intercourse and you told Mr. Maclean that if she became pregnant it would kill her. Which was it?

A. He said that first night that sexual intercourse would kill her.

Q. And did he tell you that night that the only way you could repay Mrs. Brownlee's kindness would be to have intercourse with him?

A. Yes.

Q. And you told him that you would do anything for Mrs. Brownlee in any other way to repay her kindness to you. Are you sure that that conversation took place that night?

A. Yes.

Q. So we find this man putting a proposition to you that you should part with your honour to repay the kindness of his wife, whom you'd only known a month. That's the situation, isn't it?

A. Yes.

Q. And that's the story you want this court to believe?

A. Yes. Well, he didn't say it was to part with my honour. He said it was doing an honourable thing.

Q. Did you at that time know that if you had intercourse with that man you were parting with your honour?

A. Yes, I knew I was parting with my honour.

Q. So that this is the truth — that the proposition was put to you that you should part with your honour to repay the social kindness of Mrs. Brownlee, whom you'd known only for a month.

A. Yes, sir.

Q. And you thought to pay Mrs. Brownlee's kindness to you you should enter into adultery with her husband?

A. Yes, sir.

On her next drive with Brownlee, when Vivian claimed that he embraced and kissed her, Smith asked why she had agreed to get into the back seat:

A. He said it was crowded and uncomfortable. He said it would be more comfortable for him there and he wanted to go on talking.

Q. You didn't suspect that he was going to have intercourse with you, did you?

A. No, sir.

Q. He had asked you to have intercourse with him?

A. He had asked me to be as a wife to him and a pal.

Q. Being as a wife meant, I suppose you knew, having intercourse with him?

A. Yes, sir.

Q. Still, in getting into the back seat that way you had no idea he wanted to have intercourse with you?

A. I didn't think he could have intercourse in the back seat of a car.

Q. How tall are you?

A. Five foot seven.

Q. And how tall is he?

A. Over six feet...

Q. What did you weigh at that time?

A. About 150 pounds.

Q. Well, we find him with one arm around your shoulder and the other raising your clothes, and getting on top of you, and you weighed 150 pounds, and you doing your best to save the situation?

A. Yes.

Q. The whole thing was against your will?

A. Yes, sir.

Q. And he didn't obtain complete penetration?

A. No.

Smith repeatedly focussed on discrepancies in Vivian's testimony:

Q. Now, this second night, how was the weather — this night of the 13th?

A. There was not any snow on the ground.

Q. Was it clear?

A. Yes. It was not storming as far as I can remember.

Q. Are you sure?

A. I can't be positive, but as far as I can remember it was not.

Q. Now, Miss MacMillan, the Edmonton newspapers say there was a blizzard that night. What have you got to say about that?

A. I can't believe it...

Q. You say he went into the government garage and changed into the small Studebaker, No 104 — no doubt about it?

John Caldwell (R) wouldn't marry Vivian when he learned of her affair with the premier, but he was more than willing to help her take Brownlee to court. Caldwell is shown leaving the courthouse during the trial with Vivian's brother, Harry.

A. No.

Q. What would you say if I told you that the small Studebaker was not even purchased until June 1932? What have you got to say about that?

A. Well, I know it was a smaller car than the one he was driving and the licence number was 104.

Q. You have told Mr. Maclean and told me on examination for discover and this morning that you changed to the small Studebaker, No. 104?

A. To the best of my memory.

Q. You are wrong, aren't you?

A. Yes.

Q. You advanced that as the truth, no doubt?

A. Yes, I did.

Though he hammered Vivian over minor inconsistencies, Smith couldn't induce her to recant her account. Why had she repeatedly given in to the premier's demands, even though she found the sexual act painful? "From terror, and because he told me it was my duty." Smith ridiculed her contention that Florence Brownlee's health was frail; Vivian knew, he argued, that Mrs. Brownlee skated, played golf, rode horseback and paddled a canoe. By producing a letter Alan Brownlee wrote to his mother in Vancouver in September 1931, Smith persuaded Vivian to admit that she had then been staying not in the maid's room but in Mrs. Brownlee's. "There was a bolt on the

---

Neil Maclean protested, 'I submit this court cannot render a verdict contrary to the verdict of the jury.' But Mr. Justice Ives replied, 'Oh, yes I can. I have done it on two occasions and have been upheld by the court of appeal.'

---

inside of the door; why didn't you use it?" She said, "I just did as Mr. Brownlee asked." When she couldn't remember how many times she had slept with the premier during that stay, Smith suggested, "Surely it would be engraved on your mind with photographic clearness?" Vivian answered, "I can't say that it would be, because at that time it had become practically a habit."[9] Predictably, the *Bulletin* saw the cross-examination as a contest won by the plaintiff:

> If Premier Brownlee's counsel forced her, here and there, to modify the details of her story as to the weather and the make of cars in which the alleged sex-orgies had taken place, the time of making assignations for meetings and the question of which bedroom she occupied in the premier's home, additional items of a serious nature were brought out as a result of the cross-examination.

Most damaging was Vivian's assertion that the premier had supplied her with pills to avoid pregnancy. In her examination for discovery, Vivian had testified that Brownlee had never used a contraceptive himself, but in court she told Maclean that he had given her black pills to be taken three times a day from the onset to the end of menstruation. Smith asked, "Didn't it ever occur to you that if he could prevent you from becoming pregnant by giving you some black pills that he could save the wife of his bosom by giving them to her?" Vivian answered, "I never even thought about it."

On Wednesday morning the judge caught up with the *Bulletin*. Brandishing Tuesday's edition, Smith drew Ives' attention to Cowper's story with its blatantly biased headlines, and some salacious details that the *Journal* had discreetly omitted. Ives agreed that the paper had gone far beyond any privilege extended by the court, and ordered the reporter and the publisher, Charles E. Campbell, to appear before him at 2 p.m. By then Wednesday's equally provocative edition was out. Ives found the *Bulletin* in flagrant contempt of court, fined Campbell $300 and Cowper $100, and barred the newspaper from his courtroom until the fines were paid.

So far it was Vivian's word against the premier's. Grilled by Smith, she hadn't been able to remember seeing anyone — in the halls of the legislature, the streets of Edmonton, or the country

[9]Smith read the jury a letter Vivian wrote to Mrs. Brownlee on September 27, reporting that the family was well. After mentioning that she had watered the plants, helped the maid with housework and dinner, and adopted a stray kitten, she ended, "With all the love in the world, Yours, Viv XX." (kisses)

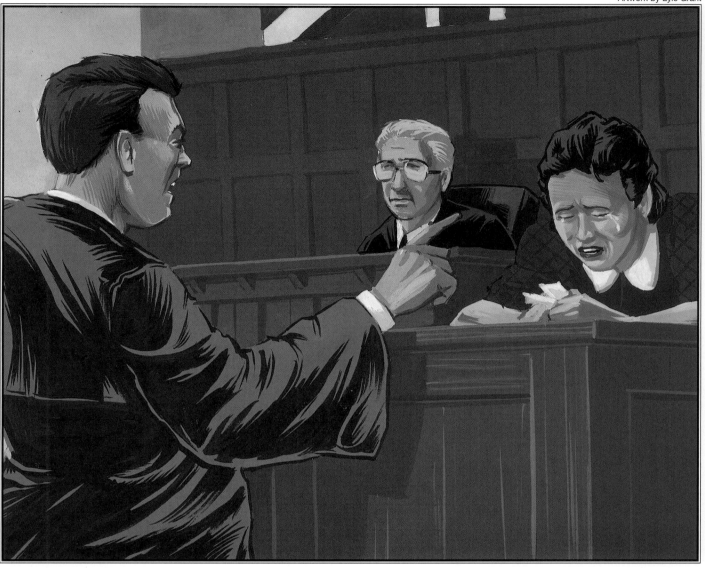

Onlookers might well have believed each of Vivian's tears was worth $5,000, but all her crying only totalled that much in the end.

roads where she said Brownlee had taken her — who might have seen the two of them alone together. Now Maclean produced a witness who had seen Brownlee picking up Vivian in his car about 10:30 on an evening in late October 1930. And, had the judge not halted Maclean's questioning, this witness might have revealed much more.

Jessie Elgert, hired as a maid by the Brownlees in January 1930, had left that job in the first week of April. She then moved to the YWCA where Vivian stayed when she first came to Edmonton, and knew her by sight. Questioned by Maclean, she testified that, about 10:30 or 11 o'clock at night in late October, she had been some fifteen feet behind Vivian, who was walking down 103rd Street. At the corner of Victoria Avenue, she said, "I saw Mr. Brownlee stop the car and continue on after she got in."

Her testimony continued:

Q. Did you recognize Mr. Brownlee?
A. Yes.
Q. Did you recognize the car?
A. Yes.
Q. How did you come to recognize that car?
A. I had been out in it myself.
Q. With Mr. Brownlee?
A. Yes.

Smith: Now, my lord, surely...

Court: We have not arrived at that point yet.

Maclean: Had you ever before driven with Mr. Brownlee?

Elgert: Yes.

Q. When you were a maid in his house?

A. Yes.

Q. And when?

A. That was sometime at the beginning of March.

Q. And where had you gone?

Court: Stop.

Cross-examination by Mr. Smith: After you left the Brownlee house you came back there and sought re-employment?

Elgert: No.

Q. You swear you didn't?

A. Yes.

Q. And all that is just as true as the other things you have just said?

A. Yes.

Maclean: Miss Elgert, did Mr. Brownlee ever ask you to come back to the house?

A. Yes, he did.

Q. How did that arise?

A. Mr. Brownlee had written and asked me to come back...

Court: You are not going any further.

Judge Ives then dismissed Jessie Elgert. In later testimony, Brownlee swore that she had left his wife's employment only to help her parents with the spring seeding, and that he had never seen her again except once, from a distance, in 1931. Cross-examining Florence Brownlee, Maclean asked, "Would you believe Jessie Elgert if she says she was out car riding with your husband? I mean going out in the country with the car parked?" Mrs. Brownlee replied, "No, I would not."

The judge also cut off the evidence of Dorothy Mackay and her mother, with whom Vivian

---

Questioned by Maclean, she recalled that on the way to the picnic in Edson, Brownlee remarked, 'You have a very beautiful daughter here, Mrs. MacMillan, what are you going to do with her?' Dismissing her studies in music as `useless,' he suggested that Vivian take a business course in Edmonton.

---

had lodged in the autumn of 1932. One night Vivian came home and threw herself on her bed, weeping; next morning Emma Jane Mackay found a torn-up note that began, "Dear Mr. Brownlee. After last night I realize of course that everything between you and I must end..." The judge disallowed the entry of the letter.

Next Maclean called Vivian's mother, Letha Maude MacMillan, who testified that the premier and his wife had visited her in Edson on August 12, 1933. Brownlee wanted to know what he was accused of; she said she couldn't discuss it, since it was in the lawyer's hands. "Mr. Brownlee suggested did I realize that Vivian's name would be ruined forever if this came out? I said, 'Do you realize what it will do your own name, Mr. Brownlee?'"

Dr. John Keith Fife testified that he had treated the plaintiff for an irritable colon. Maclean asked whether this might be caused by ergot, a drug used to induce abortion. Fife agreed that ergot would irritate the bowel. Had Vivian suffered a nervous breakdown? Yes, said Fife, in the sense that the term was commonly used to cover "nearly everything." Cross-examined by Smith, Fife denied that Vivian's illness was merely constipation.

At 2.30 p.m., Maclean declared that the case for the plaintiff was closed. Smith expressed surprise, and asked for adjournment till next morning, which was granted.

On Thursday, the crowds outside the courthouse were bigger than ever. That morning, Smith

The resignation of Premier Brownlee, carrying as it would the resignations of the entire provincial cabinet, would be something more than welcome at this juncture. That is imperative, if representative government is a popular right in Alberta, and not a concession only to be granted or denied at the will of the executive.

The scandal-sickened people of this province are entitled to immediate disassociation of their public affairs from court investigations into amorous adventures of philandering ministers.

What the caucus of UFA members of the legislature today may think about the party expediency of retiring or continuing the Government is quite aside from the point. For the reason that the UFA members cannot now claim to represent any opinions but their own. The members who are politically responsible for the humiliation with which the people of Alberta have been deluged are in no way qualified to assume a right to further dictate or participate in the conduct of public affairs.

One, and only one, further official act is due from the Brownlee Government; to vacate and vacate forthwith. Nothing can so well become it as an expeditious departure. And in going the ministers are by every implication of duty bound to advise His Honour to dissolve the present moribund legislature and give the outraged electors an opportunity to elect a body of men who will respect their sentiments and represent their views.
—*Edmonton Bulletin*, July 3, 1934

Brownlee visited Maude MacMillan, who had a sharp exchange with the premier before her daughter brought suit.

called his first witness, the premier. Testifying for more than two hours, Brownlee contradicted every incriminating detail of the plaintiff's story, down to the fact that in October he had been driving not the big Studebaker but his own brand-new Hupmobile. He had not seduced Vivian MacMillan, whom he considered almost a member of his family, like a niece. Repeatedly consulting four black-leather gilt-edged yearly diaries kept by his secretary, he not only denied every alleged instance of intercourse, but often supplied particulars of official engagements and trips that showed he was elsewhere on the dates Vivian had cited.

Smith questioned him at length about the evening of July 5, when Maclean and Caldwell followed his car. Brownlee explained that he came home from a speaking engagement in Vermilion about 9:00 p.m., and then invited Vivian for a drive to discuss whether she would join his family at Sylvan Lake, where they were then on holiday. After picking her up on 109th Street, he began to suspect that he was being followed. Circling blocks in the centre of town, he turned in sharply at the Hudson's Bay store on Jasper Avenue and caught the number of the other car as it went by. He and Vivian then walked a block to buy newspapers at Mike's News Stand and returned to the car. He asked Vivian where she wanted to get out, and she asked him to leave her at a friend's house near her lodgings. When he let her out, the other car pulled in and stopped behind them.

Smith ended by asking the premier, "Did you, on your solemn oath, at any time, endeavour to have improper intimacy with Vivian MacMillan?" Brownlee replied, "I did not."

Now Maclean could launch his attack on the quarry he had stalked for more than a year. He pointed out that on July 3 the premier could have discussed Vivian's holiday plans by telephoning or calling her into his office, rather than driving her to a country road that evening. Then he questioned Brownlee about the night of July 5 when, as he knew well, a mysterious car had pursued the premier though down-

Vivian testified that on Saturday after she moved to the YWCA, Brownlee had telephoned and said, 'A little bird told me you were here and I thought I would phone you up. I would like you to come over to my home on Sunday afternoon and meet Mrs. Brownlee and the boys.'

town Edmonton. After a dusty 360-mile drive to Vermilion and back, why would Brownlee change cars and embark on another drive with Vivian MacMillan? And where did he go? Brownlee answered, "You know. You followed me."

Q. Certainly, and then you went on Whyte Avenue and turned west, that was in the direction of your home?

A. I suppose that part would be, yes, the way south.

Q. Then you found somebody was following you?

A. I did not, not at that time.

Q. Mr. Brownlee, have you any distinct memory of that mad dash on the south side, turning corners, twisting and turning one corner after another, have you any distinct recollection of that?

A. No, there isn't very much about that.

Q. Oh, I am afraid your memory is not as good with respect to that as it is with other matters.

A. I might say, Mr. Maclean, that I was not watching the routes as closely as you were that night or probably you did.

Q. Did you ever see a terrier chasing a rat and running and twisting and turning?

A. I have never seen that.

Q. You didn't think the course that you took that night was something very much in that nature?

A. No.

Q. Then after chasing all over the city you finally parked on Jasper Avenue and found out the number of the car that had been following you and then you drove Miss MacMillan — Oh by the way Miss MacMillan said you wanted her to walk home?

A. That is not true.

Q. And you drove to where you let her out?

A. Yes.

Q. And this other car was parked about twenty feet behind?

A. When we started?

Q. When you started it was parked about twenty feet behind you?

A. Yes.

Q. Is it a fact, Mr. Brownlee, you are one of the strongest men in Alberta?

A. Physically, you mean?

Q. Yes, physically.

A. I never thought so.

Q. I think Miss MacMillan stated your wife claimed you to have the strongest grip of any man in town.

A. Does she? That is not correct.

Q. But you didn't get out of your car to see who was in this car?

A. No, I knew the number, that was all I wanted. If I had known what I know now I might have.

Q. This car had been following you all around the city for half an hour?

A. Yes.

Q. Mr, Brownlee, you found out within a day or two who was in the car who had been following you?

A. Found out whose number, what car it was, a few days after, and since that time—

Q. How long did it take you to find out?

A. As to who was in the car?

Q. Yes.

A. Oh, I couldn't say, three or four weeks.

Q. And from that time on you never asked Vivian MacMillan to go out for another drive?

A. I had no opportunity to ask Vivian between that time and the time I received your very kind letter.

The day after the letter arrived, Brownlee left to serve on the royal commission in Ottawa. He acknowledged that he had asked Attorney-General Lymburn to start investigation. Maclean asked:

Q. And the government spent about $1,400 in making the investigation?

A. Correct.

Q. So the government spent $1,400 before you put a nickel into the case?

Allan MacMillan took a second mortgage on his house to help pay his own and his daughter's legal expenses. Although they both eventually won their cases, he couldn't afford the legal costs for his own appeal and only got back what Vivian paid him.

A. If you wish to put it that way.

Q. And the government hired Harry Brace to conduct the investigation?

A. Yes.

Q. Did you pay Mr. Brace's salary on this investigation?

A. No.

Artwork by Lyle Grant

John Caldwell and Neil Maclean admitted they followed Brownlee's car around Edmonton one night, because, they said, Vivian seemed to be afraid of him and they wanted to be sure she was safe.

10Carol Snell became the mystery man in the case, although he was virtually irrelevant to it. In 1934, the defence ordered him to testify about his acquaintance with Vivian. Brownlee's solicitor, Marshall Porter, went to Halifax to take his evidence. He didn't show up for their meeting, but later agreed to meet Porter and the premier in Alberta. He was never called as a witness.

Q. Brace, what particular position is he in.

A. Mr. Brace is superintendent of insurance.

Q. And has a staff of investigators in his office?

A. Yes.

Q. And he and his staff went to work?

A. No, his staff did not.

Q. Didn't one of the staff go to Vancouver on this case?

A. Not to my knowledge. Mr. Brace only worked on this case during his spare time.

Q. Has Brace been paid?

A. I have reimbursed the government, Mr.Maclean, because I did not want any suspicion that public money had been spent on my case.

Questioned by Maclean, Brownlee denied all knowledge of how that money had been spent. He knew that Burford had been paid $25 for three months "to hold himself in readiness."

Q. Is it not a fact, Mr. Brownlee, that you kept away from all this stuff so you wouldn't know anything about it?

A. Not exactly, Mr. Maclean. I was engaged on the royal banking commission for some two months during that time that this work was done. I was not in Alberta.

Brownlee vehemently disclaimed Brace's detective, Bob Dudley: "I never met the man and never heard of him until the examination for discovery."

Q. You don't know Dudley gave $400 to Mr. Caldwell?

A. No, I don't.

Q. Spent money like a drunken sailor. Was it your money he was spending?

A. Certainly no money I have advanced has gone to Mr. Dudley.

Q. Who is paying him?

A. I couldn't say.

Brownlee admitted that his solicitor, Marshall Porter, had paid Carol H. Snell's train fare from Bear River, Nova Scotia, to Alberta, but denied asking him to approach the MacMillans**10**. Though he knew Brace had invited Allan MacMillan to Edmonton to discuss the lawsuit, Brownlee denied making any direct or indirect offer of financial settlement. Nor was his own visit to Vivian's mother on August 12 an attempt to settle the dispute by violating the ethical prohibition against dealing with plaintiffs represented by other lawyers. He simply wanted to ask her whether he was "accused of being the father of a coming child." Defying Maclean's allegations, the premier swore that on his drives with Vivian he had never kissed her, embraced her, or had any desire for her whatsoever.

Called next, Florence Brownlee testified that she was in perfect health, played sports, and lived a normal sex life. She had first met Vivian, not on September 7, 1930, but on the 17th. Her husband had mentioned that Chris Pattinson had told him that Vivian was in Edmonton, and Mrs. Brownlee invited her to the air show. She remembered it clearly because Vivian, wearing a navy blue knitted wool suit and white beret, was much "smarter looking" than she had expected[11]. Within a few months she had grown so fond of Vivian that "she was just like a daughter to me." She confirmed that her husband refused to ask Mr. Smailes to give Vivian a government job, but admitted that she had done so herself.

Staunchly supporting her husband, she contradicted every detail of Vivian's story. In September 1931, it was Vivian who suggested that her mother join Mrs. Brownlee's trip to Vancouver, and who insisted on moving in to look after the family when the maid's return was delayed. She flatly denied that her husband could have taken Vivian to his bed when she stayed in their house the following spring. Because Alan walked in his sleep, she had grown used to waking at the slightest sound: "Mr. Smith, I could even hear the dog if he paddles upstairs."

Maclean's cross-examination failed to shake Florence Brownlee. Nor did his scathing questions elicit any damaging evidence from Friday morning's defence witnesses: Emily Brown, Brownlee's secretary since 1918; civil service commissioner Fred Smailes; four janitors from the legislature; the Brownlees' former maid, Jean McCloy; Mrs. Brownlee's friend, Laura Robertson; two of Vivian's former landladies and Oran Henry Snow, secretary-treasurer of Raymond, who swore he had been in the premier's office one morning when Vivian said Brownlee had intercourse with her there. That afternoon, Smith asked Ives to let the jury inspect the premier's house. The jury not only agreed, but said they would like to view the country road where Vivian said she had parked with Brownlee. Off they went, judge, counsel and jurors, in a cavalcade of motor cars led by Vivian MacMillan, driving her father in his Chevrolet. The side road was a quagmire, and several cars were bogged down and hauled out. The *Journal* reported "the unique spectacle of the

The tendons in his right hand were sliced from an accident, so he couldn't take notes, but defence co-counsel, Calgarian Arthur Leroy Smith, KC, hammered Vivian under cross examination for two days and dissected her testimony like a surgeon in his summation, using primarily his phenomenal memory.

Brownlee established a routine which he and Vivian followed. He would walk down the hall to the bathroom, said Vivian, and run the water in the basin as a signal for her to join him. She would follow him back to his room, keeping time with his footsteps so that only one person could be heard walking on the squeaky floor.

Alberta Supreme Court in roaring motor cars smashing its way, bouncing and careering, over potholes in a thoroughfare of greasy, treacherous mud." When they all got back to court at 4:30, Ives adjourned without even taking his seat.

On Saturday, the trial ended — with a bang. First of the day's startling events was Arthur Smith's announcement that defence was dropping the counterclaim against John Caldwell and Vivian MacMillan. His excuse was that calling evidence on that issue would only complicate a clear-cut case. His reasons are still mysterious. The premier had responded to the MacMillans' statement of claim by telling the press that there was not a word of truth in the allegation: "I hope to show before I am through the real cause behind it." The real truth, as he saw it then, was the cupidity of Caldwell and perhaps the collaboration of Liberals. In his opening address to the jury, Smith had promised to produce evidence of a plot to ruin the premier, hatched by Caldwell and aided by Vivian. Why would he abandon the counterclaim, a mainstay of Brownlee's defence? Perhaps his supporting evidence had collapsed. More probably he and Porter, sure they had already won their case, decided not to muddy the waters.

Maclean immediately asked leave to amend the MacMillans' statement of claim to specify

[11]Called in rebuttal at the end of the trial, Vivian and her mother testified that the first blue tailored suit she ever wore was one she bought at the Hudson's Bay store just before she started her job at the legislature.

Furious when the jury found in favour of Vivian and Allan MacMillan, Acting Chief Justice William Ives, known in legal circles as Cowboy Billy, threw out their decision and found for Brownlee. His reversal of the jury was overturned on appeal.

damages of $10,000 for each plaintiff. He then called Vivian MacMillan, her mother, and Jessie Elgert as witnesses in rebuttal, but Ives disallowed most of his questions and no significant evidence emerged.

In his eloquent summing-up address to the jury, Smith dissected Vivian's testimony like a surgeon with a scalpel, countering each detail with contrary evidence. Citing factual discrepancies and commonsense improbabilities, he noted that "this beastly story" was so absurd that it must be produced by the plaintiff's hallucinations.

He argued that Vivian MacMillan's accusations simply didn't make sense. "Here we have a clear-cut issue of seduction or no seduction, and on that and nothing else I ask your judgment in the interest of the man whom I represent." On October 5, 1930, when Vivian claimed that Brownlee first drove her home, he had been in Winnipeg. Her subsequent story was preposterous, Smith continued.

"Here we find Brownlee urging as a reason for having this girl, that she owed it to Mrs. Brownlee whom she had known only a month... Is it sensible that anything so utterly stupid could be said by a man seeking to seduce this girl, that she should repay in this way the hospitality lasting for one month?

"I say this — mistakes if you like in time gone by about dates and so on, but if you believe that statement of Vivian MacMillan to be untrue, then it can be nothing more than a deliberate untruth. Now gentlemen, on her own story, within a matter of days or weeks, this woman had lost that which decent women hold most dear — her honour, and this being a story without an atom of truth — the beginning of that downfall, the attack on that last citadel which women protect, and it was no doubt a great and crucial moment in her life and the fact is that it cannot be disputed that on the very night she says this conversation took place John Brownlee was in Winnipeg.

"I want you to get a picture of any man leaving to drive a girl home — to take a matter of eighteen or twenty minutes —not once but constantly being gone one and a half hours at that time of the night; don't you think your wife would be suspicious?

"I only say that I do not for a moment analyse the motives that compelled this young girl to tell this story. But I also say with firmness, the story she has given is so incredible as to be beyond belief, particularly in a court of law. Here we have a motor car, and I say to you that intimacy under those conditions is an absolute physical impossibility." Surely, Smith argued, no six decent men would allow the premier to be dragged down by such specious allegations.

Then it was Maclean's turn. He argued that the case was significant because it concerned not only the career of the premier, but the honour and decency of women, and the question of whether the law was the same for the poorest and highest in the land. He suggested that the defence's abandonment of counterclaim was an admission that Vivian was not blackmailing the premier. Smith had implied that her story was the product of her imagination. Maclean argued that the defence had withdrawn from an outright accusation that she had lied: "If she is not deliberately lying ... there is only one verdict."

Maclean wondered if, while viewing the Brownlee's house, the jurors had noticed the bolt on Mrs. Brownlee's bedroom door. He challenged Smith's dismissal of backseat coupling as physically

impossible: "Ask any taxi driver, any policeman." He paid appropriate tribute to the loyalty of the premier's wife and secretary. Comparing the colliding stories given by Vivian and the premier, he suggested that small discrepancies stemmed from a truthful account rather than one carefully contrived to incriminate the premier. "Do you think that a girl standing in that box all day can con-

After Brownlee resigned, reporters from the Edmonton Journal, *the* Edmonton Bulletin *and* Canadian Press *waited at the Legislature for the announcement on his successor. L-R: Horner Ramage (EJ), George Finlay (CP), Thomas A. Mansell (EJ), Thomas B. Windross (British United Press) and Jack Oliver (EB).*

In February, the premier blamed John Caldwell and told her that a young man had nothing to offer, whereas he had everything to offer. Some weeks later his wife more astutely asked, 'Are you sure Mr. Brownlee has not done anything to you?' No, said Vivian, but the lie strengthened her resolve, she said.

coct a story which she has told the most skillful cross-examiner in western Canada, and not crack? To make this charge she has had to drag herself in the mud. Can you imagine any girl brought up as she was choosing to do this horrible thing for some dirty dollars?"

Maclean argued that if Vivian were lying, she would not have included the improbable account of how Brownlee used to summon her to the room he shared with his son. "Don't you think her story would have sounded better if she had left out all mention of that occasion or if she had said Brownlee came to her? She was in a room there by herself. It is against her interest to tell that story. Do you think she could have made up all these little details? Does it sound like a story or does it sound as if it were true? I submit to you, gentlemen, the very incredibility of the story is evidence of its truth."

The judge's instructions to the jury left no doubt where he thought the truth lay. "The story

Vivian MacMillan's lawyer, Neil Maclean (left), who took her case to the Privy Council without fee, was devastating in his cross-examination of Brownlee's civil service witnesses.

of the female plaintiff is wholly and entirely unsupported by any other evidence... The evidence, on the other hand, of the defendant is supported in many instances by that of other witnesses."[12]

At 3:55 p.m. the jury left the courtroom to debate its verdict. Outsiders could hear the jurors pleading, dissenting, cavilling and yelling. Maclean said later, "The poor bastards were screaming at each other." Almost five hours passed before they returned to the courtroom. Foreman Leonard Higgins, an Edmonton art dealer, gave the verdict: The premier had seduced Vivian MacMillan in October 1930. Vivian MacMillan suffered damage and was awarded $10,000. Her father had suffered damages in the amount of $5,000.

Judge Ives, furious that the jury had ignored his instructions, berated the jurors: "Gentlemen, I strongly disagree with your answers. The evidence does not warrant them."

Maclean moved that the jury's verdict be entered in the court's procedure book. For the defence, Marshall Porter tried a last-ditch tactic. Arguing that the plaintiffs had not proved any damages (then considered "loss of services"), he moved that the MacMillans' action be dismissed. The judge refused to enter the verdict, saying that he needed time to consider his decision.

Maclean protested, "I submit this court cannot render a verdict contrary to the verdict of the jury."

"Oh, yes I can," Ives responded. "I have done it on two occasions and have been upheld by the court of appeal."

Neither the premier nor the MacMillans were in court when the jury returned. That evening Brownlee told Lieutenant-Governor William Leigh Walsh that he intended to resign. His resignation automatically included that of his seven cabinet ministers.

If less significant, Vivian's reaction was more dramatic, according to the *Edmonton Bulletin*. She burst into tears of joy and ran into a friend's suite in the Alexander Block, where she "swooned upon a chair in a partial faint, unable to keep back the pent-up emotion that overcame her."

The judge brought down his ruling ten days later. He agreed with Porter's application. Since Vivian left her home with her parents' consent and was accompanied to Edmonton by her mother, Ives found that she was not enticed. No illness resulted from the seduction; no evidence was presented to show that the ability of the daughter to render services was in any way interfered with. Seduction by itself, without damages, was not actionable. He dismissed the MacMillans' joint action and awarded the costs of the trial to the premier. Thus the MacMillans would be liable for Brownlee's legal fees of between $1,200 and $1,500, as well as jury expenses of more than $500.

Public opinion of Ives's decision ranged from regret at the downfall of a diligent premier to indignation.[13] "What price womanhood?" raged the *Bulletin*, which set up a fund to help pay the

[12]Judge Ives's rulings during the trial had disallowed Vivian's corroborating witnesses, Jessie Elgert, Dorothy Mackay and Emma Jane Mackay.

[13] Alberta feminists didn't rally to support Vivian MacMillan. Unlike Cora McPherson, a respectable married woman whose husband had cast her aside, Vivian wasn't seen as a feminist heroine. The Canadian Civil Liberties Protective Society backed her cause only after Ives dismissed the case.

MacMillans' costs and appeals. By October, 1936 the public had donated $2,849.95.

Vivian MacMillan's subsequent appeals were based on the interpretation of Alberta's Seduction Act of 1922. Was it necessary, as Ives had ruled, to prove that a plaintiff must be injured, or unable to provide service to her father or employer? From 1934 to 1940, lawyers for Vivian MacMillan and John Brownlee would debate this question in Edmonton, Ottawa, and London.

The first appeal, to the Appellate Division of the Supreme Court of Alberta, was heard in January 1935. Maclean contended that Ives's interpretation of the Seduction Act, indeed "his conception of the whole case," was too narrow. Pregnancy and loss of services were 19th-century relics irrelevant in an age of contraceptives. Brownlee's lawyers, again led by Arthur Smith, argued that proof of pregnancy or some other damage was still necessary for the compensation of seduction under the 1922 Act. The court, split 3-2, upheld Ives's dismissal.

The "loss of services" issue fuelled two further appeals. The first was to the Supreme Court of Canada, whose 4-1 decision in May, 1937, restored the MacMillans' jury verdict and Vivian MacMillan's $10,000 judgment.[14] Brownlee appealed to the Judicial Committee of the Privy Council in London, then the court of last resort. On the grounds that proof of damage was unnecessary under the Alberta Seduction Act, the Privy Council dismissed Brownlee's appeal in June 1940.

Vivian MacMillan's personal judgment for $10,000 plus interest and legal costs was never recovered. The Premier paid $5,000 in 1941, when the litigation ended. The costs of taking her case through three courts left her only $1,500. After repaying the mortgage her father had taken out to raise the jury fees, she netted less than $500.

Neil Maclean received no compensation for the time and money he spent as Vivian's lawyer for eight years. His hopes of a federal judgeship vanished when the Brownlee trial turned the Liberals against him. Mackenzie King's man in the West was James Gardiner, who as premier of Saskatchewan had become Brownlee's friend and ally.

Vivian MacMillan won her case, from jury verdict to Privy Council judgment, at the expense of her reputation. She became Edmonton's Evelyn Nesbit,[15] slurred as "The Girl in the Red Velvet Studebaker." John Caldwell finished his studies, then left to practice medicine in Vancouver. After the trial Vivian went home to her family. She married Henry Sorensen of Edson in August 1935,

---

By ruling that some of Maclean's questions were inadmissible, Judge Ives had already made it clear that he had little sympathy for the plaintiff. But she was attractive and quick-thinking, and the jury might well believe her story. So Smith challenged her as a wanton perjurer and savaged every detail of her evidence.

---

but the marriage foundered after their son's birth. When her father retired in the early 1940s, Vivian moved with her parents to Mirror, where she worked as a store clerk. A few years later she married Frank Howie, a Calgary contractor, and bore him one son. After Howie died in 1959, she and her son moved to Arizona because she suffered from asthma. She died in 1980 and was buried beside Howie in Calgary.

When the UFA was defeated in 1935, John Brownlee returned to the United Grain Growers, first as legal advisor and then as president. Later he practised law with his son, Alan, until his death in 1961.

What is remarkable about MacMillan v. Brownlee is its shattering effect on the lives of those involved. Throughout history, men in high office have had adulterous affairs without damaging their imperial, regal or political leadership. Today such scandals are commonplace fodder for tabloids. The reaction to the Brownlee case suggests that Albertans in the Thirties followed a stricter moral code than that of other times or places.

From a sordid lawsuit marred by false oaths, reckless decisions, political cross-currents and relentless publicity, no winners emerged. Whether or not Brownlee had an affair with Vivian MacMillan, the trial ruined them both. And whatever losses were endured by plaintiff and defendant were perhaps less than those of the people of Alberta, who had lost a capable and accomplished premier.

[14]Allan MacMillan didn't appeal the rejection of his trial verdict and $5,000 award. Having lost his jury fee deposit, he couldn't afford further litigation costs.

[15]Stanford White was New York's most prominent architect, designer of Madison Square Garden. Evelyn Nesbit was the 16-year-old Girl Model of Gotham, well-known artists' model and dancer, who had moved with her impoverished mother to New York from Pittsburgh to make her fortune.

While appearing in a Broadway musical, Nesbit met White, who was 48 years old and married, and soon became his mistress, the older man providing for her and her mother. In one of his apartments, he had a red velvet swing, on which he liked to watch his young mistress swing naked. But after a year, Evelyn wanted a more permanent but equally lucrative relationship, and settled on Harry Thaw, Pittsburgh heir to a railroad fortune.

Before their marriage, the Girl on the Red Velvet Swing confessed to her future husband the nature of her relationship with White. This knowledge apparently festered in Thaw, who had demonstrated a predisposition toward violence, and who ultimately shot the architect dead in public on June 25, 1906.

At the end of a 3-month sensational trial, Thaw was found not guilty by reason of insanity. He spent 8 years in an asylum for the criminally insane. Evelyn tried to support herself, bore a son, entered a second short-lived marriage, and attempted suicide twice. Afterward she became an artist, and was seemingly happy in her later years. She died in 1967 at 82. In 1976, Michael Macdonald Mooney wrote a biography of the pair, *Evelyn Nesbit and Stanford White: Love and death in the gilded cage* (N.Y., Morrow).

RICHARD GAVIN REID

Born: Aberdeenshire, Scotland, 17 January, 1879

Died: Edmonton, 17 October, 1980, at the age of 101.

Career Apex: Premier of Alberta, 1934-1935

Major accomplishment: Holding together the sharply-divided UFA caucus from 1934, when John Brownlee resigned, until the electoral defeat of the government fourteen months later.

Quotation: *"If this [Major Douglas], the real source of Social Credit, was a polluted source, then what right had we to bother with it?"*

CHAPTER FOUR

Then out of nowhere a political tornado burst upon the province

THEY CALLED IT SOCIAL CREDIT, PROMOTED BY A RADIO SPELLBINDER NAMED ABERHART, AND IT MADE THE UFA'S DYING DAYS A VERITABLE NIGHTMARE

by GEORGE OAKE

John Brownlee was gone. Though he remained for a year a member of the Legislature, the destruction of his political career by a 22-year-old stenographer was undoubted and it shocked the nation. What Alberta did next, however, shocked it far more. The Brownlee trial set off a chain of rapid events that culminated in the election of the most radically minded government ever to hold office in Canada or perhaps even the United States. The unexpected victory of an upstart political movement was summed up by a headline in the *Boston Herald*: "Alberta Goes Crazy."

This stunning coup was achieved by William Aberhart, principal of Crescent Heights High School in Calgary. The "craze" that prompted the headline was Social Credit, a theory devised by Major Clifford Hugh Douglas, an eccentric British engineer. By adopting and misinterpreting Douglas's internationally mesmerizing scheme, Aberhart created a new political party that would govern Alberta for the next 36 years.

The first figure to fall under this new onslaught was the dour, cautious, rational person of Richard Gavin Reid, Brownlee's Resources minister and now his successor as premier. Over the next fourteen woe-filled months Reid presided over the crumbling ruin of the once-awesome United Farmers of Alberta (UFA). For two years before Reid took office he had watched the Social Credit movement grow alarmingly across his province.

Major Douglas's celebrated theory had spurred the creation of clubs and study groups all over the world. It attributed all economic ills to the machinations of money suppliers, and blamed the Depression on an international cartel of bankers, mostly Jewish, who controlled the economy. He promulgated a system of monetary reform that would restore purchasing power to the people through the redistribution of wealth. His worldwide disciples included Charles Scarborough, an Edmonton high school chemistry teacher, who met him on a voyage to England in 1925. Back in Canada next year, Scarborough heard Aberhart giving an evangelical lecture on the radio, and knew he had found the man who could sell Social Credit to the masses.

As founder of the Calgary Prophetic Bible Institute, "Bible Bill" Aberhart was becoming known throughout Alberta for his Sunday broadcasts on CFCN, then Western Canada's most powerful radio station. His soaring fundamentalist Christian exhortations reached an audience estimated in the tens of thousands. In July 1929 he met Scarborough when both were earning extra money by marking Grade 12 departmental examination papers at the University of Alberta. For three summers Scarborough spent lunch periods trying vainly to convert Aberhart to Social Credit.

In the summer of 1932, when the Communists were planning their December hunger march on Edmonton and Vivian MacMillan was about to meet and fall in love with young Johnny Caldwell, the Depression-driven suicide of one of Aberhart's students rendered him vulnerable to persuasion. Scarborough won him over by lending him *Unemployment or War*, a simplified analysis of Douglas's theory written by an English actor, Maurice Dale Colbourne. That night, in his room at St. Stephen's College, Aberhart read, finishing the book at dawn. He didn't understand it, but he sensed its promise of a new, and timely, gospel for his Depression audience.[1]

An instant convert, Aberhart borrowed more books on Social Credit from the Vancouver

[1] Several accounts say Aberhart's sudden interest in Social Credit was the product of desperation as well as conviction. His radio ratings had levelled off or even fallen as listeners became more concerned about their daily bread than Bible prophecies. Aberhart's sometimes scornful friend, H.B. "Hilly" Hill, wrote in his unpublished diary that Aberhart appeared to be searching for a new gimmick to entertain and enlarge his radio following. "About the latter part of 1932, [Aberhart] seems to have been going behind in his church," writes Hill. "Interest was waning and he cast about for something to revivify the dying enthusiasm of his large audience."

The new premier poses with the backbone of his cabinet, all holdovers from the previous administration. Seated are Premier R.G. Reid (left) and Lieut.-Gov. W.L. Walsh. Standing are (left to right) Hugh W. Allen (Municipal Affairs and Lands and Mines); George Hoadley (Health, Trade and Industry, and Railways and Telephones; John F. Lymburn (Attorney-General); Frank S. Grisdale (Agriculture); and Perren Baker (Education). J. Russell Love (Provincial Treasurer) and J.J. MacLellan (Public Works), not shown, were the only additions to the Reid cabinet.

Public Library while he holidayed at the Coast. In mid-August he broached the idea of inter-mingling economic ideas with his Sunday radio lectures to the board of his Bible Institute, who compliantly backed their apostle. On Saturday, August 20, his advertisement in the *Calgary Herald* suggested, "Every citizen of Canada should do some serious thinking regarding the present economic situation. To encourage this a series of lectures on the Bible and modern economics will be given at the Calgary Prophetic Bible Institute."

Next day he laced his usual Gospel message with brief references to his new economic theories. Carried over into his broadcasts, the mixture of politics and religion beguiled his audience, who deluged the Bible Institute with demands for more sermons. Aberhart enthusiastically complied by supplementing his broadcasts with a series of evening lectures at the Bible Institute. Thirty students enrolled in the first Social Credit study group. Supplied with charts and leaflets outlining Aberhart's version of Social Credit economic doctrine, which didn't include Douglas's anti-semitism, groups soon blossomed like fireweed in Albertan cities, towns, and villages.

By late January 1933, Thursday night lectures on Social Credit were attracting audiences of 800. Even socialist CCF supporters were becoming interested. Aberhart was invited to address 1,500 people at a meeting sponsored by the Canadian Labour Party, the League for Social Reconstruction and the Calgary UFA chapter.

To meet the growing demand, Aberhart decided to write a booklet on Social Credit, but his enthusiasm outstripped his understanding and he sought help from an unlikely source. Lettie Hill, the librarian at Crescent Heights High School, suggested Aberhart discuss the project with her husband, Henry B. "Hilly" Hill, a self-educated, disabled Great War veteran, who had read most of the radical literature of the day during a long stay in hospital. Early in 1933 Aberhart took his jottings to the Hills, who helped him to wrestle them into coherent form.

"They were written on the backs of envelopes, on pulp paper, on letter paper, on school board stationery," records Hill in his candid diary. "The writing was clear, concise, legible and grammatically awful... We corrected the notes and came to the conclusion that we had sifted the gist of what Douglas meant into pamphlet form. When we had them all completed Aberhart said, 'Now do you think that is all right, and is that what Douglas meant?'

"I said, 'Yes, in my opinion, that is what Douglas meant, but it won't work.'

"He said, 'You're crazy, Hill, of course it will work.'"

Ironically, the man who explained Social Credit to Aberhart was at that time a dedicated Communist. Hill had studied Douglas's Social Credit theories thoroughly, but rejected them after absorbing the opinions of Harold Laski and other socialists in the British *New Statesman*. Driving Aberhart home one day, he pointed out that what his passenger proposed was the forerunner of a socialistic state. "He was angry; I was a Red. It was a waste of health to argue with him," writes Hill. "He had a real horror of socialism or communism and wouldn't hear them spoken of. They were anti-Christ or something, and that was that. The old fool."

When the yellow-covered booklet, which became known as the Yellow Pamphlet, was published in May 1933 it sold for 10 cents a copy and became a runaway best-seller. And no wonder. Entitled *The Douglas System of Economics*, it proposed a monthly distribution to every citizen of non-negotiable certificates totalling $20 (soon increased to $25), as credits to be spent on necessities such as food and shelter. That promise — $25 a month for everybody — was to haunt Aberhart for the rest of his political career, which meant for life.

While $25 handouts appealed to victims of the Depression, other suggestions in the yellow booklet were more radical than anything proposed by the socialists. Hoarding of wealth and credit was to be banned. People who had money in the bank would have to turn it over to the state in return for bonds bearing 4 per cent interest, payable in Social Credit certificates. When they died, their bonds would revert to the government. Those who moved out of Alberta could redeem their bonds for Canadian dollars only when those bonds reached maturity.

The first figure to fall under this new onslaught was the dour, cautious, rational person of Richard Gavin Reid, Brownlee's resources minister and now his successor as premier. Over the next fourteen woe-filled months Reid presided over the crumbling ruin of the once-awesome United Farmers of Alberta.

The new system would create a much larger bureaucracy, which some considered Orwellian, and fundamentally change society. Under state control, citizens whose basic needs were covered by Social Credit certificates would work only eight to sixteen hours a week, spending the rest of their time learning new skills and in the constructive use of leisure. But Aberhart passionately believed in this radical, Utopian implementation of Social Credit, and he vowed to spread the new economic gospel.

When school was dismissed on June 30, 1933, he hit the road with young, tireless Ernest Manning, first graduate of the Prophetic Bible Institute.[2] Bouncing over rough country roads between meeting halls and curling rinks, just as Henry Wise Wood and John Brownlee had spread their co-operative UFA philosophy a decade or more earlier, the two apostles of Social Credit were acutely aware of their political demographics in that dusty, drought-riven summer. They headed for the area where Aberhart's Sunday broadcasts over CFCN had the greatest penetration, south of Red Deer in central Alberta.

"We organized a five-week tour, five days a week, two meetings a day," explained Ernest Manning in an interview taped for the University of Alberta Archives. "You could have afternoon meetings in those days because everything was dormant and dead anyway; you could get as big a crowd in the afternoon as you could get at night in many places... We'd go into little places with a population of maybe 1,000 or 1,200 people, and it wouldn't be unusual to get 2,000 people out for a meeting. They'd come fifty to 100 miles."

Thanks to his broadcasts, Aberhart was now a household name in south-central Alberta, and

[2] Ernest Manning, who would become the longest-serving premier of Alberta during the 20th century, was born on a farm near Carnduff, Saskatchewan, in 1908. After he happened to hear an Aberhart broadcast on CFCN early in 1926, Manning went to Calgary to learn what the Prophetic Bible Institute would offer. Aberhart baptized Manning and the two became close friends. When Manning returned to enrol in the Bible Institute he was invited to live with the Aberharts and soon became the son Aberhart never had, an unassuming alter ego to his colourful mentor.

the curious flocked to his meetings, if only to put a face to that sonorous voice they heard every Sunday. And once he corralled them in arenas or even lumber yards, he worked his magic. The complex theories of Social Credit were reduced to simple allegories and slogans that captivated audiences. "By the time the tour was over, there were literally scores of economic study groups springing up behind it, all over that part of Alberta," said Manning. As Aberhart's influence spread through the province, supporters encouraged him to enter politics, but he denied all notions of such ambition. Reassured by his claim that he was just a teacher, rather than a political rival, many UFA locals in smalltown Alberta invited him to speak.

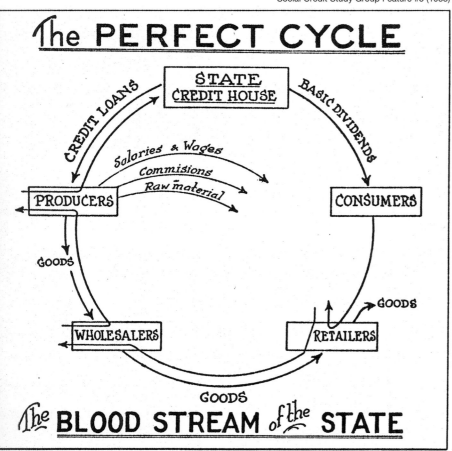

Aberhart often used the analogy of blood circulation to explain the movement of money. This depiction is from study material used by Social Credit groups that sprang up in the years before the 1935 election.

Every lecture and broadcast drew a flock of converts eager to discuss and spread Social Credit doctrine. An adept organizer, Aberhart enlisted Manning and other handpicked students at the Bible Institute to fill hundreds of requests for speakers. Rolling across Alberta like a grass fire in the autumn of 1933, Social Credit began encroaching on the hitherto resistant cities. Soon 63 study groups in Calgary were among 1,600 meeting in community halls and living rooms throughout the province. In his element, spreading the gospel of Social Credit, Aberhart was soon juggling more balls than he could handle.

One landed with a thud. In September 1933 Andrew S. Imrie, pastor of the Bible Institute Baptist congregation resigned over differences with Aberhart, a common occurrence in Aberhart's relations with various Calgary churches (see sidebar). Imrie and his followers left the Institute because they felt that mixing Social Credit with theology diluted their spiritual purpose. Aberhart responded with a series of sermons denouncing the "so-called scriptural objections to Social Credit."

He found these theological defectors less threatening than the Social Credit purists known as Douglasites. Years before Aberhart discovered Social Credit, a number of followers in communities across Alberta had adopted Major Douglas's economic philosophy. Now they saw themselves as guardians of his vision. Dismissing Aberhart and his Bible Institute zealots as interlopers, they allied themselves with Douglas's Social Credit Secretariat in London. Their studious, analytical approach attracted members from the better-educated professional classes, while Aberhart pitched his flamboyant appeal to farmers, shopkeepers and blue-collar workers.

Alarmed by his unexpected success, the Douglasites set up the New Age Club in Calgary when Aberhart and Manning set out on another whirlwind tour of southern Alberta in the summer of 1933. The club's 200 members saw Aberhart as an unsophisticated demagogue whose muddled thinking had distorted and betrayed Social Credit doctrine. Aberhart saw them as a bunch of eggheads bent on undermining all he had achieved in the past eighteen months. While the Douglasites pledged allegiance to their English mentor, Aberhart invoked God as he wrestled with contrary demons, religious or economic. At this point he considered himself not a politician but an educator, trying to force the UFA administration to embrace Social Credit in the next election, then expected the following year, 1934.

Douglasite attacks against Aberhart peaked in January 1934, when C.V. Kerslake of the Toronto-based Douglas Credit League of Canada implied that Aberhart was a bumpkin who didn't understand the British parliamentary system. Social Credit wouldn't work at the provincial level because its application would contravene the constitution, he argued. Ottawa, not Edmonton, controlled the money supply in Alberta.

Dismayed by the colonial catfight, Douglas's London headquarters intervened. On February 23, 1934, Aberhart received a letter from the secretariat asking him to remove Douglas's name from the title of the Yellow Pamphlet because Douglas refused to endorse Aberhart's Social Credit movement. Copied to the secretary of the New Age Club, Charles Palmer, and released to the press, the letter effectively called Aberhart a fake, and repudiated his interpretation of Social Credit ideas.

Aberhart reacted swiftly. Next day he ran an advertisement in Calgary's newspapers, announcing that he would give his "last address" on Social Credit at the Bible Institute on February 27. There he reduced his audience to the verge of tears by revealing that the machinations of the New Age Club compelled him to resign as president of the central council of the Douglas Social Credit League at the Bible Institute. Ironically, the fundamentalist preacher had been evicted from Social Credit, the popular movement he had virtually created, by Social Credit's own fundamentalists.

But the Douglasites' apparent victory proved hollow. Aberhart's successor as president of the central council, Gilbert McGregor, a proofreader at the Calgary *Albertan*, was only a titular head of the

organization. The central council was still a subsidiary of the Prophetic Bible Institute controlled by Aberhart. McGregor's decisions, and even his speeches, had to pass Aberhart's approval.[3]

Lacking Aberhart's single-minded purpose, the Douglasites had been co-operating with him even as they conspired to oust him. He had persuaded the New Age Club to join him in a plan designed to force the UFA government to recognize the Social Credit movement. Together the two Social Credit factions had organized a petition, signed by 54,000 people, asking Premier Brownlee to invite Major Douglas to visit Alberta.

Aberhart brought his larger-than-life physique and personality to a political landscape that had been stripped bare by drought, depression and scandal.

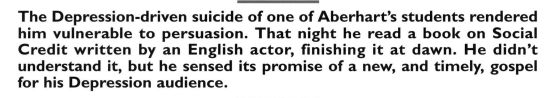

The Depression-driven suicide of one of Aberhart's students rendered him vulnerable to persuasion. That night he read a book on Social Credit written by an English actor, finishing it at dawn. He didn't understand it, but he sensed its promise of a new, and timely, gospel for his Depression audience.

Meanwhile, at Aberhart's instigation, 700 women studying Social Credit at the Bible Institute sent a telegram soliciting support from the United Farm Women of Alberta, who attended the annual UFA convention at Edmonton in January 1934. A few days later, the UFWA presented the Alberta government with a 12,000-name petition calling for an investigation of Social Credit.

Faced with these two petitions, the UFA administration could no longer ignore a movement that clearly mustered strong grass-roots support. Five days before Aberhart's resignation as president of the central council, Premier Brownlee announced that Douglas would come to Alberta in April 1934 and testify before the agriculture committee as a "reconstruction adviser."

Brownlee's decision inadvertently provided the opportunity for a showdown between the Douglasites and Aberhart, who had also been invited to testify at the committee's hearings, not by the government, but by the provincial Liberal opposition. Indeed, the premier may have hoped that the two Social Credit factions would discredit each other, taking the pressure off the government.

Aberhart, on the other hand, hoped to exploit schisms within the ruling party. Besieged by the

[3]Some historians, such as David R. Elliott and Iris Miller in *Bible Bill: A Biography of William Aberhart*, contend that Aberhart's resignation was a ploy to "test his popularity and get rid of opposition within his movement, getting his wind, while a figurehead leader, McGregor, took his place." Aberhart had a history of doing much the same thing when he ran into opposition at the long string of churches he attempted to take over before he established the Prophetic Bible Institute. First he would resign and proclaim his martyrdom, and either leave with his loyal followers for another church, or wait until clamour from the congregation forced his opponents to reappoint him.

Brownlee and McPherson scandals (see previous chapter), the UFA was already in disarray. In this charged political atmosphere, the agricultural committee began holding preliminary hearings from March 19 to 21, while Douglas was still on his way from a lecture tour in New Zealand. Those invited to testify included representatives from the New Age Club, other Social Credit purists, and at least one economist from the University of Alberta. But the audience hadn't come to hear these professionals and academics. The men in cheap gabardine suits and shirts with frayed collars who packed the public galleries were Aberhart's followers, waiting eagerly for the appearance of their champion, the first witness.[4]

Although he knew the founder of Social Credit would probably side with his foes in the New Age Club, Aberhart opened by praising Douglas. Uncharacteristically humble, he told the committee Douglas would speak with much more authority on Social Credit. If the government couldn't afford the major's expenses, he offered to pay the expected tab of $1,250, which he could raise through paid admissions to meetings.

Sitting as a member of the committee Premier Brownlee focused on what he considered Aberhart's evasive testimony. How, asked Brownlee, could an Alberta farmer, paid for his produce in Social Credit certificates which were worthless outside the province, buy machinery from Massey-Harris Company in Toronto? Aberhart plainly could not answer. Brownlee then asked Aberhart to tell the committee exactly what steps he would take if he were made general manager of a Social Credit scheme in Alberta. Aberhart, superb preacher of Social Credit though he was, professed his ignorance of its application of monetary theory to practical governmental administration. "The first step," he said, "would be to ask permission to engage Mr. Douglas to come here and organize it, and he would do the work; that is, all I would have to do is I would sit by his side, listen to him, and get all the information I could."

Brownlee kept up the pressure, finally asking what kind of state Aberhart envisioned under a Social Credit regime. Aberhart explained that, by breaking the bankers' monopoly on the issuance of credit, and setting a fair price on goods and services, the state would give more purchasing power to the ordinary citizen.

Aberhart took his jottings on Social Credit to Hilly Hill. 'They were written on the backs of envelopes, on pulp paper, on letter paper, on school board stationery,' records Hill. 'We sifted the gist of what Douglas meant into pamphlet form.' Ironically, Hill was at that time a dedicated Communist.

The premier noted the authoritarian underpinnings of Douglas's theories. "Then that is the same as the Soviet Union," he suggested. "To work out your plan then we have to put the state in a position where it is controlling the individual initiative of the man?" Aberhart replied: "It would not control the position of the individual as much as the banks do today, and the state would be a better adviser."

Aberhart returned to Calgary, chastened by the committee's and the media's dubious reception of his performance, and still uncertain of what stand Douglas would take on the split between Alberta's two Social Credit factions. When Douglas, his wife and his secretary arrived on the CNR platform in Edmonton on April 5, 1934, they were swarmed by Douglasites from the New Age Club, press and curious spectators. All eyes were focussed on the dapper 55-year-old Englishman with sad, heavy-lidded eyes and a grey moustache. Medium tall, limping from a shooting accident, Douglas still maintained the erect carriage earned in military service.

Forlorn and ignored on the margin of the crowd stood Aberhart, waiting to meet the man whose academic theory he had converted into an evangelical movement that captivated thousands of Albertans. At last a New Age executive introduced the two men, and Aberhart soon learned which faction Douglas favoured. "I think it would be much better, Mr. Aberhart, if you let me do things my own way!" he declared, and strode out with the New Agers.

Next morning by 7 o'clock the legislature steps were crowded with people waiting to hear Douglas speak. Interest in his appearance ran so high that the agricultural committee was enlarged to include the full legislative assembly, and for the first time hearings of the Alberta government

[4]An anecdote suggests that Aberhart was curiously naïve. Arriving in Edmonton, he went to see the clerk of the legislature to inquire what "fee" he would get for testifying. When the clerk told him that it was $5, plus travel expenses, Aberhart was aghast to discover that it was so little, and refused to leave until he got the cheque for $5 and his train fare. "What if the school board deducts me more than that for my time missed," he said. — John Barr, *The Dynasty, The Rise and Fall of Social Credit in Alberta* (Toronto, McClelland and Stewart, 1974).

[5]Major Douglas's first visit to Canada was arranged by Alberta Progressive MP William Irvine, later provincial leader of the CCF. Irvine met Douglas in London and was impressed with his theories. On his return to Canada Irvine approached *Ottawa Citizen* editor Charles Bowman, a strong Social Credit supporter, for financial support to bring Douglas to Canada. Bowman convinced the owners of the *Citizen*, Southam Inc., to pick up the tab for Douglas's expenses and the founder of Social Credit appeared before the House of Commons Banking and Commerce Committee in 1923. The initial visit received little press coverage, unlike his subsequent visits to Alberta that made front page news a decade later.

were broadcast over the radio.

After delivering a dense lecture on Social Credit in his clipped accent, Douglas addressed questions from the assembled MLAs. He refused to define the specific methods he would use to remedy the Depression. On the key question of whether his theories could be applied in Alberta, as Aberhart maintained, or only at the federal level, as the Douglasites insisted, Douglas was not quite conclusive. He could implement a Social Credit program provincially in three months, he declared. But then it would probably be declared illegal under Canadian law. Adoption of his theories would require alteration of the British North America Act; it might even call for a revolution. While his presentation puzzled Alberta's legislators, it reassured senior UFA ministers and officials who suspected that the British engineer was a crackpot.

But the founder of Social Credit wasn't finished yet. After addressing the legislature he left for Calgary, where the New Age Club had invited him to speak at Mewata Armouries on April 7, a move calculated to upstage Aberhart at the heart of his fief.

When word spread around the city that Aberhart had not been invited, the CPR's Ogden Shop rail workers, one of the most militant Social Credit study groups in the province, threatened to boycott the meeting. Perhaps because of their protest, Aberhart was grudgingly offered a seat on the stage behind the podium, surrounded by hostile Douglasite luminaries and various sponsors of the meeting. There he listened to Douglas's speech. After his usual convoluted explanation of monetary policy, the major advocated enlisting the armed forces in a military coup to oust the bankers.

Ignored throughout Douglas's inflammatory oration was the man seated thoughtfully behind him, Aberhart. Soon trouble erupted. "Aberhart! What about Aberhart? We want Aberhart!" chanted the angry crowd. Some of the railway workers rushed the stage, brandishing chairs. To avert a riot, the band struck up *God Save the King*. The crowd instantly stopped in its tracks and stood to attention. (Such was the power of the National Anthem in the days when Albertans respected royalty and empire.) So Aberhart did not speak.

The donnybrook so narrowly avoided in the armoury threatened to explode in the officers' mess after the meeting. Backed by the New Agers, Douglas became embroiled in a heated argument with Aberhart. Echoing the edict of his London secretariat, the major told Aberhart to strike his name from the Yellow Pamphlet. After exchanging

The English actor Maurice Colbourne (shown here with actress Angela Baddeley in Shaw's Arms and the Man) *had a pivotal influence on the history of Alberta, a place he had probably barely heard of. Colbourne's book on Social Credit converted William Aberhart and his idea for skits dramatizing Social Credit became the basis of the Aberhart's* Man From Mars *radio series that captivated thousands. Social Credit purists said that the movement's famous Yellow Pamphlet was Aberhart's version of Colbourne's version of Douglas's version of the Social Credit theory, as written by Communist Hilly Hill.*

'We organized a five-week tour, five days a week, two meetings a day,' recalled Ernest Manning. 'You could have afternoon meetings because everything was dormant and dead anyway. We'd go into little places with a population of maybe 1,000 people, and you could get 2,000 people out. They'd come 100 miles.'

---

curses, Aberhart stomped down the armoury steps, pursued by Mrs. Douglas, who invited him to "come and have dinner with us" at noon the next day.

That luncheon seemed to diffuse the hostility between the two men. When Douglas returned to the legislature in Edmonton to answer more questions on April 10, he refused to condemn Aberhart's Yellow Pamphlet outright. Asked if it fairly interpreted his theories, Douglas admitted that he hadn't read it. He couldn't explain why his London secretariat had rejected the pamphlet because at that time he had been out of England.

Impressed by Aberhart's strong support in Calgary, Douglas may have felt that his followers in the New Age Club had seriously underestimated Aberhart's power. In any event, he was no longer eager to alienate Social Credit's most effective advocate. After mollifying Aberhart and thoroughly confusing the Douglasites, he went to Ottawa, where he addressed the House of Commons banking committee on April 18.[5]

Aberhart's apparent truce with Douglas meant that the UFA plan to use the major to discredit the Calgary preacher had backfired. Even though Aberhart's testimony was curiously feeble, and

Douglas's speeches were confusing, evasive and inflammatory, the committee hearings had served only to fuel public interest in Social Credit. Rating front-page coverage in the papers, the hearings led the press to recognize Aberhart as leader of a powerful new movement in Alberta. From now on his activities regularly made the front pages.

Instead of trying to regain lost ground, the UFA compounded its problems by mishandling the aftermath of the hearings. The government announced that a report on Douglas's proposals would be published within a few weeks — which stretched to three months. When at last it appeared in June, the 127-page document turned out to be little more than a transcript of the proceedings. Its brief conclusions failed to address public demand for the recognition of Social Credit:

> Your committee is of the opinion that while the evidence given disclosed the weakness of the present system and the necessity for controlled Social Credit, it did not offer any practicable plan for adoption in Alberta under the existing constitutional condition.
>
> Major Douglas recognized this and urged that a thorough study be made, first to arrive at a definitive objective, and second, to get a clear idea of the obstacles to be overcome and the limitations to be removed in order to clear the way, and the best method of procedure to secure results.

This non-response, which lacked specific suggestions concerning change to the "constitutional condition," merely confirmed what most Albertans were thinking: the UFA government had run out of gas, just as the economy had. Lacking initiatives of its own, the farmer government refused to consider innovations urged on it by voters. As Ernest Manning later recalled: the report "... brought the whole Social Credit educational movement to a crucial point."

If Aberhart seemed out of his depth at the hearings, he quickly resurfaced. He was now clearly in command of the Social Credit movement, even though the Douglasites had forced him to resign the presidency of the central council of the Douglas Social Credit League. His successor, Gilbert McGregor, was incapable of attracting grass-roots support. Like his New Age Club colleagues, he favoured federal rather than provincial action, an unpopular stand in Social Credit's Alberta heartland. His clear, bookish speeches lacked the flashy emotional appeal of Aberhart's perorations, especially since he had no means of broadcasting them. He was also personally short

Glenbow Archives, NA-4080-3

Glenbow Archives, NA-4080-4

Social Credit cartoons never carried the clout of its radio presentations

Social Credit, which through Aberhart's genius virtually controlled the new and powerful medium of radio, never mastered the older art of political cartooning. The author of the effort at the right is not known. The one immediately below was drawn by Reverend E.G. Hansell, whom Aberhart and his lay preachers hired as the first minister of Westbourne Baptist Church and who later became a Social Credit MP. The creator of the two at the bottom of the page opposite is identified as Edward Hagell. Compared with the avalanche of ridicule and scorn about to be unleashed upon Aberhart over the next five years by cartoonists Stewart Cameron of the Calgary Herald and Arch Dale of the Winnipeg Free Press, these works are milquetoast mild.

Albertan, April 11, 1936

Pamphlet What would Social Credit Do for Us? (1934)

"No more wolves at the door"
The Solution of the Present Problem
"Purchasing power in the hands of the Consumer"

Major Clifford Hugh Douglas was the eccentric Scottish engineer whose economic theories were debated in intellectual circles, but they mostly captivated the irrepressible principal of Crescent Heights High School in Calgary.

of money, and by mid-April of 1934 he wanted out. Early in May he confronted Aberhart, and offered to hand back the presidency. Aberhart would have none of it; he preferred to be wooed by the rank-and-file. That evening McGregor resigned, and the meeting of the central council appointed an acting president.

Just as Aberhart expected, within a few days spontaneous public demand forced the council to reinstate him. He resumed the presidency with his usual gusto — and vindictiveness. He now had what he had always wanted: complete control of the movement in Alberta. He immediately swept all the New Agers from positions of power on the council, replacing them with trusted followers such as Manning. McGregor, who was still making speeches outside Calgary, was ordered to submit them for Aberhart's approval first. Humiliated, he withdrew from the movement and seldom spoke to Aberhart again.

Aberhart now took on the role of founder and sole prophet of "Social Credit for Alberta." He responded to the toothless report of the agriculture committee by issuing a series of fire-breathing pamphlets: "Social Credit: History and Character," "What Would Social Credit Do For Us?" and "The BNA Act and Social Credit," a spirited argument for the application of Social Credit at the provincial level. Wasting no time on the flagging UFA government, he and his disciples followed up the third pamphlet by approaching the other provincial parties. When the Conservatives proved dismissive and the Liberals evasive, mounting pressure from grass-roots Social Crediters urged the transformation of the movement from an educational force into a political party.

If the ruling UFA had shot itself in the foot with its report on Social Credit, it lost its right arm when John Brownlee resigned on June 30, 1934, after a jury found he had seduced Vivian MacMillan. Judge William Carlos Ives's later ruling that the seduction didn't entitle Vivian and her father to damages couldn't redeem Brownlee's reputation.

Brownlee had been the mainspring of the UFA since he took over from Herbert Greenfield in 1925. Every provincial initiative bore his fingerprints. It was Brownlee who secured Alberta's control over its natural resources; it was Brownlee who sold off money-losing provincial rail lines and balanced the books. His strong leadership held the populist party together through four years of the worst depression in Canadian memory. His departure left the UFA leaderless and in complete disarray.

The Douglasites saw Aberhart as an unsophisticated demagogue whose muddled thinking had distorted and betrayed Social Credit doctrine. Aberhart saw them as a bunch of eggheads bent on undermining all he had achieved in the past eighteen months.

While the opposition parties closed in for the kill, two new rivals lurked on the horizon. One was the Co-operative Commonwealth Federation (CCF), forerunner of the New Democratic Party, founded in Calgary in 1932 by J.S. Woodsworth, William Irvine and various farm groups that defected from the UFA. Its socialist solution for the Depression included nationalization and increased welfare. The other was Social Credit.

Beleaguered by new political heresies, shocked by the Brownlee and McPherson scandals, the confused UFA caucus met behind closed doors for three days before appointing Reid premier on July 5.[6] A thirteen-year veteran of UFA administrations, Reid had been a prominent member of Herbert Greenfield's first cabinet in which he held three portfolios, including the senior post of treasury. When Brownlee wrested control of natural resources from Ottawa in 1930, he made Reid Alberta's first minister of Lands and Mines.

The *Calgary Herald* described Alberta's sixth premier as a man who "won the respect of his

[6]Reid was by no means the unanimous choice of the UFA caucus to replace Brownlee. If Reid's rectitude and conservatism was favoured by the majority, a minority fought vigorously for the appointment of George Hoadley, the flamboyant minister of Agriculture, according to the *Calgary Albertan.*

colleagues for his steadiness and administrative ability, regarded by his opponents as thorough-going and cautious in his financial and municipal responsibilities." Reid was considered an honest, if lacklustre, replacement for the UFA's fallen titan.

An egalitarian Scot from Aberdeenshire, he had served with the Royal Army Medical Corps in the South African War. Two years on the veldt gave him a taste for the freedom of open country. He emigrated to Canada in 1903 and worked a year as farmhand and lumberjack before taking up a homestead near Mannville. A respected farmer and strong supporter of the co-operative movement, he easily won the Vermilion seat when the United Farmers entered politics in 1921. With John Brownlee and George Hoadley, the brash Agriculture minister, he formed the backbone of the UFA government headed by Greenfield. In less turbulent times, Reid might well have proved a capable premier. But now he faced an empty treasury and a firebrand opponent bent on smashing the UFA.

Forlorn and ignored on the margin of the crowd stood Aberhart, waiting to meet Douglas, the man whose theory he had converted into a movement that captivated thousands. At last he was introduced. 'I think it would be much better, Mr. Aberhart, if you let me do things my own way!' said Douglas, who then strode off.

From its original strength of 37,000 members, the UFA movement had declined to fewer than 10,000 and fragmented into four groups with widely different views. Reid and most of his cabinet, who formed the dominant faction, considered Social Credit ideas nonsensical and impossible to implement in a parliamentary system with a distinct federal-provincial division of powers. A second group, ostensibly socialist, argued that monetary reform was the first battle to be won in the long war to implement an egalitarian political system. The third faction was composed of hard-core socialists, who disliked Social Credit nostrums and believed that only socialism, or even Communism, would enable Alberta to escape the Depression. The fourth was ready to defect to Social Credit.

Faced with such divisions, Reid moved cautiously to corral his unruly flock under the tattered

In 1934, I met Mr. Aberhart...he said, "I want to form the Old Timers' Group, and some of you younger fellows wonder why I call it the Old Timers' Group, but five, six years from now, we'll be looking back at the first groups that were there... So if you'd like to become a member, and belong to this elite Old Timers' Group, he said, what each of us would have to do is go out and organize in our own poll in the city a group. We'd need 10 people in the group to really make it worthwhile and then teach another group in a neighbouring poll....
—Orvis Kennedy (taped reminiscences, courtesy of Edward Kennedy)

When the New Age Club invited Major Douglas to speak in Calgary but snubbed Aberhart, the militant Social Credit Study Group of CPR's Ogden Yards protested so vigorously that Aberhart was given a place on the platform but was not allowed to speak. A near-riot was stopped dead by the playing of God Save the King.

Glenbow Archives, NA-2888-7

Dick Reid: good man, hopeless job

Alberta's sixth premier, Richard Gavin Reid, widely recognized as a capable minister, had the hopeless job of salvaging the UFA. (Below) He consults with Robert English of the Department of Municipal Affairs. (Left) Premier Reid delivers the Silver Jubilee address on May 6, 1935. (Bottom) The family of the new premier poses for this portrait. (Left to right) George Stuart; Richard Gavin; Kathleen Margaret; James Kenneth; Marion; and Flora Marion.

UFA banner. He reinstated Brownlee's cabinet with one exception: Public Works Minister Oran L. McPherson, a political pariah since his sordid divorce case. But the new premier was vulnerable to criticism because Brownlee and McPherson were still UFA MLAs, living reminders of salacious conduct within the government.

On July 7 the *Calgary Herald* called for an immediate election: "How can O.L. McPherson imagine that he is worthy to continue high office in Alberta, a man who has been the subject of disclosures in court which, quite apart from any question of his culpability, should drive a man in any British country out of public life?" Whipped on by the press, the Liberal opposition under W.R. Howson unctuously echoed the *Herald*'s demand.

Reid would have welcomed an election to clear the air, but his cabinet and caucus urged him to wait till the scandals were forgotten. Closing ranks against the Liberals, they ignored the threat from Social Credit, whose study groups were rapidly attracting thousands of their rural supporters. UFA advisers saw Aberhart not as a politician but as a Christian evangelist whose skills could be co-opted or absorbed by their own party. They grievously underestimated the power of Aberhart's oratory and his mastery of the far-reaching new medium of radio.

Even at this juncture Aberhart was not interested in going into politics, according to Manning. "He had no ambitions to go into public life," the former premier declares in his taped interview. "He was married to his teaching profession; he loved it and didn't want to leave it."

Nevertheless, Aberhart acted like a politician in the summer of 1934, organizing his supporters and countering his opponents at every turn. The province's metropolitan newspapers, which had virtually ignored Social Credit or ridiculed it until the agriculture committee hearings, were now covering the movement's every twitch, if only to maintain subscribers. In Calgary the *Albertan* ran three series of articles explaining Social Credit. But the *Calgary Herald* and the *Edmonton Bulletin*, standardbearers for the Conservative and Liberal parties respectively, remained intractable foes,

---

The donnybrook so narrowly avoided in the armoury threatened to explode in the officers' mess. Douglas became embroiled in a heated argument with Aberhart and told him to strike his name from the Yellow Pamphlet. After exchanging curses, Aberhart stomped down the armoury steps.

---

often running personal attacks against Aberhart. These attacks seemed to increase in direct proportion to the movement's success. Finally Aberhart gave up and started his own weekly newspaper. The first issue of the *Alberta Social Credit Chronicle* appeared on July 20, 1934. It was not an easy birth. Five Calgary printing shops refused to print it without a four-week advance deposit. The first edition of 4,000 copies produced only $43 in advertising revenue.

Yet the *Chronicle* soon caught on. After the first five issues, it was enlarged from a small tabloid format to full newspaper size. It boasted 14,000 subscribers within a few months and an additional 6,000 copies were sold every week at Social Credit meetings throughout the province. Editor Charles Underwood, a devout Social Crediter, ensured the paper was unabashed partisan propaganda. Each edition contained a lead column by Aberhart. Guest columnists included people like Sir Oswald Mosley, leader of the British fascist movement, and Father Charles Coughlin, a radical Roman Catholic priest who preached against capitalists and bankers on U.S. radio.

Not content with print, Aberhart also increased his radio time with two half-hour broadcasts during the week, geared to complement more than 1,000 Social Credit study groups throughout the province. "The study groups were encouraged to meet on those evenings when the broadcast was on, and they'd listen to the half-hour lecture which he would give," Manning explained in his archival interview. "... You could get a group of people together in a community hall or a farm home or any old place at all — hundreds and hundreds of them — and they'd follow the half-hour radio lecture and sit around for a couple of hours and debate and discuss what they'd heard, and try to reach some conclusions about it."

Aberhart managed to get out on the hustings as well. Manning was usually at the wheel and during the summer of 1934 the duo, sometimes accompanied by Jessie Aberhart, travelled over 2,500 miles and made 39 speeches to about 30,000 people, according to Aberhart's estimate. He

---

On the train I had met a friend named Offenhouse... During the course of our nightcap in the smoking room of the car a chap named McNutt, who was Aberhart's son-in-law, had walked in and, seeing what we were doing, discreetly retired, or so I thought. I remarked to Offenhouse, "There goes Abie's son-in-law. Sure as hell he'll tell him Mrs. H.'s husband was drinking on the train."

Offenhouse said, "Ah to hell with Aberhart, he is a damned fool. I never heard such nonsense as he spouts." He went on to say that in his opinion Aberhart must be suffering from thwarted sex desire. His opinion was that all these religious fanatics were overly sexed and as they considered the sex act a sin, except in such instances as propagation was desired, they diverted their sex energy into religious lines... He cited instances of ministers going haywire over other women and I thought of my brother-in-law (Pearson) who was mad along those lines. Pearson should have lived in the east and had a harem...

I spent three weeks at the coast and started for home. At Kamloops, who got on the train but McNutt and he rode from there into Calgary. Lettie met me at the train and spoke to McNutt when passing...

Monday night when I got home she was there looking very perturbed... She said that Abie had been very nasty to her and had said I had made remarks about him to the effect that the only reason he had his Bible Institute was to provide himself with a harem to satisfy his insatiable sex craving... All in all he was extremely nasty to her on my account and I was quite innocent.

—Henry B. "Hilly" Hill, Diary (Glenbow Archives)

Ousted cabinet minister whacks Bulletin publisher

And the mayor of Edmonton shouts abuse from the Legislature gallery — such was Alberta in the dying days of the UFA government

A former cabinet minister socks a newspaper publisher and knocks him reeling into a pillar at the Legislature. The mayor of Edmonton shouts epithets from the public gallery at an MLA on the floor of the House. Opposition members demand prosecution of a government party organ because it contains advertisements of an "obscene nature," condom being a word that dared not speak its name in 1935 Alberta.

Had the province's lawmakers lost their senses? No, it was just the dying days of the UFA government, when tempers raged and morals were, from the evidence, somewhat low in somewhat high places.

After the McPherson divorce case broke in the newspapers (see previous chapter), Premier John Brownlee turned on the media. He warned John Imrie, publisher of the *Edmonton Journal*, that he would introduce "drastic changes" in legislation covering the rights of the press to publish allegations made in civil actions.

Brownlee was as good as his threat. He introduced amendments to the provincial Defamation Act and a new statute called the Reports of Judicial Proceedings Act. One section stipulated that newspapers must not publish statements of claim or affidavits concerning the McPherson case. The press was also prohibited from publishing any news of the actions other than the judge's remarks in disposing of the case. No independent comment on the actions would be permitted.

Both bills, however, died on the order paper in 1934 because Brownlee, himself now embroiled in a sex scandal, had "the feeling that their introduction might be construed as an effort to prejudice his court case, which was then pending," reported the *Medicine Hat News*.

The following year, however, the UFA brought them in again over the protests of the media, the opposition and the public. Newspapers lost all pretence of objectivity. "By sheer force of unreasoning party strength," began one *Edmonton*

Provincial Archives of Alberta, A 14003

Edmonton's John Imrie (left) of the Journal *and Charles Campbell of the* Bulletin *joined forces to oppose UFA legislation aimed at muzzling the press.*

Bulletin news story on April 16, 1935, "and giving a perfect example of obedience to the hand on the throttle, the UFA government in one of its last legislative acts steamrollered through the committee of the House on Monday night its two bills designed to throttle the press of the province."

However it was the Liberal opposition that delivered the sharpest blow. Leader W.R. Howson "electrified the House," said the *Bulletin*, when he argued the government should suspend the bills until it investigated the "obscene" advertisements in its own official UFA newspaper, the *United Farmer*. He then read from the party organ advertisement for condoms, whose sale was restricted in Canada by the Criminal Code, as was advertising for them. Why had the attorney-general not prosecuted such an offence? His implication was clear. It was because of the libertine lifestyle of the cabinet.

The Tories immediately concurred. "I think the attorney-general should adjourn further consideration of this bill until he has first prosecuted the press of his own party," declared Hugh Farthing, Conservative member for Calgary. Opposition members pounded their desks in agreement.

That afternoon the conflict became physical. The former Public Works minister Oran McPherson, whose "wife-swapping" divorce had been covered so graphically by the *Edmonton Bulletin* the court had reprimanded the newspaper, encountered *Bulletin* publisher Charles Campbell at the top of the broad marble staircase leading to the Legislature chamber. Heated words were exchanged and Campbell began to retreat.

"As Mr. Campbell was withdrawing," reported the *Medicine Hat News*, "Mr. McPherson struck him high up on one side of the face. Mr. Campbell reeled and fell forward towards a railing and struck his head against a corner of a pillar. The blow appeared to have temporarily affected his sight."

Liberal leader W.R. Howson shocked the legislature by speculating about condom advertisements in the United Farmer.

Public Works minister Oran McPherson's headline-making divorce triggered his government's backlash against the press.

The cause of the outburst was self-evident. Earlier in the day, the *Edmonton Journal*'s publisher Imrie had told the Legislature committee hearing testimony on the bills that first mention of the McPherson divorce case in an Edmonton newspaper had been made at the instigation of McPherson himself. The *Bulletin*'s Campbell corroborated this.

McPherson then testified that this was "absolutely false." Immediately the *Bulletin* publisher obtained a sworn affidavit from his managing editor corroborating his own testimony and refuting McPherson's. When McPherson met Campbell, he was obviously still fuming.

It remained for the *Calgary Herald* to pontificate on the incident. "If any proof were needed to give colour to the fact that these bills were conceived in spleen and anger and in the spirit of revenge," said a *Herald* editorial, "it will be

cipals of two cases now before the courts." It was a reference to the McPherson and Brownlee cases, both under appeal.

Two days later, on April 20, 1935, the controversial bills became law in Alberta. Despite the strong probability of their unconstitutionality, they were never tested in the Supreme Court of Canada, perhaps because of the plethora of *ultra vires* Alberta laws enacted under Social Credit. In the early 1970s Premier Peter Lougheed's Conservative government quietly repealed them.

As for the UFA's "obscene" advertisements, Lymburn later announced no action would be taken, though the ads would be discontinued, he said. They were.

The UFA government may have had good reason to fear more accounts of ministerial peccadilloes. Brownlee and McPherson were not the only members of the provincial gov-

---

The Liberal leader 'electrified the House' when he read out the 'obscene' advertisements in the UFA's official newspaper. It was against the law to publish such things. Why had the attorney-general not prosecuted? The implication was clear. It was because of the libertine lifestyle of the cabinet.

---

found in an occurrence which took place in the corridors of the House when a former minister of the UFA government made a physical attack on an Edmonton publisher, with intent to do him bodily harm."

Campbell didn't press charges, but McPherson wasn't finished. He was on his feet in the House the following day, and before the packed galleries charged that the incident had led to an immediate Liberal "council of war" in which Joe Clarke, mayor of Edmonton and currently a Liberal, had taken part.

Suddenly there came a shout from the gallery, "You're a liar!" It was Fighting Joe himself, incensed at McPherson's statement. As House orderlies moved in on Clarke, McPherson continued talking. Before leaving the gallery Clarke shouted again: "He's a liar and he knows it!"

By now pandemonium reigned on the floor. The Speaker called for order and promised to investigate. Attorney-General Lymburn intervened to announce that amendments would be made to the bills exempting coverage of "two prin-

ernment involved in sexual recreation, said John William Hugill, the first attorney-general in William Aberhart's Social Credit administration. "[Agriculture Minister George] Headley had the reputation of being the prime stud horse of the party, you know, and the others were all engaged in that sort of relaxation from the stress of public life," Hugill told the Glenbow Museum's George Gooderham in a taped interview.

"Mind you it's serious; it exists; you have no idea. They're at it night and day and you have to have some kind of diversion," Hugill continued. "You're living too high all the time, and what happened of course, the thing was poor old Brownlee didn't know his way about. That's all."

— *G.O.*

ᴬUnder the 1892 Criminal Code advertising for birth control was obscene, "tending to corrupt morals." Unless an accused could prove that its advocacy had been "for the public good," ie. to prevent disease, he or she was liable to serve a two-year jail term. Advertisements for condoms in the 1930s met criminal code provisions by carrying the line "for the prevention of disease only."

Social Credit introduced into Alberta the phenomenon of political hoopla

With hundreds and of eager volunteers and a substantial supply of money coming in through Aberhart's radio appeals, Social Credit was able to bring something of American-style politics into Alberta. Volunteer Social Credit canvassers, many of them young people, conducted a straw poll of the province that gave it an accurate reading on every constituency and also kept the fervour at a fever pitch in the leadup to the election. Here the party bursts forth in the Calgary Stampede parade, with streamer bedecked cars and a flower festooned float, accompanied by marching drummers. On the float (L-R) are Irene Raby, Frances Dowling, Della Leaman and Chrissie Houston.

[7]Major Douglas demanded a salary of $1,500 per annum, plus $20 a day while he was in Canada, and double first-class expenses to prepare a Social Credit plan for the province in August,1934. When Douglas heard that UFA president Robert Gardiner had made disparaging remarks about his theories, however, he withdrew his offer. UFA vice-president Norman Priestly, acting on behalf of the government, quickly replied, promising that Gardiner could be brought onside, but also informing Douglas that the UFA could not afford his terms. Ultimately, the UFA paid Douglas far more to return to Alberta.

organized his schedule so well he was always close to Calgary on Tuesdays for his mid-week broadcasts, and on Fridays to answer letters on Saturday and prepare for Sunday services at the Prophetic Bible Institute.

Meanwhile it was slowly dawning on the Reid administration that they had a new political opponent who had been campaigning for two years. On August 28, 1934, four days before massive Social Credit Labour Day picnics and parades, Norman Priestley, vice-president of the UFA, wrote to Major Douglas in England asking him to prepare a Social Credit plan for Alberta.[7]

It was clear the cautious farmer government was willing to endure another dose of Douglas, if only to discredit Aberhart. The UFA was on the ropes. "Province Reports $1,878,031 Deficit," shouted the page-one headline of the September 5 edition of the *Calgary Herald*. Brownlee's budget had predicted a surplus of $9,700. It seemed apparent to Albertans the scandal-plagued UFA administration was a failure at arithmetic as well.

Meanwhile Irvine wrote W. Norman Smith, editor of the United Farmers' official newspaper: "In my opinion there is only one hope and that is to accept the Douglas proposals officially. Then get on the air every day that Aberhart is on the air, only follow him and answer his arguments and show him up as the faker he is. This radio program should be kept going up until the provincial election."

As usual, however, Aberhart was one step ahead. In October 1934 he inaugurated his weekly *Man From Mars* radio skits, written by himself and Manning. The idea was simple and effective. An interplanetary visitor would listen in bewilderment as spokesmen for the bank-dominated establishment explained how it was essential and healthy for Albertans to live hungry and cold amidst an abundance of food and fuel and with the transportation facilities to move them.

The Martian was played by Clifford M. Willmott, a Calgary railway conductor and Social

Credit devotee. There were other characters: C.C. Heifer, a thinly disguised UFA loyalist leaning towards the CCF, and Kant B. Dunn, representing the financial establishment. Social Credit doctrine and the Social Credit version of Christianity would inevitably be threaded through the script.[8] The ingenious broadcasts, played before a live audience, kept interest in Social Credit alive throughout the winter of 1934-35 and became the opening broadside in the Social Credit political campaign.

By November, Social Credit's political role had become so self-evident that the *Edmonton*

Aberhart was as usual one step ahead. He inaugurated his weekly 'Man From Mars' radio skits in which an interplanetary visitor listened bewildered as Kant B. Dunn of the bank establishment explained how it was healthy and necessary for Albertans to live hungry and cold amidst an abundance of food and fuel.

Journal without comment listed probable Social Credit candidates at Provost, Bashaw, Consort, Rocky Mountain House, Wainwright, Coronation and Hardisty, all drawn from Social Credit clubs and study groups. Another story, datelined Stettler, read: "The Social Credit cause is developing with leaps and bounds in this district. Study groups are being organized at nearly all school houses and holding meetings every Tuesday night. During the past week units were started at Red Willow and Nevis. It is claimed the movement is finding favour with 90 per cent of the rural voters."

Meanwhile Aberhart kept insisting he was an educator and evangelist, not a politician. He told

[8] Aberhart adapted the idea from the Maurice Colbourne, author of the first book he ever read on Social Credit. Colbourne, who was a British Shavian actor, had borrowed the idea of the Martian from a George Bernard Shaw drama — and it proved to be a great hit in Alberta at a crucial point for Social Credit.

his listeners on November 13, 1934: "These broadcasts are conducted merely as an educational feature, to help the citizens of the West, and more particularly Alberta, to do a little serious thinking regarding the solution of the present unsatisfactory state of affairs in our land. In no sense of the word do we wish to make it a political broadcast."

The next month, still denying his own personal role in politics, he issued a call for "One Hundred Honest Men" to come forth as Social Credit candidates in the next election. Then at Christmas he wrote his sister: "You may some day hear of me being Premier of Alberta. I am not anxious to go into politics, but the people are urging me to do so."

By now the UFA was plainly baffled. It didn't know whether to co-opt Aberhart or fight him. It finally agreed to ask him to address its annual convention opening January 14 at Calgary. Never

---

The day after the convention Hilly Hill drove Aberhart home. 'Now is your chance to get out from under this thing,' said Hill. 'No, Hill, I can't quit in the middle of a fight,' replied Aberhart. 'I'll organize my own party, the Social Credit Party.'

---

one to miss an opportunity, Aberhart invited all 1,600 delegates to the Calgary Prophetic Bible Institute on the eve of their convention for a reception of music and dramas so he would have an extra chance to convince the delegates about the merits of Social Credit. The *Man From Mars* was on hand to amuse the delegates, as was Kant B. Dunn, now converted to Social Credit.

When the convention opened in the Central United Church auditorium the hapless Premier Reid denied that divisions within the organization "would blow the UFA to the four corners of the wind." The UFA had always been "the spearhead of reform," he declared. Then the delegates got down to work and soon had before them thorny Resolution 190: "Resolved that a system of Social Credit as outlined by William Aberhart, Calgary, be put in as a plank in the UFA Provincial platform to be brought before the electorate at the next provincial election."

The first convention of the central and southern Alberta Social Credit Leagues, which took place in Calgary on April 4 and 5, 1935, was part political pow-wow and part oldtime revival meeting.

Three hours of argument ensued, and the delegates finally confirmed the invitation to Aberhart to address them the next morning. Aberhart came in out of the -33° Celsius ice fog clutching his charts and graphs which he proceeded to hang from the pipes of the church organ. He spoke for ninety minutes, then concluded with an observation and a warning — that he doubted a UFA government would ever take Social Credit seriously, and that Social Credit would produce its own election platform and would hold a political convention in Calgary. "The battle," he concluded, "would be fought out at the ballot box."

It was a declaration of war. After lunch Irvine went to the podium and made a vigourous attack on Aberhart's ideas, contrasting them with Douglas's contention (of the moment) that Social Credit was only feasible at the federal level. While the CCF endorsed Aberhart's monetary reforms, it disliked his exotic mixture of religion and economics. Most of all, it feared that the high school principal's heady recipe might defeat them. Late the same afternoon, the vote was finally called on Resolution 190 and the UFA proved Aberhart a prophet. It went 400 to 40 against adopting Aberhart's proposals.

The day after the convention Hilly Hill drove the principal home from Crescent Heights school. Hill's diary records their conversation: "Well, those birds have turned you down," said Hill. "Now is your chance to get out from under this thing." Aberhart replied, "No, Hill, I can't quit in the middle of a fight. I'll go on and organize my own party. The Social Credit Party." Hill reminisces: "It was interesting to me as it was the first open reference he had made to any political ambitions. I said, 'I think you are wrong. You can't fight old-line finance and win. They'll get you sure. You'll lose your job as principal of the school and all your church following.'"[9]

Two weeks before the UFA convention, Aberhart told a mass meeting in Edmonton that the political future of Social Credit would depend on the results of a straw vote he was conducting across Alberta in January. Like the *Man From Mars* broadcasts, the straw poll evidenced Aberhart's ingenuity. Not only would it allow Albertans to express themselves, it kept interest in Social Credit at a high level throughout the dreary winter months.

Study group canvassers covered virtually every city block and every farmstead in the country.

[9]Hill's diary also discloses a UFA plan, masterminded by Agriculture Minister George Hoadley, to co-opt Aberhart a year earlier at the 1934 UFA convention. Hill writes: "It is regrettable that George Hoadley's instructions were not obeyed. He was in the East on government business and before he left he had instructed all his colleagues to offer Aberhart a job and contract for the next five years at $6,000 per year as provincial economic adviser. This was not done and look what happened." As Hill realized, Alberta history might have unfolded very differently had such a plan succeeded.

Glenbow Archives, NA-4103-2

Merchants lent their stores for balloting, writes John Irving in *The Social Credit Movement in Alberta* (University of Toronto Press, 1959). "One girl covered her particular neighbourhood on horseback; in some districts children wearing clothes made of gunny sacks went around canvassing." The ballots carried three questions: "Have you a vote in the next provincial election? Do you wish to see Social Credit introduced into Alberta? Will you vote 1 for a 100 per cent Social Credit candidate?"[10]

Clifford Willmott, the "Man From Mars," spent two weeks counting ballots at the Prophetic Bible Institute. When the count for an individual constituency was completed numbered pins were stuck on a large map of Alberta with flags noting the amount of Social Credit support in a specific area. "As it turned out, such a highly efficient system was actually unnecessary," writes Irving. "The results of the straw vote indicated that about 93 per cent of the people were prepared to support a Social Credit political campaign," but the poll was just one item in a big bag of tricks.

By February Social Credit was organizing itself into a political party at a fever pitch. Constituency conventions were being organized and a platform was being cobbled together. Meanwhile the UFA pondered the proposal to again import Major Douglas as UFA adviser. Finally, in evident desperation, Reid announced on February 22 that the major had been engaged to revisit Alberta and formulate a Social Credit plan for the province.

The ploy proved disastrous because voters recognized it as just that. Sniffed a *Calgary Herald* editorial, the announcement "did nothing to remove the popular impression that the invitation is a political subterfuge." When terms of the Douglas contract emerged two months later it had more to deplore. Where in 1934 Douglas's price had been $1,500 a year plus $20 per day expenses, it was now more than double that. He had negotiated a two-year contract for $5,000, payable in advance in two equal instalments. Moreover, he would receive $2,000 for each sojourn in Alberta, none to exceed three weeks.

Worse still, he wouldn't arrive in Alberta until some time in May. The farmer government's five-year mandate had only months to run and if Douglas was to turn things around they needed him immediately, not on the edge of an election. Aberhart told the *Edmonton Journal* on February 22, he would be happy to co-operate with Douglas when he arrived. He added puckishly, "But I wonder why they are bringing him out at this time."

It was by now becoming plain there were two Aberharts — the kindly, hearty Aberhart whom people knew personally, and the sneering, raging belligerent who spoke on the radio, calling his foes crooks, scheming politicians, insincere office seekers, and fornicators.

With Douglas firmly in their pocket, the UFA government targeted their chief tormentor — Aberhart. On March 7, 1935, Premier Reid invited him to Edmonton for the purpose of "preparing and submitting a comprehensive Social Credit plan for the consideration of the legislature." The hope was that Aberhart's ego would lure him into another public examination by Brownlee, who could then rip his half-formed ideas to shreds.

But the wily Aberhart didn't bite. He instead entered into a protracted correspondence with Reid, asking complicated questions about how the government would use such a plan. Finally Aberhart said he would have to canvass the constituency organizations for their advice. He did, and their answer was a resounding "No."

Yet demands for Aberhart's Social Credit plan kept recurring. The *Calgary Herald* conducted a lively, open correspondence with him, offering its pages if only he would unveil the details of his intentions. The conservative establishment knew, of course, that Aberhart had no plan, only a set of aphorisms and homilies. "One does not have to understand electricity to turn on a light switch," he would say whenever hecklers zeroed in on his vague rhetoric. Predictably he spurned the *Herald*'s offer, citing its increasingly negative coverage.

Still there had been no formal announcement of the movement's decision to run. Interestingly enough, it came from Edith Gostick, an Aberhart disciple with a peculiar ability to reduce his many critics to a state of incoherent rage. On March 4, 1935, in a speech at Lethbridge she revealed there would be a Social Credit candidate in every constituency where the straw vote indicated support. This, as it happened, meant every constituency in the province. It also meant a convention. Under Aberhart's watchful eye, two were called — one in Calgary for April 4-5, one in Edmonton for April 25-26 — because delegates couldn't afford long trips.

More than 2,000 delegates and observers filled the Bible Institute on April 5 for the world's first Social Credit political assembly. Proceedings opened with the hymn *O God Our Help In Ages Past*, a requisite at all Alberta Social Credit gatherings. Yet the mood was far from solemn, say historians David R. Elliott and Iris Miller in *Bible Bill: A Biography of William Aberhart* (Edmonton, Reidmore Books, 1987). The southern convention was a "care-free affair" and soaked in the "crusading spirit" that Aberhart could so effectively excite.

There was one sticky question: how would candidates be chosen? "If you are not going to let me have any say in the choice of my supporters, you're not going to have me as your leader," the *Calgary Herald* of April 5 quoted Aberhart as warning delegates. They thereupon endorsed a resolution empowering a special committee chaired by Aberhart to choose candidates from a list of four offered by each constituency.

"Autocratic Rule For New Party," sniped the *Calgary Herald*, describing the ideal Social Credit candidate as "one who will carry out the views of the leader to the letter. He must be docile and prepared to follow orders. Freedom is denied."Another resolution stipulated that Aberhart not run for a specific seat, thereby freeing him to campaign everywhere and escape the embarrassment of a personal defeat. The Edmonton convention came as a repeat performance.

That April Aberhart called on his followers to boycott anti-Social Credit newspapers, particularly the *Calgary Herald*. "I don't think you'll miss it if you don't have it. I think you can get the news in another way. Some of the citizens of this province cannot distinguish falsity from truth. I'm cancelling my subscription tomorrow. What about yours?"

Edith Gostick of Calgary was one of Aberhart's most devoted and strident supporters.

'I am not ambitious. The spirit of Christ has gripped me. I am only seeking to feed, clothe and shelter starving people. If that is what you call a dictator, then I am one,' Aberhart told the *Calgary Herald*.

The *Herald* replied with a stinging editorial: "Surely, it is very surprising to find the leader of a Christian movement and the head of a political party inviting his followers to injure an established industry which employs a large number of citizens... He has invoked a most dangerous precedent and has given the people of this province a foretaste of the Hitlerism which will prevail if he ever secures control of the provincial administration."

Sales of the *Calgary Herald* dropped considerably, as did those of other critical papers. One Drumheller weekly was forced out of business by Aberhart's boycott. The publisher, Archie Kay, a Social Credit convention delegate, had not supported Aberhart's candidate selection plan.

It was by now becoming plain to those who watched him that there were two Aberharts — the kindly, hearty Aberhart whom people knew personally, and the sneering, raging belligerent who spoke on the radio. "I am getting on in years," the amiable Aberhart told the *Calgary Herald* of May 7, 1935. "I am not ambitious. The spirit of Christ has gripped me. I am only seeking to feed, clothe and shelter starving people. If that is what you call a dictator, then I am one."

"But on radio," writes the historian-educator Timothy Clark Byrne, Aberhart spouted "ridicule to his critics, often using vituperative language. He labelled critics as crooks, scheming politicians, insincere office seekers, and the like. He branded one person, whom he did not name, as being guilty, not only of fornication, but also of grafting and hypocrisy." His anger towards the UFA, which had spurned him, knew few bounds.

In every radio broadcast he assailed the farm organization, referring to the United Farm Women of Alberta as the "Undernourished Fool Women of Alberta." On February 24 he fumed: "They say I won't co-operate. No, Sir, I will not co-operate with the Devil. I am going to fight the

Brownlee, Hoadley, McPherson and Company have cast over Alberta politics that lure of personal scandal which causes the most indifferent to become politically conscious.
—S. Delbert Clark, *The Canadian Forum*, December 1933.

Devil... People will not be bull-dozed, buffaloed... by the people who want to graft. God will open the Red Sea."

Against this tirade the UFA chose its scholarly vice-president Norman Priestley, a former clergyman, to refute the Social Credit leader's broadcasts point by point on radio. "For seven months Priestley argued brilliantly and tirelessly against what he, as well as other UFA leaders, considered an utterly irrational approach to economics, politics and religion," writes historian Irving. "But there can be little doubt that his clear and forceful broadcasts failed to appeal to the economically dispossessed people of Alberta. The vice-president of the UFA was certainly out-debated..."

In the run-up to the election call, Alberta's political atmosphere can only be described as frenzied. Rural church congregations were often divided into Social Crediters on one side of the aisle and UFA supporters on the other, a split fomented by Aberhart's incendiary oratory. "Aberhart has become wild and abusive. Temporarily he has stirred up some communities to a pitch of hysteria and intolerance and created an ugly spirit," wrote editor Norman Smith of the UFA newspaper in a letter to Progressive MP Henry Spencer. "I can understand more fully now how Hitler made himself a power... It takes courage in some farm communities to stand out at the moment against him. The slightest difference of opinion is treated as an insult."

In the midst of all this fervour, on May 12 Douglas returned to Alberta, following a train trip across Canada that saw him besieged by reporters, all looking for a word or phrase that would demonstrate a split with Aberhart. He realized also that his contract with the UFA government rendered him treasonous in the eyes of many Albertans. He was therefore circumspect. "Mr. Aberhart is supplying the dynamic will of the people toward reorganization of the economic sys-

Douglas departed Edmonton for Montreal, $4,500 richer. The government had also picked up the expenses of Douglas's private secretary at the Hotel Macdonald.

tem, and to that extent, he has the whole of my sympathy," Douglas told the Canadian Press in Winnipeg. But at the same time this "short jovial man," as CP described him, politely refused to endorse Aberhart's central plank of a $25 monthly dividend for citizens. "Technically, I have very little doubt it is possible, but politically I see difficulty in its execution and much political trench warfare."

Douglas was wined and dined by the government, even going so far as to play a round of golf with his UFA employers. "How do you account for the fact that [Douglas] accepted the present government's proposal," Manning asked Aberhart on a Sunday broadcast. "I do not know," Aberhart replied. "Time will tell."

But Douglas's governmental hosts were far from impressed with their new employee, as Reid made it clear in an interview for the Provincial Archives taped years later. In public he indicated that Social Credit could be applied by a province and would not require constitutional amendments. He expressed very different opinions to Premier Reid privately. Reid recalled: "On the third day of our exploratory discussions I said to him, 'Mr. Douglas, you probably realize I don't know very much about Social Credit. My mind has been filled with other things, what I may consider of more importance. But you do say that all of your policy can be brought into effect without disturbing the status-quo, of the financial set-up, the banks, for instance.'

"In reply he stated that that was correct. 'But really,' he said, 'I'm afraid it can't be done, unless we nationalize the banks.' As a matter of fact, my thoughts had reached the same conclusions so I wasn't surprised but I was amazed he admitted it... If this, the real source of Social Credit, was a polluted source, then what right had we to bother with it?" Reid concluded.

Ten days after he arrived in Edmonton Douglas submitted his interim report on a Social Credit plan for Alberta and met Aberhart for lunch at the Hotel Macdonald the next day, May 24. It was the first meeting between the two men since their cursing match in Calgary's Sarcee Armoury in 1934. Douglas obviously whispered some of the details of his report over lunch with Aberhart because the Social Credit leader was effusive when he addressed 4,000 Edmontonians at a Social Credit rally the same evening.

Imagine yourself to be a decent, hard-working farmer who has undergone every kind of agricultural ordeal: he has been made the buffeted plaything of the high tariff manipulators; he has built up markets in the United States which have been ruthlessly cut off; he has suffered drought and every other agricultural pestilence from root rot to grasshoppers; he has seen prices drop to incredibly low levels, and he has not even been able to sell what he had at those levels; he is discouraged, down-hearted and broke. He owes everybody more money than he thinks he will ever see again, and because he is a decent fellow, it worries him.

Then he tunes in on his radio, and he hears a voice explaining with unbounded confidence that his troubles can all be simply solved by a little juggling of currency and credit. Jehovah speaking from Sinai could not have spoken with more assurance, and the children of Israel were never so discouraged as the Alberta farmers are today. The Israelites had manna. The Albertans have no manna— not yet. But Mr. Aberhart has promised them something better. He has promised them money, cash money in amounts they have almost forgotten. Real, honest-to-God cash in hand, $25 a month. This is the real thing, and who will blame them if the don't tumble over themselves to get on the Social Credit bandwagon?
—G.V. Ferguson, The Canadian Forum, April 1935.

The size of the crowd "was my second delight of the day," he told the *Edmonton Journal*. "The first was when I took hold of the hand of the originator of this movement, Major C.H. Douglas. I had hoped that he would be present on this platform to speak to you, but he is in the employ of the government... I hope he will be able to speak later." Aberhart then advised the cheering audience to watch out for the Douglas Report. "Have it put in your hands," he said, "and you'll see what this genius is preparing for your welfare."

The cautious and bewildered UFA government did not release Douglas's interim report until June 5. To the government it was plainly worthless. Douglas proposed that a special credit institution, much like a bank, be created; Alberta's government would have to accumulate federal currency, stocks and bonds, to use in "foreign exchange," or interprovincial trade. He also called for a systematic news-circulation system that would be unchallengeable by critics.

In an accompanying letter to Premier Reid he suggested it might be necessary to form a coalition government, obviously with Aberhart, if Social Credit was to be realized. Finally he said a government public relations department was needed to discourage "by suitable methods loose accusations of defective administration," in other words, censorship. Douglas believed all of his ideas could be accomplished without amendments to the British North America Act, a high improbability.

Douglas was also careful not to tread too heavily on Aberhart. He noted that Aberhart's definition of the "just price" was different from Social Credit theory. Neither could he see how Aberhart's $25 dividend would increase purchasing power. However, he added, newspapers were distorting and exaggerating their differences. In his typically hyperbolic rhetoric he explained: "In view of certain mischievous comments in the public press suggesting the existence of wholly non-existent friction in regard to our personal relations, I think it is desirable to assure you that no statement in regard to matters in Alberta which is not a written statement signed by me, has any authority from me, and to suggest that even in regard to such written statements or reports, if you consider them important, that you should assure yourself that they are complete and not detached from matter that modify their meaning."

With that, Douglas departed Edmonton for Montreal, $4,500 richer, according to the *Edmonton Journal*, which further noted that the government had also picked up the expenses of Douglas's private secretary at the posh Macdonald. Premier Reid and his cabinet would eventually pay $7,000 for the "Douglas Report" whose complete text it published in pamphlet form under the title "First Interim Report on the Possibilities of the Application of Social Credit Principles to the Province of Alberta." Few read it.

Aberhart meanwhile produced a new manifesto to replace the Yellow Pamphlet that had caused so much trouble with Douglas's London secretariat in 1934. The new 64-page booklet was officially titled *Social Credit as Applied to the Province of Alberta*, but quickly became known as The Blue Manual because of its colour. It sold like wildfire at 25 cents a copy.

While the contents of the booklet were as vague as the Douglas Report, it softened some of Social Credit's more radical proposals. There was still a plan to restrict high incomes, but Aberhart was careful to dissociate his movement from fascism, socialism and confiscation, the worst nightmares of what was left of Alberta's tattered middle class in the Depression. It also purported to answer "Sixty Puzzling Questions," an attempt to address the concerns of farmers, small businessmen and others.

By July Aberhart's Social Credit party seemed unstoppable. The tacit alliance between the major newspapers and the UFA to discredit and destroy it had utterly failed. Everything the UFA tried had backfired; it now had nothing left to offer at the end of five years of Depression. Premier Reid dropped the writ on July 16 for an August 22, 1935, election. It was to prove one of the most extraordinary in Canadian history.

Reid lived to be a great age. He fought Social Credit through the Aberhart era, attempting without success to organize inter-party coalitions against the movement. He outlived Aberhart by 37 years and saw the Social Credit regime finally succumb to history as his own UFA had done, though nowhere near as precipitously. He died at Edmonton in 1980, three days before his 102nd birthday. This photo was taken three years before his death.

We were in the middle of that campaign that finally destroyed us, where we were pictured as being anything from incompetent to something worse...It was not long after this, however, before the promises of $25 a month and others similarly attractive began to show their effects. In Alberta the people were listening to the voice of the tempter. In the east, was there likely to be a change of government? And if so, what would their credit rating be?
—Richard Gavin Reid, in an interview preserved in the Provincial Archives of Alberta

Bill Aberhart slept four hours a night, worked tirelessly, fighting constantly with churches, inspectors, teachers

He paid his way through university, ran a showpiece high school, and turned a Bible class into the biggest radio audience in Alberta

William "Bible Bill" Aberhart is the stuff of Alberta mythology, a swashbuckling Bible-thumper, who to this day defines the provincial psyche in the minds of many Canadians who rely on media stereotypes.

Yet Aberhart was far from the simplistic evangelist so cherished by Hollywood screen writers and jaded newspaper columnists. The seventh premier of Alberta was undoubtedly the most radical one that Canada has ever seen.

We know the political record, but what kind of forces forged Aberhart and what kind of man not only ended the 14-year reign of the United Farmers' government in Alberta but wiped them off the political map in the process?

Some of the genes that made Aberhart such a rebel probably came from his grandparents. William and Sophia Eberhardt lived in the Grand Duchy of Mecklenburg in Western Prussia. William died during or shortly after the revolution of 1848, leaving Sophia to raise six children.

Aberhart's grandmother either fled or was expelled from Prussia, along with a second husband, Christopher Heffler, a widower some twenty years her senior, for refusing to pay taxes to the repressive government, according to David R. Elliott and Iris Miller in *Bible Bill: A Biography of William Aberhart* (Edmonton, Reidmore, 1987).

The unlucky immigrant family was apparently shipwrecked off the coast of Newfoundland and avaricious sailors demanded payment before the terrified immigrants were allowed to board lifeboats. Poorer and chastened, the family made its way up the St. Lawrence River, ending up in Hamilton, Ontario, where they journeyed by oxcart to settle in Egmontville, Huron County.

Aberhart's father, William (1843-1910), was the fourth child in the brood. He was only seven when the family arrived in Canada, but was soon put to work with the rest of the family, and as a result was illiterate. If he couldn't spell his name the same way twice — it appears on official documents variously as Eberhardt or Aberhardt, eventually settling on Aberhart — William Sr. was a hard-working man who thrived on manual labour.

Starting as a blacksmith's helper in Egmontville, he later worked in the salt mines of nearby Seaforth and slowly amassed parcels of land. By 1871 he had his own farm and had married Louisa Pepper (1848-1944) of Perth County who bore him eight children. William Sr. was well known in the community and recognized by his flowing blond beard and penetrating blue eyes.

"His beard was worn in Mennonite fashion and blew over his shoulders as he drove his high-spirited team through the countryside," write Elliott and Miller. "William Sr. took no active part in the community... other than occasionally joining his friends for drinks at the local tavern."

The child who was to be the seventh premier of Alberta was born December 30, 1878, the fourth child and third son. Powerfully built like his father, he had a voracious appetite, rose at 4 a.m. and joined his brothers in milking the family's forty cows. Later in the morning on their way to school the children delivered milk to their father's customers in Egmontville.

Such a regimen was not considered harsh and Aberhart thrived on it. At school he was only an average student, but developed special skills in penmanship and mathematics. "He had amazing powers of concentration and retention... but his dependence on his photographic memory had a deleterious effect: he never came to value inductive reasoning," write Elliott and Miller.

The Aberhart family, nominally Presbyterian, provided a good home for all their children and encouraged them to get

As a teenager, William Aberhart was already drawn to the brand of fundamentalist Christianity that would permeate the rest of his life.

an education, but there was little warmth or affection in the description of family life provided by biographers. Aberhart seemed to turn inward as a child, becoming a solitary fellow in many ways. He taught himself to play several musical instruments and developed numerous hobbies that absorbed his considerable energies.

He was also mischievous. His father caught him smoking corn silk wrapped in copy paper once, and on another occasion he is said to have coaxed some chewing tobacco out of a hired man on the farm, an experience that made him sick. He was proud of his physique and took pride in flexing his muscles for the family. To further improve his body, Aberhart constructed horizontal bars and used them in vigorous workouts. "There was much flipping over and swinging about, interspersed with not wholly successful handstands with heels to the skyward," L.P.V. Johnson and Ola MacNutt, one of Aberhart's two daughters, write in their *Aberhart of Alberta* (Edmonton, Institute of Applied Art, 1970).

Fearing broken bones William Sr. forbade any more athletic displays and ordered his son to break down the horizontal bars. "Young William stopped — that day," write Johnson and MacNutt. "But next day, in a final workout, just prior to the dismantling of the bars, he came to grief in an abortive handstand and, falling, broke his collar bone," early evidence of the stubbornness that would make him premier of Alberta. In high school Aberhart blossomed as a competitive athlete and a bit of a social butterfly. He won first place in the running high jump, long jump, senior shot-put, 100-yard dash and the bicycle race and became something of a hero on the football field.

It was in high school, however, that Aberhart experienced a spiritual crisis. John A. Irving in his *The Social Credit Movement in Alberta* (University of Toronto Press, 1959) suggests Aberhart was influenced by itinerant evangelists. Whatever the cause, Aberhart shed the nominal Presbyterianism of his family for intense Bible study and a peculiar brand of Christian fundamentalism (see Vol.5, pp.152-155).

After high school Aberhart took Normal School training and received his interim first class teaching certificate in 1899. At Wingham, Ontario, he taught all the primary grades for two school years, then a school inspector recommended him for a permanent first-class certificate, citing his ability to discipline, order and manage a school. This took him to Brantford's Central Public School, where he ran a commercial class and earned a princely $600 a year. On a weekend trip to Hamilton in the summer of 1901 he met Jessie Flatt and after initial doubts that she might be a "social butterfly" the two were wed on July 19, 1902. Their first daughter, Khona Louise, was born in 1903, and she was joined two years later by another girl, Ola Janet.

Mrs. Aberhart, by all accounts a fun-loving young

Aberhart's "Back To the Bible" radio program had endeared him to most of southern and central Alberta by the time he entered the political arena.

woman, found herself married to a bit of a prude. By now he disapproved of frivolities, the theatre, cards, drinking and smoking. He was chiding his parents as religious backsliders and running his classes with military discipline, assigning numbers to his students, and stamping their homework assignments, "Checked by Wm. Aberhart." Slight misdemeanours brought strappings, more serious offences recommendations for suspension or expulsion. Though this may have appalled his biographers of a later era, it didn't disturb his superiors who named him principal of Central High at a salary of $1,000.

Principalship and fatherhood were not enough. He became an itinerant Sunday preacher as well, strongly influenced by men like Arno C. Gaebelein, editor of the fundamentalist magazine *Our Hope*, and Dwight L. Moody, the former shoe salesman who started the Bible institute that bears his name. "He looked longingly at the course of Knox College Divinity School," says the Johnson-MacNutt biography, "but it would require four years of study and financing by the church" which could not finance a candidate with a wife and two children. Author John Irving has another explanation. He quotes an unidentified contemporary as asserting: "[Aberhart] got in wrong with the ministers and officials of the church because of his high-handed methods and his tendency to condemn all who were not of his opinion."

Undaunted, Aberhart enrolled in a correspondence program from Queen's University, carried all his responsibilities and earned first-class honours in mathematics. He also failed Greek twice, Hebrew once and received only 35 per cent in political science. After four years of study he was awarded a Bachelor of Arts in 1911.

He then sought entry to Knox College at the University of Toronto, but fate intervened. Teaching colleagues who had gone West told of his talents to the Calgary School Board, which offered him $1,400 to take over its new Alexandra School. His staff and fifty students at Brantford's Central High petitioned the school board to keep him, but Brantford couldn't match the price. When he arrived in Calgary, during the Easter holidays of 1910, he headed for church wearing his customary silk top hat and frock coat, only to discover that such formal attire produced bemused

The energetic principal also plunged into Calgary's religious life. He started teaching a Bible class for men at Central Methodist Church, soon became substitute preacher at Trinity Methodist, a working-class congregation, then got part-time preaching assignments in other Methodist, Presbyterian and Baptist churches. He started a Bible class at St. Andrew's Presbyterian, which his family attended, endearing himself to the congregation though not to the minister, who found his teachings about the second coming of Christ far too radical.

So Aberhart took his admirers and Bible students with him to Trinity Methodist Church two blocks away, where his Bible classes so captivated his students they seemed unwilling to leave when the class was over. His family now attended fashionable Grace Presbyterian, where he became president of the men's fellowship group and established a popular advanced Bible class.

What is known of William Aberhart's family life gives no clue as to the reason for his religious conversion. The future "Bible Bill" is standing to the left of his father.

But all did not go well at Grace either. He once used a $2 donation from his Bible class offering to help a hospitalized member of the congregation, found himself being criticized for unauthorized use of church funds, and was asked by the minister, the Rev. Alexander Esler, to leave. This took him to Calgary's Wesley Methodist, where his Bible class was swelled by members from St. Andrew's and Grace.

So it went and by 1915 Aberhart had become a familiar figure in Calgary — 37 years old, six-foot-four, 240 pounds and bald as a billiard ball. His administrative genius and charismatic teaching abilities were always subject to the caveat of his radical religious ideas. People either loved or hated him. That year, however, he achieved a career coup, the principalship of the newly organized Crescent Heights High School at an initial salary of $2,250, gradually increased to $4,200. It took the next thirteen years for the school to be completed and become the crown jewel of the Calgary Board of Education.

stares in the pews of that frontier city.

He was made principal of Victoria School for the remainder of the school year, and the Aberharts moved into their new two-storey house at 1216 13th Avenue SW, where they would live for the next seventeen years. In September Aberhart was made principal of Alexandra (later Mount Royal) School. Two years later he became the principal of King Edward School, at $2,100 a year.

But as usual Aberhart provoked two reactions. Irving quotes two anonymous teachers who served under him. "He was held in the very highest esteem by his fellow teachers who early recognized him as a leader among them," said

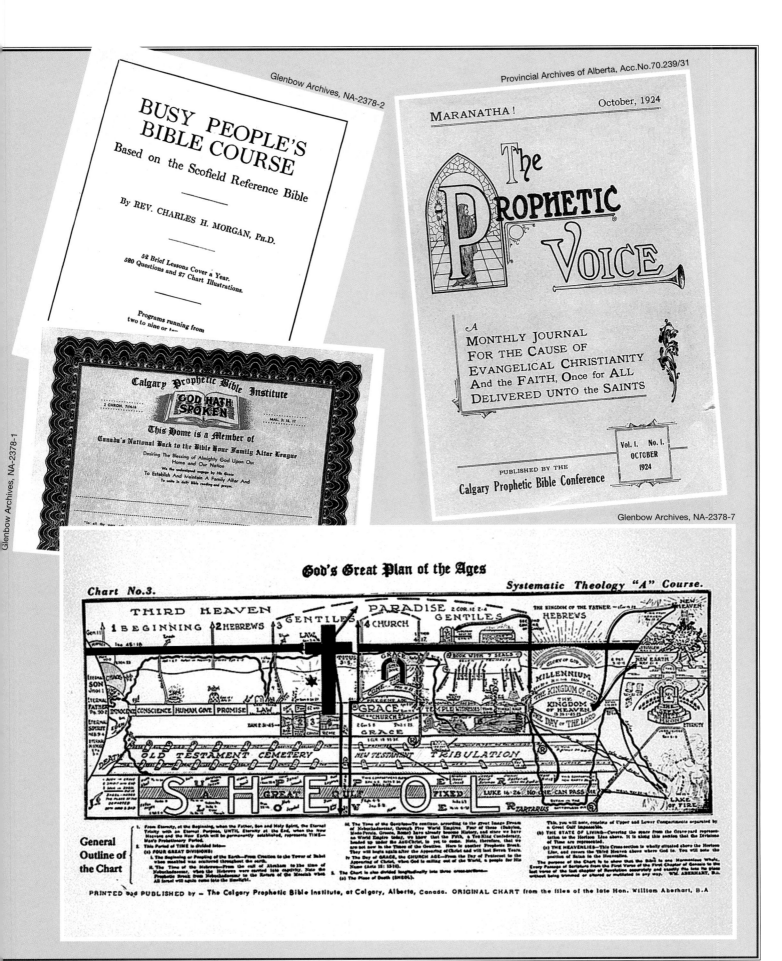

BUSY PEOPLE'S BIBLE COURSE

Based on the Scofield Reference Bible

By REV. CHARLES H. MORGAN, Ph.D.

52 Brief Lessons Cover a Year.
520 Questions and 27 Chart Illustrations.

Programs running from
two to nine or ten...

MARANATHA!   October, 1924

The PROPHETIC VOICE

A MONTHLY JOURNAL
FOR THE CAUSE OF
EVANGELICAL CHRISTIANITY
And the FAITH, Once for ALL
DELIVERED UNTO the SAINTS

Vol. I.   No. I.
OCTOBER
1924

PUBLISHED BY THE
Calgary Prophetic Bible Conference

Calgary Prophetic Bible Institute

GOD HATH SPOKEN

2 CHRON. 7:14-15   MAL. 3: 16, 17

This Home is a Member of
Canada's National Back to the Bible Hour Family Altar League

Desiring The Blessing of Almighty God Upon Our
Home and Our Nation
We the undersigned engage by His Grace
To Establish And Maintain A Family Altar And
To unite in daily Bible reading and prayer.

God's Great Plan of the Ages

Chart No.3.   Systematic Theology "A" Course.

General
Outline of
the Chart

PRINTED and PUBLISHED by — The Calgary Prophetic Bible Institute, at Calgary, Alberta, Canada. ORIGINAL CHART from the files of the late Hon. William Aberhart, B.A.

one. "Students, too, respected and admired their principal. He was always eminently fair in his dealings with young people, and former pupils recall that he was never too busy to listen patiently to both sides of a story."

The other, described by Irving as thoughtful and well-informed, considered Aberhart "a good dog-trainer, or perhaps we should say a good drillmaster. He wanted his students to learn their tricks mechanically, and never mind the reasons for them."

Meanwhile, the Bible classes continued to thrive and create controversy with various church establishments. He became the first preacher at the new Westbourne Baptist and moved his Bible classes there after a wrangle with Trinity Methodist. By now the pattern was becoming familiar. When he arrived at each new church Aberhart would roll up his sleeves, take on all jobs and all opposition. Inevitably, a theological or personality dispute developed

continued to thrive and grow, the classes being held in the public library.

In 1918 they acquired the name, the Calgary Prophetic Bible Conference, and the following year they had to rent space in the Grand Theatre and later the Palace Theatre which had a 2,200-person capacity, Aberhart filling it every Sunday.

By then he found himself in another war at Crescent Heights where eight senior teachers rebelled against their principal's high-handed ways and called for a full investigation. School inspectors transferred three male teachers to other schools and the school board made it plain that any more staff problems at Crescent Heights would result in a call for resignations, including the principal's. Aberhart did not change either his attitude or his methods by a whiff.

He lived in a whirlwind — four hours' sleep a night, teaching at and running Crescent Heights each day, evenings and weekends devoted to Bible classes and preaching, long discussions with his students, endless games of chess, of which he was so enamoured that he wrote a manual on the game.

Aberhart's family appears to have supported of his ambitions, although they did not share his evangelical fervour. (L-R): Daughters Ola Janet MacNutt and Khona Louise Cooper; Aberhart's wife, Jessie.

Somehow his family life remained strong. On the rare nights he was free, he liked to hole up in his second-floor study and read or prepare lessons into the early morning hours. The Johnson-MacNutt biography paints an almost fawning portrait. "As husband and wife,

and Aberhart moved to a new spiritual home.

At Westbourne, however, he was virtually in control of the church, though not an ordained minister, or a deacon, or even a Baptist. Naturally, the Baptist Union of Western Canada, under which Westbourne Baptist operated, took exception to this. Led by Thomas Underwood, a prominent Baptist and former Calgary mayor, the central body stipulated that Westbourne should show its loyalty to the church union by removing Aberhart if it expected funding. Tempers rose and one Sunday the Westbourne congregation found the church doors locked against them. A notice on the doors stated that this was the action of the trustees from First Baptist Church, which had sponsored the Westbourne congregation.

This launched a four-year feud between Aberhart and the Baptist establishment during which Aberhart's Bible class

William and Jessie Aberhart added practical understanding to their mutual love and respect," they write. Jessie was the mistress of her own home. "She won this autonomy by competence and understanding, by the will to make a happy restful home for her sometimes harassed husband."

The Elliott-Miller work seeks evidence of underlying strife but has trouble finding it. "Although the Aberharts gave the impression of being a markedly happy and united family, close friends claimed otherwise," they write. There was some tension regarding their religious values... Aberhart's strong evangelical urge was not shared by his family and he did not press the issue..." Jessie's interests, they say, were more "urbane." She belonged to the Women's Canadian Club, the Red Cross, the YMCA and YWCA.

In 1920, Aberhart came in contact with Pastor Harvey McAlister, a member of Canada's first Pentecostal family who had revived charismatic Christianity in Canada with its phenomenon of speaking in tongues. The McAlister ideas interested Aberhart, especially total immersion baptism, long practised by the Baptists but which Aberhart, raised Presbyterian, had not experienced. Thus on May 20, 1920, he was baptized by total immersion at Westbourne Baptist Church, a spiritual bath that seemed to renew his religious fervour. One effect was to gradually turn Westbourne Baptist Church and his Prophetic Bible Conference into a theological sect of its own.

By the mid-1920s the Prophetic Bible Conference had a membership in the thousands and Aberhart consented to hiring a full-time minister at Westbourne. In 1924 he established a bimonthly magazine, *The Prophetic Voice*, dedicated to "the Cause of Evangelical Christianity and the Faith, Once For All Delivered Unto the Saints." This further enlarged his following.

But it was only a beginning. The phenomenon of radio had arrived in Alberta by 1922. W.W. Grant, owner of CFCN Calgary, was probably the first person to suggest Aberhart hit the airwaves. At first Aberhart was reluctant. "If I broadcast, people won't come to the theatre, and there will be no col-

Aberhart tentatively broached the idea of a new building to his burgeoning radio audience. The money rolled in. Soon a lot was purchased at 516 8th Avenue SW for $5,300. His radio appeals eventually raised $30,000. When accountants estimated a further $35,000 was needed to complete the building, Aberhart was unfazed. He issued bonds at eight per cent interest and boasted of the deal during his Sunday religious broadcasts. "The banks will give you five per cent, but I will give you eight," he declared. The issue was over-subscribed.

On Sunday, October 2, 1927, the Calgary Prophetic Bible Institute threw open its doors leading to a main auditorium accommodating 1,200 people. There were also numerous classrooms.

"Aberhart preached three times on opening day," writes Harold J. Schultz in his 1959 Duke University doctoral thesis, *William Aberhart and the Social Credit Party*.

Westbourne Baptist's deacons closed the doors of their old church and moved into the institute at Aberhart's invitation. They even volunteered to pay $600 a month in upkeep. However four months later the Westbourne deacons left in a huff when they couldn't maintain the $600 pay-

Many teachers respected and admired Aberhart, and students said he always had time to listen to them. Others called him 'a good dog-trainer' or maybe, said some, 'a good drillmaster.'

lection," he said. He was finally persuaded to try one experimental broadcast from the Palace Theatre.

"Aberhart, with extreme reluctance, went on the air," writes Irving. "'He trembled,' one of his followers has said, at the thought of broadcasting. Indeed, he was in abject terror as he faced the microphone." Much to his surprise financial contributions poured in after the broadcast and he was deluged in mail from people all over Alberta. W.W. Grant got a five-month contract to produce the *Back to the Bible Hour*.

No radio show in Alberta would ever equal it. "At the height of his fame," says Irving, "CFCN estimated that 350,000 people were listening to the Sunday afternoon broadcasts, which were then being heard throughout the three prairie provinces, as far west as the Okanagan Valley of British Columbia and in the American mountain states." Radio turned the evangelist into a star; Aberhart became larger than life in the eyes of his listeners. His ratings in Alberta were higher than those of the famous American comedian Jack Benny who followed Aberhart on CFCN.

Meanwhile, back at Westbourne, all was not well. The Rev. E.G. Hansell found himself administering to a flock of less than 200 by April 1926. But Aberhart had lost interest in Westbourne. He had a new crusade. He wanted to build his own temple, free of meddling pastors and hand-wringing deacons, a Bible institute in which one man was in charge.

ment and returned to their old church, taking most of their flock with them.

"Aberhart's first interest now became the Bible school and he undoubtedly would have enjoyed resigning from Crescent Heights to give full time to it," writes Schultz. "Somehow he managed to keep on at high school and still give full time to the Institute... He was president of the Calgary Prophetic Bible Institute Church, Dean of the Institute and 'apostle' of the church."

But the untiring evangelist had gained complete control over his religious domain just four months before the 1929 stock market crash. Soon the Depression began to set in and it affected, among other things, his radio audience and their contributions. This, say Elliott and Miller, played a part in his eventual embrace of Social Credit.

It also raised the central questions about the man. Was he a real believer or a mere opportunist? Was he zealous saint or ideological tyrant? Certainly there was much of the bully in the way he ran his church, his school and the legislature of Alberta, and yes, he could be mean-spirited, as so many encounters with rival pastors and other teachers have shown. Yet he could laugh at his own expense, and was always willing to ditch the prosaic for the exotic, if he found another yellow brick road to glory. Not even history can say.

—*G.O.*

CHAPTER FIVE

In the tumultuous election of '35, Albertans vote for a revolution

IT'S ABSURD, IT'S RURAL, IT'S GOING NOWHERE, SAID THE NEWSPAPERS, BUT IT TOOK 56 OF 63 SEATS, MOSTLY ON THAT PROMISE OF $25 A MONTH

by RIC DOLPHIN

Twenty-five dollars a month was a lot of money in 1935. It was the mortgage payment on the kind of house that would admit one to the comfortable middle class; it was the monthly instalment on a brand-new Ford car; it was the kind of money that could propel a family from destitution to sufficiency or from sufficiency to plenty. To a populace that had suffered five winters without Christmas, twenty-five dollars a month was the tinkle of sleighbells on the rooftop, the promise of Santa Claus and sugarplums.

In the election summer of 1935, the greatest concern to the great majority of Alberta voters was getting out of the hole of the Depression. And the only party that was making a tangible promise in this regard was William Aberhart's Social Credit, with its assurance of a "basic dividend" of twenty-five dollars a month to each of the province's 400,000 adults — this, and a lot of other stuff about "the unearned increment of real credit secured by association of the consumers" that even its leader didn't seem to fully understand.

That this was this golden carrot that accounted for the unprecedented landslide victory of Social Credit on August 22, 1935, was doubted by no political commentator at the time and no historian ever since.

"Ask your local Social Credit supporter why he is voting Social Credit," wrote a woman from Balzac who identified herself simply as a "Farmer's Wife," in one of the many letters to the *Calgary Herald* in the weeks before the election. "All he knows is that his 'Moses' has promised him twenty-five dollars per month. How is he to get it, who from, or who has to suffer doesn't worry him. Santa Claus has told him to trust and believe, ask no questions, and all will be well."

This woman, doubtless a stalwart of the rapidly evaporating United Farm Women of Alberta, was raising a voice in the wilderness in the summer of 1935. By the time the election writ had been dropped on July 16, the UFA, once a radical force that had defeated the Liberals in 1921 by 39 seats to 14 on the promise of curing the near-depression of the postwar years, had become the Grinch who Stole Christmas — and a rather lecherous Grinch at that. In a province where the average farm income was now $250 a year, there weren't many farmers and farmers' wives who weren't ready to give Santa Claus a chance.

At the ever more crowded Social Credit rallies in the towns around Alberta that summer, even the better-off women could be heard discussing the new linoleum they'd be putting in the kitchen when the dividend payments came through, or the brand-new Beatty washing machine that at least one rural candidate had promised them they'd be able to afford after the election. There would be a record number of women voters in this election.

But while never failing to respond to the No.1 question that came in about Social Credit — when do the dividends start coming? (answer: about 18 months after the election) — Aberhart and his lieutenants insisted, as they would for years after, that the twenty-five dollars had not been intended as a main plank of their platform. It had just popped up in passing, a "by the way" comment in an Aberhart speech. Even the amount was unsubstantial. Aberhart had more than once called it twenty dollars. During one appearance in Edmonton in August, he casually allowed that it could be raised to as much as seventy-five.

Begun as an underground network of study groups, no one in 1935 knew how many supporters the Social Credit movement had. As a result Aberhart's political asperations were not taken serious by many in the established parties right up until the date of the election itself. What was well known, however, was that the near-legendary oratorical skills of the seasoned radio evangelist could and did draw big crowds.

On the eve of the election, Arch Dale let Winnipeg Free Press *readers know what he thought the chances were that Albertans would receive the promised $25-a-month dividend.*

Ernest Manning, Aberhart's Boswellian foil on the radio shows and destined to become Alberta's longest-serving premier, later recalled that the Social Credit leader had thrown out the figure when he was asked how he would supercharge the purchasing power of the consumer. "In those days," said Manning, "with living costs being very low, twenty-five dollars a month was about what you'd need for the bare necessities of life. So he said, about twenty-five dollars a month would be a reasonable dividend. That was the start of the famous twenty-five dollars a month for everybody, which was seized on immediately as a firm, magic figure. It was talked about all over Canada and all over the world, I guess."

But apart from the twenty-five dollars other factors plainly contributed to the August 22 election phenomenon. One was the element of surprise. The result came like a bombshell. Almost no one, in or out of the movement, realized the massive proportions of the electoral turnaround. One exception, significantly, was Aberhart himself, who two days before the vote called the number of Social Credit seats almost exactly. Despite the fevered interest in the Social Credit theory, despite the thunderous outdoor rallies that could draw four thousand or five thousand supporters a time in little towns like Derwent or Marwayne, despite Aberhart's bully pulpit on Calgary's CFCN (and later Edmonton's CFRN) that drew an estimated 300,000 listeners every Sunday, none of his opponents or the newspapers that supported them could quite bring themselves to believe that what they saw as a square-headed Biblical literalist with his pie-in-the-sky promises and a platoon of untried politicians could do much more than form an absurd rump.

"In spite of the seeming popularity of the Social Credit movement and the reaction against the idiocy of the Depression," wrote the southeastern Alberta Social Credit candidate Norman James, voicing a common view, "I really didn't have much hope of winning, though I talked bravely and glibly of its being 'in the bag.' My opponents were old campaigners with well-oiled machinery to use. We were greenhorns, blundering along with nothing much but an objective."

In fact, of all the contemporary observers one journalist alone sensed the scale of the voter revolution. That was Fred Kennedy, a reporter with the Conservative *Calgary Herald*, assigned in 1930 to keep an eye on Aberhart's Prophetic Bible Institute.[1] He wasn't to file any stories, merely write confidential reports for *Herald* publisher Colonel O. Leigh Spencer, a Tory concerned by the

[1] Kennedy would become the only reporter Aberhart ever trusted, probably because they had one thing in common: Christianity. A devout Catholic, Kennedy was chairman of the Calgary Separate School Board, an unusual situation for a reporter even in those days. In many ways Kennedy would become Aberhart's severest critic because he would accost him, often to his face, on Aberhart's failures to follow elementary moral principles, like keeping promises and telling the truth. Unlike other journalists, however, Kennedy realized the ultimate secret of Social Credit success. Right or wrong, it had a plan; the Liberals, Conservatives and UFA did not. Their ultimate message to Albertans was: keep on suffering.

developing political content of Aberhart's sermons.

In his capacity as a spy, Kennedy became intimate with the nascent Social Credit movement and familiar with the tendencies and capacities of its leader. Kennedy watched as the Bible study groups became Social Credit study groups, then *de facto* a province-wide network of campaign committees. The city newspapers, making a mistake they would repeat throughout the century, dismissed the movement as essentially "rural" (read: rube, bumpkin, ignorant). Kennedy knew better. While a Calgary-wide survey conducted by four other *Herald* reporters in late 1934 found less than a half-dozen people who admitted to being Social Crediters, he discovered that on Tenth Avenue alone there were ten house meetings of Social Crediters, attracting on average 20 people, each person contributing a campaign contribution of ten cents. In his autobiography, *Alberta Was My Beat: Memoirs of a Western Newspaperman* (Calgary, The Albertan, 1975), Kennedy writes:

> If 160 persons had been attracted to the movement on a single avenue, then it could be assumed that the overall total for the city could reach fantastic proportions. What puzzled me was that if I could find 160 potential Social Credit party supporters in a ten-block area, how was it that four reporters could find less than half a dozen in a three-day survey?
>
> I found part of the answer in the next few days when I casually button-holed several neighbours whom I had noticed at the various house meetings. All stoutly declared that they had attended out of curiosity only, but their protestations lacked substance. It was the start of a political phenomenon which was to endure until the landslide Social Credit victory in the 1935 elections. Then and only then did people admit that they were Social Crediters.

As the movement grew — "like a prairie fire in late summer," to quote the cliché of that year — Kennedy's prognostications became more dire. But he remained a Cassandra in his own camp. In the newsroom his talk of a Social Credit landslide was met with derisive hoots. The *Herald*, of which Aberhart had urged a boycott in April, continued its campaign against the Social Crediters, its pages inevitably favouring letters from those excoriating the movement over those praising it.

In early August, Leigh Spencer told Kennedy that although he was sure the UFA "was in for a shellacking," he felt equally sure the Liberals would win the election, just as they had resound-

---

Aberhart and his lieutenants insisted that the twenty-five dollars a month had not been intended as a main plank of their platform. Even the amount was unsubstantial. Aberhart had more than once called it twenty dollars. In Edmonton he'd casually allowed it could go as high as seventy-five.

---

ingly done elsewhere. Begging to differ, Kennedy said that based on his observations in the city and the country, the Social Crediters would win between 45 and 50 of the 63 seats.

"This election has already been decided," Kennedy recalls telling Spencer. "The people of Alberta are in desperate straits and they are willing to listen to, and believe, anything which might lead to some improvement in the economy."

"But the whole thing is crazy," said the publisher.

"They're selling that line to people whose kids have hunger creases in their bellies," replied Kennedy, a witness to the appeal of twenty-five dollars a month.

Meanwhile, over the radio and at the growing number of Social Credit picnics and rallies, the Aberhart voice, somehow both stentorian and folksy,[2] came bellowing into the ears of a silent majority that the supposedly knowledgable refused to believe existed.

"Blessed is he that considereth the poor," preached Aberhart, quoting Psalm 41. "The Lord will deliver him in time of trouble. The Lord will preserve him and keep him alive. He shall be blessed upon the earth." The psalm laid the foundation for a homily on the biblical use of the word "Ho!"—a rarely used expression of sheer joyful anticipation. Aberhart continued:

> A friend of mine was telling me up the country there that he came across a woman and two children. And he said she had such a worn-out-looking face. Hope was gone. The two

Just as always the pendulum swings from one extreme to the other; people turned in disgust from the Brownlee scandal to this old-time religion.
—Muriel Clipsham, Reminiscences of an Alberta School Teacher, 1926-1934 (Glenbow Archives manuscript)

[2]After meticulously preparing his speeches in standard English, Aberhart would revise them with ungrammatical flourishes and the droppings of g's from the ends of words to enhance the folksiness of delivery.

little ones were poorly dressed. They were half sobbing and half crying at her knee and she hadn't anything to give them. And this man gave her something and he said, "Lady, have you ever heard of Social Credit?" She hadn't. He says, "When we get Social Credit in this country we'll guarantee that your children will not be hungry. They won't cry any more. But you will be properly looked after, fed, clothed and sheltered."

And her eyes brightened up a bit, and she said 'Oh-ho!' And then the tears streamed down her face. That's the way she expressed it. She couldn't give it with the full accent, but it was the same words. *Oh-ho-ho*. This is the laugh of joyous anticipation. Joyous anticipation. And some politician says all they want it for is the twenty-five dollars a month. Well, if you're in her shoes you'd be mighty glad to have it for twenty-five dollars a month.

"A new Christianity, a new type, a true type, is appearing," preached Aberhart, outlining a universalism that would lose him support among the stauncher fundamentalists, but gain him much more among the more liberal churchmen. "The old prejudiced denominationalism is giving place to the era of Christian brotherhood. Let the critics howl; they can never stop it. We shall combine and co-operate so that we may become our brothers' keepers."

Such was the message and along with it Aberhart contributed something else, notably a powerful organizational genius. He once said, "I've been organizing all my life. There's nothing I'd rather do than organize. It's a hobby with me." This campaign was the culmination of that hobby. By August 1935 there were 1,600 Social Credit study groups around the province. All were collecting campaign donations, which were spent on radio air time for Aberhart, and on the expense of sending the party's better speakers — Aberhart's "one hundred honest men" — to meetings in the far-flung towns. These gatherings, more like revival meetings than political rallies, attracted a steady stream of cash and a river of converts.

One was Alfred J. Hooke whose long Social Credit career began when, as a young Rocky Mountain House school principal, he answered Aberhart's radio appeal for volunteer speakers. In his biography, *30 + 5: I Know, I Was There*, Alf Hooke writes:

His system worked well, although the requests came in so thick and fast that some of us, who by this time were also becoming known to the public, were addressing meetings every night of the week... It was not unusual to drive over exceedingly bad roads to find the little rural school jammed to the doors by eight o'clock. Every means of conveyance had been used by people to get there — a few cars, plenty of Bennett buggies [automobiles drawn by horses because the owners could not afford gasoline], saddle horse and every sort of horse-drawn vehicle were parked around the school yards.

Benches were arranged in appropriate parts of the room where babies and young children slept while the meeting was in progress. In places of affluence one occasionally found two Coleman gas lamps burning, one placed where it could be advantageously used by the speaker and the other suspended from the ceiling over the audience. On many occasions, however, one found that a single coal oil lamp sitting on the teacher's desk was the only illumination in the entire room.

In the spring of 1935, after the members of the study groups had graduated to being members of a political party, nomination conventions were held in each of the province's sixty-three constituencies. Not one but four candidates were chosen in each riding. Aberhart and his advisory board would ultimately pick the right one from among each four. Since, however, the winner for each riding was not to be told of the choice until the election call, this meant that four candidates were campaigning in each riding up until July 16. During this lead-up, the opposition suffered the disadvantage of not knowing which candidate to attack. It also meant that Aberhart, as the dominant member of the advisory board, would be able to hand pick his caucus, having had a five-week period to gauge them for loyalty and performance.

When the candidates were announced, they turned out to be a strong and diverse cross-section that included many teachers, a few lawyers, Mormons and United Churchmen,[3] businessmen and tradesmen. In the rural ridings at least (and there were 51 ridings outside Calgary and Edmonton), the candidates tended to be well-respected members of the community with no previous experience in politics. Emblematic was Dr. Wallace Warren Cross, the gallant and humanitarian Hanna physician who would serve as Alberta's minister of Health for twenty-two years. Edmonton's nationally recognized cancer treatment and research centre honours his name.

Aberhart's decision to take the gloves off and "go political" was probably made final in January of 1935 when the UFA convention formally rejected Social Credit theory as he had outlined it to them. The convention showed him two things: that the UFA was losing ground among its grassroots to Social Credit, and that the UFA leadership was running scared. "It will be known as the convention where the UFA committed suicide," noted the *Social Credit Chronicle* prophetically. "It is likely," writes Ernest Watkins in his 1980 history, *The Golden Province: Political Alberta* (Calgary, Sandstone Publishing, 1980), "that Aberhart looked at the UFA as an organization to be captured."

By the election call in July most of it had been captured. Socialists in particular, drawn by Aberhart's left-sounding entreaties against the "Fifty Big Shots" who controlled the economy (a

---

Despite the fevered interest in the Social Credit, the thunderous outdoor rallies and Aberhart's radio pulpit with its 300,000 listeners, neither his opponents nor their supporting newspapers could believe that what they saw as a square-headed Biblical literalist with pie-in-the-sky promises could create more than an absurd rump.

---

phrase originally coined by the socialists), and the evils of a market-driven economy, not to mention his inevitable recitals of the party motto to end "poverty in the midst of plenty." MP Henry Spencer (Progressive, Battle River), wrote to a friend: "I supported the Douglas theory thinking that while it was not the goal, it might be an easier step towards the economic freedom towards which we are working than by direct socialization which might be hardest to meet with general support. It was a plan I felt might be our economic salvation along with public ownership of our great national resources and natural monopolies."[4]

The odds-on favourite to win Alberta, however, were not the socialists, but the Liberals, led by the stolid war veteran and Edmonton lawyer William R. Howson. The Liberals were a party of lawyers, led by a lawyer and buoyed by the fact that every other province now had a Liberal government and that Mackenzie King's federal Liberals were on the verge of sweeping away the R.B. Bennett Tories. They therefore behaved through most of the campaign with the sort of clubbish self-assurance that won them points only in the sorts of circles in which they moved.

Alf Hooke recalls the ribbing he took when his university pal Jack Marshall, one of six Liberals running in Edmonton, found out Hooke was a Social Credit candidate. Marshall, who was blind, asked Hooke to drive him one evening to a public meeting at Edelweiss Hall in Edmonton. "Now don't get me wrong," Marshall told Hooke, "I don't want you to chauffeur me for nothing; I promise here and now to pledge to you my first twenty-five-dollar Social Credit dividend."

The meeting, like most, seemed populated largely with Social Credit supporters, there to see their featured speaker, Joe Unwin of Edson, who was also a friend of Marshall's and Hooke's. When it came to question time, Unwin decided to have some fun in front of this favourable audience with Marshall.

"Mr. Marshall," said Unwin, rising to his feet, "I listened to your speech with all the intelligence God gave me and could not find one grain of good argument amongst all the chaff."

"Well, Joe," said Marshall without hesitation, "I don't think you have an argument with me; but no doubt you have one with God."[5]

Unfortunately the Liberals couldn't quite decide which way the wind was blowing and followed it in most every direction. "The Liberal party is asking you to join in giving Alberta a new

[3]H.C. Malliah's study of the legislators of Alberta, *A Socio-Historical Study of the Legislators of Alberta, 1905-67* (University of Alberta, PhD. Thesis, 1970), showed that United Church membership predominated among Social Credit MLAs. Owen Anderson's analysis of the membership of the party indicated almost thirty per cent of members belonged to either the Anglican or United Church, while only about eleven per cent were members of fundamentalist sects.

[4]In their strategic effort to gain the widest possible support, the Social Crediters also adopted a full platform of non-ideological promises that covered much of what the other parties were promising. The platform included voter recall of candidates, state medicine, improved irrigation, lower freight rates, the creation of a provincial police force and the eradication of weeds.

[5]The morning after the election, Hooke got a call from his Liberal friend Jack Marshall. "Congratulations, you old so-and-so," Hooke remembers Marshall saying. "Didn't I tell you we expected a landslide? but I didn't realize until now how many blind people there are in Alberta. At least I have a right to be blind."

start, a New Deal," said Howson during an early Rooseveltian moment. Later, when it seemed the Social Credit movement might be gaining critical mass, the Liberals began promising that if elected they would "employ three of the most expert Social Credit advocates to carry on full investigations into the proposed claims of Social Credit and evolve and submit a plan suitable for the Province of Alberta which the Liberal party pledges itself to submit to the Legislature for its consideration."

Most socialists had by now joined the three-year-old CCF, the Co-operative Commonwealth Federation (see previous chapter), which had been created by the Progressive movement, the federal wing of the UFA. This inevitably linked the CCF to the incumbent provincial government, a handicap that spelled doom and drove less doctrinaire socialists into the Social Credit camp. The Canadian Labour party was on a different deck of the same boat, while the Communists focused their attention on organizing protest demonstrations among the unemployed.

The Conservatives under ex-Edmonton mayor David M. Duggan suffered from an association with the unpopular federal government of R.B. Bennett, and won few points by championing of the systems of law and commerce that, to the disgruntled farmers and small businessmen of Alberta, had proven themselves impotent. Duggan's party was just out of style. Its chief plank, announced by Duggan, would be an "unequivocal" opposition to Social Credit. Even William Lyon Mackenzie King, about to return as prime minister, was rattling on about major revolutions in the financial realm which made him sound like a closet Social Crediter.

When they weren't deploring what Social Credit would or would not do, the older parties

A torrent of letters to the editor

DAY BY DAY THEY REVEAL THE DEEP DIVIDE AND EMBITTERED OPINION

The outpouring of views, for and against, on the revolutionary tenets of Social Credit, reached feverish proportions during the four weeks leading up to the election of August 22, 1935. Nowhere was this outpouring more comprehensively, and sometimes eloquently, recorded than in the letters pages of the Calgary Herald. *The following are excerpted:*

The so-called Social Credit, as propounded by the Calgary leader, is so much like the many attempts of amateur scientists to work out a scheme of 'perpetual motion,' I cannot refrain from drawing attention to it... We have a very amateur economist bringing on a big scheme to make the credit of the province rotate, which is supposed to drive the industries of the province and make everyone happy. To the many who are so gullible to take him seriously, his scheme seems to be perfect, but when examined one only needs half an eye to see that the same fallacy is in vogue as in the perpetual motion failures: i.e., the credit never gets back to the starting point and the whole plan fails.

—J.B. McCubbin, Ghost Pine Creek, July 20, 1935.

Notwithstanding the great possibilities of Social Credit some would, indeed, sell their birthright for a proffered mess of communistic potage, and would fain feed on the husks in the swine trough of an ephemeral materialism, but the British people as a whole will not take dictation from the hircine pagans and politicians of Moscow, nor will they sink to the level of the decadent races of Europe; they will find a

way out of the Depression, and still maintain the solidarity of the empire as well as remain true to the Word of God and loyal to his Imperial Majesty King George V... Social credit is not heterodox exploiting capitalism; it represents true brotherhood speaking in terms of the golden rule; it is 'orthodox' capitalism, indeed; and its peculiar excellence and promise for the future lie in the facts that like the British Empire it is not only 'button-holed' with the triple crosses of the Union Jack, but also founded on the eternal principles of justice and brotherly love which are delineated in Holy Writ...

— "W.A.C.," Drumheller, July 25, 1935.

The late P.T. Barnum, the great American circus king, once said, "A fool is born every minute." Judging from the Social Credit craze sweeping Alberta, it looks as though Barnum was right.

—John Glambeck, Milo, July 25, 1935.

The age of supply and demand is gone, it just does not work. We have the supply, also the demand, but the bridge between the two is missing. That 'bridge' is purchasing power. Some of the people who have the work idea should use spoons and forks when they start to make roads, then they would keep everyone working.

—Mrs. Scott, Calgary, July 27, 1935.

Only Social Credit believes that money can be created —

made comparatively modest promises of their own — balancing the budget (Conservatives), fixing the roads and improving crop insurance (UFA), or socialization of banks and industry someday (CCF and Labour). The underlying message of them all was one of perseverance, prudence, and retrenchment. Red Deer Liberal candidate George Clarke typified this approach when he urged upon voters Sir Wilfrid Laurier's slogan, "Toleration, Moderation and Conciliation." But the Alberta electorate of 1935 was in no mood to tolerate, moderate or conciliate anything. It was thinking in terms of revolution and Social Credit seemed more likely than any to bring one about.

The newspapers meanwhile played right into Aberhart's hand. By conducting a concerted attack on him personally and on Social Credit generally, they tended to affirm his portrayal of a country run by eastern "big shots." The two biggest papers — the *Edmonton Journal* and the *Calgary Herald* — were both Conservative and both owned by Southam, an eastern-based company. Apart from its own house organs, the movement had no press support whatever. The result was a text-book demonstration of ineffectual journalism. In voting for Social Credit, the public was implicitly voting no-confidence in its press.

The newspapers tried different lines of attack. The *Edmonton Journal* began by patiently explaining the fallacies inherent to Social Credit policy and referred darkly to unnamed sources who had told it business was preparing to move out of town if the Social Crediters won. On its news pages it incorporated criticisms and jibes about the movement whenever available . A feature story on a venerable 87-year-old French woman, for example, led with her statement that "this Social Credit, it is cra-zee!" An article on the life of the crusty old meatpacker John Gainer

and purchasing power distributed — and that one part of the people will be ready to work and feed the other part for worthless, created paper money. The right to any other man's commodity or productions can only be had by exchange of some other kind of one's own commodity or production. Any other way is simply confiscating, by taking the one man's production and giving it unconditionally to another man. Producers would soon become wise and give up producing any more than their own needs.

—*Alfred Hunter, Calgary, July 27, 1935.*

When we consider how ordinary and normal thoughts and emotions spread from one man to many, and sway multitudes to the same views and actions, it is no longer a mystery that morbid conditions of the mind should become at times no less epidemic than physical diseases.

—*Joseph Smith, Innisfail, August 3, 1935.*

In conclusion I submit the following postcard sent to me as being typical of the manners and methods of the intelligent and 'outstanding' supporters of Mr. Aberhart. Social Crediters take great exception to alleged mud-slinging by opponents, but I doubt very much if any non-Social Crediter, at his worst, could produce anything to equal this effort: I suppose you thought you were smart with your letters in the *Herald*. Your brainless reasoning is that of a fool. You are to be pitied. The printing machine ought to have blow up when it printed yours. I wonder how much you are paid to write such lies. You are not fit to lick Mr. Aberhart's feet. Signed, E.P., Drumheller.

—*C.E. Atter, Pine Lake, August 3, 1935.*

The people hope that Social Credit will bring back the youths from the relief camps and hold out some hope for their own youths. They believe that it is more important to balance the rations of a people than it is to balance the budget of a state. They wish to hand on the heritage given in their hands with most of its real value unimpaired. They hope to take the humiliation and stigma from the word 'unemployed' before a vast political machine with vested interests is set up to control a part of their people. They haven't any doubt of its permanency if once set up. They hope to keep a large part of their people from being formed into a vast armed force, either for law and order or against it. They want adequate insurance against the four horsemen. They believe that if Social Credit will accomplish some of these things the price isn't too high to pay.

—*F.J. Kelly, Wayne, August 3, 1935.*

So far as I am personally concerned, I can only see three things in Social Credit: taxation, plus inflation, plus coercion. But then, you see, I am only a hard working business man who has never found any person give me something for nothing — except abuse.

—*"Ignoramus," Calgary, August 3, 1935.*

The only people afraid of Social Credit coming in are racketeers and people with guilty consciences. All honest folk have nothing to be afraid of.

—*Fred Carroll, Calgary, July 27, 1935.*

—*R.D.*

included the exchange: "Do you think that business could be done on a sound basis under Social Credit?" "No, I think Social Credit is a fraud."

The *Herald* employed the pen of young cartoonist Stewart Cameron, who skilfully depicted Aberhart as a thick-lipped, pince-nez'd buffoon. One of the cartoons showed Aberhart slicing a German sausage. "No matter how you slice it," read the caption, "it's still baloney."

Non-Alberta newspapers helpfully (for Aberhart, anyway) joined fervidly in the attack. "It is a cruel fanaticism," editorialized the *Winnipeg Free Press*, "for nothing is surer than its folly and nothing more inevitable than its ultimate disillusionment." Aberhart replied: "They spat upon my Saviour. They scorned him. They crowned him with a crown of thorns." The crowds screamed their concurrence.

This religious undercurrent made the campaign "undoubtedly one of the bitterest ever fought in the Dominion of Canada," said Alf Hooke. Aberhart opened it with a military metaphor. "We are going over the trenches now," he told his radio audience. "If you falter, we will fail, and remember the enemy will take advantage of your faltering." His troops heard the bugle call. Social Credit candidates routinely put in eighteen-hour days in which as many as ten speaking locales were achieved. In his final thrust, Aberhart worked himself harder than his captains and between his many appearances from Cardston to the far north of the province he appeared in a permanent state of exhausted distraction.

"Those closest to Aberhart say that he could hardly believe at this stage that it was possible for him to win the election," write David Elliott and Iris Miller in *Bible Bill: A Biography of William Aberhart* (Edmonton, Reidmore Books, 1987). "It was even hard for him to get used to the idea that he was actually in the game of politics."

On the stump he was as spellbinding as ever, even impressing the newspaper reporters who followed in his train but were bound by their editors to minimize his appeal. "Once he rose to speak," recalled one of those reporters, "the audience was his until he chose to stop talking. But his strength, to them, lay simply in the fact that he was bringing good news; he told them what they wanted to hear, that heaven and earth were to be had for the asking... He had a loud voice, a noble brow and a massive frame, and was a practised pedagogue and preacher."

Time and again Aberhart exhorted his listeners with his favourite Social Credit-adapted parable. "Are conditions not similar today to those when the Master took a whip of small cords and drove the money changers out of the temple? Do not the common people need leaders and shepherds today, the same as in the days when the Christ had compassion on them and fed the 5,000 with five loaves and two small fishes? There is salvation. God can and will work even a miracle to bring his people into the place of joy and prosperity. Is that not a message for all believers in Social Credit?"

He was not running for a seat himself. This, he told the people, was so he'd be "free to go into any part of the province" during the campaign. But the decision also served a strategic purpose of denying the opposing parties an opportunity to directly challenge Aberhart in a home riding on the Social Credit theory that he could never fully state because he could never fully understand it. Clifford Wilmott, Social Credit's "Man from Mars", who spoke at rallies to make a point about the alien nature of the established financial system, said later that if Aberhart had run in a particular constituency the opposition would have done everything it could to defeat him. After the election,

it was understood, any one of a dozen of his handpicked candidates could be counted upon to step down to allow the general a seat in government.

Very soon Aberhart's view of Canada's predicament persuaded most voters — a circle of entrenched privilege ran Canada, and it was fiercely resisting the threat to it posed by a militant populace now enlightened by Social Credit. (If you doubted this, just read the papers!) "It wasn't uncommon to get 1,500 people out to a meeting," recalled Ernest Manning. "They'd come in from thirty to forty miles. We used to use skating rinks and curling rinks for meetings because you couldn't accommodate the people. On the other hand, the government members and the opposition party members would go out and have a handful of people in a little hall. It was just obvious where the enthusiasm and support of the people was."

Soon the intensity of feeling would take physical form. Meetings were sometimes disrupted by minor fistfights. Rancour supplanted neighbourliness. Social Credit supporters and their opposition counterparts refused to stop if they saw someone from "the other side" broken down on the road. The two factions would sit on opposite sides of the church.

Ex-premier John Brownlee, bravely running for re-election in Ponoka despite the sex scandal, made an especially attractive target. At a meeting in Morrin, his speech was drowned out by a group of single men from a nearby relief camp, all chanting, "How is Vivian? How is Vivian? How is Vivian?"[6] Brownlee later told of a meeting in Waterglen in Ponoka constituency where some

Concerned as much about style as he was about content in his campaign speeches, Aberhart made an off-the-cuff remark about a $25-a-month dividend that would be seized on by voters as the promise that decided the elections. Here he is speaking at Willingdon.

[6]Vivian, of course, is Vivian MacMillan (see this section, ch.3). This episode was described by Art Roberts, whose interview with Warren Caragata is preserved in the Provincial Archives of Alberta. He was one of a group from a nearby single men's relief camp who came into Morrin to attend political meetings.

Memoir of the great campaign of 1935

SOCIAL CREDITER NORMAN JAMES RECALLS THE TURMOIL, ABUSE AND FUN
AND THAT AWFUL NIGHT WHEN THE OPPOSING WORK GANG DUG UP THE ROAD

Norman B. James, an amiable English-born farmer from Youngstown, Alberta, was among the sixty-three candidates fielded by Social Credit in the frenetic 1935 election. In his 1949 book, The Autobiography of a Nobody, *James describes in humorous detail the ordeal of his progress from lay preacher for Bill Aberhart's Prophetic Bible Institute to MLA in the Social Credit benches. The following are excerpted from his memoirs of the 1935 campaign, beginning with the nomination of the initial four candidates, at a meeting in Oyen, east of Hanna,*

Provincial Archives of Alberta, A2807

It did not take us long to get down to business. Having selected a chairman and gone through the usual preliminaries, nominations for candidates were called for; and by the time they were all in, there were twelve aspirants. We were a weird lot. There were three or four school teachers, an auctioneer, a druggist, a postmaster, and some farmers — and myself.

With such a powerful array of talent preceding me I didn't think I was in much danger of being the victim, so I let my name stand.

After the nominations, we were all invited to the platform and sat in a row behind the chairman. I hid behind the piano. Then the fun began. Each one had to make a four-minute speech to explain his existence (if reasonably possible) and prove that he was the only possible solution to the problem of choosing a candidate. I still sat behind the piano.

Norman B. James's autobiography gives a backbencher's-eye-view of the 1935 election campaign.

After listening to the marvellous records of their lives and accomplishments, I felt more sure than ever that I was out of my class and safe. What they hadn't accomplished individually and collectively wasn't worth mentioning. Some of them even dared to bring in their ancestors. By the time they got through, I was convinced that if any one of them was selected, we'd have a combination of Lincoln, Washington and Gladstone to represent us in the Legislative Assembly.

After the eleven had got through, the chairman counted down his list and discovered that one was missing. Someone suggested that he look behind the piano. I came out rather shame-facedly and stood before them. I knew I just couldn't compete with such talent, so I didn't try. My little speech

went something like this:

"Ladies and gentlemen, you have heard the splendid records of these gentlemen and have been told all about their accomplishments. They have bared their lives for your inspection, and I feel that, after what we have heard this afternoon, we must have come to the conclusion that any one of them would make a fitting candidate (I didn't state for what), and I don't intend to compete with them by telling you what I have done or left undone in my past. In fact I think the less you know about my past, the better it will be for you — and me too."

And I went back behind the piano. After this we were released and I felt that, as far as I was concerned, the danger was past and I could relax.

While they were distributing the ballot papers, I collected my wife and went out for a cup of coffee. After a time other delegates came in and sat with us. The ballots were still being counted so we didn't hurry back. About an hour later, another bunch came in, showing traces of excitement, and I wondered what was happening. One of them spied me and came over, and I got the shock of my life. It appeared that my name was on top of the list and that, along with three others, I was elected to go before the Advisory Board who were to choose the final candidate.

I wasn't yet the candidate. I was only one of four possibilities, so the Opposition couldn't concentrate on my personal character — or lack of it. That came later. The four possible candidates used to travel in pairs at that time, and share the honours and abuse, and it speaks rather well for the cause we represented that every one of the four played the game fairly and squarely and never tried to take an unfair advantage of the others.

Some day I may devote a whole book to these meetings. Not that they were important in themselves, though school house meetings have a far greater influence on world affairs than "experts" ever dream of. But they gave an insight into the character of the very ordinary farming population. I think that city people do not fully appreciate the natural wit, humour and deep thoughtfulness of the rural population... No flash in the pan answer was good enough for them. "Smartness" was not appreciated. They wanted to KNOW.

I am not a philosopher, but I think that the reason for this was that these people had had to fight. They had had to fight first of all the forces of nature to wrest from the land the living that they had to have, and secondly they had to fight the "city slicker," represented by political parties and the "financial interests," who waited until they had accumulated something and then snatched it away from them. These conditions had MADE them think, and the result was all to the good.

Then came the time when the announcement was made as to who the real candidate was to be. On the evening in question [July 16, 1935], I was scheduled to address a meeting in a neighbouring constituency. I was in the middle of my alleged speech when the news was telephoned through that I had been selected by the advisory board as the candidate for our constituency. The applause was rather overwhelming, but I have wondered since whether it was joy over my appointment or relief at getting away from my

allowance that was three miles long and being ploughed up very efficiently, was consequently impassable. As it was the only road I could take, I started down it, and promptly got stuck.

My wife decided that her best plan was to get out and cross the fields and wait for me at the end of the road. I have a sneaking idea that the language I was using had something to do with the decision. This being a special occasion she was dressed appropriately in a spotless white dress. When I eventually met her at the other end, her dress was no longer spotless for what the dust hadn't done to ruin her "get-up" the barbed wire had finished. She was a sorry sight. I was in no better shape. I had spent some of the time under the car, some in the ditches and the balance shovelling huge clods of earth out of my way.

I did somehow get through and went on, much to the disgust of the road gang who, incidentally, belonged to one of the opposition parties, and who had, by a strange coincidence, chosen this day to tear up the road. I understand that after I got through they all quit and went home.

In consequence of this delay, we reached Oyen an hour

Election night being a special occasion my wife was dressed appropriately in a spotless white dress. Her dress was no longer spotless for what the dust hadn't done to ruin her 'get-up' the barbed wire had finished. She was a sorry sight. I was no better. I had spent some time under the car, some in the ditches and the balance shovelling huge clods of earth out of my way.

---

speech for a time.

After that, all the vials of Opposition wrath naturally fell on my luckless head... It was some small consolation to find that I was only slightly worse than any of the other Social Credit candidates. We seemingly, and without knowing it, were just about the worst bunch of criminals unhanged, and the worst criminal of the lot was William Aberhart... Besides the greater crimes of which I was accused, were the milder inaccuracies such as, that I was an old bachelor living alone in an old tumble-down shack, and that I wore a wig. I think these two slanders made my wife more indignant than any of the more vicious scurrilities I ran into... The election campaign was merely an episode to be recorded. In some ways it was a distinctly unpleasant episode, and by the time I got through I felt I needed fumigating, and that some others had got past the stage where fumigating would do any good.   In other ways, though, it was really good fun, and the rushing around, speeches, applause and abuse were, after I got over the first fright, rather exhilarating than otherwise.

After lunch we started back to Oyen to be at headquarters to hear the returns come in. We figured we would be in plenty of time, but we figured wrong. We got about half way, and were sailing along comfortably, nicely dressed for the occasion in our very best, when we came to a road

or two after the returns had started to come in. We were to sneak into the hotel and get a general clean-up, but no sooner did we hit the main street than we were surrounded and almost swamped by a delirious and cheering mob. It appeared that I was already piling up such a huge majority that the opposition was already practically out of the running. I did, after a time, get my wife to the hotel so that she could do the mysterious things women can do to come up spruce and smiling under any circumstances, but I never got a chance to get anywhere but the committee rooms until late that night.

The place was a regular bedlam as the results came pouring in, and after the result was assured, it took me half an hour to get the lipstick off my face. After this my wife and I were escorted from home to home "just for a cup of tea." I do like an occasional cup of tea, but I've been allergic to the island of Ceylon ever since that night. By the time I got back to the hotel I felt as if I had been submerged in tea. Even at that I was in better shape than some. They had also been submerged — but not in tea.

It was a wild night, but in a way the circumstances warranted the celebration. It was perhaps the most complete victory that any political party — and we had become just that whether we liked it or not — had ever accomplished.

Social Crediters in attendance declared that he should not be allowed to speak as "he had nothing to offer Alberta." Brownlee ignored the remarks and rose anyway. He recalls what followed:

> It was a large hall and it was packed... During the first forty-five minutes of my address, I didn't touch on Social Credit and no one could have had a better hearing... After three quarters of an hour I stated that, as their member in the legislature, they would expect me to discuss my attitude to Social Credit. So I began to tell them in all sincerity what I thought of Social Credit. A group of big fellows near the door then left the hall, slamming the door violently as they went out. Some of them got into cars and started to blow horns. Others got logs and began pounding the walls and doors of the building from outside, while they hooted and yelled. Some of my supporters went outside and the rough stuff stopped. But the meeting inside was in a tumultuous uproar.

In concert with the newspaper offensive against Social Credit, the chambers of commerce and boards of trade in the larger centres abandoned previous policies of neutrality and took direct aim at Aberhart and his theories. They and their allies produced pamphlets full of dire predictions and unflattering cartoons seeking to discredit a man they freely compared to Hitler or Mussolini.

"Eloquent words may sway people, but cannot coerce the facts," said the Edmonton chamber in a statement carried on the front pages of the *Journal* and the *Calgary Herald*. "We venture to think that the hope of creating something out of nothing, which is the essence of the whole plan, rests on a fundamental fallacy as to the nature of banking credit."

June 1935 marked the beginning of the professional relationship between ex-Disney cartoonist Stewart Cameron and William Aberhart, the former as perpetual critic, the latter his perpetual victim. Cameron would continue to monitor Aberhart's political career for the Calgary Herald and became a relentless irritant in Aberhart's life.

Provincial Archives of Alberta, Stewart Cameron Collection

The Economic Safety League was the most prominent of these pamphleteering groups. Formed by the Medicine Hat and Drumheller boards of trade, the ESL was headed by former Lieutenant-Governor Dr. William Egbert, and accorded itself a certain amount of intellectual heft by hiring University of British Columbia economist Henry Angus. The newspapers, naturally, gave front-page play to the ESL's every utterance.

The ESL pamphlet cleverly began with a biblical quotation ("Come let us reason together." — Isaiah 1:18), then painstakingly went through the entire Social Credit manifesto, knocking it down pin by pin, arguing that the whole scheme would result in massive taxation and confiscation of property, and likening Aberhart to the driver of a bus who decides to veer off a cliff by way of an experiment in getting all those aboard to their destination much sooner. Mimicking Aberhart's penchant for parodic initials, the Economic Safety League (whom Aberhart later called the Elevated Society of Lunatics) referred to Social Credit as the SFN (Something For Nothing) party, and to its promise of twenty-five dollars a month as an appeal to the desperate fool.

"Often," read the ESL pamphlet, "when no sensible answer can be made to his critics, the professor, urging us to cut our suspenders and take a leap in the dark, says, 'Can we be worse off than we are?' That is the kind of reasoning a man usually resorts to when about to court suicide... It would take Alberta ten years to recover from one year of Aberhart."

The *Social Credit Chronicle*, reacting with its customary pointed humour — a humour that sounded a lot like Aberhart's — dismissed the pamphlet. "They say that our [blue] pamphlet proposes to 'interfere with well-recognized forms of personal liberty.' About the only personal liberty that most of us have left today is that we are free to starve. It is quite true that Social Credit will interfere with that particular kind of liberty."

· The opposition forces also took their desperate campaign against Social Credit onto Aberhart's own well-worn turf — the radio. "The time has come," intoned Conservative leader Duggan on Edmonton's CJCA, "for straight-thinking, and for practical people in Alberta to rise against the menace of Social Credit as a provincial scheme without a plan, against the peril of notions which threaten ruin to the province into which have gone the fortunes, the hopes, the buildings, the life-work of our citizens."

"While he may allow his deluded dupes to regard him as a Moses, a Joshua, and what not," stormed Calgary Conservative J.J. Zubick, a businessman, on CFCN, "that while he may countenance this near blasphemy of near-worship, the cold facts of his public utterances reveal him as something suggesting the modern version of the Pharisee who went into the temple and prayed thus, 'God I thank Thee that I am not as other men are.'"[7]

All of this *sturm und drang*, while Wagnerian in its racket, proved nothing more than racket. Aberhart's excellently laid campaign only mounted in momentum as election day approached, to the accompaniment of an endless stream of anecdotal homilies. "Pat and Mike had a keg of beer and one five-cent piece," he'd tell the crowds. "They decided to go into the business of selling beer by the roadside. No customers appeared, so Pat and Mike decided to develop a self-contained economy by buying and selling to one another. Pat handed over the nickel and got in exchange a glass of beer. Mike passed back the nickel and got a keg of beer. The double exchange was repeated until the keg was empty... All that turnover and only one nickel!" (The beer, however, was gone, something Aberhart didn't seem to take into account.)

A UFA member later described a meeting in Wetaskiwin where he had finished his speech and called for questions. "I sell a steer," said a young farmer, "for hardly enough to pay the freight. Now would you tell me what I have got to lose in trying Social Credit whether I believe it or not?" The question was cheered by the farmers in the audience. The UFA member described this as a typical experience.

"The night before the election I addressed a meeting in the Elks' Hall in Red Deer, the hall being filled to capacity and overflowing into the street," wrote Alf Hooke. "A couple of blocks

Calgary Herald, August 8, 1935, p.3

CALGARY BOARD OF TRADE
TAKES STAND ON
SOCIAL CREDIT

It having been represented to the Calgary Board of Trade that people were looking to it for some statement regarding Social Credit, the Council of the Board, after very prolonged and careful consideration of the arguments for and against the proposals, has decided to submit the following as its considered conclusions on the subject:—

1. The proposals must necessarily involve crushing taxation entirely beyond the capacity of the people of Alberta to pay.

2. Any attempt to fix just prices can only result in incredible confusion and paralysis of business to the detriment of every producer and consumer.

3. The suggestion that dividends can be paid out of cultural heritage and undeveloped natural resources is impracticable and impossible.

4. The Social Credit monetary proposals will lead to a condition similar to that which occurred in Germany, involving the Province, the farmer, the wage earner, etc., in financial disaster.

5. The Social Credit proposals will isolate Alberta and render it impossible for either the farmer or the business man to buy or sell to advantage.

6. Finally, such an experiment as is outlined by the Social Credit proposals will lead to chaos, and entail great suffering, from which the Province would not recover for many years.

Inserted By The

ECONOMIC SAFETY LEAGUE
CALGARY

Hon. Dr. W. Egbert
President

Jesse Gouge
Secretary

Of the many groups who came into existence for the sole purpose of opposing Social Credit's political bid, none was as active as the Economic Safety League, spearheaded by former lieutenant-governor William Egbert. In fact they were so far above the pamphleteering pack as to be honoured by Aberhart himself with the epithet Elevated Society of Lunatics.

away, the Liberals, who had expected a landslide, had gathered to hear imported high-powered speakers. When I was speaking a note was handed to me from the audience which read: 'The Liberals have four speakers, and twelve people in the audience. One of them left with me and is now listening to you.'"

In the last week of the campaign opposing Social Credit was like opposing the tide, but even then such polling as existed was primitive and its opponents didn't seem to realize this. Aberhart did. On August 20, working at Crescent Heights High School in a show of preparation for the fall term, Aberhart was asked by librarian Lettie "Hilly" Hill what the party's chances were.

"Oh, the election is all over, it's in the bag, so to speak," he said, and estimated the Social Crediters would win between fifty-five and sixty seats. "It's a fact all right. You see I've got the greatest political organization that this province or country has ever seen." He was stating the truth with scientific accuracy.[8]

That same day the Liberals were estimating they would win forty-five seats, the UFA was saying it would hold onto between twenty-two and twenty-five seats. The Alberta newspapers, farthest of all from reality, still spoke as though the big battle lay between the Liberals and UFA. In London the *Times* was more cautious. One of the many overseas papers following the election, it observed: "Under the counter-attack and the campaign of the other political parties, the popular support of the Social Credit League is said to be waning, but it still causes anxiety."

August 22, election day, was hot, with temperatures in the mid-80s Fahrenheit. Voter turnout was even hotter. New voting booths had to be manufactured on the spot to meet the demand in some constituencies. In some areas with high concentrations of non-English speakers, write Elliott and Miller, the most frequently asked question was "Vich vun twenty-five dollar man?"

"There were actually polls where there wasn't a single vote for anybody except the Social Credit candidate," Ernest Manning remembered. "Which means that even the scrutineers and

---

By August of 1935 there were 1,600 Social Credit study groups around the province. All were collecting campaign donations which were spent on radio air time for Aberhart, and travel expenses for party speakers in the far-flung towns. These gatherings, more like revival meetings than political rallies, attracted a steady stream of cash and a river of converts.

---

election people of the other parties ended up voting for the Social Credit candidate. With that type of atmosphere around, it was quite evident that the movement was going to elect a lot of members." Alf Hooke, who won his Red Deer constituency with 3,565 votes to the next-placing Liberal candidate's 788, wrote:

At the same time as the Red Deer results were pouring in, the radio was giving an account of every other constituency in the province and similar results were being recorded almost everywhere. Every now and again the radio announcers would give out excitedly that a phone call had just been received saying that a baby boy had just been born to Mr. and Mrs. So and So and christened William Aberhart So and So. How many I don't recall.

In 1930 the total vote cast in the province was 188,219 but in 1935, even though our population [772,000] had increased but slightly, 301,752 cast their ballot. Of this total Social Credit candidates received 163,700, more than all the other parties combined.

The UFA government was swept into oblivion, as not a single candidate came anywhere near election. Out of a total of sixty-three members, Social Crediters elected fifty-six; the Liberals five; and the Conservatives two. The first Social Credit government in the world was now to begin its reign.

At the Calgary Prophetic Bible Institute on election night, Aberhart seemed stunned. He leaned against his podium as if his legs were weak. "I want to personally give thanks to the Almighty God for His guidance and direction in this whole matter," he said in the short speech broadcast over CFCN. "I assure you that it is our intention to submit our deliberations to His

[7]Zubick, a Russian immigrant who had edited a newspaper in rural Saskatchewan until the Depression folded it, also attempted to paint the Social Crediters as a nest of racists by reading a letter he'd received from a William B. Sendall of Brooks. "Dear Mr. Bohunk," wrote Sendall, "I heard your foul mouthings over the air last Wednesday and I wish to tell you that of all the vile lowdown sneaking creatures of the earth, you are the lowest. You and your filthy countrymen will be the first ones to apply for a basic dividend when Social Credit gets control of the province and the hell hounds who are paying you to spew such rot over the air."

[8]When the final votes were tallied, Social Credit had taken 55 seats in the legislature, the Liberals had 5 and the Conservatives, 2. The UFA returned no members, and did not return as a political force in the 20th century.

Long-time Health minister George Hoadley moved to Toronto, where he served as president of the Dominion Health Study Plan. He later moved alone to Victoria, having separated from his wife, Lily, and died in December 1955 at the age of 88.

Former Education minister Perren Baker retired from public life in 1935. In 1941 he moved with his second wife, Edna, to Vancouver, where he died in February 1974 at the age of 96.

After retiring from politics, former attorney-general J.F. Lymburn returned to his law practice with the firm of Lymburn, Reid and Cobbledick in Edmonton. He was active in the Presbyterian Church until his death at 89 in November 1969.

Divine guidance. Since He seems to be calling us to a place of leadership we trust our people will put their trust in Him and not fail. Follow your government with your prayers. Remember our theme song: *O God Our Help in Ages Past*. Fear not, thank you, ladies and gentlemen."

The morning after the election, *Herald* publisher Leigh Spencer walked into the newsroom and announced, "I have just been in touch with Mr. Aberhart. The only person on this staff he will talk to is Kennedy." Thus Fred Kennedy, the man whose disbelieved prophecies had now come resoundingly true, became the first reporter to interview Aberhart following the election. After Kennedy had "asked the questions I was supposed to ask and he supplied the answers," the two men had a candid chat.

"Kennedy," said Aberhart, "you've had quite a bit of experience in politics. I have been too busy with my high school and my Bible school to bother much about it. What do you see in all this?" Flabbergasted that the man who had beaten some of the most seasoned politicians in the country knew nothing about politics, Kennedy proceeded to answer some of Aberhart's questions on the details of house procedures and so forth. Then he said to the premier-elect, "I wouldn't want to be in your shoes at this moment for a million dollars."

"Why not?"

"By way of the ballot," said Kennedy, "untold thousands of Albertans have turned to you for help. You are the modern Moses who is supposed to lead them out of the financial and economic wilderness. Many of them are suffering from hunger and want. They are broke. The cities are broke and the province is broke. You promised these people monthly dividends and a lower living cost and you must deliver. On the face of it you have set yourself an impossible task. You will be badgered and heckled and badgered again every day of your life from now on, not only by your political opponents but by your own people."

As Kennedy remembers it, "his face darkened." With good reason, it would turn out. He was about to launch the most controversial government ever elected in Canada that would draw the press of the world into Alberta. But that is a story for another volume.

Denial that he ever had predicted that the world would end in 1934, or that wheat would reach $4.85 per bushel in that year was made Friday by William Aberhart, leader of the Social Credit movement in this province, when interviewed by the Journal. He was questioned regarding a denial made in the course of a speech at Rossington.

"I have never made the statement that the world would end in 1934. I could not possibly know. The end of the world probably will not be for thousands of years yet," he said.

Mr. Aberhart said that what he had stated on this subject was that according to the Bible, the price of wheat would be $4.85 a bushel when the troublous times predicted in the Scriptures arrive.
—*Edmonton Journal*, July 19, 1935

Index

Note: Page numbers in italics refer to photos. Page numbers followed by n refer to text appearing in the margins.